BOOK
OF
INDIAN ERAS
WITH
TABLES FOR CALCULATING
INDIAN DATES.

BOOK
OF
INDIAN ERAS,

WITH

TABLES FOR CALCULATING

INDIAN DATES.

BY

ALEXANDER CUNNINGHAM, C.S.I., C.I.E.,
MAJOR GENERAL ROYAL ENGINEERS (BENGAL)

Every nation forms an era from some remarkable event, such as a change in religion, the accession of one family to the throne, upon the extinction or expulsion of another, a great earthquake or a flood —ABUL FASL

GYAN

Published by

GYAN

Gyan Publishing House
5, Ansari Road
Daryaganj, New Delhi-110002
Phone: 011-47034999, 9811692060
E-mail: books@gyanbooks.com

Distribution Network
gyanbooks.com
India, USA, Canada, UK, Australia, France

ISBN : 978-81-212-2426-0 (HB)
First Published, 1883

2nd Impression 2021

Printed at: Gyan Press, Delhi.

Book of Indian Eras
Author: Alexander Cunningham

BOOK

OF

INDIAN ERAS,

WITH

TABLES FOR CALCULATING

INDIAN DATES.

BY

ALEXANDER CUNNINGHAM, C.S.I., C.I.E.,

MAJOR-GENERAL, ROYAL ENGINEERS (BENGAL).

Every nation forms an era from some remarkable event, such as a change in religion, the accession of one family to the throne, upon the extinction or expulsion of another, a great earthquake or a flood.—ABUL-FAZL.

CALCUTTA:

THACKER, SPINK AND CO.

1883.

PREFACE.

MOST of the Tables in this Book were prepared for my own use so far back as 1859. I had long felt the want of some handy and ready means of calculating Indian dates, as the process described in Warren's Kâla Sankâlita and Prinsep's Useful Tables is both cumbrous and troublesome. It struck me that, by substituting decimal parts of days for the Hindu *gharis*, *palas*, and *vipalas*, and by lessening the number of items to be taken out from the tables, the process would be made much more easy. The road in both is the same, but I believe that I have made it both shorter and smoother. The best test, however, of the advantage of my process will be to compare it with one of Warren's own examples for finding the initial day of both the Solar and Luni-Solar Calendars for the year of Kâli-Yuga 4923 complete = A.D. 1822.

The following is my process :

	SOLAR AHARGANA. *Surya Siddhânta, Table XII.*		LUNI-SOLAR AHARGANA. *Surya Siddhânta, Table XIII.*
4900 years =	1789,168·9067 days	and	1736,398·5710 days.
23 „ =	8,400·9514 „	„	8,150·4422 „
4923 years =	1798,168·8581 days	and	1744,549·0132 days.

Deduct constant ...	... 2·1475	
Solar Ahargana ...	1798,166·7106	÷ 7 = 6·7 or 7 days over = Friday, 12th April 1822, 1st day of solar year.
Luni-Solar Ahargana	1744,549·0132	
	53,617·6974	
Dd. 1800 Lunations ...	53,155·0582	
Table XIV ...	462·6392	
Dd. 15 Lunations ...	442·9587	

Conjunction 19·6805 or 20 days earlier = Saturday, 23rd March.
Beginning of Luni-Solar year 1 day later = Sunday, 24th March.

The following is Warren's process. See his Kâla Sankâlita, p. 240, and Tables, pp. 65 and 66.

Wanted the beginning of the *Solar year* 4923 Kâli-Yuga, according to the Surya Siddhânta—

	Years.	Days.	G.	V.	P.
	4000	1461,035	1	33	20
	900	328,732	52	51	0
	20	7,305	10	30	28
	3	1,095	51	29	22
		1798,168	51	29	22
Subtract Sodhyam	...	2	8	51	15
Divided by 7	...	1798,166	42	38	7
Remainder	...	6 over,			

which, counted from Friday, gives *Suta-dina* = Thursday.

[*N.B.*—Here *Thursday* is a misprint for *Friday*, as the large fraction of a day, upwards of 42 *gharis*, or more than two-thirds of a day, is practically a whole day; so that the remainder of 6 days + 42 *gharis* is reckoned as 7 days, as noted by Warren himself on page 65 at the foot of Example II, where he states that by the Surya Siddhânta the initial day is *Friday*.]

Warren's Luni-Solar example is on page 66 of his Tables.

Wanted the beginning of the *Luni-Solar year* 4293 Kâli-Yuga, according to the Surya Siddhânta—

Years.	Days.			Years.	Days.	G.	V.	P.
4923 =	1.798,166		... ...	4000	1417,468	13	16	49
(1)	1.754,549		... ...	900	318,930	20	59	17
	53,617		... ...	20	7,087	20	27	59
(2)	35,436		... ...	3	1,063	6	4	11
	18,181		... ...		1.744,549	...	48	17
(3)	17,718	(2)	100 Lunar years		35,436	42	19	55
	463	(3)	50 ditto		17,718	21	9	57
(4)	354	(4)	1 ditto		354	22	1	23
	109	(5)	3 Lunar months		88	35	30	20
(5)	88							
Remainder	21		... ...		1.798,147	1	49	56
					+1			
			Luni-Solar Ahargana ...		1.798,148			
			Divide by 7					
					256,878 weeks + 2 days.			

Remainder 2, counted from Thursday, gives *Saturday* for the Suta-dina, or day of conjunction.

In the tables for finding the corresponding dates for any Hijra day I believe that I have made the process more certain as well as more easy, by the adoption of a table, No. XV, showing the number of each day in the Muhammadan year. By this means the corresponding Christian day of any Muhammadan date can be ascertainted with absolute certainty in a few minutes.

The tables connected with the Christian year appear to me to be much simpler than any others that I have met with. I prepared them for my own use in 1859, and I have since had so many opportunities of testing their accuracy as well as their easy working, that I have no hesitation in putting them forward as really useful and handy Tables.

For the Tables of the Seleukidan era, I must crave some indulgence, as the subject is one of much difficulty, partly owing to the meagreness of trustworthy data, and partly to the adoption of the Julian reckoning in the western half of the Syro-Macedonian Empire after its annexation to Rome. As my object is to treat of Indian eras only, I have retained the use of the cycle of Meton with its embolismic months, as I feel quite satisfied that the Julian reckoning was never adopted in the eastern provinces subject to the Bactrian Greeks and Parthians.

The present work differs from others on the same subject, not only in the greater completeness as to the number of eras treated of, but also in the greater handiness and simplicity of its Tables for calculation. I believe, therefore, that this "Book of Indian Eras" will help to supply a want, which has long been felt, in its numerous tables for the calculation of any Indian dates by easy and simple processes.

The most useful works on Indian Measures of Time that I am acquainted with, are the following:—

Warren's Kâla Sankâlita, 1825.
Jervis's Weights, Measures, and Coins of India.
Prinsep's Useful Tables, 1834.
Cowasjee Patell's Chronology, 1866.

Colonel Warren, who belonged to the French family of De Warenne, was one of the officers of the Great Trigonometrical Survey. His work gives an elaborate exposition of the Hindu solar and luni-solar measures of time with an account of the Vrihaspati Chakra, or Jupiter cycle of sixty years, and a memoir on the lunar year of the Muhammadans. At the end he has given a series of very useful tables for facilitating the computation of Indian dates. The Kâla Sankâlita is valuable for its accuracy, but its Tables are rather cumbrous and troublesome for any large number of calculations. My own Hindu Tables are simpler and easier to work with than Warren's, but they are essentially the same, and were, in fact, based upon his elaborate and more cumbrous processes.

Jervis's Measures of Time form only part of his large work on Indian Weights and Measures. His Muhammadan calendar is excellent; but his list of the corresponding years of the Vikramâditya Sambat is entirely vitiated by his adoption of the wrong initial point of the era as 56 B.C., instead of 57 or 56¾. His account of the 60-year cycle of Jupiter is limited to the corrupt form in use in Southern India.

James Prinsep's Useful Tables are founded almost entirely on Warren's Kâla Sankâlita. But his tabular forms are much more handy than those of Warren, and his calendric scales for ascertaining corresponding dates by simple inspection are a really useful invention. For his own use he hadwooden cylinders prepared round which the scales were pasted, so that the initial day of any Hindu or Muhammadan year could be set at once to its corresponding date in the Christian calendar. There are several misprints; but the only serious one is in the table of Hindu sidereal years, where the initial days of the Christian years on the left hand from A.D. 1753 onwards are continued in Old Style, while the initial days of the corresponding Hindu years are given in New Style right down to the end. Thus the present year A.D. 1882 is made to begin on Friday (which is O.S.), instead of on Sunday (N.S.), while *Tuesday* the 10th April is given as the beginning of the Hindu year in N.S.

Cowasjee Patell's Chronology is an extremely useful practical work, as it gives a large number of corresponding lists of years of different eras "in use among Parsis, Jews, Greeks, Hindus, Muhammadans, Chinese, Japanese, &c. The brief accounts of the eras are generally taken from Prinsep, as well as the rules for calculating the dates. The Tables are singularly free from misprints; but whilst I was calculating my own Tables and comparing them with his, I found the following errata, which may be worth noting by all those who possess a copy of his work.

In A.D. 141 and again in A.D. 543, the name of the intercalary month has been omitted:

In A.D. 999, *for* 19th March, *read* 21st March.
——— 1168, *for* 15th March, *read* 12th March.
——— 1169, *for* 4th March, *read* 1st March.
——— 1344, *for* 15th March, *read* 16th March.
——— 1597, *for* 7th April, *read* 7th March.
——— 1655, *for* 26th February, *read* 28th March.
——— 1899, *for* 1st April, *read* 11th April.
——— 1983, *for* 15th April, *read* 13th April.

A very curious coincidence of dates came accidentally to my notice during the past cold season. At Boram Deo in the Central Provinces I found several inscribed Sati Pillars, two of which gave the name of the year of the 60-year cycle of Jupiter in addition to the Samvat date. These two inscriptions are recorded as follows :—

A.—Swasti Samvat 1430 samayo
Sidhârthi nâma Savachhara.

B.—Samvat 1445 Bhâva nâma
Samvatsara Aswina badi 13 Some.

As Boram Deo is in Chattisgarh or Mahâ Kosala, which formed the old kingdom of the Chedis or Kalachuris, I thought it most probable that these dates were reckoned in the Chedi or Kalachuri Samvat of which the initial point, as I have previously shown, was A.D. 249 = 0· Reckoning from this starting point, the date of A would be 1430 + 249 = 1679 A.D., which was actually the year Sidhârthi, according to the computation of the cycle in use in Southern India.

Similarly the date of B would be 1445 + 249 = 1694 A.D., which was actually the year Bhâva of the Southern reckoning.

Here then I thought that I had found a clear proof that the Chedi or Kalachuri era had continued in use down to A.D. 1694. But when I proceeded to calculate the week day of B, I found that it did not agree with A.D. 1694. It then struck me that the Samvat might be that of Vikramâditya, according to which the date of A would be 1430 – 57 = 1373 A.D., which to my surprise proved to be also the year Sidhârthi of the Northern reckoning of the 60-year cycle. Similarly the date of B would be 1445 – 57 = 1388 A.D., which was also the year Bhâva of the Northern reckoning. On calculating the week day of B, I found that it agreed exactly with the Vikramâditya Samvat, as the 13th of Aswina-badi in Vik. Sam. 1445 was actually a Monday. Without this mention of the week day, the true equivalent of these two dates would, therefore, have been doubtful, and I should certainly have been inclined to refer them to the Chedi era.

Of course, this coincidence could only happen within the limit of the 86-year period in which these two dates are included, as the omission of every 86th name of the Jupiter Cycle in the Northern reckoning would make all the earlier northern names later, and all the latter ones earlier.

Since the text of this book was printed, a notice of my attempt to fix the date of the Gupta era has been published by Dr. Thibaut, Principal of the Benares College.* His remarks are confined to the calculations

* *Indian Antiquary*, Vol. XI, p. 322.

based on the 12-year cycle of Jupiter, as he considers it highly probable that the modern system of Hindu astronomy, with its fairly accurate knowledge of the planetary revolutions, "was not well established before A.D. 400." This I fully admit as far as the existing Siddhântas are concerned. But the fact that the Macedonian months were in use in Northern India, certainly during the 1st and 2nd centuries A.D., offers, in my opinion, a clear proof that the people of North-Western India had adopted the Macedonian era of the Seleukidæ. Now the Greeks of Alexander's army must have brought with them the calendar of Meton, which was a luni-solar cycle of 19 solar years of 365¼ days each, or 235 lunar months.* But this is the very cycle that is still used by the Hindus themselves, and I have very little doubt that they must have corrected the old erroneous reckoning of Garga by the Greek calendar of Meton.

If this conclusion be right, then the Hindus of the 1st and 2nd centuries A.D. must have had a nearly accurate knowledge of the length of the solar year, the amount of error being only one day in 76 years. It seems to me, therefore, not improbable that a fairly accurate adaptation of the cycle of Jupiter to the reckoning of the solar year may be as old as the time of the Indo-Scythians, who made use of the Macedonian calendar in their inscriptions. Of course this is not a proof that the reckoning of the Arya and Surya Siddhântas was in use at so early a period. But it is, in my opinion, a very strong argument that a nearly accurate reckoning must already have been adopted.

I am perfectly aware that the date of the Gupta era is still unsettled; but there is one fact that is strongly in favour of the early period that I have arrived at,—namely, the date of A.D. 319, which is assigned by Abu Rihân for the extinction of the Gupta dominion. Now the last of the great Gupta kings was almost certainly Skanda Gupta, and as we have a copperplate inscription dated in the year 146, during his reign, the initial point of the era cannot well be placed later than 319—146=173 A.D., that is within seven years of my proposed date. I, therefore, adhere for the present to the year 166 A.D. as a convenient date, which cannot be far from the truth. In fact the two inscriptions of King Jaika, if they belong to the same person, are very strongly in favour of my date. One of these is dated in the year 794 of the Vikramâditya Samvat, or A.D. 737-38, and the other, from Morbi, is dated in 595 of the Gupta era. Deducting 595 from 738, we get the year 143 A.D., which is 23 years earlier than my date. But if we accept my date as a near approximation to the truth, we obtain 166 + 595 =761 A.D., as the date of the

* See my account of the Seleukidan era in this volume.

Morbi inscription, which would give King Jaika a reign of 23 years from 738 to 761 A.D.*

In Table XVIII I have added a list of eclipses, both lunar and solar, from the beginning of the Christian era down to A.D. 2000. These have been taken from the celebrated French work "L'Art de verifier les dates"—Vol. I, 8vo., 1818. In the original work the hour of each eclipse is given for the meridian of Paris. These I have omitted for want of space. While copying out the dates, I have noted a few errors and omissions, namely :—

A.D. 1341, *for* Lunar Eclipse, 13th May, *read* 31st May.
A.D. 1392. *for* Lunar Eclipse, —— Sept., *read* 2nd Sept.
A.D. 1488, *for* Solar Eclipse, 9th July, *read* Lunar.
A.D. 1916, *for* Lunar Eclipse, 8th January, *read* 18th.

To show how easy it is to make mistakes in dates, it will be sufficient to state that the Emperor Bâber has given the wrong date for his own famous battle of Khânwa, in which he defeated Râna Sangrâm of Mewâr. Bâber says that it took place on Saturday, the 13th of the second Jamâdi, A.H. 933, which both Erskine and Dowson make the 16th March A.D. 1527.† That the name of the week day is correct we learn from Shekh Zein-uddin, who repeats the name in the following quotation from the Korân: "Since God has given a blessing on your Saturday." But the 13th of the second Jamâdi was a Sunday as will be seen from Bâber's own statements of other dates in the same year. Thus he calls—

24th Muharrám 933		... ...	a Wednesday.
15th Safar	„	... ...	Wednesday.
16th Rabi I	„	... ...	Friday.
9th Jamadi I	„	... ...	Monday.
14th „	„	... ...	Saturday.

All of these dates bring us to Monday as the 30th or last day of Jamâdi I, and to Tuesday as the 1st of Jamâdi II. Consequently, Saturday was the 12th and not the 13th of that month—a fact which has escaped the notice of both Erskine and Dowson.

With reference to the intercalary months of the Hindu luni-solar year, I may mention that there is a great divergence between the published lists of Jervis and Cowasjee Patell.‡ At page 91 I have quoted the native rule as given by Warren and Prinsep, and the following example will show that the table published by Jervis is certainly wrong :

* For these two inscriptions of Jaika, see my accounts of the Gupta and Vikramâditya eras in this volume.

† Baber's Memoirs, translated by Erskine, p. 258.

Jervis's Weights, Measures, and Coins of India, p. 94 ; Cowasjee Patell's Chronology.

In the Saka year 1091, or A.D. 1168, the month of Srâvana was intercalary as recorded in an inscription of Vyaya Pandya Deva.* At that date the luni-solar year began on the 1st March, and the solar year on the 24th March. The 23rd March was, therefore, the 31st day of the solar month of Chaitra, and the 1st March was the 8th day of the solar Chaitra. Now, according to the native rule when the luni-solar year begins on the 6th, 7th or 8th of the solar month of Chaitra, then the month of Srâvana will be intercalary. Turning to my Table XVII, page 175, it will be seen that in the year A.D. 1168, or Saka 1091, the month of Srâvana was intercalary. That it was an intercalary year is proved absolutely by the initial date of the following year Saka 1092, which is 20 days later, and therefore the year 1091 just ended must have consisted of 13 lunar months.

But Jervis makes the year 1091 Saka a common year, and assigns the intercalary month of Srâvana to the year 1093 Saka. The Patell's year of intercalation are correct, and so also are his names of the intercalary months so far as I have had leisure to test them.

ALEXANDER CUNNINGHAM.

* Pali, Sanskrit, and Old Kanarese inscriptions. By J. F. Fleet. No. 141.

CONTENTS.

INDIAN ERAS.

TABLES.

Christian Era.

Seleukidan Era.

Indian Eras.

Muhammadan Era.

ERRATA.

Page 7, line 22, *for* 'K*âli*-Yuga,' *read* '*Kali*-Yuga,' and the same correction in other places.
Page 25, No. 43, *for* '*Sanmya*,' *read* '*Saumya*.'
Page 42, line 2, *for* '165-164,' *read* '166-165.'
———, line 10, *for* '165-164,' *read* '166-165.'
———, line 11, *for* '161-160,' *read* '162-161.'
———, line 12, *for* '139-138,' *read* '140-139.'
———, line 13, *for* '129-128,' *read* '130-129.'
Page 58, line 24, *for* 'any,' *read* 'my.'
Page 73, line 2, *insert* '*Guru*,' *after* '*Dhamma*.'
———, line 19, *for* '1929' *read* '1029.'
Page 83, line 23, *for* 'Sunh,' *read* 'Sanh.'
Page 86, line 36, *for* '*of* the year,' *read* '*to* the year.'
Page 164, opposite A.D. 820, *insert*, in 1st and 3rd columns of Jupiter-Cycles, two black circles, to show that two names have been omitted.
Page 168, opposite A.D. 945, in column 3, *for* '23,' *read* '22.'
Page 169, opposite A.D. 972, in column of initial days, *for* '*Tu.* 19,' *read* '*Mo.* 18.'
———, opposite A.D. 974, *for* '*Mo.* 26 Feb.' *read* '*Th.*'
Page 186, opposite A.D. 1496, *for* '*We.* 16 Mar.' *read* '*Tu.* 15.'
Page 224, line 2, should *read* "in which *each* year has a separate name."

N.B.—Page 45—add at foot:

If the correction of Kallippus of 1 day in 76 years had been adopted by the Seleukidæ, then the year 2 of their era would have begun on the 2nd October 312 B.C., and every succeeding 77th year would also have begun on the same day of the corresponding Christian year. Thus the following years of the Seleukidan era would all have begun on the 2nd October:—

An. Sel.	1,	77,	153,	229,	305,	381,	457,	533,	609
In B.C.	312,	236,	160,	84,	8,	A.D. 69,	145,	221,	297

The fact that the battle of Arbela was fought on the 2nd October 331 B.C., near the end of the month of Gorpiæus, shows that the Macedonians of Alexander's army had not adopted the corrected Calendar of Kallippus, otherwise the 2nd of October would have been the 1st of Hyperberetæus.

N.B.—P. 95—add the following paragraph:—

When the given date falls in an intercalary year *after* the intercalary month, then 30 days must be added to the number of days given in Table X. Thus, if the given date should be 10th Mâgha-sudi, and the year be an intercalary one, 30 days must be added to the number of 305 days given in the Table, unless the intercalary month should happen to be Phâlguna, which being later in the year, would not affect the month of Mâgha.

BOOK

OF

INDIAN ERAS.

ANCIENT INDIAN MODES OF RECKONING TIME.

The natural divisions of time—years, months, and days—have, in all ages, been determined by the motions of the sun and moon. In India the day was reckoned from sunrise to sunrise; the month, from one moon to another moon; and the year, from the beginning of one season until its return.

The most ancient year probably consisted of 360 days, which approximated roughly to twelve revolutions of the moon and one of the sun. In one of the hymns of the Rig Veda the sun's annual course through the heavens is described as his *twelve-spoked wheel.** The 360 days, with as many nights, are called his 720 children. In another part of the same hymn the sun's annual course is somewhat differently described: "The felloes are 12, the wheel is 1, 3 are the axles: within it are collected 360 spokes."† Here the spokes represent the number of days; the axles are the three seasons of Heat, Rain, and Cold; and the 12 felloes are the 12 months.

But the great difference of 11 days between 12 lunations and 1 revolution of the sun must soon have led to the establishment of the old cycle of 5 solar years and 62 lunations. Taking the solar year at 365¼ days, and the moon's revolution at 29½ days, the 5 solar years would have been 1826¼ days, while the 62 lunations would have been 1829 days. The difference of 2¾ days in the lustrum of 5 years would have made a yearly difference of upwards of half a day. The five years consisted of three ordinary years of 12 lunar months, and of two years, the 2nd and 5th, each with an intercalary, or thirteenth month.

---

* So also in the Surya Siddhânta, xii, 19, Varâha Mihira speaks of the year as a 'wheel.'

† Wilson's Rig Veda, II, 143; and also II, 131.

B

This intercalary, or thirteenth month, is very plainly alluded to in the Rig Veda,* where Varuna is said to know the 12 months, "and that which is supplementarily engendered," or, as Dr. Max Müller has it: "He knews the 12 months with their offspring, and knows the month which is produced in addition." †

Dr. Max Müller also notes that, "In the hymns of the Yajur Veda the 13th month is changed already into a deity. Oblations are offered (Vâjasan Sanhitâ, vii, 31) to each of the twelve months, and at the end one oblation is made to Anhasaspati, the deity of the intercalary month. In the Brâhmanas likewise the thirteenth month is mentioned, and in the Jyotisha the theory of intercalation is fully explained." It seems certain therefore that the intercalary month was well known as early as the Vedic Period.

Each year of this five-year cycle, or lustrum, had a separate name. This important fact was first made known by Colebrooke from the White Yajur Veda. The same names are also given by Varâha Mihira, who says:‡ "The first year of each lustrum, called *Samvatsara,* is (ruled by) Agni; the second, *Parivatsara,* by the Sun; the third, *Iddvatsara,* by the Moon; the fourth, *Anuvatsara,* by the Creator; and the last, *Udavatsara,* by Rudra." But the passage in the Yajur Veda goes on to say: "May mornings appertain to Thee, may days and nights, and *fortnights,* and months, and seasons, belong to Thee." Here then we see that, as early as the time of the Yajur Veda, the whole system of lunar months, with their light and dark fortnights, and of intercalary months, to adapt the lunar months to solar reckoning, had already been established.§

We have another testimony to the early use of the lunar fortnights in a passage of Quintus Curtius, whose information must have been obtained from some of the writers who accompanied Alexander the Great.‖ "Their months consist of fifteen days; but they keep the

---

* Wilson's Rig Veda, I, 65.

† History of Ancient Sanskrit Literature, p. 212.

‡ Dr. Kern's Translation of the Brihat Sanhita, C. viii, 24.

§ Yâjnavalkya also [C. ii, 6] says, that a petition made to the king should give the year, month, *half-month,* and day.

‖ Vita Alexandri, C. viii, 9: "Menses in quinos denos descripserunt dies: anni plena spatia servant. Lunæ cursu notant tempora, non, ut plerique, cum orbem sidus implevit, sed cum se curvare cœpit in cornua."

full year. They reckon time by the course of the moon; not as most people do, but by half-moons."

We also learn the same thing from the inscriptions of Asoka, which are about eighty years later than Alexander. Thus in the separate edicts at Dhauli we find mention of the month of Tishya (*Mâsi-cha Tise*), of the lunar fortnight (*athami pakhaye*, or the 8th day of the *paksha*), and of the three seasons (*tisu chatum-Mâsisu*, or the three four-monthly periods). On three days the slaughter of animals also is forbidden, namely, on the day of 'fullmoon,' *punnamâsi* (called also *pannadasam*, or the 15th day), on the 14th day, and on the day after the conjunction.

The old year was divided into three seasons of Heat, Rain, and Cold, called *Grishma, Varsha,* and *Hemanta,*—all of which names are found in the Indo-Scythian inscriptions. They are also commonly known as *Dhûp-kâl, Barkha-kâl, Sît-kâl.** So in Ceylon the rainy season, or *Wasso,* still consists of four months, and extends from July to November. In ancient times, however, *Wasso* or *Varsha* extended from June to October; but owing to the greater length of the Indian year the seasons fall back about one day and-a-half in every hundred years. At the present time the solar year begins on the 13th of April instead of on the 21st of March. In consequence of this difference the beginning of *Varsha,* or the rainy season, in the times of Alexander and Asoka, would have fallen just one month earlier than at present.

In the Indo-Scythian inscriptions from Mathura, the fortnights are not designated as light and dark, or the waxing and the waning of the moons, but are numbered throughout each season as the 1st, 2nd, 3rd, &c., fortnights of the hot, the rainy, or cold season. Thus one of Vasudeva's inscriptions is dated in

Sam. 83—*Gr.* 2—*Di.* 10

that is, *Samvatsara* 83, *Grishma* 2 *Paksha, Divasa* 10; or, "on the 10th day of the 2nd fortnight of Grishma in the year 83." But as the names of the Hindu months of Chaitra, Vaisâkha, Ashâdha, and Srâvana are found in the Indo-Scythian inscriptions from Gândhâra, along with the Macedonian names of Daisios, Apellaios, and Artemisios, during the reigns of Kanishka and Huvishka, it is difficult to say which of the

---

* Abul Fazl, Gladwin's Translation of Ain-i-Akbari, I, 266, gives these three names, and significantly adds, "throughout Hindustan they do not reckon more than three seasons of the year."

two systems of naming the lunar fortnights may be the older. I have a suspicion, however, that the indigenous nomenclature may have been by numbering, and that the other method of waxing and waning fortnights may have been borrowed from the Greek *μηνος ισταμενου* and *μηνος φθίνοντος*.

The oldest eras described by the astronomers are the *Saptârshi-Kâl*, or cycle of the seven Rishis; the *Bârhaspatya-Mânas*, or sixty and twelve year cycles of Jupiter; and the *Kâli-Yuga*, or beginning of the Kâli-Age. Not one of these mounts up to the exaggerated periods of thousands of millions of years like the monstrous systems invented by the astronomers. The oldest of them, the *Saptârshi-Kâl*, ascends only to B.C. 4077, or perhaps to 6777 B.C., while the *Bârhaspatya-Mâna* and the Kâli-Yuga reach only a little beyond 3000 B.C. In Alexander's time the Hindus did not claim a greater antiquity than B.C. 6777. I have therefore a very strong suspicion that the present extravagant system of Yugas and Mahâyugas, Manwantaras, and Kalpas, was an invention of the astronomers, which they based on their newly-acquired knowledge of the precession. The problem was a simple one: Given the precession of 49·8 seconds, as determined by Hipparchus, the period of one revolution through the whole circle of 360° would be $26{,}024\frac{16}{166}$ years. To obtain a whole number of years the fraction was got rid of in the usual way by multiplying 26,024 by 166, and adding 16 to the product, a process which gives a period of exactly 4,320,000 years, or just one *Yuga*.

It may be objected that the Hindu astronomers did not adopt the precession of Hipparchus. But this will not alter the case, as their own determinations of the precession give precisely the same result. The precession fixed by Parâsara is 46·5 seconds, and that of Aryabhata 46·2 seconds. Following the same process as before, we obtain for Parâsara $27{,}870\frac{150}{155}$ years as the period of one revolution, and $28{,}051\frac{146}{154}$ years for Aryabhata, both of which periods give the same whole number of 4,320,000 years. Exactly the same result is also obtainable from the European precession of 50·1 seconds, which gives a period of $25{,}868\frac{44}{167}$ years for one revolution, and a whole number of 4,320,000 years.

But if this be the true origin of the Hindu *Yuga* and the monstrous system of *Mahâyugas, Manwantaras,* and *Kalpas*, it follows that some other mode of reckoning must have been in use before the Christian era. Now the only early eras used in Northern India, of which detailed accounts still remain, are the cycle of the seven Rishis, the two cycles of Jupiter, and the Kâli-Yuga. The Saptârshi-Kâl is unknown in Southern India; but the Kâli-Yuga and the 60-year cycle of Jupiter are well known, besides the two cycles of Parasurâma and Grahaparivrithi, which are peculiar to Southern India. The eras of Buddha and Mahâvira, both of which are prior to Vikramâditya, must have been used by the Buddhists and the Jains at an early period. The former was certainly current amongst the Buddhists in the time of Asoka; and the latter was probably in use about the same period. In the Mathura inscriptions of the Indo-Scythian kings, which are found upon the statues of both Jains and Buddhists, the dates are invariably expressed in an era which may have originated with Kanishka, but which was most probably only an Indian adoption of the Seleukidan era as suggested by Mr. Thomas.

In dealing with Indian dates there is one fact that must never be forgotten, namely, that every year that is mentioned by number, that number refers to years actually elapsed, just as Europeans reckon their ages. When a man says that he is 50 years old, he means literally that 50 full years have passed since his birth, and that he is then in his 51st year. So when a Hindu records the year 80 of the Vikrama Samvat, or any other era, he means that 80 full years of that era have actually elapsed, and that the current year is the 81st.

Only one inscription to my knowledge has yet been found dated in any of the intercalary months. This is no doubt due to the entire want of festivals in these months, and as grants of land are usually made on the festival days, there are of course few inscriptions recorded in the intercalary months.

I.—SAPTÂRSHI-KÂL;

OR,

CYCLE OF THE SEVEN RISHIS.

The Sapt-Rishi-Kâl, or "Cycle of the Seven Rishis," called also the *Saptârshi* and *Sat Rikhi Kâl*, is so named after the seven stars of the constellation of the Great Bear. It is the only mode of reckoning employed in the Râja Tarangini, or History of Kashmir, and it is still used in the hill states to the south-east of Kashmir between the Chenâb on the west and the Jumna on the east. The general use of this cycle did not escape the notice of Abu Rihân, who has preserved much valuable information regarding the different centenary cycles in use at the time of Mahmud's invasion of India.

"In India," he says, "the vulgar reckon by ages, and these ages follow one after another. This they call the *Samvatsara* of a hundred. When one century is passed they drop it, and begin another. They call this the *Lok-Kâl*, or 'People's Era.'" * Now this last is the same name that is used by Kalhana Pandit of Kashmir, who says: †

Laukikebde chaturvinsate Sakakâlasya sampratam.
Saptatyâtyadhikam yâtam sahasram parivatsarah.

"The 24th year of the *Laukika* corresponds with the year 1070 of the Saka-Kâl."

From this statement we learn that the year 1 of the *Laukika* coincided with 1047 of the Saka, or A.D. 1025; and as the cycle was a centenary one, the first year of each century must have corresponded with the 25th year of each Christian century. This is placed beyond all doubt by the following facts:—

1.—In the Temple of Baijnâth, in the district of Mandi, there is an inscription which bears the two dates of Sake 726 and Lok-Kâl 80. Deducting 79 from each date we obtain the Sake year 647, or A.D. 725, as the first year of the Lok-Kâl century.

---

* Reinaud, Fragments Arabes et Persaus, p. 147.

† Râja Tarangini, I, 52.

2.—Captain Patrick Gerard of the Gorkha Battalion, then stationed at Kotgarh on the Satlej, heads one of his notes as follows:—"*Kacha Sambat*, or year 2, or 1826-27, Kotgarh, June 25th, 1826." By this account the year 1825 A.D. was the first of the *Kacha Sambat*, or *Sapt-Rishi-Kâl*, of 100 years.

I first became acquainted with the survival of this mode of reckoning in 1846, when I was employed in the Kangra district. It was commonly called the *Sat-Rikhi-Kâl*, but was also well known as the *Pahâri Samvat*, or "Hill era." In the same year I obtained further information about it from Wazir Gusâun, the astute minister of the Mandi state, who accompanied me to Ladâk. From him I learned to read the dates on the Sati Pillars of the Mandi Rânis. Again, in 1859, on my return from Burma, I made new enquiries in Kashmir and Kângra, in Mandi and Kullu, as well as in Kotgarh and Râmpur on the Satlej. I then found that the Pandits of Kashmir still preserved the fanciful mode of reckoning the Lok-Kâl, which was invented by the astronomers, and afterwards adopted by Kalhana Pandit in the Râja Tarangini. All other accounts agree in making the Sapt Rishi cycle older than the Mahâbhârata. But the astronomers differ altogether from the common opinion which has been generally adopted throughout India. According to the almost universal belief of the people the period of the Great War, or the era of Yudhishthira, was also the beginning of the Kâli-Yuga. That this was also the popular belief in former days is proved by the explicit statement of Abul Fazl,* that "In the beginning of the fourth or present *Yuga*, Râjâ Yudhishthira was universal monarch, and the commencement of his reign became the epoch of an era, of which to this time, being the fortieth year of the reign, there have elapsed 4696 years." Now the fortieth year of Akbar was A.D. 1595, which, deducted from 4696, gives B.C. 3101 as the period of Yudhishthira as well as of the Kali-Yuga. In another place also he states that the Mahâbhârata was "carried on in the latter end of the Dwâpara-Yuga. And in a third place he says that the war happened one hundred and five years before the end of the Dwâpara-Yuga, and 4831† years before the fortieth year of Akbar. But Abul Fazl had also heard of the date invented by the astronomers, as near the close of his work he places the reign of Kansa, râjâ of Mathura, "above 4000 years before the fortieth of Akbar," that is between 2400 and 2500 B.C.

---

* Gladwin's Ain-i-Akbari, I, 263: see also II, 88-91.

† This number should be 4801, or 4696 + 105, and not 4831.

On one point all accounts agree—namely, "that the Munis (or Seven Rishis) were in Maghâ when king Yudhishthira reigned over the earth." * But the popular belief assigns the same position of the Seven Rishis to be beginning of the Kâli-Yuga also.

According to the astronomers the era of Yudhishthira varied from 600 to 666 years after the beginning of the Kâli-Yuga. But their determinations depend on such groundless assumptions that they can only be looked upon as mere astronomical fancies. Both Parâsara and Aryabhata assume that the revolutions of the Seven Rishis began with the commencement of the Kalpa of 4,320.000,000 years; and that the number of their revolutions in this period was 1.599,998. But they differ slightly in the number of years elapsed before the beginning of the Kâli-Yuga, which the former makes 1,972.944,000, while the latter has 1,969.920,000. According to Parâsara—

As 4,320.000,000 : 1.972.944,000 :: 1.599,998 : 730,719·0866
or 10,000 : 4567

that is, at the beginning of the Kâli-Yuga the Seven Rishis had accomplished 730,719 complete revolutions plus ..... ·0866 of a revolution. Multiplying this fraction by 2,700 years, or one whole revolution, we get years 233·8200 of a revolution expired before Kâli-Yuga began. Then as the Great War took place when the Seven Rishis were in Maghâ (the 10th Nakshatra), we must deduct the 233·82 from 900, by which we obtain 666·18 years of Kâli-Yuga expired at the date of Yudhishthira.

By a similar process for Aryabhata, we get 662·4 years of Kâli-Yuga expired as the date of Yudhishthira; and by repeating the process for Varâha Mihira, we get 653 Kâli-Yuga as his date of the Mahâbhârata. The last is the date adopted by Kalhana Pandit, who says: † "When 653 years of the Kâli-Yuga had expired, the Kurus and Pândavas flourished."

This fanciful date invented by the astronomers is noticed by Abu Rihân as the *Pându-Kâl,* or "era of the Pandus," which was different from the Kâli-Yuga; but he omits to mention its starting point.‡

The theory of the astronomers is in direct opposition to the explicit statements of the Purânas, which are in complete accord with the common belief.§ Thus the Vishnu Purâna says:—" When the first two

---

* Râja Tarangini, I, 56. † Râja Tarangni, I, 51.

‡ Reinaud, Fragments Arabes et Persaus, p. 137.

§ Vishnu Purana, IV, C. 24, or Hall's Edition, Vol. IV, p. 233.

stars of the Seven Rishis (the Great Bear) rise in the heavens, and some lunar asterism is seen at night at an equal distance between them, then the Seven Rishis continue stationary, in the conjunction, for a hundred years of men. At the *birth of Parikshit* they were in *Maghâ;* and the *Kâli-age then commenced,* which consists of 1200 (divine) years. When the portion of Vishnu (that had been born from Vasudeva) returned to heaven, then the Kâli-age commenced."*

The Bhâgavata Purâna agrees with the Vishnu Purâna in placing the Seven Rishis in Maghâ at the time of the Great War. Thus Suka, *addressing Parikshita,* says: "Of the Seven Rishis, two are first perceived rising in the sky; and the asterism, which is observed to be at night even with the middle of those two stars, is that with which the Rishis are united, and they remain so during a hundred years of men. *In your time,* and *at this moment,* they are situated in Maghâ."

"When the splendour of Vishnu, named Krishna, departed for heaven, then did the Kâli-age, during which men delight in sin, invade the world. So long as he continued to touch the earth with his holy feet, so long the Kâli-age, comprising 1200 (divine) years, began." So also Nrisinha "expounds the Sâkalya Sanhita, and rejects Varâha's rule as disagreeing with the Purânas."†

Varâha himself quotes Vriddha Garga for his account of the cycle of the Seven Rishis.‡ His words are: "1, 2. I shall tell, according to the theory of Vriddha Garga, the course of these Seven Seers, by whom the northern region is, as it were, protected; through whom she shines, as if adorned with a string of pearls, like a maiden with joyful countenance, wearing a wreath of white water-lilies; those Seven Seers, by the turning round of whom the northern region seems dancing, the pole-star being the regulator.

"3. The Seven Seers were in Maghâ when king Yudhishthira ruled the earth, and the period of that king is 2526 years before the Saka era.

"4. They remain moving for a hundred years in each lunar mansion, and rise constantly in the north-east, together with Arundhati."

---

* Wilson's Vishnu Purâna by Hall. † Colebrooke's Essays, II, 313-14-15.

‡ Dr. Kern's Translation of the Brihat Sanhita, C. xiii, 1—4.

But unluckily for Varâha Mihira his commentator, Bhatta Utpala, has given us the very words of Garga, who simply says: *

"At the *junction of the Kâli and Dwâpara ages*, the virtuous sages, who delight in protecting the people, stood at the asterism, over which the Pitris preside (that is *Maghâ*)."

On comparing this quotation with Varâha's statement, we see at once that he has suppressed Garga's mention of the beginning of the Kâli-Yuga to suit his own astronomical fancies. Now Garga states most explicitly that the Seven Rishis were in Maghâ at the beginning of the Kâli-Yuga, and says nothing whatever about Yudhishthira. But the fact that the Rishis were in Maghâ at the time of the Great War was too well known to be altered, and so Varâha accepts this, while he quietly ignores Garga's statement about the Kâli-Yuga. Well might Nrisinha reject "the teaching of Varâha as differing from the Purânas."

The quotations which I have already given from Abu Rihân and Kalhana Pandit show that the fanciful vagaries of the astronomers regarding the date of the Mahâbhârata had already been partially adopted in the 11th and 12th Centuries A.D. But the learned Muhammadan author goes on to show that the use of the Sapt-Rishi cycle had certainly extended to Multân and Sindh.† He says, that "writers differ with regard to the beginning of the year as well as with regard to the initial point of the cycle." He states also that he has "seen the Indians, when they wished to mark the date of the taking of Somnâth, write down 242, 606, and 99, and then add them together, which gives the year of Saka. Abu Rihân explains that 242 shows the number of years (of Saka) which preceded the epoch when the Indians first began to use the centenary cycle, and that this usage commenced with the era of the Guptas. Further, that the sum of 606 shows the number of complete centenary cycles of 101 years each; and lastly, that 99 is the number of years elapsed of the current cycle." These numbers added together give 947 as the year of Saka in which Somnâth was captured, equivalent to the year beginning in April A.D. 1025, and ending in April 1026, which is correct, as Somnâth fell in January 1026.

In confirmation of the accuracy of this process Abu Rihân quotes the following formula from the astronomical tables of Durlabha of Multân:—"Set down 848 and add the Lok-Kâl or vulgar reckoning; the sum will show the year of the Saka era." Abu Rihân then gives

* Colebrooke's Essays, II, 313. † Reinaud, Fragments Arabes et Persaus, p. 147.

the following example:—"Set down the actual date (year 953 of Saka in which he was writing) of Saka, and deduct 848, the remainder 105 will be the Lok-Kâl, and the year of the fall of Somnâth will be 98."

In the first example, the capture of Somnâth is assigned to the year 99 of the Lok-Kâl, and in the second example, to the year 98: but the latter is no doubt a mistake for 99.

As the Lok-Kâl of this description differs from that which has been in use for many centuries throughout Kashmir and all the hill states of the Punjâb and Cis-Sutlej districts, it appears to me either that the Lok-Kâl of Sindh and Multân must have had a different starting point from that of Kashmir, or that Abu Rihân must have been puzzled by conflicting accounts which he obtained from various persons who, perhaps, had but little knowledge of the subject. The latter, I conclude, to have been most probably the case, as Abu Rihân candidly acknowledges the imperfectness of his account, and warns the reader that the results which he gives are uncertain, as several of the numbers (of the centenary cycles) exceed 100.

The Lok-Kâl, or "common era," called also the *Sapt-Rishi-Kâl*, or "era of the Seven Rishis," is a cycle of 2700 years divided into twenty-seven centenary periods, a new reckoning being started at the beginning of each century. The theory of the cycle is, that the Seven Rishis, or stars of Ursa Major, remain for one century in each of the twenty-seven *Nakshatras*, or lunar mansions. All authorities agree in making Aswini the first of the Nakshatras, and in stating that the Mahâbhârata took place when the Rishis were in the lunar constellation Maghâ, the tenth of the series. The Purânas, and the practice of all the people who still use this cycle, excepting only the Kashmiris, agree in making the era of Yudhishthira the same as the Kâli-Yuga. All, however, agree in stating that, at the time of the Mahâbhârata, the Seven Rishis had already passed 75 years in Maghâ. But as Varâha places the Great War 653 years after the beginning of the Kâli-Yuga, or in 2449 B.C., that year should have been the 76th of the tenth Nakshatra, and the 976th year of the cycle. This would fix the first year of each centenary period to the 25th year of each century B.C., and to the 76th year of each century A.D. But to prevent the confusion that would thus have arisen, Varâha simply ignored the generally accepted belief that the Rishis had spent 75 years in Maghâ when the Mahâbhârata took place and retained the initial points of the Saptârshi centuries—only bringing Maghâ down from B.C. 3177 (or 3102 + 75) to B.C. 2477. Accordingly, Varâha's followers place the initial point of the Vrihaspati Chakra in 3377 B.C. in Aswini, so that each century begins in the 26th year of each century of the Kâli-Yuga exactly as Dr. Bühler was informed. This also accords with the statement of my Kashmiri informant that the Rishis had completed three revolutions less 25 years in the Dwâpara-Yuga before the Kâli-Yuga began; that is, their Chakra preceded the Kâli-Yuga by 275 years, equivalent to B.C. 3377, or 3102 + 275 years.

The following is a translation of the reply which I received from the Brahmans of Kangra in A.D. 1859 regarding the *Sapt-Rishi-Kâl*:— "At the beginning of the Kâli-Yuga, the Seven Rishis (or Stars of Ursa Major) had been 75 years in one Nakshatra (Maghâ), and they remained in the same for 25 years longer. These 25 years are the amount of difference between the total number of Kâli-Yuga years elapsed and the number of centuries or years of the Hill cycle [*Pahâri Samvat*] up to the present date. Thus the present year, 1859 of the Christian era, is Kâli-Yuga 4960, and 35 of the 50th Hill cycle, or exactly 25 years short of the number of Kâli-Yuga years."

From another informant I received the following account:—"The Seven Rishis remain for one hundred years in each Nakshatra. They entered into Maghâ 75 years before the beginning of the Kâli-Yuga, and they remained in Maghâ for 25 years of the Kâli-Yuga;" that is until 3077 B.C., when they entered into another Nakshatra.

Similar information was received from the Brahmans of Mandi and Bisahar. But from Kashmir the reply was somewhat different. It was obtained by Mirza Saifuddin after consultation with pandits and astronomers: "The present year 1859 is 4960 of the Kâli-Yuga, and Samvat 35 of the Haft Rikheshar. The Kâli-Yuga is said to be 25 years in advance of the Haft Rikheshar. The seven stars complete one revolution in each Nakshatra in 100 years. When they had completed three revolutions less 25 years in the Dwâpara-Yuga, then the Kâli-Yuga began, and only 2425 years of the first Chakra belong to the Kâli-Yuga. Each whole period of 2700 years is called a *Chakra*, or cycle, in which the Seven Rishis pass through the 27 Nakshatras from Aswini to Revati. Of the second Chakra of 2700 years 25 Nakshatras were completed in the Christian year 1825, or 4926 Kâli-Yuga." This tallies exactly with the information lately obtained in Kashmir by Dr. Bühler, who writes: "I have found in the manuscript several more dates in the Saptrishi era with the thousands added, and all agree with the verse which places the beginning of the era in *Kâli 26*, Chaitra-sudi 1." In these accounts from Kashmir the computation of Varâha Mihira is adopted, which places the era of Yudhishthira in 653 of the Kâli-Yuga, when the Seven Rishis are said to have been in Maghâ, in direct opposition to the commonly received reckoning which places the era of Yudhishthira at the beginning of the Kâli-Yuga.

The informants in Kangra, Mandi, and Bisahar agreed with the Kashmir correspondent in fixing the beginning of the year at the *norâtra*, or new moon of Chaitra; that is Chaitra-sudi 1.

So universal is the belief that the date of the Kâli-Yuga is the same as that of the Mahâbhârata, that the native almanacs state it as a positive fact. Thus Professor Bhândârkar quotes the following from an ordinary Hindu Panchânga of Bombay: "In the Kâli-age there are six founders of eras. First, there was Yudhishthira in Indraprastha, whose era lasted for 3044 years. The second was Vikrama at Ujayani, whose era had a run of 135 years. The third was Salivâhana at Pratisthâna." Here the era of Yudhishthira is made the same as that of the Kâli-Yuga, which also dates from 3044 years before the era of Vikrama.

The first mention of the Lok-Kâl, or cycle of 100 years in the Râja Tarangini, is the year 89, corresponding with A.D. 813-14. Before this period only the lengths of reigns are given, but from A.D. 813 downwards the date of each king's death is carefully recorded, with the name and day of the month as well as the year of the cycle.

I have been thus particular in pointing out the true beginning of each century period of the Lok-Kâl or Sapt-Rishi Chakra in the year 25 of each Christian century, because both Troyer and Wilson, after translating correctly Kalhan's statement that the year 24 of the *Laukika* coincided with 1070 of the Ṣaka (or A.D. 1148) have most deliberately and unaccountably thrown over the native historian's statement and adopted some fancied dates of their own. Thus the 89th year of the Kashmirian cycle, which, as we know from the Baijnâth inscription as well as from Kalhana himself, corresponded with A.D. 813, Troyer refers to A.D. 816, and this error of three years pervades all the dates throughout the first six books of his translation. So also Wilson's Chronology of Kashmir is throughout twenty-one years in advance of the true dates. How all this happened I cannot even guess, but can only repeat the old saying "*aliquando bonus dormitat Ḥomerus.*"

The astronomers have been much puzzled to account for the alleged centennial motion of the Seven Rishis from one Nakshatra to another, which they admit is not visible to the human race. Thus the commentator Sridhara Swâmi explains, that "the two stars which rise first are Pulaha and Kratu; and whichever asterism is in a line south from the middle of those stars is that with which the Seven Rishis are united, and they so remain for one hundred years." Other explanations are cited by Colebrooke, who closes his account with the opinion of Kamalâkara, who observes, that "no such motion of the stars is perceptible. Remarking, however, that the authority of the *Purânas* and *Sanhitâs*, which affirm their revolution, is uncontrovertible, he reconciles faith and experience by saying, that the stars themselves are fixed; but the Seven Rishis are invisible deities, who perform the stated revolution in the period specified." *

The mythologists, however, give a different explanation. According to them the Seven Rishis, having given offence to their teacher in the Satya-Yuga, were cursed by him and condemned to spend the remainder of their lives as antelopes, wandering from one Nakshatra to another every hundred years. Hence they were named the *Sapta-Mriga*, or "Seven Antelopes." This name recalls the *Septem Triones* of the Romans. Some say that the Rishis were doomed to take the shapes of different animals every hundred years.

But however obscure may be the origin of the cycle, there is no doubt about its antiquity, as both Varâha Mihira and Bhattotpala refer to the description of it given by Vriddha Garga, whose date is fixed by Dr. Kern to the first century B.C. By his account the cycle must have been in use before the beginning of the Kâli-Yuga, as he notes that the Seven Rishis had then passed 25 years in the Nakshatra or Lunar asterism of Maghâ. Then as Maghâ was the 10th of these asterisms, the beginning of that Chakra or cycle of 2700 years must be dated back by 975 years to B.C. 4077. But the genealogical lists of the Purânas point to a still earlier period, as they place Krishna in the 52nd generation after Brahmâ. Allowing twenty-five years to a generation the Hindu date of the creation would be thrown back by upwards of 1300 years before the Kâli-Yuga, or to B. C. 4400.

On referring to the accounts of ancient India handed down to us by Alexander's companions, I find a curious statement which seems to bear directly on this question of the starting point of Indian chronology.

---

* See Colebrooke's Essays, II, 314 and 316.

The statement is preserved by Pliny, Solinus, and Arrian. The first says, "Colliguntur à Libero Patre ad Alexandrum Magnum reges eorum CLIV, annis sex millia CCCCLI adjiciunt et menses tres,"—that is, "they reckon from Bacchus to Alexander the Great 154 kings, who reigned for 6451 years and 3 months." As Alexander entered the Panjâb in 326 B.C., and left it towards the end of the same year, this account fixes the starting point of Indian chronology to the year 6451¼ + 326 = 6777 B.C.

Now it is a curious coincidence that if another *Saptârshi Chakra* of 2700 years be added to 4077 B.C., or the beginning of the Chakra indicated by Vriddha Garga, the initial year will fall in 6777, the very year which was said by the Indians of Alexander's time to be the initial point of their history. This coincidence is certainly very remarkable, and as it is the result of the addition of such a large period as 2700 years, it would seem to point to the conclusion that so early as the time of Alexander the *Saptârshi Chakra* of 2700 years was the common mode of Indian reckoning. This indeed has already been inferred from the statement of Vriddha Garga himself.

The reckoning of the Lok-Kâl, as now used in Kashmir and the other hill states, is by the common luni-solar years beginning on Chaitra-sudi 1, or the new moon of Chaitra. The cycle consists of 27 centuries, each counting from 1 to 100 years, when a new reckoning is begun. The first year of each century corresponds with the 25th year of each Christian century. According to Abu Rihân the people of Multân had only recently adopted the Kashmiri reckoning from Chaitra, while in Sindh and Kanauj they still reckoned the year from *Mânkhir* (that is from Mârgasiras or Agrahayana). *

For ascertaining any dates recorded in the Lok-Kâl the corresponding year of the Kâli-Yuga must be obtained from the General Table, and the calculation must be made according to the rules laid down for the luni-solar calendar. In the Râja Tarangini the years are always mentioned by their numbers, and so they are in the Baijnâth and Mandi inscriptions. But the name of the century, which should be that of the Nakshatra, is never given.

In Abu Rihân's account of the centenary cycle, there are several discordant numbers which I find it difficult to reconcile. He states that when the Indians wished to note the date of the taking of Somnâth [January 1026 A.D.], they set down the figures 242, 606, and 99, which added

* Reinaud, Fragments Arabes et Persaus, p. 146.

together gave 947 of the Saka era [equivalent to A.D. 1025-26]. He explains the numbers by referring 242 to the number of years which had passed before the Indians began to use the centenary cycle, which came in with the era of the Guptas.* In a previous passage, however, he makes this period only 241 years. The figure 606 indicates the number of complete centuries (counting 101 years to each century), and the last figure 99 represents the number of years elapsed (éconlees) of the current cycle. Now it seems to me that Abu Rihân has not properly understood the number 606, which I would explain as follows: The unit 6 seems to me to refer to the period which had elapsed between the establishment of the so-called Gupta era in A.D. 319, and the beginning of the centenary reckoning in A.D. 325. According to this explanation, the account will stand thus:—

A.D. 78-79, establishment of the Saka era.
241 years.
319 establishment of the so-called Gupta era.
6 interval.
325 beginning of the centenary cycle.
600 years elapsed.
925
99 years of current cycle elapsed.
1024-25 A.D

But as the 99th year is said to have elapsed (éconlee), the current year of the cycle would have been 100 and not 99. Accordingly, the year A.D. would have been 1025-26, which is correct, as the fall of Somnâth took place in January 1026.

The following table will be of use in showing at a glance the initial year of each century, as well as its Nakshatra or Lunar asterism according to the different reckonings of Vriddha Garga and the Purânas on one hand, and of Varâha and the later astronomers on the other. The numbers placed against the names of the asterisms show the number of each century, while the beginning of the *Chakra*, or complete cycle of 2,700, is indicated by the No. 1 placed against Aswini. Thus, on the left hand, it will be seen that the cycle of the commonly received account began in the years 6777, 4077, and 1377 B.C., and in 1325 A.D., while those of Varâha Mihira's reckoning began in 3377 and 677 B.C. By the former it will be seen that the Seven Rishis were in Maghâ between 3177 and 3077 B.C., that is in B.C. 3101 at the beginning of the Kâli-Yuga; while by the latter, they are placed in Maghâ just 653 years later, between B.C. 2477 and 2377, that is, in B.C. 2448.

* Reinaud, Fragments Arabes et Persans, p. 146.

	According to Vriddha Garga and the Purânas.	LOK-KAL, or SAPTARSHI CYCLE. Initial years of Centuries.				According to Varâha Mihira and the later Astronomers.	
		B. C.	B. C.	B. C.	A. D.		
1	Aswini	6777	4077	1377	1325	U. Ashadha ...	21
2	Bharani	6677	3977	1277	1425	Sravanâ	22
3	Krittikâ	6577	3877	1177	1525	Dhanishthâ ...	23
4	Rohini	6477	3777	1077	1625	Satabhishâ ...	24
5	Mrigasiras ...	6377	3677	977	1725	P. Bhadrpadâ ...	25
6	Ardrâ	6277	3577	877	1825	U. ——	26
7	Punarvasu ...	6177	3477	777	1925	Revati	27
8	Pushyâ	6077	3377	677	2025	Aswini	1
9	Asleshâ	5977	3277	577	2125	Bharani	2
10	MAGHA... ...	5877	3177	477	2225	Krittikâ	3
11	P. Phalguni ...	5777	3077	377	2325	Rohini	4
12	U. ——	5677	2977	277	2425	Mrigasiras ...	5
13	Hastâ	5577	2877	177	2525	Ardrâ	6
14	Chitrâ	5477	2777	B.C. 77	2625	Punarvasu ...	7
15	Swâti	5377	2677	A.D. 25	2725	Pushyâ	8
16	Visâkhâ	5277	2577	125	2825	Asleshâ	9
17	Anurâdhâ ...	5177	2477	225	2925	MAGHA... ...	10
18	Jyeshthâ ...	5077	2377	325	3025	P. Phalguni ...	11
19	Mulâ	4977	2277	425	3125	U. ——	12
20	P. Ashâdha ...	4877	2177	525	3225	Hastâ	13
21	U. ——	4777	2077	625	3325	Chitrâ	14
22	Sravanâ	4677	1977	725	3425	Swâti	15
23	Dhanishthâ ...	4577	1877	825	3525	Visâkhâ	16
24	Satabhishâ ...	4477	1777	925	3625	Anurâdhâ ...	17
25	P. Bhadrpadâ ...	4377	1677	1025	3725	Jyeshthâ ...	18
26	U. ——	4277	1577	1125	3825	Mulâ	19
27	Revati	4177	1477	1225	3925	P. Ashâdha ...	20

II.—BÂRHASPATYA-MÂNA,

OR

60-YEAR CYCLE OF JUPITER.

THE *Bârhaspatya-Mâna*, or Cycle of Jupiter, is a period of sixty years, or five revolutions of the planet, each year of which has a different name. This era was considered by Warren to be "very ancient;"* but James Prinsep, misled by Csoma de Körös and Bentley, thought it was a "comparatively recent introduction."† The former understood from the Tibetan authorities that the Vrihaspati Chakra was introduced *into India* about the year 965 A.D., a date which tallied very closely with Bentley's assumed epoch of Varâha Mihira in A.D. 966-67. Happily, Bentley's vagaries have long ago been set to rest, while Colebrooke's date of Varâha Mihira, the author of the Sûrya Siddhânta, has been satisfactorily established. As Varâha died in A.D. 587, his writings describing the Cycles of Jupiter must be referred to the middle of the Sixth Century A.D. But as he quotes Vriddha Garga as his authority,‡ the Jovian Cycle must have been in use before the Christian era.

There are three different modes of reckoning the cycle of sixty years, of which the oldest is certainly that preserved by Varâha Mihira, as the first year of the Kâli-Yuga, by his account, is the twenty-seventh year of the Jovian Cycle. The second is the reckoning of the Jyotishtava, which is clearly only a correction of Varâha Mihira's method, as it makes the first year of the cycle correspond with the first year of the Kâli-Yuga. Both of these reckonings have been in use in Northern India, where the necessary omission of every eighty-sixth year of the Jovian Cycle has always been preserved. The third method is the reckoning followed in the south of India, by which the Jovian year is considered exactly the same as the solar year, and the

---

* Warren's Kâla Sankâlita, p. 199. † Prinsep's Useful Tables, p 27.

‡ Davis in Asiatic Researches, III, p. 78.

names are taken in succession, without any correction for the difference between the period of one revolution of the sun and that of one-twelfth part of a revolution of Jupiter. By this mode of reckoning the actual Cycle of Jupiter is entirely lost sight of, and the sixty names become simply the appellations of as many solar years.

The Bârhaspatya-Mâna has been fortunate in finding two such capable expounders as Davis and Warren, to whose works I may refer for a complete exposition of the cycle. It will be sufficient here to note the rules for finding the years of the cycle according to the two slightly different modes of the Northern reckoning.

The Sûrya Siddhânta rule, as explained, is as follows:—Divide the expired years of the Kâli-Yuga by 86, add the quotient to the dividend; divide the sum by 60, and the quotient gives the number of cycles expired. Then, if the proposed year should fall less than 31 from the last expunged year of the Chakra, add 28 to the remainder; but if it should be more than 31, add only 27; and the remainder so increased will indicate the current year of the Chakra. Take the year 223 A.D. = 3324 Kâli-Yuga, as an example:

÷ 86) 3324 (38 + 3324 = 3362
÷ 60 ——
56 + 2 over
add 28
——
30th year of 57th cycle.

A reference to the general table will show that this result is correct, reckoning from Prabhava.

The rule followed in the second method is thus laid down in the Brihat Sanhita:*

"Multiply the years expired since the era of the Saka King by 11 and the product by 4; add 8589; divide that sum by 3750. To the quotient add the Saka years; divide the sum by 60 (to find the cycles).

Taking the same year as before A.D. 223 − 78 = 145 Saka—

145
× 11
——
1595
× 4
——
6380
+ 8589
——
÷ 3750) 14969 (4

4
+ 145
——
149
÷ 60 ——
Cycles 2+29 years complete
or 30th year current as before.

* Dr. Kern's Translation of the Brihat Sanhita, c. viii, 20-21.

The Jyotishtava rule is practically the same as that of the Varâha Sanhita; the only real difference being in the amount of the *Kshepa*, or sum added :—" Multiply the Saka year by 22, add 4291 to the product, and divide by 1875. Next add the quotient to the Saka year, and divide the sum by 60. The remainder will be the last expired year reckoning from Prabhava."

Taking the same year as before A.D. 223 − 78 = 145 Saka,

Then 145 Saka	145 Saka
22	4
290	149
290	÷ 60 —
3190	Cycles 2 + 29 complete years, or 30th year current as before.
4291	
÷ 1875) 7481 (4	

In these last two methods the multiplying by 11 and then by 4 of the first is equivalent to multiplying by 44, which is exactly double the multiplier 22 of the second; just as the divisor 3750 of the first is double 1875 of the second. In other words, $\frac{11 \times 4}{3750} = \frac{22}{1875}$. There is a slight difference in the *Kshepa*, or addition, as the half of 8589 is $4294\frac{1}{2}$, or a little more than 4291. As James Prinsep has remarked, the factor $\frac{22}{1875}$ " is equivalent to dividing by 85·227, the period when a year is to be expunged by this system."

But the same result may be obtained by a further simplification of the process, as follows :—To the Saka date add 195, then divide the sum by 85, and add the quotient to the Saka year. Then divide by 60: the quotient will give the number of cycles expired, and the remainder the number of expired years of the current cycle. Thus taking the same year 145 Saka, the process is

145	145
+ 195	+ 4
85) 340 (4	149
	60 —

Cycles 2 + 29 years expired.

By the Telinga reckoning of Southern India the cycle began twelve years before the Kâli-Yuga, the first year of which corresponds with

Pramatha, the thirteenth year of the cycle. The rule for ascertaining the cycle year for any particular date is simply to divide the expired years of the Kali-Yuga by 60, and the quotient will give the number of expired years.

Take the same year A.D. 223 + 3161 = 3324 Kali-Yuga.
÷ 60 ——
Cycles 55 + 24 years.

add 12 for the years before Pramatha, and the result is 36 years of the cycle expired, and the 37th year current as in the general table.

As the years of the 60-year Cycle of Jupiter are only occasionally mentioned in the inscriptions of Northern India, I have not thought it worth while to give the Jyotishtava reckoning in addition to that of the Sûrya Siddhânta. In fact, the difference between the two is never more than one year, and that only between the two periods of omitted years. In the Second Century A.D., the omitted year of the Sûrya Siddhânta reckoning took place in 136, while that of the Jyotishtava was two years later—in 138. In A.D. 394, the omissions took place together. In A.D. 479 the Jyotishtava omitted year preceded that of the Sûrya Siddhânta by one year, but in the present Century the Jyotishtava omitted year, No. 48 in 1848, preceded the other, No. 1 of 1856, by thirteen years. The current years of the two cycles, however, generally correspond, excepting in the short periods between the two omissions, when they differ by only one year. The years 847 and 907 A.D. were initial years of cycles in all three modes of reckoning: and the numbers of all the years coincided from A.D. 825 (the 39th year) down to A.D. 909.

The Telinga computation, though useless as an astronomical cycle, is of great value in fixing the dates of inscriptions where the numerical figures are at all doubtful, or where the name of the era may be uncertain. Of the latter class there is a very curious example in an inscription translated by Dr. Hall.* The record is dated "in the *Saka* year twelve hundred and seventy-five, called *Chitrabhânu*, in the light fortnight of *Mârgasirsha*, its fifth day, and Saturday." Now nothing can apparently be clearer than this date, which corresponds with A.D. 1353; and yet it is absolutely certain that the word 'Saka' cannot be intended for the *Saka* era,† as the name of *Chitrabhânu*, which is the 16th year of the Jovian Cycle, corresponds exactly with 1275 of the

* Bengal Asiatic Society's Journal. XXVIII, pp. 4-5.

† I have since found an inscription dated in Vikrama Saka.

Vikramâditya era according to the Northern reckoning, while the Saka year 1275 is the 33rd year of the Jovian Cycle in the North, and the 27th year in the South, both many years distant from Chitrabhânu. But besides this evidence there is also that of the week day, *Saturday*, which agrees with Mârgasiras-Sudi 5 in the Vikramâditya era, and not in the Saka era, when that date fell on a Monday. Another reason for accepting the earlier date is the fact that Mâlwa had already become a province of the Muhammadan empire of Delhi long before Saka 1275, or A. D. 1353, whereas in Vikrama Samvat 1275, or A.D. 1218, Mâlwa was still under Hindu rule, as the invasion of Iltitmish did not take place until A.D. 1230.

A good example of the Southern mode of reckoning is found in the date of the Kardla copper-plates, in 894 Saka in the year *Angiras*, on Wednesday, the full moon of Aswina, during an eclipse of the moon.* The year *Angiras* is the 6th of the cycle corresponding with 894 Saka (or A.D. 972) of the Southern reckoning. According to the Northern reckoning the year was Srimukha, or the 7th. But, strange to say, the full moon of Aswina was not a Wednesday according to Cowasjee Patell,† who makes the luni-solar year of Saka 894 begin on Tuesday the 19th March 972 A.D. The full moon of Aswina is the 192nd day of the ordinary year, which number divided by 7 gives 3 over, or Thursday the 26th of September for the day of full moon. Now we know that there was an eclipse of the moon on Wednesday the 25th of September A.D. 972, which actually was the full moon of Aswina according to the Northern reckoning of the Sûrya Siddhânta. I have calculated the date by both reckonings, and I find that, by the Southern reckoning, the 1st Vaisâkh of the solar year fell on Friday the 22nd March, and the 1st Chaitra-Sudi of the luni-solar year 4·49 days earlier, or on Monday the 18th March 972 A.D., and not on the 19th as given by Cowasjee Patell. According to the Northern reckoning the 1st Vaisâkh of the solar year fell on Saturday the 23rd March, and the 1st Chaitra-Sudi of the luni-solar year 4·808, or five days earlier,—that is, on Monday the 18th March. By both reckonings, therefore, the full moon of Aswina fell on a Wednesday. But the cycle year of Jupiter agrees with the Southern reckoning.

The cyclic names, however, sometimes disagree one year with the reckoning of the other eras. Thus there are no less than three inscriptions, all dated in the Saka year 730, whilst each has a different year of the Jovian Cycle assigned to it. These are Vyâya the 20th year, Sar-

---

* Royal Asiatic Society's Journal, III, 104.

† Patell's Chronology, p. 136.

vajit the 21st, and Sarvadhâri the 22nd. The second name agrees with the date according to the Northern reckoning, and the last according to the Southern account. But the first, which occurs in the Nâsik inscription, and should therefore belong to the Southern reckoning, is two years out, and is therefore most probably a mistake.

Amongst eighty inscriptions which I have noted as containing year names of the Jovian Cycle, there are only five which conform to the Northern reckoning. The latest is a short record on a pillar in the cloisters of the Lâl Darwâza Masjid at Jaunpur,* in which the date is stated to be "the year Plava of Samvat 1353." Both dates correspond with A.D. 1296. By the Southern reckoning Plava coincides with Samvat 1358.

In the annexed table I have given the Sanskrit names of all the sixty years, with their numbers counting from Prabhava. The numbers only are given in the general table for want of space. In the inscriptions the names only are given; so that whenever the name of a Jovian year is found in an inscription, it will be necessary, in the first place, to refer to this table for its number.

I have also given translations of the Tibetan names, which were derived from the Chinese, for all the sixty years. They are formed by a combination of the names of the twelve animals of the smaller cycle of twelve years with the five elements. The first cycle dates from A.D. 1027, and not from 1026, as stated by Csoma de Körös, and adopted by Prinsep.† At page 181 of his Grammar, Csoma correctly states that "the present year 1834 being the 28th year of the 14th cycle," which gives A.D. 1807 as the first year; and therefore in taking 1026 as the first year of the first cycle, he is one year in error.

Prinsep quotes Csoma's account of a period of 403 years, termed *Me-kha-gya-tsho,* as preceding the introduction of the Kâla-Chakra, or 60-year Cycle of Jupiter in Tibet; and he adopts his opinion that it has reference to the Hijra era. "If," says Csoma, "we add these 403 years to 622, the first year of the Hijra, we have exactly the year 1025, whence with 1026 commences the first cycle of 60 years of the Tibetans." But the correct date was 1027, and the number 403 most probably had reference to the years passed from the Kashmiri Lok-kâl of A.D. 625

* See Archæological Survey of India, XI, 126.

† Tibetan Grammar, p. 195; Prinsep's Useful Tables, p. 30, quotes Csoma; Bengal Asiatic Society's Journal, III, 6, but the passage is not there.

down to A.D. 1027, when the Cycle of Jupiter was introduced. The name was only a symbolical mode of reckoning the number 403: as *mé*, "fire" = 3; *kha*, "vacuity" = 0; *gya-tsho*, "ocean" = 4; or put together 403. It had therefore nothing to do with "the entrance of the infidels into Makha."

Csoma, in his Chronology, states, that the Baidurya Karpo was "written in the first year of the twelfth cycle, or A.D. 1687." This is correct, as the unit of each initial year of a cycle should be a 7. So also the period elapsed from the introduction of the Kâla-Chakra down to 1687 is said to be 660 years, which gives A.D. 1027 as the first year of the first cycle.

It is perhaps only accidental that the year 1027 is also the beginning of the 60-year cycle in Southern India. But the coincidence is curious. In China the cycle began in 1024 A.D., a fact which is proved by the numbers attached to the Tibetan names in the accompanying table, which shows that three years of the Chinese or Tibetan cycle names had already passed when the Indian cycle, commencing with Prabhava, began.

In my work on Ladâkh I have made the same mistake of one year as was done by Csoma himself. I stated correctly (p. 396) that the year A.D. 1851 was the 45th year of the 14th cycle; for, deducting 44 from 45 and from 1851, we get the first year = 1807. But in the list of initial years I have given A.D. 1026 down to 1806, instead of A.D. 627 to 1807, owing to my faith in Csoma's accuracy.

BÂRHASPATYA-CHAKRA.

Names of the 60 years of the Jovian Cycle.

No.	SANSKRIT.	TIBETAN.	No.
1	Prabhava	Fire-hare	4
2	Vibhava	Earth-dragon	5
3	Sukla	Earth-serpent	6
4	Pramoda	Iron-horse	7
5	Prajâpati	Iron-sheep	8
6	Angiras	Water-ape	9
7	Sri Mukha	Water-bird	10
8	Bhâva	Wood-dog	11
9	Yuvan	Wood-hog	12
10	Dhatar	Fire-mouse	13
11	Iswara	Fire-ox	14
12	Bahudhânya	Earth-tiger	15
13	Pramâthin	Earth-hare	16
14	Vikrama	Iron-dragon	17
15	Vrisha	Iron-serpent	18
16	Chitrabhânu	Water-horse	19
17	Subhânu	Water-sheep	20
18	Târana	Wood-ape	21
19	Pârthiva	Wood-bird	22
20	Vyaya	Fire-dog	23
21	Sarvajit	Fire-hog	24
22	Sarvadhârin	Earth-mouse	25
23	Virodhin	Earth-ox	26
24	Vikrita	Iron-tiger	27
25	Khara	Iron-ape	28
26	Nandana	Water-dragon	29
27	Vijaya	Water-serpent	30
28	Jaya	Wood-horse	31
29	Manmatha	Wood-sheep	32
30	Durmukha	Fire-ape	33
31	Hemalamba	Fire-bird	34
32	Vilambin	Earth-dog	35
33	Vikârin	Earth-hog	36
34	Sarvari	Iron-mouse	37
35	Plava	Iron-ox	38
36	Sobhakrit	Water-tiger	39
37	Subhakrit	Water-hare	40
38	Krodhin	Wood-dragon	41
39	Viswavasu	Wood-serpent	42
40	Parâbhava	Fire-horse	43
41	Plavanga	Fire-sheep	44
42	Kîlaka	Earth-ape	45
43	Sanmya	Earth-bird	46
44	Sâdhârana	Iron-dog	47
45	Radhakrit	Iron-hog	48
46	Paridhâvin	Water-mouse	49
47	Pramâdin	Water-ox	50
48	Ananda	Wood-tiger	51
49	Râkshasa	Wood-hare	52
50	Anala	Fire-dragon	53
51	Pingala	Fire-serpent	54
52	Kâlayútka	Earth-house	55
53	Siddhârtha	Earth-sheep	56
54	Randra	Iron-ape	57
55	Durmati	Iron-bird	58
56	Dundubhi	Water-dog	59
57	Udgârin	Water-hog	60
58	Raktâksha	Wood-mouse	1
59	Krodha	Wood-ox	2
60	Kshaya	Fire-tiger	3

III.—BÂRHASPATYA-MÂNA,

OR

12-YEAR CYCLE OF JUPITER.

THE smaller Cycle of Jupiter consists of a period of twelve years, or one-fifth of the greater Cycle. It was described by Davis at some length, but is only briefly noticed by Warren.* I have already given a detailed account of this Cycle in my attempt to fix the initial point of the Gupta era.† Varâha Mihira notices it in the following terms: "Each year (during which Jupiter completes a twelfth part of his revolution) has to bear the name of the lunar mansion in which he rises. The years follow each other in the same order as the lunar months." They are also named after the lunar months with the prefix of the word 'Mahâ.' Thus Lalla says:

Maghâ-cha Maghâyam yuktà Maghâyam-cha Gururgada Mahâ-Mâgha.

"When both the Moon and Jupiter are in the asterism Maghâ, on the day of full moon of the month Mâgha, then the year is called *Mahâ-Mâgha.*"

The statement of Varâha, quoted above, that the year has to bear the name of the *mansion* in which Jupiter rises requires some explanation. The twenty-seven Nakshatra, or lunar mansions, are divided into twelve groups, nine of which comprise two mansions only, and the remaining three each three mansions. One Nakshatra in each of these twelve groups gives its name to the luni-solar months, and consequently to the years of this cycle.

According to the rule for naming the several years of the 12-year Cycle of Jupiter, the year is called after the Nakshatra in which the planet rises heliacally. But in practice the names of the Jovian years

---

* For the former, see Asiatic Researches, III, 217; and for the latter, the Kâla Sankâlita, p. 197.

† See Archæological Survey of India, Vol. X, Appendix.

are made to coincide with those of the luni-solar months. So that should the planet rise in Bharani the year is not called Bhârani, but Aswini, which is the name-giving Nakshatra of the group to which Bharani belongs.

Bhattotpala quotes Garga to the effect that 170 solar years being equal to 175 Jovian years, the two names of Aswayuja and Chaitra must be omitted.

This proportion was afterwards altered by Varâha, who made 172 years of Jupiter equal to $170\frac{5}{11}$ solar years, on which account two of Brihaspati's years are to be omitted in that period. His words are:

"*Saptatyabda sate ekâdasa bhagaih panchabhira adhike gate Guru yukta Nakshatra mâsa samjna varsha dwayamâdhikam bhavati.*"

Practically, every eighty-sixth name is expunged, and consequently the omissions are confined to six names out of the twelve; or, in other words, the omissions fall only on the alternate names in regular succession. Thus the six omitted names are Srâvana, Aswayuja, Mârgasiras, Mâgha, Chaitra, and Jyeshtha. The rule for finding the year of the 12-year cycle is only a slight extension of that for the 60-year cycle.

Rule.—Find the equivalent year of the Saka era, and multiply it by 22, then add 4291 to the product, and divide by 1875. Add the quotient without fractions to the Saka date, and divide the sum by 60. This quotient gives the number of expired cycles, and the remainder the number of expired years of the current cycle counting from Prabhava. To find the year of the 12-year cycle divide the last remainder by 12; the quotient will give the number of Jupiter's own revolutions completed, and the remainder will be the number of years expired of the current 12-year cycle, counting from Mahâ-Srâvana as the first. The following example will show the working of the rules: Take A. D. 166 = 88 Saka.

I.

88 × 22 = 1936
+ 4291
———
÷ 1875) 6227 (3
88
—
91
÷ 60 —
Cycle 1 + 31 years.

II.

31
12—

Cycles 2+7 years completed, or the 8th year current, which counted from Srâvana gives Jyeshtha, as in the General Table.

But the same result may be obtained by the shorter process which I have proposed in my account of the 60-year cycle. Thus, to the Saka date add 195, then divide the sum by 85, and add the quotient to the Saka. Then divide by 60; the quotient will give the number of cycles expired, and the remainder the number of expired years of the current cycle. The above example will therefore be as follows :—

Saka 88
+ 195
———
÷ 85) 283 (3 + 88 = 91
÷ 60—
1-31 as before.

Very few inscriptions have hitherto been discovered dated in the 12-year Cycle of Jupiter. But four of these, which are found coupled with the concurrent dates of the Gupta era, are of unusual importance from the aid which they may give in fixing the initial point of the Gupta era, which will be discussed hereafter. These four dates are found on the copperplate inscriptions of Raja Hastin and his son Sankshoba. They are as follows :—

Year	156 of Gupta	=	Mahâ Vaisâkha.
„	163 [read 173]	=	Mahâ Aswayuja.
„	191 ...	=	Mahâ Chaitra.
„	209 ...	=	Mahâ Aswayuja.

Another inscription of the same family on a stone pillar gives the name of Mahâ Mâgha, but without any concurrent date.

Mr. Fleet has published* two ancient inscriptions of the Kadamba Râjas of Banawâsi in the Dakhin, which are apparently dated in this 12-year cycle of Jupiter. Both inscriptions are of Raja Mrigesa, the earlier one being dated in the *year Pausha*, which is said to be the third year of his reign, and the later one in the year *Vaisâkha*, which is said to be the eighth year of his reign. From these two statements we learn that the third year of his reign must have begun in Mahâ Mârgasiras, as shown by the succession of the names of the years as follows :—

Mahâ	Mahâ	Mahâ	Mahâ	Mahâ	Mahâ
Mârgasiras —	Pausha —	Mâgha —	Phâlguna —	Chaitra —	Vaisâkha.
3rd year.	4th year.	5th year.	6th year.	7th year.	8th year.

* Archæological Survey of India, Vol. X, 126-27.

Here unfortunately there is nothing to fix the date beyond the fact that between the years named Mahâ Pausha and Mahâ Vaisâkha there was no name omitted. But I think that something may perhaps be gained from the inscriptions to assist in finding an approximate date.

Sir Arthur Phayre has published a Burmese inscription from Pugân, which appears to me to be dated in the 12-year Cycle of Jupiter, as well as in the common era in use in Burma. It opens with the date thus: "In the era 551, the *Tharawan* year." Tharawan is the Burmese pronunciation of *Srâvana.* But the year 551, or A.D. 1189, was Mahâ Jyeshtha. If we might read 553, or A.D. 1191, then the year would correspond with the Indian year of Mahâ Srâvana.

I have quoted these examples from Banawâsi in the Dakhin, and Pugân in Burma, to show how widely spread was the use of the Cycles of Jupiter in ancient times.

The people of Tibet and Ladâk also make use of a cycle of twelve years for the computation of short periods, such as a person's age, or the date of any recent event. In this cycle each year is named after a different animal, as follows:—

	Tibetan.			*Tibetan.*	
1.	Byi-lo ...	... Mouse-year.	7.	Ta-lo ...	... Horse-year.
2.	Lang-lo...	... Ox ,,	8.	Lug-lo ...	... Sheep ,,
3.	Stag-lo ...	... Tiger ,,	9.	Spre-lo ...	... Ape ,,
4.	Zos-lo ...	... Hare ,,	10.	Bya-lo ...	... Bird ,,
5.	Brug-lo...	... Dragon ,,	11.	Khyi-lo ...	... Dog ,,
6.	Brul-lo ...	... Serpent ,,	12.	Phog-lo...	... Hog ,,

The only difficulty that I see about accepting the 12-year Jovian Cycle of Varâha for the five centuries which preceded him is the statement of Garga about the omission of Chaitra and Aswayuja, as if in his time they were the only years subject to retrenchment. But as Garga mentions that 172 of Jupiter's years were equal to 170 solar years, while Varâha makes them equal to $170\frac{5}{11}$ solar years, the two cycles are practically the same in other respects. It does not, however, follow that no other years were subject to omission because Chaitra and Aswayuja alone are mentioned. My impression is, that the same six months that are omitted by Varâha's rule were also subject to omission in Garga's time. But even admitting that Chaitra and Aswayuja were the only two years that were expunged from the time of Garga down to Varâha Mihira, I see no difficulty in adjusting the times of omission so as to make them the only expunged years. As Chaitra and Aswayuja are also omitted years in Varâha's scheme, they will of course remain constant, as the average period of omission is in both cases the 86th year. If then we accept the year 310 A. D. in which Chaitra was omitted as common to both systems, we have only to take the Aswayujas and Chaitras which fall *nearest* to the 85-year periods, either those preceding (A) or those following them (B), and the result will be the same excepting only as regards the names of the other omitted years. This will be seen at once by the following arrangement of the names :—

Varâha Mihira.			*Proposed Arrangements.*					
A. D.	**Interval**		**A. D.**	**Interval**	**A**	**A. D.**	**Interval**	**B**
310		Chaitra	310		Chaitra	310		Chaitra
	85			77			89	
395		Jyeshta	387		Aswayuja	399		Aswayuja
	85			89			89	
480		Srâvana	476		Chaitra	488		Chaitra
	85			89			77	
565		Aswayuja	565		Aswayuja	565		Aswayuja
	85			77			89	
650		Agrahayana	642		Chaitra	654		Chaitra
	85			89			89	
735		Mâgha	731		Aswayuja	743		Aswayuja
	85			89			77	
820		Chaitra	820		Chaitra	820		Chaitra
	510	years		510	years		510	years
÷ 6			÷ 6			÷ 6		
Mean	85	interval	Mean	85	interval	Mean	85	interval

From this table it will be seen that a regular succession of Chaitras and Aswayujas might be omitted while still retaining a uniform mean period of eighty-five years. It will also be seen that at every third period the *names* of the omitted years, as well as the dates of omission, agree with those of Varâha Mihira.

IV.—KÂLI-YUGA.

THE Kâli-Yuga, or fourth age of Hindu Chronology, dates from the year 3102 B.C.; the year 1, expired or completed, being B. C. 3101. The Four Yugas, or ages, which comprise one Mahâ-Yuga, consist of the following periods :—

		Years.		
Krita-Yuga	..	1.728,000 ÷ 360 =	4800	years of Gods.
Treta-Yuga	..	1.296,000 ÷ 360 =	3600	„
Dwâpara-Yuga	..	864,000 ÷ 360 =	2400	„
Kâli-Yuga	..	432,000 ÷ 360 =	1200	„
One Mahâ-Yuga	..	4.320,000 ÷ 360 =	12000	years of Gods.

Regarding the origin of the Mahâ-Yuga I have already expressed my opinion that it was the invention of the astronomers founded on the precession of the equinoxes. It may be objected that the division into four Yugas and their duration are mentioned both in the Code of Manu* and in the Mahâbhârata. But what is the age of Manu's Code? The references to female heretics who wear an unlawful dress, or a dress unauthorized by the Vedas [v, 89, 90], of "female anchorets," or nuns [viii, 36, 37], and of "heretical books," or books of a false religion [ii, 11, and xi, 66], point so clearly to Buddhism, that the Code in its present form must certainly be posterior to the spread of Buddhism under Asoka.

The era of the *Kâli-Yuga* was in use down to the time of Varâha Mihira, who first introduced the use of the Saka era into Astronomical works. Aryabhata, who was not more than fifty years prior to him, still computed by the era of the Kâli-Yuga.† The initial point of the era seems to have been a traditional date of the period of the great war, which had been handed down perhaps for ages. This date of 3102 B.C.

* Mânava Sanhita, or Mânava Dharma-Sâstra, I, 67 *et seq.*

† Weber's History of Indian Literature, p. 260.

as the year 0 of the Kâli-Yuga was accepted by all; and from it the calculations of Aryabhata, and Varâha Mihira for the solar and luni-solar periods were computed.

Where the Kâli-Yuga era is used alone, the day of the month may be expressed either according to the solar calendar, or to the luni-solar one. Frequently the year is given in two different eras; one of which may be usually connected with the solar calendar and the other with the lunar. In the North of India the Kâli-Yuga and the Saka years are generally, but not always, connected with the solar reckoning, while in the South of India the Saka era is usually accompanied with the luni-solar reckoning. The Samvat of Vikramâditya is the only era that is exclusively luni-solar.

V.—CYCLE OF PARASURÂMA.

THE era of Parasurâma is a cycle of 1000 years, which is said to have begun in B.C. 1175¾ complete, or 1176 B.C. current. It has been described by Warren in his Kâla Sankâlita,* where he states that its use is confined to the Southern part of the Peninsula, called Malayâlam, comprising Malabâr and Travancore down to Cape Comorin. "The commencement of the year 977 of the 3rd cycle is said to have coincided with the 1st of (the solar month) Aswina of 1723 Saka, and the 14th September A.D. 1800." Here the Christian year is wrong, as it should be 1801, to agree with Saka 1723. According to Cowasjee Patell, the initial day of the year 977 was the 15th September 1801. The year is a solar one. This cycle is also called the Quilon or Kollam era. Dr. Burgess calls it the Kollam Andu era, and says that the last expired cycle began on the 25th August, A.D. 825.† Cowasjee Patell gives the 29th August of the same year. The initial dates of the different cycle are therefore

I	Cycle	...	...	...	B.C.	1176
II	„	...	...	...	„	176
III	„	...	...	...	A.D.	825
IV	„	...	...	...	„	1825

It is never used in Upper India, and indeed is scarcely known, except by name, even to the astronomers.

* Kâla Sankâlita, by Colonel Warren, p. 298.

† *Indian Antiquary*, 1882, p. 271.

VI.—NIRVÂNA OF BUDDHA.

THE *Nirvâna*, or death of the last Buddha Sâkya Muni, has been in use from a very early date down to the present day. According to the Buddhist Chronicles of Ceylon and Burma, the Nirvâna took place in 544 B.C. But as the inauguration of Asoka is referred to the year 218 after the Nirvâna, it seems probable that there must be an error in the date of the Nirvâna itself to the extent of sixty-six years, as the chronology of the reign of Asoka is now pretty well ascertained. His father's death took place in the year 214 of the Nirvâna, or B.C. 264, and his inauguration as king four years later, after he had prevailed over his brothers.

Only two inscriptions have yet been found which are dated in this era. The first is contained in the rock edicts of Asoka at Rupnâth and Sahsarâm. The second occurs in an inscribed slab which I found in the Temple of Surya in the city of Gaya. The date of Asoka's inscription is the year 256, or the 42nd year after the death of his father; his own reign being stated in the chronicles at 4 years + 37 years, or altogether 41 years complete, and 42 current. The second date is 1813 of the *Bhagavat Parinirvritte Samvat*, or Nirvâna, or Thursday the 1st of Kârtika-badi.

In Northern India the true date of the Nirvâna was lost at a very early period. Thus, in the time of Hwen Thsang, A. D. 630—645, the Buddhist schools held widely different opinions, varying from 900 and 1000 years up to 1200, 1300 and even 1500 years prior to that date,* which would place the Nirvâna of Buddha either in 250, or 350, or 550 or 650 and 850 B.C. The same extravagant antiquity was also asserted in the time of FaHian, who places the Nirvâna during the reign of Ping-Wang, Emperor of China, in B.C. 770—719.† A similar antiquity was still claimed as late as the Twelfth Century A. D., during the reign of Asoka

---

* Julien's Hwen Thsang, II, 335.

† Record of Buddhistic Kingdoms, translated by Giles, C. vii.

Balla Deva. Two of his inscriptions are dated in the years 51 and 74 of the Lakshmana Sena era, or in A. D. 1157 *and* 1180. A third inscription, which is dated in the year 1813 of the *Parinirvritte* of *Bhagavata*, shows that the time the Nirvâna was believed to have occurred, was about 656 to 633 B.C.

But these extravagant periods are disproved by Brahmanical as well as by Buddhist records, after making the necessary correction for the dates of Chandra Gupta and Asoka.

The following is the account given in the Brahmanical Purânas :—

VAYU PURANA.		MATSYA PURANA.	
Ajâta Satru, 25—8 =	17 years.	Ajâta Satru, 27 - 8 =	19 years.
Harshaka	25 "	Vansaka	24 "
Udayâswa	33 "	Udâsin	33 "
Nandi Vardhana	42 "	Nandi Vardhana	40 "
Mahanandi	43 "	Mahanandi	43 "
	160 "		159 "
Mahapadma + 9 Nandas	100 "	Mahapadma + 9 Nandas	100 "
Chandra Gupta	24 "	Chandra Gupta	24 "
Bindusâra	28 "	Bindusâra	94 "

Accession of Asoka 312 years ... ... or 311 years after the *Nirvâna* of Buddha.

Now the period stated in all the Buddhist records is 214 years, the difference of nearly 100 years, being in the reigns between Ajâta Satru and Chandra Gupta. In favour of the Buddhist records I may remark that Buddhaghosha, " the Brahman youth, born in the neighbourhood of the terrace of the Great Bo-tree, . . . who had achieved the knowledge of the three Vedas,"* must have been cognizant of the northern chronology when he translated the Singhalese *Attha-katha*, in which he has adopted the same dates as are found in the Mahawansa and Dipawansa. Admitting the correctness of this suggestion, it follows that Buddhaghosha either gave a preference to the Singhalese chronology, or that it did not differ from the northern chronology in his time, that is in A.D. 400. But whatever may be the true explanation of the difference, the fact remains that the Buddhists are unanimous in placing the Nirvâna of Buddha 214 years prior to the accession of Asoka. Accepting this as the most probable account of the interval, we obtain for the Nirvâna the corrected date of 264 + 214 = 478 B.C., instead of 544 B.C., being a difference of 66 years.

* Mahawansa.

A novel theory has lately been put forward to account for the discrepancy by referring the Nirvâna to the time of Buddha's attainment of Buddhahood under the sacred tree. As this took place when he was 29 + 6 = 35 years old, the difference is only 80 − 35 = 45 years, instead of 66 years. Mr. Curter, who proposes this explanation, appears to think that Sâkya obtained Buddhahood at 29 years of age. But he only left his home at that age, and had to sit for six years under the Bodhi tree at Uruvilwa before he attained Buddhahood.* The Buddhavansa (which he quotes) states vaguely that Gotama did not live to 100 years.

Mr. Curter's figures are—

Gotama's birth	...	...	...	572 B.C.
Nirvâna at 29th year	=	...	...	543 „
Death according to the Inscriptions			...	483 „

I must say that I remain quite unconvinced. The period that requires correction is not that between Buddha and Asoka, but the still later period of the impossible reigns of Mutasiwo and his sons for 162 years, or exactly 81 years to one generation. If the Buddhist dates of Chandra Gupta and Asoka can be corrected to the extent of 66 years, the date of Buddha's Nirvâna must be subject to the same correction, as the period between them does not seem to be capable of extension. On the contrary, the Northern Buddhists seem to have usually curtailed it to 100 years as stated by Hwen Thsang, as well as in the Asoka Avadâna.† A single northern work, the Avadâna Sataka, extends the period between the Nirvâna and Asoka to 200 years.

For these reasons I retain the year 544 B.C. as the accepted date of Buddha's Nirvâna, according to the Buddhist chronology of Ceylon and Burma. At the same time I think that there must certainly be an error in this date to the extent of about 66 years as shown by the subsequent dates of Chandra Gupta and Asoka.

---

* *Academy*, 19th March 1881, and *Indian Antiquary*; May 1881, p. 153.

† See Burnouf.

VII.—NIRVÂNA OF MAHÂVIRA.

The Jains make use of an era dating from the *Nirvâna*, or death of their last teacher Mahâvira. According to the Swetâmbara sect this event took place 470 years before Vikrama, or in B. C. 527. The Digambaras, however, make it 605 years before Vikrama. As the difference between the two dates is exactly 135 years, it seems probable that the Digambara date of 605 years before Vikrama should be altered to 605 years before Sâka, which would agree with that of the other sect. I have made many enquiries on this subject from learned Jains in Northern India, and the answer has been uniformly the same, "470 years before Vikramâditya." This also is the date given by the Jains of Gujarât.* The same date is used throughout the Theravali of Merutunga, who says: "Before the commencement of the reign of Vikrama, Sri Vera's Nirvâna took place 470 years."† Colonel Miles also, in his account of the Jainas of Gujarât and Mârwâr, uses the same date.‡ Colonel Tod makes the era 477 years before Vikrama.

---

* Dr. Stevenson's Kalpa Sutra, Preface, p. viii, and note, p. 96.

† Dr. Bhau Dâji, Bombay Asiatic Society's Journal, IX, 149.

‡ Royal Asiatic Society's Transactions, III, 358.

VIII.—ERA OF THE SELEUKIDÆ.

THE initial point of the Seleukidan era has been fixed by Fynes Clinton to the 1st of October 312 B.C., in the beginning of Olympiad XVII, 1.* According to Ulugh Beg this era began 12 years after the death of Alexander, and 340,700 days before the Hijra of Muhammad, 16th July A.D. 622. Now 311 complete years B.C. plus 621 complete years A.D. = 932 Julian years, contain 340,414 days, which deducted from 340,700 leave 286 days to be accounted for. As the Hijra era dates from 16th July there are 196 days in A.D. 622, which leave only 90 days prior to the beginning of B.C. 311; so that, according to Ulugh Beg, the Seleukidan era must have begun on the 3rd of October B.C. 312. The other datum of 12 years after the death of Alexander does not refer to the actual date of Alexander's death, but to the initial day of the 425th year of Nabonasar, 12th November 324 B.C., in which year Alexander died. Twelve years later places the beginuing of the Seleukidan era near the end of the year 312 B.C.

This era dates from the defeat of Nikanor, the general of Antigonus, by Seleukus, who thus became master of Babylon in Olympiad XVII, I. The initial date of the era in B.C. 312 is also established by the dates ou several coins, of which one of Hadrian bears the date ΙΙΚΥ, and another of Caracalla bears the date of ΗΚΦ. As Hadrian began to reign on the 11th August 117 A.D., and Caracalla on the 8th April 217 A.D., the first year of the era referred to must have included the dates of 8th April and 11th of August 311 B.C.†

The names of the months were the same as those of the Macedonian Calendar. But as the Seleukidan year began in October, the first month must have been Hyperberetæus. The order of the Macedonian months has been gathered by Clinton from Josephus and Suidas,

---

* Fasti Hellenici, III, p. 311.

† Ordo Sæclorum, by Henry Browne, pp. 487 and 488. See also Fasti Hellenici, III, p. 373.

who compare them with the Hebrew and Roman months.* Clinton gives an extract from Cardinal Norisius, who quotes Hieronymus to show that in Antioch and other Syrian cities the year began with Hyperberetæus :— " In quarto mense qui apud nos vocatur Januarius, apud Orientales enim populos, October erat primus mensis, et Januarius quartus Est (Shebat) in acerrimo hyemis, qui ab Ægyptüs Mechir, à Macedonibus Περιτιος, à Romanis Februarius appellatur." So also Corsini and Scaliger make Hyperberetæus the first month. The following are the names of the months with the corresponding months of the Jewish Calendar as found in Josephus and other authors—

	MACEDONIAN.	HEBREW.	ENGLISH.
1	Hyperberetæus ...	Tisri	October
2	Dius	Marcheswan ...	November
3	Apellæus ...	Kisleu ..	December
4	Audynæus ...	Tebeth ...	January
5	Peritius	Shebat ..	February
6	Dystrus	Adar ...	March
7	Xanthikus ...	Nisan ..	April
8	Artemisius ...	Ijar ...	May
9	Dæsius	Swan ...	June
10	Panemus ...	Thamuz ...	July
11	Löus	Ab ...	August
12	Gorpiæus ...	Elul ..	September

Now the Macedonian Calendar, like that of the Athenians, was a luni-solar cycle of 19 solar years, or 235 lunar months ; and as more than a century had elapsed from the time of Meton when Seleukus established his era, there can be no reasonable doubt that the Metonic cycle was adopted in Syria. This is proved by the following facts :†

1. " Whenever Macedonian months are compared with Attic or lunar months, it nowhere appears that they differ in their dimensions or contents.

2. " Seleukus Nikator, the founder of the kingdom of the Seleukidæ, gave order to affix the Macedonian names to the Syrian months, which were unquestionably lunar.

* Clinton, Fasti Hellenici, III, p. 353.

† These proofs are taken from Browne's Ordo Sæclorum, p. 461.

3. "Ptolemy, in his Almagest, gives the dates of various eclipses and occultations observed at Babylon between the years B.C. 721 and 229. The last three dates, B.C. 245, 237, 229, bear the names of Macedonian months, and by calculation prove that the Babylonians under the Seleukidæ measured time by lunar months with Macedonian names.

4. "The date on the Rosetta stone, IX Ptolemy Epiphanes, 18th Mechir = 4th of Macedonian Xanthikus, being reduced, proves the same thing."

These facts show most decisively that the Syro-Macedonian calendar of the Seleukidæ was luni-solar, and not solar, as is frequently stated.* Thus James Prinsep, copying an article from the Companion to the Almanac for 1830, says:—"Their year was solar, and consisted of 365 days, with the addition of a day every fourth year." But the calendar of 365¼ days is the Julian calendar, which was not adopted in Syria until some time after the Christian era, when it had become a Roman province.

As the Syro-Macedonian months were lunar, there must have been seven intercalary months inserted at certain periods in each cycle of 19 years. According to the Greek cycle of Meton, these insertions took place in the 3rd, 5th, 8th, 11th, 13th, 16th, 19th years of the cycle. "The name of the old Macedonian intercalary month is inferred from 2 Maccabees, XI, 21, where the date of a manifesto issued by Lysias, General of Antiochus Eupator, is given as 24th Διοσκορινθιου, but in the Vulgate 24 *Dioscori;* and from the Etymol^m Mag^m we learn, that Διόσκορος was the name of a month. A missive of Antiochus, evidently written not much later, is dated 15th Xanthikos. Hence it is inferred that the place of this intercalary month Διόσκορος was the same as that of the Jewish month, *i.e.*, before Nisan."†

The introduction of the Julian reckoning must have been confined to Syria and the western provinces of the Seleukidan empire, which had been annexed to Rome. But in the Eastern provinces, which then formed the Parthian empire, the luni-solar reckoning still maintained its place. This is proved most conclusively by the following facts. It was the custom of the later Parthian kings to date all their large silver coins with the month and year of their issue. The names of all the twelve Macedonian months have thus been found on the coins of the Parthian

* Cowasjee Patell, p. 26, of course copies Prinsep. † Ordo Sæclorum, p. 461.

kings. There are a few slight differences, such as Xandikus for Xanthikus, and Soloiûs for Loüs. But on one coin of Vologeses III, I find the name of EMBOΛI, which can only be that of the intercalary or *embolismic* month.* This is accompanied with the date OY or 490, or A.D. 178-9, in which year there was an intercalary month according to my table. It is clear, therefore, that, up to this late period, the people of the Parthian empire still continued to use the luni-solar reckoning of the Macedonian Calendar.

I have been thus particular in describing the Syro-Macedonian Calendar of the Seleukidæ, as we know that it was in use in the north-west of India, during the period of Indo-Scythian rule, from which we may infer, with some certainty, that it must have been the common reckoning of their predecessors, the Bactrian Greeks. Mr. Thomas has already shown that this is highly probable; but nothing has yet been found to determine it absolutely.

In the Indo-Scythian inscriptions, the names of four different Macedonian months have been found,—namely, Panemos, Daisios, Apellaios, and Artemisios. The occurrence of these names shows incontestably that the Macedonian Calendar must have been introduced into Kabul and North-Western India by the Bactrian Greeks, and as the province to the west of the Indus had belonged to Seleukus, I conclude that the era of the Seleukidæ must have been adopted there also. Unfortunately, the year dates hitherto discovered are all small numbers, which might refer to some recently established era of the Indo-Scythians, or, as suggested by Mr. Thomas, they may possibly refer to the Seleukidan era by leaving out the hundreds, which was the common Indian mode of reckoning the year of the Saptârshi-kâl. With the Indo-Scythian inscriptions, for instance, the dates of 9, 11, 18, and 28 of Kanishka, and of 33, 39, 47, and 51 of Huvishka, might either be referred to a new era, such as the Saka-kâl of 78 A.D., or to the years 9, 11, 18, &c., of the fifth Seleukidan century, by leaving out 400. In the former case, the year 9 of Kanishka would be 78 + 9 = 87 A.D., while in the latter case it would be referred to the year 409 of the Seleukidan era, equal to A.D. 97-98.

It is doubtful, except in a few instances, whether any coins of the Greek kings are dated. The three letters PMI on the exergue of the coin of Platon can only be explained as a date, although the usual order of IMP is reversed. As a date they represent 147, which can only be

* This coin is engraved in Longperier's unpublished book on the Parthian coinage, Plate XIV, Fig. 9.

referred to the Seleukidan era, and would, therefore, be equivalent to B.C. 165-164. The letters OΓ, or 73, are found on a coin of Eukratides, and the letters ΠΓ, or 83, on several coins of Heliokles. That these are most probably dates has been proved by Mr. Thomas, by a reference to a coin of Heliokles in the British Museum, bearing the full date PΠΓ, or 183.* I have since acquired a tetradrachm of Eukratides with the detached letters NA, which may also be read as a date, or 51 = 151 of the Seleukidan era. According to these dates we have—

	An. Sel.	B. C.
Platon in	147	= 165-164.
Eukratides in	51 or 151	= 161-160.
Ditto	73 or 173	= 139-138.
Heliokles	183	= 129-128.

After this the dates on the Greek coins would seem to be, as Mr. Thomas suggests, only regnal years of the different kings.

Having accepted these dates—and I do not see how they can be disputed—I feel that the dates found in the Indo-Scythian inscriptions along with the names of the Macedonian months must also be referred to the Seleukidan era. I am quite prepared, therefore, to accept all the dates of the Indo-Scythian inscriptions from Kabul and Taxila and Mathura as belonging to the Seleukidan era, with the hundreds omitted after the Indian custom. This also would appear to be Mr. Thomas's conclusion, when he says: "The question thus arises whether this latter practice (of using the Macedonian names of the months) does not imply a continued use of the Seleukidan era, in association with which the names must first have reached India."

Under this view, the following will be the dates of the Indo-Scythian Princes Kanishka, Huvishka, and Vâsu Deva:

A.D. 80 *Kanishka,* S. 9 = 409 – 312 = 97 A.D.
S. 28 = 428 – 312 = 116 —
A.D. 120 *Huvishka,* S. 33 = 433 – 312 = 121 A.D.
S. 51 = 451 – 312 = 139 —
A.D. 150 *Vâsu Deva,* S. 87 = 487 – 312 = 175 A.D.
S. 98 = 498 – 312 = 186 A.D.
A.D. 190, close of Indo-Scythian rule in Northern India.

The accuracy of these dates is confirmed by the discovery of gold coins of Wema Kadphises, Kanishka and Huvishka in the Ahin-posh Stûpa, along with some Roman gold coins of Domitian, Trajan, and

* Bactrian Coins and Indian Dates, in Royal Asiatic Society's Journal, New Series, Vol. IX, p. 3.

Sabina, the wife of Hadrian. Sabina died in A.D. 137, and as there was only one coin of Huvishka amongst twenty-one specimens, the Stûpa was probably built not later than 130 A.D.

Under these circumstances it appears to me that some account of the era of the Seleukidæ is absolutely necessary for any work treating of early Indian dates. I have therefore drawn up the accompanying tables of the initial days of all the years of the era from its commencement down to the close of the Parthian empire in the early part of the Third Century A.D. I have studied the accounts given by Clinton in his Fasti Hellenici, and by Browne in his Ordo Sæclorum, and I have examined most of their authorities in the original. I have also computed many of the test calculations for myself, some of which will be noticed presently.

The old Greek year consisted originally of 360 days, divided into 12 months of 30 days each. But as many of the Greek festivals depended on the moon, it was soon discovered that the true length of a mean lunation was about 29½ days, and that of a solar year about 365 days. Various methods were adopted from time to time for accommodating the computation by lunar months to the solar year. In the time of Perikles the *enneateris*, or cycle of 8 solar years, was in use. This consisted of 8 lunar years of 354 days each, with the addition of 3 intercalary months, in the 3rd, 5th, and 8th years, making a total of 99 lunations or lunar months. But as 8 solar years of 365¼ days contain 2922 days, while 99 lunations of 29½ days amount to only 2920½ days, there was a deficiency of one day and-a-half in every cycle of 8 years.

To remedy this defect Meton proposed in B.C. 432 his famous cycle of 19 solar years of 365¼ days each, which differs by only a small fraction from 235 lunations. Meton's value of the 19 solar years as 6940 days was a little in excess of the truth, as a year of 365¼ days gives only 6939·75 days in 19 years. As this excess of ¼ day amounted to a whole day in 76 years, Kallippus, in B.C. 330, introduced the cycle of 76 years, or four Metonic periods, from which he retrenched the extra day. But beyond this, according to Clinton, "he appears to have made no change in the εννεα-και-δεκαετηρις of Meton." It is supposed, from the account of Timocharis of the 36th and 47th years being *anni communes*, that he closed the 6th Metonic cycle at its 8th year, or B.C. 330, which, accordingly, became an *annus communis* as the 1st of the Kallippic cycle of 76 years, which could not have happened if the original Metonic cycle had not been interrupted. But Clinton quotes a marble which renders this arrangement doubtful. It is quite certain that it could not have been adopted in Syria, as we know that the year 148 of the Seleukidan era, or B.C. 165-64, was intercalary,* which is true of the Metonic cycle, but disagrees with that of Kallippus. As the Parthian coin of Vologases III shows the same accordance with the Metonic reckoning, there can be no doubt that the Kallippic correction had not been introduced into either Syria or Parthia. Clinton also deduces from "the three years described by Ptolemy as 67, 75, and 82 of the Chaldæans, commencing respectively October 15, October 16, and October 1, that the Macedonians must have received the cycle in the 9th year of a Metonic εννεα-και-δεκαετηρις, which would be the second of a Kallippic. For this reason I have adopted the Metonic cycle in the accompanying tables, which show the initial day of every year down to the close of the Parthian empire. I have numbered the Metonic cycles I, II, III, IV, &c., and should it be required to convert any date into the Kallippic reckoning, it is only necessary to throw back every date in each period of 76 years by one day; or, as the Kallippic correction was established in B.C. 330, to antedate by one day every initial day in the Metonic Cycles IV, V, VI VII; by two days those of Cycles VIII, IX, X, XI; by three days those of Cycles XII, XIII, XIV, XV; and so on, deducting one more day for every four Metonic cycles.

In the old cycle of 8 years the lunar months consisted nominally of 30 days each, one day being "omitted between the 20th and 30th of every alternate month. But in those months from which a day was deducted, the last day was still called τριακὰς, and the day omitted was perhaps the 29th, or any other day but the 30th."† Meton also retained the nominal value of the month at 30 days, but he proposed a new scheme for the days to be omitted. As 235 lunations at 30 days each amounted to 7050 days, or 110 days in excess of the 6940 days assigned to 19 solar years, he devised the cumbrous and inconvenient plan of omitting every 63rd day throughout the cycle; but it is not known whether he included or excluded the seven intercalary months. These omitted days, or ἡμέραι, ἐξαιρέσιμοι, are shown in the table, which is altered from Clinton's Attic tables to suit the Macedonian Calendar.

The seven intercalary months of the Metonic cycle were added at the end of the 3rd, 5th, 8th, 11th, 13th, 16th, and 19th years. But in the Macedonian Calendar the embolismic month was placed in the middle of the year immediately preceding Xanthikos.‡ Clinton supposes that the embolismic months were also subject to the retrenchment of the 63rd

---

* See 2 Maccabees, XI, p. 21. † Clinton, Fasti Hellenici, I, p. 336.

‡ Clinton, III, 353, quoting Macrobius, who states that the intercalations were placed at the end of February of Greeks as well as Romans.

day, should it happen to fall upon them. But this cannot have been the case, otherwise the number of omitted days would have amounted to 111·9, or nearly 2 in excess of the required number of 110. Meton's scheme consisted of a cycle of 19 years, each of 12 months of 30 days, with seven intercalary months also of 30 days, making altogether 7050 days, from which 110 days were to be deducted to obtain the required number of 6940 days, by omitting every 63rd day. Now if the embolismic months had been subject to curtailment, the number of omitted days would have been 112. But if they were not subject to these omissions, the required number of 6940 days would have been obtained by passing them over, and striking out tho. day from the following month. This arrangement is shown in Table VII, where the embolismic month of 30 days is placed in the middle of the year between Dustros and Xanthikus.

But there is another grave objection to Clinton's scheme, namely, that it would make all the last four months of the cycle full months of 30 days, and as the first two months of each cycle were necessarily full months, there would have been no less than six consecutive full months all lumped together. I look upon this result as quite fatal to his scheme.

Now, the arrangement which I propose, as shown in Table VII, is quite free from this defect, as it has not even a single instance of three full months coming together, and only one of three hollow or short months,—namely, in the last year of one cycle and first two years of the succeeding one. According to Clinton's scheme, if a new moon had fallen in the first day of the first of the six consecutive full months, a new moon would have occurred three whole days before the beginning of the seventh month. By my arrangement, the new moon would only differ one day and-a-half from the *νουμηνια*.

To test the tables, I will take the date of the battle of Arbela, which took place on the twelfth day after an eclipse of the moon, the two armies having been drawn up facing each other on the eleventh night after the eclipse. Now the day of battle has been fixed to the 2nd of October B.C. 331 by the mention of this eclipse. The eclipse took place on the night of 20th of September at full moon, and the new moon which opened the next Macedonian year, must, therefore, have fallen on the 5th of October. According to my table, the new year's day fell on the 4th October. We know that the battle took place very near the end of the Macedonian month, as Aristander had foretold that "a battle would be fought in that very month."* The 2nd of October was the 29th of Gorpiæus, or the last day but one of the month.

---

* Arrian, Hist., Allexandri, III, 7.

IX.—ERA OF PARTHIA.

—:oo:—

THE notice of a Parthian era was discovered* by George Smith amongst the cuneiform records at Babylon. Three Parthian tablets were obtained at Babylon itself, but only one of them was perfect. This gave a double date as follows:—

"Month ——— 23rd day, 144th year, which is called the 208th year, Arsakes, king of kings."

George Smith gives the year 248 B.C. as the first year of the Parthian era. But as the first year of the Seleukidan era did not begin until October 312 B.C. or 311¼, only three months of the year 248 at the very utmost can be assigned to the first year of the Parthian era. But if, as is quite possible, the Parthian era did not begin until about the middle of the Seleukidan year, its initial point would have been in April 247 B.C., or even later, instead of in October 248, and it would not have ended until April 246 or later. Now Antiochus II Theos died in January 246,† and as Strabo, Appian, and Suidas, all agree in assigning the revolt of the Parthians to the period immediately following the death of Antiochus II, I think there is a very strong reason for adopting some middle month of the year 247 B.C. as the initial point of the Parthian era. I had already adopted the year 246 for the rise of Bactrian independence, on the testimony of the authors above quoted, in my account of the Coins of Alexander's successors in the East.‡ And as I have shown that the date of the death of Antiochus may easily have fallen within the first year of the Parthian era as now established by the cuneiform inscriptions, I think that the year 247 has a better claim to be considered the starting point of Parthian independence than the previous year 248.

---

* Assyrian Discoveries, p. 389.

† Clinton, Fasti Hellenici, III, 350.

‡ See Numismatic Chronicle, New Series, 1868, p. 257.

X.—VIKRAMADITYA SAMVAT.

—:oo:—

The Vikramâditya Samvat, or era of Vikramâditya, is reckoned from the vernal equinox of the year 57 B.C., and the completion of the Kâli-Yuga year 3044. It is used all over Northern India, except in Bengal, where the Saka era has been generally adopted. It is used also in Telingâna and Gujarât; but in the latter province the year does not begin until seven months later than in the north, or with the 1st of Kârtik-Sudi, which now falls during October, but which, at the beginning of the Christian era, fell between the middle of September and the middle of October.

This era is said to have been established by Vikramâditya, a king of Ujain, to commemorate his victory over the Sakas. The earliest date yet found in any inscription, with the name of Vikramâditya attached to it, is one of Raja Jâika, whose name is already well known from the Morbi inscription bearing the date of 585 of the Gupta era. In this new inscription the date, as read by Pandit Bhagwân Lâl, is thus expressed :

"In the Vikrama Samvatsara 94, in addition to 700, on the 30th day (*amâvâsyâ*) of the dark half of the month of Kârtika, Sunday, in the afternoon (?) on the occasion of a solar eclipse."

The text of this inscription has now been published by Dr. Bühler, who gives the following translation of the date:*

"When seven hundred years of Vikrama exceeded by ninety-four (in figures) 794 (*had passed*) in the second half of the month Kârtika, at the new moon, on a Sunday, under the constellation Jyeshthâ, on the occasion of an eclipse of the sun."

---

* Reinaud Fragments Drabes et Persans, pp. 145-146.

*

Now the last day of Kârtika in the Vikrama Samvat 794 was the 28th of October A.D. 737, which day was a Monday, and not a Sunday as stated in the inscription, and there was no eclipse on that date; Dr. Bühler, therefore, suggests that, as "the figure for the year *probably* refers, as usual in Indian dates, to completed years, the grant must have been issued at the end of Kârtika (in Gujarât the first month) of Vikrama Samvat 795." Now this is *absolutely impossible.* All Indian *dates* are given in completed years, and the Gujarât year of Vikrama Samvat 794 began on the 30th September 737 A.D., and ended on the 18th October 738. On this point there is no possibility of mistake, as the date is recorded in words as well as in figures. It is true that there was an eclipse of the sun on the 18th October 738, but that date, according to Hindu reckoning, was the last day of Aswina, and was a Saturday and not a Sunday. At present the Vikramâditya years begin with the 1st of Kârtika; but Abu Rihan mentions that in Sindh the year began with the following month of *Mânkhir*, or Mârgasiras.* Now, if this was the case in the neighbouring country of Gujarât, the month of Kârtika would have fallen in the end of the year 794; and if there had been no intercalary month, the last day of Kârtika would have been the actual eclipse day, 18th October 738 A.D. But, according to the usual reckoning, the month of Ashâdha was intercalary in that year, so that the last day of Kârtika fell on the 16th of November. As it is quite clear that there must be a mistake somewhere, I think it probable that it may be in the name of the month; I would, therefore, propose to read Aswina 794 for Kârtika 794, which would agree with the real eclipse day of 18th October 738. But as that day was a Saturday, a very inauspicious day, the writing of the grant was probably made on the following day, or Sunday, which was the first day of Kârtika, and this might have led to the substitution of the name of Kârtika for that of Aswina as the actual day of the eclipse.

But a very much earlier date, presumably of Vikramâditya, has been brought to notice by Dr. Bühler in one of the Gujarât inscriptions of Jayabhata, which, although no era is named, must also certainly be referred to the Vikramâditya Samvat.† He reads the year as "Samvat 486, Sunday, the tenth day of the bright half of Ashâdha-Sudi, when the sun entered the sign of the Scorpion."

The Vikrama Samvat year 486 began in Gujarât, according to the present reckoning, on the 1st Kârtika-Sudi, or 28th September A.D. 429,

---

* *Indian Antiquary*, Vol. XII, p. 156.

† *Ibid*, Vol. V, p. 114.

so that the 10th of Ashâdha-Sudi would have fallen in the following year, A.D. 430. As there was no intercalary month in that year, the 10th of Ashâdha-Sudi was the 99th day calculated from the 1st Chaitra-Sudi, or Tuesday, 11th March 430, which brings the date to Tuesday the 17th June, thus agreeing with the Tuesday already calculated by two Bombay authorities for Dr. Bühler. But as the day was a Sunday, according to the inscription, it seems to me not improbable that the date may not have been read quite correctly. The only year which I can find that agrees with the week day indicated is Vikrama Samvat 497, in which year the 10th of Ashâdha-Sudi fell on Sunday, the 15th June A.D. 441. If the figure for 80 was injured below, as the figure for 400 certainly was, then the decimal figure read as 80, might have been 90 and the Samvat year might, perhaps, be 497.

In the Jain books also there is very early mention of the Vikrama Samvat. Thus the Satrunjaya Mahâtmya professes to have been written 477 years after Vikrama, or in A.D. 420, when "Silâditya, king of Vallabhi, expelled the Buddhists from Saurashtra, recovered Satrunjaya and other places of pilgrimage from them, and erected many Jain temples."* The era of Vikrama also is said to have been established by Vikramârka Raja 470 years after Mahâvira, or in 527 — 470 = 57 B.C. From the way in which he is spoken of as "honouring the advice of Siddha Sena Suri as the words of Jaina," it would appear that Vikramârka was a Jaina, which would account for the use of his era in the Jaina books, as well as for the non-mention of it in early Brahmanical inscriptions.

Most of our early writers, as Colebrooke, Wilford, Tod, and Jervis, have vitiated their chronology by placing the initial point of the Vikramâditya era in 56 B.C., instead of in 57 B.C., as shown by Prinsep.† The following examples from Colebrooke and Tod show how necessary it is to be strictly exact in dealing with dates:

1. In one of "Three grants of land found at Ujjayini," the recorded date is an eclipse of the moon in Srâvana of 1200 Samvat. Using the erroneous equation of 56, Colebrooke identifies this eclipse with that of the 16th July 1144 A.D.‡ But the true date was 1200 — 57 = 1143 A.D., in which year there was an eclipse of the moon on 28th July, which day was also the full moon of Srâvana.

---

* Dr. Bhau Dâji, in Bombay Asiatic Society's Journal, Vol. VI, 29-30.

† See Prinsep's Useful Tables, p. 82, where the origin of the error is pointed out.

‡ Colebrooke's Essays, Vol. II, p. 264.

2. But Tod's mistake is even more curious. He quotes the well-known Balabhi inscription, which gives the month of Ashâdha of the year 1320 of Vikrama along with the year 945 of the Balabhi era. He accordingly takes the year 375 [or 1320 — 945] of Vikrama as the initial point of the Balabhi era, from which, deducting 56, he obtains A.D. 319. Here his equation of 56 gives a true result, because he is dealing with an inscription from Gujarât, where the Vikrama year does not begin until 1st Kârtika-Sudi. In the same inscription the Hijra date is also given as 662. Now, as this year did not begin until the 4th November 1263, it is obvious that the Hindu month of Ashâdha, or June-July, must belong to A.D. 1264, and not to A.D. 1263. We thus learn that the Vikrama Samvat year referred to in the inscription must have begun in October, as is still the practice in Gujarât, and that the year 1320 must be reckoned from 1st Kârtika-Sudi, or from October A.D. 1263 to October 1264, and not from March 1263 to March 1264. The equation for the Gujarât reckoning of the Vikrama Samvat is, therefore, 56¼, or, in round numbers, 56, which gives A.D. 1264 as the equivalent of the Vikrama Samvat 1320, as well as of the Hijra year 662. If the year of Vikrama had been reckoned from the last new moon preceding the vernal equinox, the date of the inscription would have been 1320 — 57 = 1263 A.D., so that the month of Ashâdha (or June-July) would have fallen four months before the beginning of the Muhammadan year 662.

XI.—GRAHA-PARIVRITHI CYCLE.

THIS is a cycle of 90 years, which is in use only in Southern India. Warren has described it from the account of the Portuguese Missionary Beschi, who lived for forty years in Madura. It begins in the Kâli-Yuga 3078, or B.C. 24. As the second cycle would have fallen in A.D. 76, it seems probable that it may have some connection with the Jyotishi cycle of Jupiter, which dates from the same period.

XII.—SÂKA ERA.

THE *Sâka-kâl*, called also *Sâka-bhûpa-kâl* and *Sâkendra-kâl*, or the "era of *the Saka King*," is perhaps more widely used than any other era. Abu Rihân says that it was specially employed by the astronomers. But Aryabata and his predecessors would appear to have made use of the Kâli-Yuga for all their calculations, and it was Varâha Mihira who first made use of the Sâka-kâl in astronomical works. Abu Rihân, who correctly describes it as dating 135 years after Vikramâditya, says, that "Saka was the name of a king who reigned over the country situated between the Indus and the Sea; Vikramâditya marched against him and killed him in a battle fought near Korur, between Multân and the Fort of Luni." The town of Kahror still exists in the neighbourhood of Multân and Bahâwalpur. But this Vikramâditya, as Abu Rihân remarks, could not, owing to the long interval of 135 years, be the same as the famous prince who established the Vikrama Samvat. The name of the Saka king was Sâlivâhan, and accordingly the era is now very generally called Sâka Sâlivâhana. It is also known as the Sâka Samvat.

The reckoning of the Sâka era begins with the vernal equinox of the Kâli-Yuga year 3179, or A. D. 78. But as the Indians count only by completed years, the year 1 begins with the vernal equinox of Kâli-Yuga 3180, or A. D. 79. In Northern and Southern India it is usually employed along with the luni-solar calendar; but in Bengal it is generally used with the solar calendar.

In converting Sâka dates into Christian reckoning, 78 years must be added to the given date; and *vice versâ* to convert Christian dates into Sâka reckoning, 78 years must be deducted from the former.

XIII.—GUPTA ERA.

—:o:—

THE *Gupta-kâl*, or Gupta era, is not mentioned by any native writer, although it is found in several ancient inscriptions, as well as on the coins of the Gupta kings. It is however noticed by Abu Rihân, who makes the singular mistake of dating it from the epoch of their extermination, and of confounding it with the era of Balabhi. Now the initial point of the Balabhi era is known absolutely from Colonel Tod's inscription, which makes the year 1 = 319 A.D., which is precisely the same date that is assigned to it by Abu Rihân, who says, that it is posterior to Sâka by 241 years, or 241 + 78 = 319 A.D. But as he goes on to say "Apparemment Ballaba suivit immediatement les Guptas," it is clear that the Guptas must have reigned *before* A.D. 319.

The confusion about the two eras has probably arisen from the fact that the Balabhi kings, in all their copper-plate grants, continued to use the Gupta era instead of making use of the Balabhi era itself. The following dates of the Gupta-kâl are found on the coins and inscriptions of the Gupta kings and in the records of their contemporaries :

1.	SAMUDRA-GUPTA	Copper-plate, S. 40.
2.	CHANDRA-GUPTA	Inscriptions, S. 82-93.
3.	KUMARA-GUPTA	Inscription, S. 96-98-126.
4.	SKANDA-GUPTA	Inscriptions, S. 137-138-141-146. Coins, S. 144-145-149.
5.	BUDHA-GUPTA	Inscriptions, S. 165. Coins, 174-180 odd.
6.	RAJA HASTIN	S. 156-and year Mahâ Vaisâkha. S. 163 (read 173) year Mahâ Aswayuja. S. 191 ——— Mahâ Chaitra.
7.	RAJA SANKSHOBA	S. 209 ——— Mahâ Aswayuja.

The last four dates, which are recorded in two different reckonings, I have already made use of in my attempt to fix the initial point of the Gupta-kâl.* The title of mahâ, prefixed to the names of the four years, shows that the reckoning belongs to the Lesser Bârhaspatya Chakra, or

* Archæological Survey of India, Vol. X, Appendix.

12-year Cycle of Jupiter. This cycle I have already described; and as the General Table gives all the names of the years in due order, marking each period of the omission of a name by a black circle, it will be easy to follow the arrangement by a reference to the Tables.

As the 12th part of one revolution of Jupiter is considerably more than four days less than one solar year, a difference which amounts to one whole year in a little more than 85 solar years, the rule is to omit every 86th name. Now the double dates which I have given above show that, from the year 156 to 209 of the Gupta era, there was no name of the Jovian Cycle omitted. As this fact seemed to me to offer a ready means of obtaining an approximate date for the beginning of the Gupta-kâl, I drew up a Table showing the names of all the years of the 12-year cycle from the beginning of the Christian era down to the present day. Now as there was no omitted name between the years 156 and 209 of the Gupta era, or for a period of 54 years, the first date of Mahâ Vaisâkha, or Gupta-kâl 156, must lie within the period of 32 years (86 − 54) succeeding one of the omitted names. On referring to the General Table, where the names of the years of the 12-year cycle are all given, it will be seen that the date of 156 Gupta-kâl must, therefore, lie within some one of the following periods:

1.—A.D. 225 to 257, or 225 + 32.
2.—A.D. 310 to 342, or 310 + 32.
3.—A.D. 395 to 427, or 395 + 32.

In the first period the only dates on which Mahâ Vaisâkha falls are three, namely, A.D. 227, 239, 251. But as these dates would place the beginning of the Gupta era in A.D. 73, 81, or 95, they may be given up as too early.

In the second period the dates of Mahâ Vaisâkha are A.D. 310, 322, 334. If 310 be taken as 156 of the Gupta-kâl, then the year 1 will fall in 310 − 155 = 155 A.D. This would place the date of Budha Gupta's Pillar in 154 + 165 = 319 A.D., but as the week day of 12th Ashâdha-Sudi in Budha Gupta's inscription fell on a Tuesday in that year, and not on a *Thursday* as required, that date must be given up.*

If the middle number 322 be taken as 156 of the Gupta-kâl, then the year 1 will fall in 322 − 155 = 167 A.D., and the date of Budha Gupta's Pillar in 166 + 165 = 331 A.D., in which year the 12th of Ashâdha-Sudi did fall on a *Thursday*.

* Budha Gupta's inscription on the Pillar at Eran bears the date of Samvat 165, Thursday, 12th Ashâdha-Sudi.

If the third number 334 be taken as 156 of the Gupta-kâl, then the year 1 will fall in 334 – 155 = 179 A.D., and the year 165 of Budha Gupta's Pillar in A.D. 178 + 165 = 343, in which year the 12th Ashâdha-Sudi fell an a *Monday*.

In the group of 85 years from A.D. 310 to 395, there is therefore only one year, A.D. 322, that will satisfy the two requirements of being a Mahâ Vaisâkha year itself, and of having a *Thursday* as the week day answering to 12th Ashâdha-Sudi of the year 165 of the Gupta era.

In the second group of 85 years from A.D. 395 to 480, the only dates on which Mahâ Vaisâkha falls within the limit of 54 years preceding 480, are the two years 405 and 417 A.D., from which, deducting 155, we get the years 250 and 262 as two new starting points for the Gupta era.

First, taking 250 as the year 1 of the Gupta-kâl, the year 165 will be A.D. 414, in which year the 12th of Ashâdha-Sudi fell on a Tuesday, and not on a Thursday.

Next, taking 262 as the year 1 of the Gupta era, the year 165 will fall in A.D. 414, in which year the 12th of Ashâdha-Sudi fell on a Thursday, as required.

We have thus in the two groups of years, extending from A.D. 310 to 395, only two dates which fulfil the two conditions of the Mahâ Vaisâkha year, and the 12th of Ashâdha-Sudi being a Thursday. These two dates place the 1st year of the Gupta-kâl either in A.D. 167, or in A.D. 262.

It is needless to try a third group of years, as the only possible Mahâ Vaisâkha dates would fall in A.D. 488 and 500, which would place the 1st year of the Gupta era in A.D. 333 or 345, both of which are certainly too late.

When I submitted these results to my learned friend Pandit Bâpu Deva, he pointed out that the 12th of Ashâdha-Sudi in A.D. 331 was a Friday, and not a Thursday. But it is so only by the reckoning of the Surya Siddhânta, which I have purposely rejected in dealing with these Gupta dates, as Varâha Mihira, the author of the Surya Siddhânta, lived at least two centuries later than Budha Gupta; so that it is quite impossible that his corrected tables could have been used in computing the calendar of the Gupta period. My calculations have been made from the tables of Aryabhatta, according to which the 12th of Ashâdha-Sudi in A.D. 331 was actually a Thursday. I am of course aware that Aryabhatta is also later than Budha Gupta; but as his length of year differs from that of his predecessor Parâsara by little more than half a second, the adoption of Aryabhatta's table will not affect the week day. The case is different with Varâha Mihira, as his year is considerably longer than that of Parâsara and Aryabhatta. This difference was duly noticed by James Prinsep, who remarks that "Warren's Kâla Sankâlita gives the beginning of the Hindu solar year invariably *one day earlier* than the reckoning followed in the tables of the Sudder Dewânee. This arises from his using the Tamil year of the Arya Siddhânta, while the Surya Siddhânta is used in Bengal."

In A.D. 331, the Hindu luni-solar year began on the 23rd February, according to Cowasjee Patell, who, throughout his chronology, has used the tables of Aryabhatta. In this year the month of Bhâdrapada was intercalary; but as this month is later than Ashâdha, the date will not be affected by the intercalation. Now the 12th of Ashâdha-Sudi is the 101st day of the Hindu luni-solar year; and as the 23rd of February was a Tuesday, the 101st day was a Thursday in A.D. 331, according to Aryabhatta's tables. But according to Varâha Mihira, the Hindu luni-solar year began one day later, on the 24th February, and consequently the 101st day would be Friday, 4th June.

The result of this examination is that there are only two possible dates for the commencement of the Gupta era, which fulfill the conditions of the two tests which I have applied,—namely, A.D. 167 and A.D. 262. We have accordingly to choose between these two dates that which agrees best with some of the other conditions.

By the first date, the period of Samudra Gupta, the son of Chandra Gupta I, the presumed founder of the era, would fall between the year 200 and 230 A.D., which agrees with the fact that he was a contemporary of the Devaputra Shâhi, Shahân Shâhi, or the king of the Great Yue-chi Indo-Scythians.

By this earlier period also the date of Dhrûva-bhatta would fall in 166+447=613 A.D., or just 28 years before Hwen Thsang's visit to Balabhi in 641, during his reign.

Taking the later date of A.D. 262, the period of Samudra Gupta would fall about A.D. 290 to 330, which would place him some considerable time after the Great Yue-chi had already got rid of their kings and had established military chiefs (? Satraps).

This later period also would fix the date of Dhrûva-bhatta in 261 + 447=708 A.D., or just 68 years after Hwen Thsang's visit, which is much too long a period for the reign of a single king.

For these reasons I much prefer the earlier date of A.D. 167 as the first year of the Gupta era. This earlier date also is attended by a curious coincidence, which seems to me to offer a very strong confirmation of its accuracy. This is the correspondence in time of the death of Skanda Gupta with the foundation of the Balabhi era. His latest inscription is dated in S. 146, or A.D. 312, according to the earlier initial point which I have adopted. But one of his silver coins in my cabinet is dated three years later, or in S. 149, or A.D. 315, which is within four years of the establishment of the Balabhi era. I think it very probable, therefore, that the foundation of this era may have been brought about by the opportunity of Skanda Gupta's death. This would agree very well with the statement of Abu Rihân, "that the fall of the Guptas corresponded with the establishment of the Balabhi era."*

In my attempt to fix the date of the Gupta era I overlooked a very important inscription of Silâditya V., the father of Dhrûva-bhatta of Balabhi. This inscription is dated in S. 441, while the son's inscription is only six years later. Supposing its dates to be recorded in the Gupta era, then Silâditya V. would have been reigning in 166 + 441 = 607 A. D., and his death may be placed about A.D. 610, or three years before the date of his son's inscription in S. 447, or A.D. 613. Now Silâditya V. was the tenth generation of the Balabhi kings, and if we place the foundation of the Balabhi monarchy in A.D. 319, the ten *generations* will have reigned from A.D. 318 to 610, or for 292 years, which gives an average of 29¼ years to each *generation*. During this period there were 18 *reigns*, which give an average of nearly 16¼ years to each *reign*.

That the era used by the Balabhi kings was that of the Guptas seems to be almost certain, as the Senapati Bhatâraka, the founder of the Balabhi dynasty, is said to have been the governor of Surâshtra during the last two years of Skanda Gupta's reign. If then we accept the

* See Archæological Survey of India, Vol. X, p. 125.

year A.D. 319 as the date of the foundation of the Balabhi monarchy, as well as of Balabhi itself, the Gupta era must be placed at least 146 years earlier, or in A.D. 173, according to the date of Skanda Gupta's latest inscription; or 149 years earlier, or in A.D. 170, according to the date of his latest coin. This direct succession of the Guptas by the Balabhis, already noted by Abu Rihân, is confirmed by the traditions of the people, which state that, on Skanda Gupta's death, the Senapati "assumed the title of king of Surâshtra," and "founded the city of Valabhinagar."* From these statements I gather that the Valabhi era must almost certainly be dated from the foundation of the city of Valabhi, which followed immediately after the death of Skanda Gupta. For this reason, therefore, I think that the date of A.D. 166, which I have already deduced for the beginning of the Gupta era, from the copper-plate inscriptions of Raja Hastin and his son Sankshoba, compared with the week day date of Budha Gupta's Pillar at Eran, has a better claim for acceptance than any other that has yet been proposed.

The new inscription of Jaika (which has not yet been published) has induced Dr. Bühler to fix the beginning of the Gupta era about A.D. 206-209. But even the earlier date of 206 would place Silâditya V. in 206+441=647 A.D., just six years later than the visit of Hwen Thsang, who found his son Dhrûva-bhatta on the throne.

This inscription of Dhrûva-bhatta I had previously overlooked until my attention was drawn to it by Dr. Burgess.

It tells altogether in favour of any earlier date, for the inscription of Dhrûva-bhatta himself is dated in 447, or only six years later than that of his father.

As the latest possible date for Silâditya V. is 640 A.D. (the year before Hwen Thsang's visit), the latest possible starting point for the Gupta era is 640−446=194 A.D.

According to my present calculation of the initial point of the Gupta era in A.D. 166=0, and 167=1, the date of Silâditya V. will fall in 441+166=607 A.D., and that of his son Dhrûva-bhatta in 447+166=613, A.D.

The published inscription of Jaika, from Morbi, is dated in the year 585 of the Gupta-kâl, or era of the Guptas. It records a grant made

---

* *Indian Antiquary*, 1873, p. 312. Notes by Major Watson.

on the occasion of a solar eclipse; but the inscription itself is dated on the 5th of Phâlguna-Sudi, which was not therefore the date of the grant, as a solar eclipse can only happen on *badi* 14th or the last day of the waning moon. According to my calculation of the initial point of the Gupta era, the year 585 will correspond with $585+166=751$ A.D., in which year there was an eclipse of the sun on the 25th of August.

It is true that this date is about five months earlier than the actual date of the record. But this is not a difficulty of any consequence, as we have a similar interval between the actual date of a grant and the date of its record on copper in the Râjim inscription of Tivara Deva, king of Kosala. His grant was made on the 12th of the solar month of Jyeshta, but was not recorded until the 8th of Kârtika, or just four days less than five months later. The day of the month I have read myself, as it is not given by Wilson in his Translation, see Asiatic Researches, Vol. XV. The eighth day of Kârtik is recorded both in words and in figures.

XIV.—CHEDI, OR KALÂCHURI-SAMVAT.

—:o:—

THERE is a considerable number of inscriptions of the Kalâchuri Rajas of Chedi, with various dates from S. 792 to S. 934, which, from the style of their characters, as well as from the names of other kings mentioned in them, cannot possibly be referred to the era of Vikrama. The actual name of the era was discovered by Mr. Beglar in several inscriptions from the district of Raypur to the east of Nâgpur. In some it is named the *Chedi*-Samvat, and in others the *Kalâchuri-Samvat.* All the then available dates have been discussed in my account of the Kalâchuri inscriptions.* From these I deduced that the initial point of the era must have been A.D. 249, "as that year gives the correct week days by computation for *four* of the recorded dates." Since then I have been able to correct two of the discrepant dates noticed in my account, while I have myself found two new dates. As all of these give the correct week day when calculated from the initial point of 249 A.D. = 0, and 250 = 1, I feel satisfied that this is the true starting point of the Chedi era.

During my late tour in the Central Provinces I obtained the two new inscriptions of the Kalâchuri or Chedi-Samvat already mentioned. The date of the earlier one is given as *Samvat* 866, *Mârga-Sudi 9, Ravau,* or "Sunday the 9th of the waxing moon of Mârga, 866." Taking my previously ascertained starting point of the era in A.D. 250 = 1, the date will be 866 + 249 = A.D. 1115, in which year Jyeshta was intercalary, and the 9th of Mârga-Sudi fell on a Sunday.

The date of the second inscription is *Samvat* 934, *Kârttika-Sudi* 5, *Budhe,* or "Wednesday the 5th of the waxing moon of Kârttika in the year 934." Adding 249 to 934 we get the year A.D. 1183, in which the 15th of *Kârttika-Sudi* was a Wednesday.

---

* Archæological Survey of India, IX, 112, et *ante.*

One of the discrepant dates, noted in my previous account, was that of the Benares inscription of Karna Deva, which I gave as "Samvat 793, Phâlgun-Badi 9th Monday." But as the 9th of Phâlgun-Badi in 793 + 249 = A.D. 1142 was a Sunday, I have come to the conclusion that I may perhaps have misread 793 for 792.

This conclusion was suggested to me by the fact that Wilford read the unit as 2, and that the 9th of Phâlguna-Badi in the preceding year, or 792 + 249 = A.D. 1141, was actually a Monday.

The other correction is in the day of the month in the year 898, which I read as Aswina-Sudi 7, instead of Aswina-Sudi 2, which a fresh examination has shown it to be. As the 7th was a Saturday (as noted in my previous account), the 2nd was of course a Monday, as stated in the inscription. We have thus got no less than eight dates, all of which agree in placing the initial point of the Chedi or Kalâchuri era in A.D. 249—the year 250 being reckoned as 1.

There are three inscriptions which give the name of "*Kalâchuri-Samvat,*" dated respectively in 896, 898, and 910, but the first two only name the week day. Two other inscriptions, dated in 919 and 933, give the name of "*Chedi-Samvat,*" but they do not give the week days.

The initial point of the Chedi or Kalâchuri-Samvat is therefore satisfactorily established by the eight following inscriptions, in which the calculated week days agree exactly with the recorded ones:—

INSCRIPTION.		CHEDI S.	A. D.	
Benares	...	792	1041	Phâlgun-Badi 9, Monday.
Nâgpur museum	...	866	1115	Mârga-Sudi 9, Sunday.
Rajim	...	896	1145	Mâgha-Sudi 8, Wednesday.
Seorinârâyan	...	898	1147	Aswina-Sudi 2, Monday.
Tewar	...	902	1151	Ashâdha-Sudi 1, Sunday.
Bhera-Ghât	...	907	1156	Mârgasiras-Sudi, Sunday.
Bhera-Ghât	...	928	1177	Mâgha-Badi 10, Monday.
Sahaspur	...	934	1183	Kârttika-Sudi 5, Wednesday.

I must mention, however, that there are two other inscriptions in which the calculated week day differs by one day from that recorded. These are—

Bharhut	...	909	1158	Srâvana-Sudi 5, Wednesday, comes out Thursday.
Tewar	...	928	1177	Srâvana-Sudi 6, Sunday, comes out Monday.

The Rajas of Chedi are mentioned in the inscriptions of the neighbouring kings from A.D. 520 downwards. But the earliest Prince mentioned in their own inscriptions is Kokalla I., the contemporary of Bhoja of Kanauj, whose dates we know to have ranged from A.D. 875 to 900. From his time down to the close of the dynasty, the Kalâchuri Princes played a principal part in the history of Central India. Their capital was at Tripura, now Tewar, six miles to the west of Jabalpur. But there was an eastern branch of the family which ruled at Ratanpur, of whom very little is at present known. A list of the Rajas of this family is given in the Gazetteer of the Central Provinces. Some of the names correspond with those found in the inscriptions; but the dates are all wrong, as they have been referred to the Samvat of Vikramâditya, instead of to the local Chedi era of the country.

XV.—ERA OF BALABHI.

—:o:—

THE initial point of the *Balabhi-kâl*, or era of Balabhi, is fixed by the account of Abu Rihân, as well as by the other dates recorded in Tod's inscription, to the year 319 A.D. According to the former, it was 241 years posterior to the Sâka, or $78 + 241 = 319$ A.D. According to the inscription, Sunday the 13th Ashâdha-Badi of the year 945 of *Srimad Balabhi*, fell in the year 662 of *Muhammad*, 1320 of *Vikrama*, and 151 of the *Siva Singha Samvat.** The first year of the Balabhi era was fixed by Tod by deducting 975 from 1320, which gives 375 of the Vikrama Samvat as the year 1 of the Balabhi Samvat. Then, deducting 56 from 375, he obtained 319 A.D. as the equivalent in the Christian era.

Now the difference between the Christian and the Vikrama starting points being nearly 57 years, the equivalent for Vikrama 375 should be 318, and not 319. But as we know from Abu Rihân that the Balabhi era actually began in 319, some explanation is required to show how Tod's erroneous factor of 56 gave the right year A.D. The explanation is a very simple one,—namely, that the Vikramâditya years in the province of Gujarât, where the inscription was found, began then, as they do now, with the month of *Kârtika* or October, and consequently the true factor for converting the Vikrama date into the Christian equivalent was 56½, or 56 as used by Tod. The proof of this is equally simple. The Hijra year 662 did not begin until the 4th of November 1263 A.D. This being the case, the month of Ashâdha (or June-July) of the Christian year 1263 had already passed by, and therefore the Ashâdha of Samvat 1320 of the Northern reckoning cannot belong to that year. But if we take the Southern reckoning prevalent in Gujarât, then 56 will become the nearest factor, and Tod's $375-56$ will give the correct year A.D. 319. Then deducting 56 from the given Samvat year 1320, we get A.D. 1264 as the concurrent Christian year. This agrees exactly with the given year of Muhammad, 662, which began on 4th November 1263, and ended on the 23rd October 1264.

So far as I am aware Tod's inscription is the only one that has yet been found dated in the Balabhi era.

---

* Tod's Rajasthan, I, 801.

XVI.—SRI-HARSHA ERA.

—:o:—

The *Sri-Harsha-kâl*, or "Era of Sri-Harsha," is mentioned only by Abu Rihân. Its initial point shows that it was established by the famous king Sri Harsha Vardhana of Kanauj, from the 1st year of his reign. It was used in Mathura and Kanauj, and Abu Rihân gives its initial point from the Almanacs of Kashmir as 664 years posterior to Vikramâditya, or 664−57 = 607 A.D.* I brought to notice some years ago one inscription of Bhoja Deva of Kanauj, which is certainly dated in this era. This inscription is at Prithudaka, or Pehoa, and is dated both in words and in figures in the year 276. Referring this to the era of Sri-Harsha we get 606+276 = 882 A.D.†

But the inscriptions found in Nepâl by Pandit Bhagwân Lâl offer still earlier instances of the use of this era.‡ The earliest of these records, bearing the name of Ansu Varma, are dated in Samvat 34, 39, and 45. Now Ansu Varma was on the throne when the Chinese prilgrim Hwen Thsang visited Nepâl in A.D. 637, which was in the very middle of his reign, as his earliest inscription above quoted is dated in A.D. 640 (606+34) and his latest in A.D. 651, which was near the close of his reign, as an inscription of his successor, Jishnu Gupta, is dated in S. 48, or A.D. 654. Three inscriptions of Siva Deva are dated respectively in S. 119, 143, 145, and one of Jaya Deva in S. 153, or A.D. 759. Now Jaya Deva's mother is said to have been the grand-daughter of the "Great Aditya Sena, the illustrious lord of Magadha," of whom I have an inscription dated in S. 55, as I read the two figures. This would place Aditya in A.D. 661, or 64 years prior to his grand-daughter, the wife of Siva Deva.

---

* Renaud, Fragments Arabes et Persans, p. 139.

† See Archæological Survey, X, 101, for other inscriptions of Bhoja Deva; Gwalior A.D. 876; and Deogarh A.D. 862. The Raja Tarangini also places him between 883 and 901 A.D.

‡ *Indian Antiquary*, Vol. IX, p. 169, *et seq.*

In A.D. 880 the Newâr era was introduced into Nepâl by Râghaba Deva. He is the sixth Prince in the Nepâl list after Jaya Deva; and if Jaya reigned until about 170 of the Harsha era, or A.D. 776, there would remain only 104 years to be divided over the five intervening reigns.

None of the inscriptions describe the era by name, but call it simply Samvat. But, from the mention of Ansu Varma as the reigning king of Nepâl by Hwen Thsang, it is quite clear that the dates which I have quoted must belong to the Sri-Harsha era. According to the lists Ansu had one predecessor Siva Deva Varma, who, as he belonged to the old family that had been expelled, was very probably restored by the powerful king of Kanauj, whose era he adopted.

There are two copper-plate inscriptions of the family of the Kanauj kings, who reigned from about 750 to 1,000 A.D. The earlier plate is of Mahendra Pâla Deva, the son of Bhoja Deva, whose date I have fixed from several other inscriptions as extending from A.D. 870 to 900. The date of Mahendra's plate may be read as 315, which, referred to the Sri-Harsha era, would place him in A.D. 921. The later plate is of Sri Vinayaka Pâla Deva, the grandson of Mahendra Pâla. Its date seems to be 386, which would place him in A.D. 992.* Shortly after this, Kanauj was conquered by the Râthors, who introduced the Samvat of Vikramâditya.

---

* For the first plate, see Bengal Asiatic Society's Journal, XXXIII, 321, and for the second plate, see the same Journal, XVII, 71.

XVII.—HIJRA ERA.

—:o:—

THIS era dates from the morning after the flight (*Hijra*) of Muhammad from Mekka to Medina, which took place on the night of the 15th July A.D. 622. The year 1, therefore, began on *Friday*, 16*th July* 622. The year is a simple lunar one of 12 lunations or lunar months, of 30 and 29 days alternately. The common year, therefore, consists of only 354 days. But as a month of 29½ days is somewhat less than one mean lunation, an intercalary day is added to the last month in the 2nd, 5th, 7th, 10th, 13th, 16th, 18th, 21st, 24th, 26th, and 29th years of each period of 30 years, so that the year consists of $354\frac{11}{30}$ days, which makes the mean lunation $29\frac{191}{360}$ days, or 29·5305555. This differs from the mean synodical revolution of European astronomers by only ·0000332 of a day. The Muhammadan lunar year of $354\frac{11}{30}$, or 354·3666 days, is, therefore, 0·970202 of the solar year of 365·25 days of the Julian reckoning.

To find whether any given year is intercalary, divide it by 30, and if the remainder be either 2, 5, 7, 10, 13, 16, 18, 21, 24, 26, or 29, then the year is an intercalary one of 355 days; but if it be any other number, the year is a common one of 354 days.

But to save the trouble of calculation for finding on what day of the Christian era any particular Hijra date falls, I have prepared two tables, by which the corresponding date can be obtained in a much shorter time by inspection.

Thus, to find the corresponding date of Timur's capture of Delhi, which he has himself recorded as "Wednesday the 8th of the 2nd Rabi 801 A. H.," first look in Table XVI for the initial day of the Muhammadan year in Christian reckoning, which was Friday the 13th September 1398. Then turn to Table XV, and look for the place of II Rabi 8, from which run the eye upwards to the horizontal line of week days, beginning with Friday, where the intersection will be found to fall on Wednesday, thus agreeing with the week day given by Timur. Next look to the Roman numerals on the right, where it will be seen that "II Rabi 8" was the 6th day of the 13th week, or the 97th day of the Muhammadan year. Then calculate from the 13th September 1398 as the 1st day as follows:—

In September	... ...	18 days.
„ October	... ...	31 „
„ November	... ...	30 „
„ December	... ...	18 „
	Total ...	97 days.

The corresponding Christian date was, therefore, the 18th December 1398, which, by the tables of the Christian calendar, was a Wednesday.

The following dates taken from several different authors agree with the tables:

						Page.
A. H.	422	Muharram	1	= Tuesday	*Baihaki*, H. M. Elliot, II,	61
	633	Shabân	29	= Tuesday	*Minhâj*, H. M. Elliot, II,	330
	638	Muharram	8	= Monday	... ...	338
	640	Rajab	9	= Friday	... ...	343
	645	Muharram	2	= Thursday	... ...	347
	655	I Rabi	6	= Sunday	... ...	356
	656	Muharram	6	= Sunday	... ...	358
	801	II Rabi	8	= Wednesday,	Timur's own date of capture of Delhi, H. M. E., III ...	443

Dowson erroneously gives 17th December 1398 as the European date of the capture instead of 18th. The 17th December was Tuesday—

A. H. 912	II Jamadi	8	Monday	Babar's Memoirs,	page 201
925	Muharram	1	Monday	... ...	„ 246
925	I Rabi	11	Sunday	... ...	„ 260
932	Safar	1	Friday	... ...	„ 290
933	I Rabi	16	Friday	... ...	„ 347
936	Muharram	3	Tuesday	... ...	„ 425
949	Rajab	5	Sunday	Akbar born.—Blochmann.	
963	II Rabi	2	Friday	Akbar placed on throne at Kalanor by Bairâm.	

Occasionally, however, the week days of both inscriptions and books will be found to differ *one* day from the week days of the tables. If this should be the case in several instances of the same writer, the discrepancy must be due to his having used a slightly different order of the intercalary years. The numbers of the intercalary years which I have used in the accompanying Tables are those of Ulugh Beg, which are the most generally accepted,—namely—2—5—7—10—13—16—18—21—24—26—29. But according to Jervis the Indian Almanacs give three of the numbers differently, or one in each decade of each cycle. These different numbers are 8, 19 and 27, instead of 7, 18 and 26. The result is, that where the years 8, 19 and 27 are made intercalary, those years will begin one day *earlier* than in the Tables, and every day throughout each of those years will also be one day earlier. In the accompanying Tables I have placed Roman numerals against the intercalary years of the accepted reckoning, and stars against the three years which differ.

I have found this discrepancy of a single day in the following dates:—

			Recorded Date.	*Date by Tables.*		
A. H. 630	Safar	20	Tuesday	Monday	Minhâj, H. M. Elliott, II,	327
634	Rajab	6	Friday	Thursday	... ...	...
882	Muharram	1	Wednesday	Tuesday	Pandua inscription.	
899	Ramzân	4	Monday	Sunday	Babar's Memoirs ...	7
926	Muharram	1	Saturday	Friday	... ...	281
934	Muharram	1	Saturday	Friday	... ...	373
977	I Rabi	17	Wednesday	Tuesday	Jahângir born.	
1000	II Jamâdi	6	Saturday	Friday	Tabakâti Akbari.	

It must be confessed, however, that not one of the above dates falls in the 8th, the 19th, or the 27th years, so that I can only suggest carelessness on the part of the writers as the probable explanation of the discrepancies. The following more glaring instances will be sufficient to show that even the best Muhammadan authors are not free from errors of this kind:

Minhâj—A. H. 634, I Rabi 18—*Sunday,* should be *Wednesday.*
———A. H. 637, Ramzan 27—*Monday,* should be *Friday.*
Baber—A. H. 933, Muharram 25—*Monday,* should be *Thursday.*

This last mistake has been noticed by Erskine.

In using the general table of the initial days of the Hijra years, it is only necessary to remember that all the dates up to the beginning of A.D. 1753 are given in Julian reckoning or Old Style, and from that date in Gregorian reckoning or New Style. The week days of course remain unchanged, whichever reckoning is used. The correction of the calendar took place in Engalnd in A.D. 1752, when eleven days were struck out after the 2nd September, making the next day the 14th instead of the 3rd. This change occurred towards the end of the Hijra year 1165. In the table I have given the beginning of the year 1166 in the New Style as Wednesday the 8th November 1752. By the Old Style reckoning the date would have been Wednesday, 28th October.

To find the day of the week on which any given year of the Hijra began, the following rule is given by Woolhouse—

1*st.*—Find the year of the current cycle by dividing the proposed Hijra year by 30.

2*nd.*—Divide the number of cycles thus obtained by 7, to obtain the number of the period.

Now take the year 1000 A. H. as an example—

	1000 A. H.		33 cycles.
30	———	7	———
Cycles	33 + 10 = current year of cycle.		4 + 5 = number of period.

Then look in the following table for the intersection of the current year of the cycle, or 10, with the number of the period, or 5, and it will be found that the initial day is Saturday, which is correct:

Current year of the cycle.				Number of the period of 7 cycles.						
				0	1	2	3	4	5	6
0	8	...	...	Mon.	Sat.	Thur.	Tues.	S.	Frid.	Wed.
1	9	17	25	Frid.	Wed.	Mon.	Sat.	Thur.	Tues.	S.
*2	*10	*18	*26	Tues.	S.	Frid.	Wed.	Mon.	Sat.	Thur.
3	11	19	27	S.	Frid.	Wed.	Mon.	Sat.	Thur.	Tues.
4	12	20	28	Thur.	Tues.	S.	Frid.	Wed.	Mon.	Sat.
*5	*13	*21	*29	Mon.	Sat.	Thur.	Tues.	S.	Frid.	Wed.
6	14	22	30	Sat.	Thur.	Tues.	S.	Frid.	Wed.	Mon.
*7	15	23	...	Wed.	Mon.	Sat.	Thur.	Tues.	S.	Frid.
...	*16	*24	...	S.	Frid.	Wed.	Mon.	Sat.	Thur.	Tues.

The calculation of this table is based on the fact that as the cycle consists of 30 years, the whole series of week day changes will be exhausted in each period of 30 × 7 = 210 years. Thus the year 1 A.H. having begun on a Friday, the following years would also begin on Friday :—

				O.S.
A. H. 1	=	Friday, 16th July	622	A.D.
211	=	Friday, 13th April	826	„
421	=	Friday, 9th January	1030	„
631	=	Friday, 7th October	1233	„
841	=	Friday, 5th July	1437	„
1051	=	Friday, 2nd April	1641	„
1261	=	Friday, 10th January	1845	N.S.

As the calendar was corrected in England in A. D. 1752, during the currency of the Hijra year 1165, the last entry is given in New Style, or Gregorian reckoning.

But the initial week day of any given year of the Hijra can also be obtained by a short calculation, starting from any cne of the above periods. Thus taking the year 1000 A. H. as before, and remembering that the intercalary days are inserted in the following years of each cycle—

2 . 5 — 7 . 10 — 13 — 16 — 18 — 21. 24. 26. 29

The calculation is as follows :—

1000 A. H. — 841 = 159 years.
× 4 = No. of days in each year in excess of 50 weeks.
——
636 days
150 years = 5 cycles = 55 days, at 11 intercalary days per cycle of 30 years.
In 9 years over 5 cycles = 3 intercalary days [2nd, 5th, 8th years]
—— ——
159 Total 694 days.
÷ 7 ——
Weeks 99 + 1 day = Saturday.

that is, one day over Friday = Saturday, the same as derived from Woolhouse's Table.*

When a full table is not at hand for finding a date by simple inspection, either of the above methods will be found very useful, as both are absolutely correct.

* Woolhouse's account of the Hijra Era will be found in "Weights and Measures of all Nations."—*Weale*, 1856.

XVIII.—THE BURMESE COMMON ERA.

—:o:—

THE common era of Burma which is now in use is the luni-solar calendar, which was introduced from India in A.D. 638. The length of the year is exactly the same as that of the Surya Siddhânta, namely, 365·875648 days. The solar year is reckoned in the same way as that of the Hindus, and accordingly it now begins on the 12th and 13th of April, which is the calculated date of the sun's entrance into Aries according to Hindu reckoning. The luni-solar year has 12 lunar months of 29 and 30 days alternately, with an intercalary month at seven fixed periods in each cycle of 19 years. The years in which these intercalary months are inserted are the

2nd, 5th, 7th, 10th, 13th, 15th, 18th.

But the extra month is always inserted in the same part of the year after the month of Wahso, and is consequently named the second Wahso. The names of the 12 months are the following:—

1.	Tâgu	... Chaitra	... March-April.
2.	Kasong	... Vaisâkha	... April-May.
3.	Nayong	... Jyeshtha	... May-June.
4.	Wahso	... Ashâdha	... June-July.
5.	Wahgoung	... Srâvana	... July-August.
6.	Tauthalin	... Bhâdrpada	... August-September.
7.	Thadinkyut	... Aswina	... September-October.
8.	Tasoung-mong	... Kârtika	... October-November.
9.	Natdart	... Agrahayana	... November-December.
10.	Payatho	... Pausha	... December-January.
11.	Tabodweh	... Mâgha	... January-February.
12.	Taboung	... Phâlguna	... February-March.

The year begins with the new moon immediately preceding the commencement of the solar year, and ends with the 30th day of Taboung.

The initial point of the era is Saturday the 21st March A.D. 638 of the Julian reckoning, or 24th March A.D. 638 of the Gregorian reckoning. In computing any date the calculation is much simpler than that of the usual rules for the Hindu luni-solar year, as the reckoning is referred to the beginning of the era, and not to the beginning of a yuga or mahâ-yuga several thousands of years back. The process is otherwise the same as that for any day of the Hindu luni-solar year, with the exception that the fixed position of the intercalary month saves some trouble.

To ascertain whether any particular year will be intercalary or not, it is only necessary to divide the number by 19, and if the remainder be either 2, 5, 7, 10, 13, 15, 18, then an intercalary month will be added in that year; but if it be any other number, the year will be an ordinary one.

In India the only examples of Burmese dates that have hitherto been met with are in the few Burmese inscriptions found at the Mahâbodhi temple at Buddha Gaya. Three of these, which refer to the Great Temple itself, are of so much importance that I gladly take this opportunity of giving my readings of their dates. The longest inscription is on a stone slab which was found by the Burmese embassy fixed in one of the inner walls of the Mahant's residence. Three translations of it have been published,—*1st*, by Ratna Pala, a Singhalese Pali scholar; *2nd*, by Colonel Burney; and *3rd*, by Mr. Hla Oung, a Burmese scholar. The inscription professes to record the history of the original building and the successive repairs of the temple. Two dates are given in figures, accompanied, in each case, by the day of the week as well as the day of the month. The following is a brief abstract of this valuable record :—

1—Asoka built the first temple.

2—Temple rebuilt by Naik Mahanta.

3—Temple restored by Raja Sado-Meng.

4—Raja Sempyu-Sakhen-tara-Mengi deputed his guru Sri Dhamma Râja Guna to superintend the restoration of the temple work not completed.

5—Varadasi Naik Thera petitioned the Raja to undertake the work, which was then entrusted to "the younger Pyu-Sakheng" and his minister Ratha.

This last work was begun in the Sakka Raj year 441, on Friday the 10th of Pyadola, and finished in 448, on Sunday the 8th of Tachung Mangla (or Tasoung-Mong).

Here I have given my own reading of the dates as 441 and 448, for the following reasons:

A copper gilt canopy, which was found by Mr. Beglar carefully buried eight feet under the ground level to the west of the Great Temple, bears two inscriptions in Burmese and mediæval Indian characters,

The Burmese inscription is much injured, but I can still read the name of *Sri Dhamma* in it. The Indian inscription, which is nearly perfect, opens as follows :—

Sam 391, *Sri Dharma Raja Guru.*

Here the date which is very clearly inscribed can only be referred to the Burmese common era of A.D. 638, which fixes the period of Dharma Raja Guru's visit to 391 + 638 = A.D. 1029. Now the account of the later mission of "the younger Pyu-Sakheng" shows that it must have followed not long after Dharma Raja Guru's Mission. I therefore read the two dates as 441 and 448, in preference to the very much later dates of 667 and 668, which had been generally adopted previously. I have tested all the possible readings of these dates as 641, 647, 661, 667, 648, and 668, by the week days mentioned in the inscription. Not one of them stands this test, whereas the two dates of 441 and 448 which I have adopted do actually agree with the week days recorded in the inscription. The evidence in favour of my readings is, therefore, doubly strong. The later history of the temple will therefore be as follows :

Burmese era 391 = A.D. 1929—Dharma Raja Guru's Mission.

———— 441 = A.D. 1079—Restoration of temple begun by the younger Pyu-Sakheng.

———— 448 = A.D. 1086—Completion of the work.

These readings of the dates allow a period of 6 years and 10 months for the restoration, instead of the short period of only 10 months allowed by the former readings.

The two dates noted in the inscription correspond, according to my calculations, with the following European dates :

1. Sakka Raj year 441, Friday, 10th of Pyadola was Friday, 6th December A.D. 1079.

2. Sakka Raj year 448, Sunday, 8th of Tachung Mangla was Sunday, 18th October A.D. 1086.

XIX.—NEWAR ERA.

—:o:—

THE Newâr era is peculiar to Nepâl, where it was introduced in A.D. 880 by Raja Râghava Deva. Pandit Bhagwân Lâl Indarji has published several inscriptions dated in this era. The earliest date is S. 533, or A.D. 1413, of Raja Jyoti Malla, who may be the Jestili Mall of Prinsep's List. The next is one of Siddhi Nri-Sinha, dated in S. 757, or A.D. 1637. This Prince must be the Siddha Nara Sinha of Prinsep's List, whose reign is assigned to A.D. 1654—1685. But this inscription places him at least seventeen years earlier. He was the grandson of Jayakusa Malla by his daughter, to whom was left the district of Pâtan. A third and a fourth inscription furnish another correction. These are records of Pratâpa Malla of Kâthmându, dated in S. 769 and 778, or A.D. 1649 and 1658, which serve to place this Raja seven years earlier than in Prinsep's List.

Prinsep obtained his information from Dr. Bramley, who was Residency Surgeon in Nepâl. The year begins in October, and 951 years had expired in 1831. The Newâr era is used upon the coins of the Newâri Rajas of Bhatgaon, Kâthmându, and Pâtan. Marsden has published coins of Jaya Prakâsa Malla II. of Kâthmându, dated in S. 819 and 823, or A.D. 1699 and 1703, which agree with the dates of 1606 and 1706 given in Prinsep's List. This era was discarded in A.D. 1768 by the Gorkha conqueror Prithi Nârâyana Sâh, who introduced the use of the Sâka era, which is still placed on all the coins of Nepâl.

XX.—CHÂLUKYA ERA.

—:o:—

In the Châlukya inscriptions the dates are generally recorded in the Sâka era. But in the year *Nala* of the Jovian cycle of 60 years, or A.D. 1076,* the Châlukya king Vikramâditya Tribhuvana Malla established a new era called the *Châlukya Vikrama Varsha.* From his own inscription we learn that he set aside " the ancient Saka, and established the Vikrama Saka in his own name."† He reigned for fifty-one years from Saka 998 to 1049. His era dates from his accession in Saka 998, or A.D. 1076. He was one of the most powerful of the Châlukya kings, and his era seems to have been adopted by some of the neighbouring princes. Thus the Kadamba king Tailapa Deva dates one of his inscriptions on " Monday, the full moon day called Herjuggi (or Aswina) of the *Sarvadhâri* Samvatsara, which was the thirty-third year of the glorious *Châlukya Vikrama Varsha.*" Sarvadhâri, the twenty-second year of the cycle, fell in A.D. 1108 in Southern India, and as it was the thirty-third year of the new Châlukaya era, the first year must have fallen in 1108 − 32 = 1076 A.D.

After the death of Vikrama in A.D. 1127 the power of the Châlukyas began rapidly to decline, and in Saka 1084, or A.D. 1162, their throne was seized by Vijala Kalâchuri, after which their era would seem to have fallen into disuse.

---

* Brown's Cyclic Tables, pp. 2, 57.

† Royal Asiatic Society's Journal, IV, 14.

XXI.—ERA OF LAKSHMANA SENA.

THE earliest notice of this era by name occurs in an inscription from Buddha Gaya published by James Prinsep, in which the date is thus given:

Sri Mat Lakshmana Sena Deva pâdânam-
-atita râjye Sam 74, *Vaisâkha-badi* 12, *Guran.*

"The reign of Sri Mad Lakshmana Sena Deva having *passed*," or as Babu Râjendra Lala translates it—

"After the *expiration* of the reign of the auspicious Lakshmana Sena Deva."

This era, therefore, was established on the death of Lakshmana Sena, the son of Ballâla Sena, Râja of Bengal. It is still used in Tirhut and Mithila in almanacs, but always along with the better known eras either of Vikrama or Sâka. Unfortunately the people, who thus use it, know nothing about it, and the equivalent dates give slightly varying results. I believe, however, that I have succeeded in clearing up the difference. I number the following statements for easy reference hereafter :—

1. The earliest mention of the era is by Colebrooke, who speaks of "Lakshmana Sena as a renowned monarch who gave his name to an era of which 692 years are expired."* The Preface containing this statement is dated 17th December 1796 : the year in which this era was established must have been A.D. 1104, and A.D. 1105 would have been the year 1 expired.

2. The next mention is by Buchanan, who says that, according to the almanacs of Mithila, A.D. 1810 was the 706th year of the era of Lakshmana Sena, which, as he remarks, places its beginning in A. D. 1104.†

3. In another place, however, he gives a slightly different statement as follows : "In Mithila the year is lunar (*i.e.* luni-solar) and commences

* Preface to the Digest of Indian Law—Essays, I, 472.

† Buchanan's Eastern India, III, 41 and 139.

on the first day after the full moon of Ashâdha. Here they say that Sak was the same as Sâlivâhan, and this year 1810 is reckoned the 1732nd year of his era. It is also the 1866th year of Samvat, who, according to them, is the same with Vikram. In these two points they agree with the Brahmans of the South, and differ totally from those of Bengal. They have still another era called after Lakshman, king of Gaur, and of which this is the 705th year."

4. Babu Râjendra Lâla mentions the *Saduktikarnâmrita* as bearing the two dates of Saka 1127 and Lakshmana Sena era *rasa*+*eka*+*ninsa*.* The book was written by Sridhara Dâsa, son of Vatsa Dâsa, a general under Lakshmana Sena. The words expressing the date are unfortunately defective.

5. Babu Râjendra also notes that the *Dâna-Sâgara* was written in Saka 1019, or A.D. 1097, by Halâyudha, the spiritual adviser of Lakshmana Sena.† I mention this for two reasons: *1st*, because it shows that Lakshmana Sena I. was reigning *before* A.D. 1105, when the era was established; and *2nd*, because this Lakshmana must be a different prince from the Lakshmana of No. 4, who can only have been Lakshmana Sena II., or Lakshmaniya.

6. A copper-plate inscription of Siva Sinha Deva, Raja of Tirhut, gives the following dates: — "*Lakshmana Samvat* 293, *Srâvana-Sudi* 7, *Gurau*," coupled with "*Saka* 1321, and *Samvat* 1455." The Saka date is equivalent to A.D. 1399, but the Vikrama date of 1455 gives A.D. 1398. The difference between the two dates is only 134 years instead of 135. This difference was also noticed by Buchanan, who states that Kamalakânta, the most learned Brahman in the Rangpur district, made the Samvat era begin 134 years before that of Saka.‡ In the Mithila district he found the same, as he notes (see No. 2) that the year 1810 A.D. was reckoned as Sake 1732 and Samvat 1866, withonly 134 years' difference. As the Sake date is the correct one, I have adopted it in preference to the Samvat date, which is but little used in Bengal. But the best proof of its accuracy is the fact that it agrees with the week day mentioned in the copper-plate. The dates are Thursday the 7th Srâvana-Sudi, 1321 Sake, or A.D. 1399. As the proof of this is very simple, I give it here as another example of the general accuracy of the

---

* Notices of Sanskrit Manuscript, III, pp. 134, 149.

† Bengal Asiatic Society's Journal, 1865, p. 137.

‡ Eastern India, III, p. 506.

tables for working out any luni-solar date. Sake 1321 = Kâli-Yuga 4500—

	Solar Ahargana.	*Luni-solar Ahargana.*
4500 years	= 1643,664·4042 days	... 1594,651·7489 days.
Deduct constant	—2·1475	....
	1643,662·2567 days ÷ 7 =	6·2 days over
	1594,651·7489	= Thursday, 27th March 1399, 1st day of Solar year.
	49,010·5078	
1600 lunations =	47,248·9406	= 27th March
		— 19 days.
	1761·5672	—
59 lunations =	1742·3046	8th March = 1st day of luni-solar year.

Luni-solar year begins 19·6626 days earlier.

and as Srâvana-Sudi 7th is the 125th day of the year, it fell on Thursday, 10th July 1399, O. S.

7. There is another inscription dated in the era of Lakshmana Sena, which also gives the week day. Prinsep read it as Sam. 74,* which would be equivalent to A.D. 1180 and Kâli-Yuga 4281. This is the inscription referred to in the beginning of this account as being dated from the close of the reign of Lakshmana Sena. But taking Prinsep's reading of the year as S. 74, my calculation shows that the week day does not agree with *Thursday*, Vaisâkha-Badi 12.

8. I possess a third inscription dated in *Sri Mal Lakshmana Senasyâtita râjye Sam* 51. "In the year 51 *after the close* of the reign of Sri Lakshmana Sena." Then follow some letters and figures which, no doubt, give the month and the day; but I have not yet been able to read them.

In noticing the almanacs of Mithila, which mention this era, I have said that the equivalent dates give slightly varying results. This is even the case with the two notices of Buchanan, who in one place gives the year 705 of the Lakshmana era as the equivalent of A.D. 1810, and in the second place, 706.

9. Babu Râjendra Lâla Mitra has collected several instances of the use of this era by the people of Tirhut.† He quotes Babu Rajakrishna Mukarji as having brought to notice the fact that it was still current

* Bengal Asiatic Society's Journal, Vol. V, p. 657.

† *Ibid*, 1878, p. 396.

in Tirhut, and that A.D. 1874 was the year 767 of the Lakshmana era. Deducting 766 from each number we get A.D. 1108 as the year 1 of the era.

I also obtained several equivalent dates from some manuscript Tirhut almanacs in the possession of Pandit Babu Lâl of Darbhanga.

10. The oldest of these was dated in Saka 1698, and Lakshmana Sam. 669, and Vikrama Sam. 1833, equivalent to A.D. 1776. Deducting 668 we get A.D. 1108 = the year 1 of the Lakshmana era.

11. A second almanac, dated in Lakshmana Samvat 732, gave the equivalent dates of Sake 1762, and Vikrama Samvat 1897, both corresponding with A.D. 1840. Deducting 731 we get A.D. 1109 = the year 1 of the Lakshmana era.

12. A third almanac, dated in Lakshmana Samvat 773, gave Saka 1802 as the equivalent corresponding with A.D. 1880. Deducting 772, we get 1108 = the year 1 of the era.

13. A fourth almanac, dated in Lakshmana Samvat 730, gave Vikrama Samvat 1895 corresponding with A.D. 1838. Deducting 729 we get 1109 A.D. = the year 1 of the era.

On comparing the dates derived from the almanacs, it will be seen that not only do they differ amongst themselves, but there is not one of them that agrees with the date derived from the copper-plate inscription, which places the year 1 of the era in A.D. 1107. These various dates are as follow :—

No.	1	Colebrooke	... A.D.	1796 = 692	L.S.	or	A.D.	1105 = 1
„	2	Buchanan	... „	1810 = 706	„	or	„	1105 = 1
„	3	Do.	... „	1810 = 705	„	or	„	1106 = 1
„	6	Copper-plate	... „	1399 = 293	„	or	„	1107 = 1
„	9	Almanac	... „	1874 = 767	„	or	„	1108 = 1
„	10	Do.	... „	1776 = 669	„	or	„	1108 = 1
„	12	Do.	... „	1880 = 773	„	or	„	1108 = 1
„	11	Do.	... „	1840 = 732	„	or	„	1109 = 1
„	13	Do.	... „	1838 = 730	„	or	„	1109 = 1

The differences are not very great; but in dealing with the establishment of an era, the strictest accuracy is imperatively necessary. What may be the cause of these differences I can only guess at. I notice that Buchanan refers the beginning of the year to the full moon of Ashâdha.* But I was informed in Tirhut that the Lakshmana Samvat

* Eastern India, III, 139.

begins with 1st Mâgha-Badi, while both the Vikrama and Saka years begin with the 1st Chaitra-Sudi. Babu Râjendra also states that the Lakshmana year is a luni-solar one, "commencing from the 1st of the month of Mâgha," that is, *Mâgh-Badi* 1, or middle of January.

Before closing this account I must notice a very serious error into which Babu Râjendra has fallen about Lakshmana Sena himself. After having translated the Buddha Gaya inscription dated in S. 74, which declares that the era of Lakshmana Sena began "after the expiration" of his reign, he on the very next page makes the era date from the beginning of his reign.* Thus he says, "*Beginning* with (A.D.) 1106 Lakshmana had a very prosperous reign of many years." And again he says, "A period of 30 years would not be too much . . . and Lakshmana's reign may very fairly be assumed to have extended to the close of the fourth decade of the 12th Century." So that the year 1706 A.D. was both the *beginning and the end of Lakshmana's reign.* Again on page 402, in his list of the Sena Rajas, he gives A.D. 1106 as the beginning of Lakshmana's reign. Lastly, in page 397, in speaking of the Tarpondighi inscription, which is dated in the 7th year of Lakshmana's own reign, he notes that no attempt had been made to trace the initial date of the era.

How the learned Babu came to the conclusion that the year A.D. 1106 was the beginning of Lakshmana Sena's reign I cannot even guess. He himself publishes the notice that the *Dâna-Sâgara* was written in Saka 1019, A.D. 1097, by Halâyudha, the spiritual adviser of Lakshmana Sena. This alone is sufficient to establish the fact that Lakshmana Sena was reigning at least nine years before the adoption of his era. But there is another fact recorded by one of the earliest Muhammadan historians, Minhaj-us-Siraj, which points very clearly to an earlier period for the reign of Lakshmana Sena. This is the statement that Lakshmaniya, the last Hindu king of Gaur, had reigned for 80 years previous to the conquest of Bengal by Bakhtiyar Khalji in A.D. 1195.

---

* Bengal Asiatic Society's Journal, 1878, p. 398.

XXII.—SIVA-SINGHA SAMVAT.

—:o:—

This era is known only from its mention in Colonel Tod's inscription from Balabhi. From the discussion on the date of this inscription in my account of the Balabhi era, it will be seen that its initial point corresponds with A.D. 1114. It seems probable that it may refer to the expulsion of the Jaina Rajas from the Peninsula of Gujarat.

M

XXIII.—FASLI ERA OF BENGAL.

—:o:—

THE *Fasli* Era owes its origin to Akbar's love of innovation. It should properly be dated from the time of his own accession, or the 2nd of Rabi-us-Sâni in the Hijra year 963, or 14th February 1556; but the actual solar reckoning of the Fasli system in Bengal begins with the 1st Vaisâkh of the Hindu solar year, on Saturday the 28th March, O.S., or Saturday the 6th April, N.S.* In the account published by James Prinsep, the different reckonings of the Fasli calendar in various parts of India are all noticed. It is altogether a mongrel era, the first 963 years being purely lunar ones of the Hijra Calendar, after which the years are purely solar ones, the Bengâli sanh beginning with the 1st of the Hindu Vaisâkh, the Fasli of Northern India with the 1st of the lunar Aswina, and the Vilayati with the 1st of the solar Aswina.

There is also a later Fasli *era* in the Dakhin, which was established by Shah Jahân in A.D. 1636 or at 1046. The beginning of the year has been fixed by the Madras Government to the 12th of July.

---

* James Prinsep gives 11th April 1556 as the 1st of Vaisâkh, but this is clearly a mistake, as his own Tables give the same date for the beginning of the Fasli year in 1856. —*Useful Tables*, p. 36.

XXIV.—ILÂHI ERA.

—:o:—

THE *Târikh Ilâhi*, or "Ilâhi Era," was established by Akbar so late as the 30th year of his reign in A.H. 992, or A.D. 1584. The courtly Abul Fazl says, that it was established "in order to remove the perplexity that a variety of dates unavoidably occasions. He disliked the word *Hijra* (flight), but was at first apprehensive of offending ignorant men, who superstitiously imagined that this era and the Muhammadan faith were inseparable." "Amir Fateh-Ullah Shirâzi corrected the calendar from the tables of Ulugh Beg, making this era to begin with His Majesty's reign, and contemplating the character of the monarch, named it *Târikh Ilâhi*, or the Mighty Era." "The years and months are both natural solar, without any intercalations. The names of the months and days correspond with the ancient Persian. The months are from 29 to 30 days each. There is not any week in the Persian month, (the) 30 days being distinguished by different names, and in those months which have 32 days, the last two are named *Roz-o-Shab* (day and night), and in order to distinguish one from the other are called first and second."

The Ilâhi era dates from Akbar's accession to the throne, which, according to the Tabakât-i-Akbari, was Friday the 2nd of Rabi-us-Sâni, A.H. 963, or 15th February 1556, O. S.* It was employed extensively, though not exclusively, on the coins of Akbar and Jahângir, and appears to have fallen into disuse early in the reign of Shah Jahân. Marsden has published a coin of this king with the date of Sunh 5 Ilâhi, coupled with the Hijra date of 1041. But in this case the Ilâhi date would appear to be only the *jalus*, or year of the king's reign.†

In the account quoted above from Abul Fazl, which Prinsep has also copied, the lengths of the months are said to be "from 29 to 30 days each;" but in the old Persian Calendar of Yazdajird, they were

---

* Nizâmuddin in Elliot's Muhammadan Historians, V, p. 241.

† Numismata Orientalia, Vol. II, p. 640.

30 days each, the same as amongst the Parsis of the present day. The names of the twelve months, all of which are found on the coins, are as follows:—

1.—Farwardin.	5.—Mirdâd.	9.—Ader.
2.—Ardi-behisht.	6.—Shariur	10.—Dê
3.—Khurdâd.	7.—Mihir.	11.—Bahman.
4.—Tir.	8.—Abân.	12.—Isfandarmaz.

The Ilâhi era, as well as the old Persian era, had a different name for each of the 30 days of the month—

Days.

1. Hormazd.	11. Khurshid.	21. Ram.
2. Bahman.	12. Mhor.	22. Guvâd.
3. Ardi-behisht	13. Tir.	23. Depdin.
4. Shatiur.	14. Gosh.	24. Din.
5. Aspandâd.	15. Depmehel.	25. Ashasang.
6. Khurdâd.	16. Mihir.	26. Ashlâd.
7. Amerdâd.	17. Serosh.	27. Asmân.
8. Depâdar.	18. Rashne.	28. Zamiâd.
9. Adur.	19. Farwardin.	29. Maharesphand.
10. Abân.	20. Bahrâm.	30. Anirâm.

The following is Abdul Kâdir's account of the establishment of this era: * "The era of the Hijra was now abolished, and a new era was introduced, of which the first year was the year of the Emperor's accession (963). The months had the same name as at the time of the old Persian kings, and, as given in the *Niçabuççibyan*, fourteen festivals also were introduced corresponding to the feasts of the Zoroastrians; but the feasts of the Musalmans and their glory were trodden down, the Friday prayer alone being retained, because some old, decrepit, silly people used to go to it. The new era was called Târikhi Ilâhi, or 'Divine Era.' On copper coins and gold-mohurs, the era of the Millenium was used, as indicating that the end of the religion of Muhammad, which was to last one thousand years, was drawing near."

I have read somewhere that in A.H. 992, when the Hijra millenary began to draw towards its close, and Akbar was meditating the establishment of the Ilâhi era, one of his courtiers stated openly that the eras even of the greatest kings did not last beyond 1,000 years. In proof of this he cited the extinction of some Hindu era, which was abolished at the end of 1,000 years.

---

* Blochmann's Ain-i-Akbari, p. 195.

XXV.—CHRISTIAN ERA.

—:o:—

The era which has been adopted by all Christian nations is reckoned from the supposed date of the birth of Christ, and has, therefore, been called *Anno Domini*, or the "year of our Lord." The era was first brought into use by Dionysius Exiguus, a Roman Abbot, who fixed the birth of Christ in the 45th year of the Julian era, or A.U.C. 753 of the Roman Calendar. "Previous to this, the Christian Churches had for about a century dated from the Diocletian era, or year of Martyrs." The true date of the nativity is now admitted to be four years earlier, or in 4 B.C. of the present Christian reckoning. But the use of the Christian era did not become general until A.D. 730, in the time of Pope Gregory II.

The year was the same as the Julian year, and consisted of 365¼ days, the fraction being arranged by making three consecutive years of 365 days, and adding a whole day to the 4th year. But after the lapse of many centuries it was discovered that this value of the solar or sidereal year was too much. In A.D. 1582, when the amount of excess was ten days, the calendar was corrected by order of Pope Gregory XIII by striking out ten days in October from the 5th to the 14th. In England the correction was not made until A.D. 1752, when, the error having still further increased, eleven days were struck out from 3rd to 14th September. The true length of the year is 365·24219 days, but for convenience it is made 365·2425 days, or three days less than the Julian reckoning in 400 years. This is effected by omitting the extra day in the three odd hundred periods of four centuries. Thus the years 1600 and 2000 are leap years, but 1700, 1800 and 1900, are common years.

The accompanying tables for ascertaining the week day of any date either before or after Christ, and according to either the Julian or Gregorian reckoning, were prepared by myself more than twenty years ago. Since then I have had ample opportunities of testing their usefulness in facilitating the very common operation of finding the week day of any given date. According to my experience, their use is both more rapid and less troublesome than any others that I have tried. Every week day is shown at once by simple inspection. I have also invented the following short process for finding the initial day of any year of the Old Style or Julian reckoning.

Rule.—Set down the date and add one-fourth, rejecting fractions. Deduct two years, if leap year, but only one year if an ordinary one. Divide by 7, and the remainder, counted from Sunday as 1, will be the initial day of the year. The following examples will be sufficient. Both results agree with the table—

A.D. 1600, leap year.	A.D. 1625, ordinary year.
÷ 4—	÷ 4—
400	406
2000	2031
−2	−1
1998	2030
÷ 7—	÷ 7—
285+3 = Tuesday.	290 = Saturday.

There is an old memorial verse, which is much used for ascertaining the initial day of each month when the initial day of the year is known. The capital letters are the Dominical letters showing the days of the week, counting from Sunday as 1.

> At Dover Dwell George Bruce, Esquire,
> Good Christopher Finn, And David Fryer.

Here we see at once the initial day of each month. But as the same may also be obtained at once from an inspection of the table, the chief use of this memorial verse is when the table is not at hand.

The tables themselves are so clear and simple that they scarcely require any explanation. But suppose it be required to find the week day of the 20th October 1712 A.D. First look in Table III of the Julian Calendar for the year 1700 A.D., then run the eye down until it meets the horizontal line opposite of the year 12, and the intersection will show the initial day of the year 1712 as Tuesday. Next look in Table II at top for the horizontal line of week days, beginning with Tuesday, which is the third one of the seven, and as 1712 was a leap year, look for the name of October in the right hand column. Then, taking the 20th day of October, and running the eye upwards until it meets the horizontal line of week days, of which Tuesday was the 1st of January in that year, it will be seen that Monday was the 20th of October, as recorded at the head of the Spectator " Monday, October 20th, 1712."

As a second example let it be required to find the week day of the 7th November 1752 after the Gregorian reckoning or New Style had been adopted in England. First look in Table IV of the Gregorian Calendar for the initial day of A.D. 1752, which will be found to be Saturday. Then with this as the first day of January look in Table II as before for the month of November and the seventh day, which will be Tuesday. The Adventurer is dated " Tuesday, Nov. 7th, 1752."

As a last example, I will take a still earlier date recorded by Bacon, " 1617, Feby. 6th, Friday." Here the date being prior to the 25th March the true year was 1618, as now reckoned. The initial day in Julian reckoning was Thursday, and the year being an ordinary one, the names of the months must be read from the left side of Table II, which gives Friday as the 6th February 1618.

XXVI.—SAURA-MANA;

OR,

SOLAR RECKONING.

THEORETICALLY the Hindu solar year should begin with the sun's entrance into Aries; but owing to the greater length of the Hindu year, the 1st of Vaisâkh has gradually receded, so that the first day of the solar year now falls on the 12th or 13th of April. The Indian computations were all made from the beginning of the Mahâ-Yuga, and owing to the difference in the length of the solar year as laid down by Aryabhatta and Varâha Mihira, there is often a discrepancy of one day in the beginning of the Hindu year in the places which make use of their different tables. The actual difference is, however, not so much, being only about one-third of a day in 4000 years. According to Warren the number of days assigned by Aryabhatta to a Mahâ-Yuga of 4,320,000 years is 1,577.917,500 in the south of India, and 42 more in the MSS. preserved in Bengal. The former gives a year of 365·2586805 days, and the latter of 365·258692 days.* But the Surya Siddhânta of Varâha Mihira gives 1,577.917,823 days to the Mahâ-Yuga, which makes the year somewhat longer, or 365·2587564 days.

As the number of revolutions was complete at the beginning of the Kâli-Yuga, it is not necessary to go back, as the Hindu astronomers do, to the beginning of the Mahâ-Yuga. It will be sufficient to begin the computation from the commencement of the Kâli-Yuga itself. In the accompanying Tables, Nos. XI, XII, and XIII, I have given the number of days elapsed from the beginning of the Kâli-Yuga down to K. Y. 5100, according to both computations now in use, that of the Surya Siddhânta in Northern India and that of Aryabhatta in Southern India. The fractions of days are given in the convenient form of decimals instead of the troublesome *gharis*, *palas*, and *vipalas* of the native astronomers.

As an example of the working of the Tables I will take the year A.D. 1857, to find on what day the 1st Vaisâkh fell. According to the

---

* Bentley, p. 139, makes the Bengali year slightly different as 365·258690 days.

Surya Siddhânta reckoning, the Kâli-Yuga year 4958 (or 3101+1857) began on the 11th of April, while Warren's Tables also give the same date. The process in both reckonings is as follows:—

		Surya Siddhânta.	*Arya Siddhânta.*
Years.		Days.	Days.
4900	contain	1.789,767·9067	1.789,767·5346
58	„	21,185·0078	21,184·9934
4958	contain	1.810,952·9145	1.810,952·5280
Deduct constant		—2·1475	—2·1475
		1.810,950·7670	1.810,950·3805

After striking out the weeks by dividing both by 7, there remains 1·7 days over, and 1·3 days over.

As the week days are counted from Friday, the first day following was Saturday, which in the year 1851 A.D. was the 11th of April. Should the large fraction of ·767 of a day be reckoned as a whole day, then the initial day of the solar year in Northern India would be Sunday, 12th April 1857, and this I find is the actual date given for Bengal in the Calcutta Gazetteer of that year.

The initial day of the year having been fixed, it is a very simple process to find any particular day of a given month, by an inspection of the Table of solar months, with the collective number of days for the whole year. The months themselves are of varying lengths with broken periods; but for the calendar they are made to consist of whole numbers. Then suppose it be required to find the day of the Christian year corresponding with the 10th of Kartika of the solar year 4958, Kâli-Yuga, a reference to the Table will show that the day required is the 197th day of the year, which is to be reckoned from the 12th of April as the first day. A reference to the Christian Table of days shows that the 12th of April is the 71st day, to which adding 196, we get the 267th day of the Christian year, or the 22nd of November 1857.

XXVII.—CHANDRA-MÂNA.

—:o:—

THE *Chandra-Mâna,* or luni-solar calendar of the Hindus, is a much more elaborate system of reckoning. The object of the Chandra-Mâna is to combine the solar and lunar reckonings, so that the years may be reckoned by the course of the sun, while the months are regulated by the revolutions of the moon. For this purpose a cycle of 19 solar years was adopted, as being equal, or nearly so, to 235 lunations or revolutions of the moon of 29·5306 days. The periods do not quite tally, as 19 solar years are equal to 6939·9163 days according to Varâha Mihira, and 6939·9149 days according to Aryabhatta, while 235 lunations are equivalent to only 6939·6910 days. The difference is nearly one-fourth of a day in 19 years.

The year consists of 12 lunar months of 30 and 29 days alternately, making altogether 354 days. The deficiency of eleven days less than the solar year, is made good by the addition of seven intercalary months in each cycle of 19 years, which are inserted in the

3rd, 5th, 8th, 11th, 14th, 16th, 19th years.

As these intercalary months also consist of 30 or 29 days, the cycle of 19 years is thus made to consist of $19 \times 12 = 228 + 7 = 235$ lunations. The Hindu luni-solar year, therefore, agrees very closely with the Greek cycle of Meton, which also consisted of 19 solar years, or 235 lunations. The seven intercalary months of Meton were inserted in the following years:

3, 5, 8, 11, 13, 16, 19.

The only difference between this arrangement and that of the Hindu series is in the 5th intercalation, which was made in the 14th instead of in the 13th year. But in spite of this close agreement, I think it almost certain that the two cycles were independently developed, although they may perhaps have had a common origin. The difference in the *mode* of intercalation is so great that it seems quite impossible that one can have been borrowed from the other. In the Greek cycle, the intercalary month has a fixed position, while in the Indian cycle both the name and the position are constantly changing. The name of the intercalary month is determined in the following manner—" When two new moons fall within the same solar month, as for instance on the 1st and 30th of Chaitra, then the name of Chaitra, or the corresponding lunar month, is repeated, the year being then intercalary with 13 months. The extra month is called *adhika* (or added), and the other *nija* (or ordinary). By the rule of the Surya Siddhânta, the intercalated month is to be placed in the middle of the ordinary month. In Southern India the whole intercalary month is placed before the ordinary one.

The common rule followed for intercalation is thus given by Warren. When the luni-solar year begins—

On the 1st of the solar Chaitra, then	*Chaitra*	will be intercalary.
On the 2nd or 3rd	Vaisâkha	"
On the 4th or 5th	Jyeshtha	"
On the 6th, 7th, or 8th	Srâvana	"
On the 9th or 10th	Bhâdrapad	"

" It happens once within each term of 160 years that there is no new moon in one of the last six lunar months, which from the sun being in perigee contain only 30 and 29 days each." " To obviate this, that month is expunged, while two others for the opposite cause are repeated. This double intercalary year with its expunged month is called *Kshaya Samvat-sara.*"

In the General Table, which gives the names of the intercalary and expunged months, I have adopted the calendar published by Cowasjee Patell. The initial days of the years I have calculated myself throughout up to A.D. 540. The early calculations have been made with the solar reckoning of Aryabhatta: but from 541 down to the end, according to the solar reckoning of Varâha Mihira. Cowasjee Pateil's Tables are calculated according to Aryabhatta, whose reckoning is still used in Southern India.

As the luni-solar year begins with the new moon immediately preceding the 1st of the solar Vaisâkh, the first step to be determined is the number of days by which the one precedes the other. For this purpose the beginning of the solar year has to be fixed, as already shown in the account of the Saura-Mâna, using the Solar Ahargana of the Surya Siddhânta for the North Indian dates and Aryabhatta's Solar Ahargana for South Indian dates. The next step is to find the number of days of the luni-solar Ahargana in the given period, and to deduct this total from the number of days of the Solar Ahargana already found. The remainder is to be reduced by continued subtraction of whole lunations, until the last remainder is less than one lunation. Then that last remainder shows the exact number of days by which the new moon precedes the 1st day of the Solar Vaisâkh.

As an example of the process I will take the date of Kâli-Yuga 4958, or A.D. 1857, of which the initial days have already been found in my account of the Saura-Mâna or solar reckoning. As the Luni-Solar Ahargana of the Surya Siddhânta is used in the South as well as in the North, one process will be sufficient—

4900 years of luni-solar reckoning	=	1736,398·5710 days.
58 " "	=	20,553·2892
4958 years	=	1756,951·8602 days.
Deduct from the Solar Ahargana already found for N. India		1810,950·7670 days.
Difference		53,998·9068 days
Deduct 1800 lunations		53,155·0582
		843·8486
Deduct 28 lunations		826·8564
Days		16·9922

The new moon, therefore, precedes the beginning of the solar year by 16·99, or 17 days. Then as the 1st of the Solar Vaisâkh fell on the 11th of April 1857 in North India, the new moon will have fallen on the 24th March, and the beginning of the luni-solar year, or the 1st Chaitra-Sudi, on the following day or 25th March. In Southern India it would have been the same according to my reckoning from Aryabhatta's length of the solar year; and this also is the day given by Warren. But according to Cowasjee Patell, it was the 26th March.

I have tested these Tables for several dates at distant intervals and have found them correct—

1. On the 5th February B. C. 21 there was an eclipse visible in India. By the Tables the first day of the solar year was Wednesday,

14th March, and the first day of the luni-solar year was Tuesday the 6th March, from which date counting backwards 29½ days for the previous conjunction of the sun and moon, we get the 5th February.

2. In A.D. 314, on the 3rd of March, there was a grand eclipse of the sun visible over E. Asia. According to Cowasjee Patell, the first day of the luni-solar year A.D. 314 was the 3rd of March.

3. In A.D. 490, on the 7th March, there was an eclipse of the sun visible over S. E. Asia. According to Cowasjee Patell, the first day of the luni-solar year was the 8th March, which is right according to the rule that the first day of the new year is the day after the conjunction.

4. On the 4th March 1840, I saw an eclipse of the sun in N. India. According to Cowasjee Patell, and also according to my own reckoning, the luni-solar year began on the 3rd April 1840, which is exactly one conjunction later.

5. In my account of the Bârhaspatya-Mâna, I have given another example of the correct working of the Tables for an eclipse of the year 792 A.D., which is mentioned in one of the Indian inscriptions.

6. But perhaps the most striking illustration of the general accuracy of the Tables is the eclipse of the moon, which is recorded to have happened in the month of Srâvana Samvat 1200. The inscription in which this is found is one of "three grants of land found at Ujjayani," on which Colebrooke makes the following remarks:*

"One of three grants or patents records a donation of land made by the reigning sovereign of Dhârâ, on the anniversary of the death of his father and predecessor, in 1191 of the Samvat era; confirmed by the prince, his son, at the time of an eclipse of the moon in Srâvana 1200 Samvat. It appears from calculation that a lunar eclipse did occur at the time—*viz.*, on the 16th of July A.D. 1144, about 9½ P.M., apparent time at Ujjayani."

Now it is quite true, as Colebrooke says, that an eclipse of the moon did occur on the 16th July 1144, but that day was certainly not the full moon of Srâvana in that year. The true date was the 28th

* Colebrooke's Essays, II, p. 264. He has used the erroneous equation of 56 instead of 57 to reduce the Samvat year to Christian reckoning.

July 1143, on which day was the full moon of Srâvana, and also a lunar eclipse. The following is the calculation according to the Tables. Samvat year 1200 + 3044 = 4244 Kâli-Yuga = A.D. 1143.

	Solar Ahargana.	*Luni-solar Arhargana.*
4200 years =	1534,086·7772 days.	1488,341·6323 days.
44 years =	16,071·3852 „	15,592·1504 „
4244 years =	1550,158·1624 days.	1503,933·7827 days.
Deduct constant	2·1475	
	1550,156·0149 ÷ 7 leaves 6 days over = Thursday, 25th March, O. S.,	for first day of solar year.
Luni-solar Ahargan	1503,933·7827	
	46,222·2322	The full moon of Srâvana } or Srâvana-Sudi 15th
1500 Lunations	44,296·8820	is the 133rd day of the Hindu year,
	1926·3502	which, counted from Thursday the
	1919·4882	25th March, gives 28th July A.D.
		1143, on which day there was an
6·86 = 7 days earlier	6·8620	eclipse of the moon.

In the North the luni-solar year begins with the new moon, or 1st day of *Chaitra-Sudi*, and as this is the latter half of the month, this Hindu year has the strange anomaly of beginning in the middle of a month. The first half of Chaitra, or the period of the waning moon, called *Badi*, or *Krishna Paksha*, belongs to the past year. This mode of placing the *Badi*, or waning half of the moon, in the beginning of the month is known as the *Krishnadi* reckoning; while the opposite practice of putting the *Sudi*, or *Sukla Paksha*, half of the moon, as the beginning of the month, is known as the *Sukladi* reckoning. The names *Badi* and *Sudi* are contractions of *bahula-paksha-dina*, the "day of the dark half," and *sukla-paksha-dina*, the "day of the bright half," the first and last syllables only being retained.

Table X shows the number of days in the Hindu luni-solar year when not intercalary. When the year is an intercalary one, and the day required falls later than the intercalary month, then 30 days must be added to the number given in the Table.

The years of intercalation being fixed by the rules laid down for the 19-year cycle, the name of the intercalated month has yet to be found. As there are 30 days in six of the lunar months, while the time of one lunation is only 29½ days, it would of course occasionally happen that two new moons would fall in the same month, one at the beginning, and the other at the end. But as this is not allowed, a peculiar arrangement has been adopted for avoiding it. In whatever month two new moons would naturally fall, that month is doubled; or, in other words, an intercalary month of the same name is added called Adhika Vaisâkha, Adhika Srâvana, &c.

To ascertain which month will be Adhika, or intercalary, Warren's Kâla Sankalita should be consulted, and also the brief abstract given by Prinsep. The process is troublesome, and in the present work I have adopted the names of the intercalary months as given by Cowasji Patell. The years of the intercalations are shown to be correct by the shifting of the initial days backwards and forwards, all of which I have myself calculated.

TABLE I.

CHRISTIAN CALENDAR.

Week Days for one year.

In COMMON YEARS the Months are to be read on this side.								In LEAP YEARS the Months are to be read on this side.
	S	Mo	Tu	W	Th	Fr	Sat	
	Mon	Tu	W	Th	Fr	Sat	S	
	Tu	W	Th	Fr	Sat	S	Mo	
	Wed	Th	Fr	Sat	S	Mo	Tu	
	Thu	Fr	Sat	S	Mo	Tu	W	
	Fri	Sa	S	Mo	Tu	W	Th*	
	Sat	S	Mo	Tu	W	Th	Fr	
JANUARY	1	2	3	4	5	6	7	
	8	9	10	11	12	13	14	JANUARY
OCTOBER	15	16	17	18	19	20	21	APRIL
	22	23	24	25	26	27	28	JULY
	29	30	31	...	...	...	...	
———								———
FEBRUARY	...	...	...	1	2	3	4	
MARCH	5	6	7	8	9	10	11	FEBRUARY
	12	13	14	15	16	17	18	AUGUST
NOVEMBER	19	20	21	22	23	24	25	
	26	27	28	29	30	31	...	
———								———
	...	...	...	...	...	...	1	
APRIL	2	3	4	5	6	7	8	SEPTEMBER
JULY	9	10	11	12	13	14	15	DECEMBER
	16	17	18	19	20	21	22	
	23	24	25	26	27	28	29	
	30	31	...	...	...	...	...	
———								———
	...	...	1	2	3	4	5	
AUGUST	6	7	8	9	10	11	12	MAY
	13	14	15	16	17	18	19	
	20	21	22	23	24	25	26	
	27	28	29	30	31	...	...	
———								———
	...	...	...	...	...	1	2	
SEPTEMBER	3	4	5	6	7	8	9	
DECEMBER	10	11	12	13	14	15	16	JUNE
	17	18	19	20	21	22	23	
	24	25	26	27	28	29	30	
	31	...	...	...	...	...	...	
———								———
	...	1	2	3	4	5	6	
	7	8	9	10	11	12	13	
MAY	14	15	16	17	18	19	20	OCTOBER
	21	22	23	24	25	26	27	
	28	29	30	31	...	...	...	
———								———
	...	...	...	...	1	2	3	
JUNE	4	5	6	7	8	9	10	
	11	12	13	14	15	16	17	MARCH
	18	19	20	21	22	23	24	NOVEMBER
	25	26	27	28	29	30	31	

CHRISTIAN ERA.

TABLE II.

JULIAN CALENDAR.

CHRISTIAN CENTURIES. B. C. A. D. CHRISTIAN CENTURIES.

	B. C.							OLD STYLE — CHRISTIAN YEARS.				A. D.							
B. C.	3400	3300	3200	3100	3000	2900	2800					0	100	200	300	400	500	600	A. D.
	2700	2600	2500	2400	2300	2200	2100					700	800	900	1000	1100	1200	1300	
	2000	1900	1800	1700	1600	1500	1400					1400	1500	1600	1700	1800	1900	2000	
	1300	1200	1100	1000	900	800	700												
	600	500	400	300	200	100	0												
B. C.	INITIAL DAYS.											INITIAL DAYS.							A. D.
	Fr	Th	W	Tu	Mo	S	Sa	0	28	56	84	Th	W	Tu	Mo	S	Sa	Fr	L. Y.
L. Y.	W	Tu	Mo	S	Sa	Fr	Th	1	29	57	85	Sa	Fr	Th	W	Tu	Mo	S	
	Tu	Mo	S	Sa	Fr	Th	W	2	30	58	86	S	Sa	Fr	Th	W	Tu	Mo	
	Mo	S	Sa	Fr	Th	W	Tu	3	31	59	87	Mo	S	Sa	Fr	Th	W	Tu	
	S	Sa	Fr	Th	W	Tu	Mo	4	32	60	88	Tu	Mo	S	Sa	Fr	Th	W	L. Y.
L. Y.	Fr	Th	W	Tu	Mo	S	Sa	5	33	61	89	Th	W	Tu	Mo	S	Sa	Fr	
	Th	W	Tu	Mo	S	Sa	Fr	6	34	62	90	Fr	Th	W	Tu	Mo	S	Sa	
	W	Tu	Mo	S	Sa	Fr	Th	7	35	63	91	Sa	Fr	Th	W	Tu	Mo	S	
	Tu	M	S	Sa	Fr	Th	W	8	36	64	92	S	Sa	Fr	Th	W	Tu	Mo	L. Y.
L. Y.	S	Sa	Fr	Th	W	Tu	Mo	9	37	65	93	Tu	Mo	S	Sa	Fr	Th	W	
	Sa	Fr	Th	W	Tu	Mo	S	10	38	66	94	W	Tu	Mo	S	Sa	Fr	Th	
	Fr	Th	W	Tu	Mo	S	Sa	11	39	67	95	Th	W	Tu	Mo	S	Sa	Fr	
	Th	W	Tu	M	S	Sa	Fr	12	40	68	96	Fr	Th	W	Tu	Mo	S	Sa	L. Y.
L. Y.	Tu	M	S	Sa	Fr	Th	W	13	41	69	97	S	Sa	Fr	Th	W	Tu	Mo	
	Mo	S	Sa	Fr	Th	W	Tu	14	42	70	98	Mo	S	Sa	Fr	Th	W	Tu	
	S	Sa	Fr	Th	W	Tu	Mo	15	43	71	99	Tu	Mo	S	Sa	Fr	Th	W	
	Sa	Fr	Th	W	Tu	Mo	S	16	44	72	100	W	Tu	Mo	S	Sa	Fr	Th	L. Y.
L. Y.	Th	W	Tu	Mo	S	Sa	Fr	17	45	73		Fr	Th	W	Tu	Mo	S	Sa	
	W	Tu	Mo	S	Sa	Fr	Th	18	46	74		Sa	Fr	Th	W	Tu	Mo	S	
	Tu	Mo	S	Sa	Fr	Th	W	19	47	75		S	Sa	Fr	Th	W	Tu	Mo	
	Mo	S	Sa	Fr	Th	W	Tu	20	48	76		Mo	S	Sa	Fr	Th	W	Tu	L. Y.
L. Y.	Sa	Fr	Th	W	Tu	Mo	S	21	49	77		W	Tu	Mo	S	Sa	Fr	Th	
	Fr	Th	W	Tu	Mo	S	Sa	22	50	78		Th	W	Tu	Mo	S	Sa	Fr	
	Th	W	Tu	Mo	S	Sa	Fr	23	51	79		Fr	Th	W	Tu	Mo	S	Sa	
	W	Tu	Mo	S	Sa	Fr	Th	24	52	80		Sa	Fr	Th	W	Tu	Mo	S	L. Y.
L. Y.	Mo	S	Sa	Fr	Th	W	Tu	25	53	81		Mo	S	Sa	Fr	Th	W	Tu	
	S	Sa	Fr	Th	W	Tu	Mo	26	54	82		Tu	Mo	S	Sa	Fr	Th	W	
	Sa	Fr	Th	W	Tu	Mo	S	27	55	83		W	Tu	Mo	S	Sa	Fr	Th	

...TIAN CENTURIES.

					Sat.	Fri.	Wed.	Mon.	A. D.
			400		0	100	200	300	
		100	0		400	500	600	700	
					800	900	1000	1100	
					1200	1300	1400	1500	
					1600	1700	1800	1900	
					2000	2100	2200	2300	
					2400	2500	2600	2700	

B. C.	INITIAL DAYS.				CHRISTIAN YEARS.				INITIAL DAYS.				A. D.
	Sa	Th	Tu	Mo	...	28	56	84	Sa	Th	Tu	S	L. Y.
L. Y.	Fr	W	Mo	Sa	1	29	57	85	Mo	Sa	Th	Tu	
	Th	Tu	S	F	2	30	58	86	Tu	S	Fr	W	
	W	Mo	Sa	Th	3	31	59	87	W	Mo	Sa	Th	
	Tu	S	Fr	W	4	32	60	88	Th	Tu	S	Fr	L. Y.
L. Y.	S	Fr	W	Mo	5	33	61	89	Sa	Th	Tu	S	
	Sa	Th	Tu	S	6	34	62	90	S	Fr	W	Mo	
	Fr	W	Mo	Sa	7	35	63	91	Mo	Sa	Th	Tu	
	Th	Tu	S	Fr	8	36	64	92	Tu	S	Fr	W	L. Y.
L. Y.	Tu	S	Fr	W	9	37	65	93	Th	Tu	S	Fr	
	Mo	Sa	Th	Tu	10	38	66	94	Fr	W	Mo	Sa	
	S	Fr	W	Mo	11	39	67	95	Sa	Th	Tu	S	
	Sa	Th	Tu	S	12	40	68	96	S	Fr	W	Mo	L. Y.
L. Y.	Th	Tu	S	Fr	13	41	69	97	Tu	S	Fr	W	
	W	Mo	Sa	Th	14	42	70	98	W	Mo	Sa	Th	
	Tu	S	Fr	W	15	43	71	99	Th	Tu	S	Fr	
	Mo	Sa	Th	Tu	16	44	72	100	Fr	W	Mo	Sa	L. Y.
L. Y	Sa	Th	Tu	S	17	45	73		S	Fr	W	Mo	
	Fr	W	Mo	Sa	18	46	74		Mo	Sa	Th	Tu	
	Th	Tu	S	Fr	19	47	75		Tu	S	Fr	W	
	W	Mo	Sa	Th	20	48	76		W	Mo	Sa	Th	L. Y.
L. Y.	Mo	Sa	Th	Tu	21	49	77		Fr	W	Mo	Sa	
	S	Fr	W	Mo	22	50	78		Sa	Th	Tu	S	
	Sa	Th	Tu	S	23	51	79		S	Fr	W	Mo	
	Fr	W	Mo	Sa	24	52	80		Mo	Sa	Th	Tu	L. Y.
L. Y.	W	Mo	Sa	Th	25	53	81		W	Mo	Sa	Th	
	Tu	S	Fr	W	26	54	82		Th	Tu	S	Fr	
	Mo	Sa	Th	Tu	27	55	83		Fr	W	Mo	Sa	

N. B.—The initial day of each even century, 400, 800, &c., is Saturday; that of the odd centuries is either Friday, Wednesday, or Monday, as noted at the head of the column.

TABLE IV.

Number of Days in the CHRISTIAN Year.

Day of Month.	January.	February.	March.	April.	May.	June.	July.	August.	September.	October.	November.	December.
1	1	32	60	91	121	152	182	213	244	274	305	335
2	2	33	61	92	122	153	183	214	245	275	306	336
3	3	34	62	93	123	154	184	215	246	276	307	337
4	4	35	63	94	124	155	185	216	247	277	308	338
5	5	36	64	95	125	156	186	217	248	278	309	339
6	6	37	65	96	126	157	187	218	242	279	310	340
7	7	38	66	97	127	158	188	219	250	280	311	341
8	8	39	67	98	128	159	189	220	251	281	312	342
9	9	40	68	99	129	160	190	221	252	282	313	343
10	10	41	69	100	130	161	191	222	253	283	314	344
11	11	42	70	101	131	162	192	223	254	284	315	345
12	12	43	71	102	132	163	193	224	255	285	316	346
13	13	44	72	103	133	164	194	225	256	286	317	347
14	14	45	73	104	134	165	195	226	257	287	318	348
15	15	46	74	105	135	166	196	227	258	288	319	349
16	16	47	75	106	136	167	197	228	259	289	320	350
17	17	48	76	107	137	168	198	229	260	290	321	351
18	18	49	77	108	138	169	199	230	261	291	322	352
19	19	50	78	109	139	170	200	231	262	292	323	353
20	20	51	79	110	140	171	201	232	263	293	324	354
21	21	52	80	111	141	172	202	233	264	294	325	355
22	22	53	81	112	142	173	203	234	265	295	326	356
23	23	54	82	113	143	174	204	235	266	296	327	357
24	24	55	83	114	144	175	205	236	267	297	328	358
25	25	56	84	115	145	176	206	237	268	298	329	359
26	26	57	85	116	146	177	207	238	269	299	330	360
27	27	58	86	117	147	178	208	239	270	300	331	361
28	28	59	87	118	148	179	209	240	271	301	332	362
29	29	...	88	119	149	180	210	241	272	302	333	363
30	30	...	89	120	150	181	211	242	273	303	334	364
31	31	...	90	...	151	...	212	243	...	304	...	365

TABLE V.
ATTIC CALENDAR.

Omitted days in the Macedonian Cycle of 19 years.

Years of Cycle.	Huperberetaios.	Dios.	Apellaios.	Audunaios.	Peritios.	Dustros.	DIOSKOROS.	Xanthikos.	Artemisios.	Daisios.	Panemos.	Lōos.	Gorpiaios.	No. of omitted days.	Length of year.
	I	II	III	IV	V	VI	Emb	VII	VIII	IX	X	XI	XII		days.
I	...	...	3	...	6	...	—	9	...	12	...	15	...	5	355
II	18	...	21	...	24	...	—	27	...	30	...	...	3	6	354
E. III	...	6	...	9	...	12	Emb	15	...	18	...	21	...	6	384
IV	24	...	27	...	30	...	—	...	3	...	6	...	9	6	354
E. V	...	12	...	15	...	18	Emb	21	...	24	...	27	...	6	384
VI	30	...	...	3	...	6	—	...	9	...	12	...	15	6	354
VII	...	18	...	21	...	24	—	...	27	...	30	...	...	5	355
E. VIII	3	...	6	...	9	...	Emb	12	...	15	...	18	...	6	384
IX	21	...	24	...	27	...	—	30	...	...	3	...	6	6	354
X	...	9	...	12	...	15	—	...	18	...	21	...	24	6	354
E. XI	...	27	...	30	...	...	Emb	3	...	6	...	9	...	5	385
XII	12	...	15	...	18	...	—	21	...	24	...	27	...	6	354
E. XIII	30	...	...	3	...	6	Emb	9	...	12	...	15	...	6	384
XIV	18	...	21	...	24	...	—	27	...	30	...	...	3	6	354
XV	...	6	...	9	...	12	—	...	15	...	18	...	21	6	354
E. XVI	...	24	...	27	...	30	Emb	...	...	3	...	6	...	6	384
XVII	9	...	12	...	15	...	—	18	...	21	...	24	...	6	354
XVIII	27	...	30	...	...	3	—	...	6	...	9	...	22	5	355
E. XIX	...	15	...	18	...	21	Emb	...	24	...	27	...	30	6	384
Total number of days omitted ...														110	...
Total number of days in Cycle of 19 years ...														...	6940

TABLE VI.

INITIAL DATES

Of two Attic and Macedonian Cycles of Meton preceding the Era of the Seleukidæ.

B.C. 348 to 330. | **B.C. 329 to 311.**

Olymp.	Attic. Year of Cycle.	Attic. B.C.	Macedonian. Year of Cycle.	Macedonian. B.C.	Olymp.	Attic. Year of Cycle.	Attic. B.C.	Macedonian. Year of Cycle.	Macedonian. B.C.
108.1	E. viii	19 June 348	i	12 Oct. 348	112.4	E. viii	19 June *329	i	12 Oct. *329
2	ix	7 July 347	ii	2 Oct. 347	113.1	ix	7 July 328	ii	2 Oct. 328
3	x	27 June 346	E. iii	21 Sep. 346	2	x	27 June 327	E. iii	21 Sep. 327
4	E. xi	15 June *345	iv	9 Oct. *345	3	E. xi	16 June 326	iv	10 Oct. 326
109.1	xii	4 July 344	E. v	28 Sep. 344	4	xii	4 July *325	E. v	28 Sep. *325
2	E. xiii	23 June 343	vi	17 Oct. 343	114.1	E. xiii	23 June 324	vi	17 Oct. 324
3	xiv	12 July 342	vii	6 Oct. 342	2	xiv	12 July 323	vii	6 Oct. 323
4	xv	30 June *341	E. viii	26 Sep. *341	3	xv	1 July 322	E. viii	27 Sep. 322
110.1	E. xvi	19 June 340	ix	13 Oct. 340	4	E. xvi	19 June *321	ix	13 Oct. *321
2	xvii	8 July 339	x	3 Oct. 339	115.1	xvii	8 July 320	x	3 Oct. 320
3	xviii	27 June 338	E. xi	23 Sep. 338	2	xviii	27 June 319	E. xi	23 Sep. 319
4	E. xix	16 June *337	xii	11 Oct. *337	3	E. xix	17 June 318	xii	12 Oct. 318
111.1	i	6 July 336	E. xiii	30 Sep. 336	4	i	6 July *317	xiii	30 Sep. *317
2	ii	26 June 335	xiv	19 Oct. 335	116.1	ii	26 June 316	xiv	19 Oct. 316
3	E. iii	15 June 334	xv	8 Oct. 334	2	E. iii	15 June 315	xv	8 Oct. 315
4	iv	3 July *333	E. xvi	26 Sep. *333	3	iv	4 July 314	xvi	27 Sep. 314
112.1	E. v.	22 June 332	xvii	15 Oct. 332	4	E. v	22 June *313	xvii	15 Oct. *313
2	vi	11 July 331	xviii	4 Oct. 331	117.1	vi	11 July 312	Sel. 1	4 Oct. 312
3	vii	30 June 330	E. xix	24 Sep. 330	2	vii	30 June 311	2	24 Sep. 311

The 7th Attic year of Meton's Cycle ended at Midsummer, 310 B.C.
⁂ October 310 was in the 8th Attic year.
*** The stars denote leap years of Julian reckoning.**

TABLE VII.

SELEUKIDAN ERA.

Initial Days—CYCLE OF METON.

Days in Year.	Year in Cycle.	I CYCLE. An Sel	I CYCLE. B. C.	II CYCLE. An Sel	II CYCLE. B. C.	III CYCLE. An Sel	III CYCLE. B. C.	IV CYCLE. An Sel	IV CYCLE. B. C.	V CYCLE. An Sel	V CYCLE. B. C.	VI CYCLE. An Sel	VI CYCLE. B. C.	VII CYCLE An Sel	VII CYCLE B C.
Days.															
355	i	3	13 Oct. 310	22	13 Oct. 291	41	13 Oct. 272	60	13 Oct. *253	79	14 Oct. 234	98	14 Oct. 215	117	14 Oct. 196
354	ii	4	2 Oct. *309	23	3 Oct. 290	42	3 Oct. 271	61	3 Oct. 252	80	3 Oct. *233	99	4 Oct. 214	118	4 Oct. 195
384	E. iii	5	21 Sep. 308	24	21 Sep. *289	43	22 Sep. 270	62	22 Sep. 251	81	22 Sep. 232	100	22 Sep. *213	119	23 Sep. 194
354	iv	6	10 Oct. 307	25	10 Oct. 288	44	10 Oct. *269	63	11 Oct. 250	82	11 Oct. 231	101	11 Oct. 212	120	11 Oct. *193
384	E. v	7	29 Sep. 306	26	29 Sep. 287	45	29 Sep. 268	64	29 Sep. *249	83	30 Sep. 230	102	30 Sep. 211	121	30 Sep. 192
354	vi	8	17 Oct. *305	27	18 Oct. 286	46	18 Oct. 267	65	18 Oct. 248	84	18 Oct. *229	103	19 Oct. 210	122	19 Oct. 191
355	vii	9	6 Oct. 304	28	6 Oct. *285	47	7 Oct. 266	66	7 Oct. 247	85	7 Oct. 228	104	7 Oct. *209	123	8 Oct. 190
384	E. viii	10	26 Sep. 303	29	26 Sep. 284	48	26 Sep. *265	67	27 Sep. 246	86	27 Sep. 227	105	27 Sep. 208	124	27 Sep. *189
354	ix	11	15 Oct. 302	30	15 Oct. 283	49	15 Oct. 264	68	15 Oct. *245	87	16 Oct. 226	106	16 Oct. 207	125	16 Oct. 188
354	x	12	3 Oct. *301	31	4 Oct. 282	50	4 Oct. 263	69	4 Oct. 244	88	4 Oct. *225	107	5 Oct. 206	126	5 Oct. 187
385	E. xi	13	22 Sep. 300	32	22 Sep. *281	51	23 Sep. 262	70	23 Sep. 243	89	23 Sep. 224	108	23 Sep. *205	127	24 Sep. 186
354	xii	14	12 Oct. 299	33	12 Oct. 280	52	12 Oct. *261	71	13 Oct. 242	90	13 Oct. 223	109	13 Oct. 204	128	13 Oct. *185
384	E. xiii	15	1 Oct. 298	34	1 Oct. 279	53	1 Oct. 260	72	1 Oct. *241	91	2 Oct. 222	110	2 Oct. 203	129	2 Oct. 184
354	xiv	16	19 Oct. *297	35	20 Oct. 278	54	20 Oct. 259	73	20 Oct. 240	92	20 Oct. *221	111	21 Oct. 202	130	21 Oct. 183
354	xv	17	8 Oct. 296	36	8 Oct. *277	55	9 Oct. 258	74	9 Oct. 239	93	9 Oct. 220	112	9 Oct. *201	131	10 Oct. 182
384	E. xvi	18	27 Sep. 295	37	27 Sep. 276	56	27 Sep. *257	75	28 Sep. 238	94	28 Sep. 219	113	28 Sep. 200	132	28 Sep. *181
354	xvii	19	16 Oct. 294	38	16 Oct. 275	57	16 Oct. 256	76	16 Oct. *237	95	17 Oct. 218	114	17 Oct. 199	133	17 Oct. 180
355	xviii	20	4 Oct. *293	39	5 Oct. 274	58	5 Oct. 255	77	5 Oct. 236	96	5 Oct. *217	115	6 Oct. 198	134	6 Oct. 179
384	E. xix	21	24 Sep. 292	40	25 Sep. 273	59	25 Sep. 254	78	25 Sep. 235	97	25 Sep. 216	116	26 Sep. *197	135	26 Sep. 178

6,940 days in 19 years.

* The stars denote leap years of Julian reckoning.

TABLE VII.—(Contd.)

SELEUKIDAN ERA.

Initial Days—CYCLE OF METON.

Days in Year.	Years of Cycle.	VIII CYCLE.		IX CYCLE.		X CYCLE.		XI CYCLE.		XII CYCLE.		XIII CYCLE.		XIV CYCLE.	
		An Sel	B. C.	An Sel	B. C.	An Sel	B. C.	An Sel	B. C.	An Sel	B. C.	An Sel	B. C.	An Sel	B. C.
Days.															
355	i	136	14 Oct. *177	155	15 Oct. 158	174	15 Oct. 139	193	15 Oct. 120	212	15 Oct. *101	231	16 Oct. 82	250	16 Oct. 63
354	ii	137	4 Oct. 176	156	4 Oct. *157	175	5 Oct. 138	194	5 Oct. 119	213	5 Oct. 100	232	5 Oct. *81	251	6 Oct. 62
384	E. iii	138	23 Sep. 175	157	23 Sep. 156	176	23 Sep. *137	195	24 Sep. 118	214	24 Sep. 99	233	24 Sep. 80	252	24 Sep. *61
354	iv	139	12 Oct. 174	158	12 Oct. 155	177	12 Oct. 136	196	12 Oct. *117	215	13 Oct. 98	234	13 Oct. 79	253	13 Oct. 60
384	E. v	140	30 Sep. *173	159	1 Oct. 154	178	1 Oct. 135	197	1 Oct. 116	216	1 Oct. *97	235	2 Oct. 78	254	2 Oct. 59
354	vi	141	19 Oct. 172	160	19 Oct. *153	179	20 Oct. 134	198	20 Oct. 115	217	20 Oct. 96	236	20 Oct. *77	255	21 Oct. 58
355	vii	142	8 Oct. 171	161	8 Oct. 152	180	8 Oct *133	199	9 Oct. 114	218	9 Oct. 95	237	9 Oct. 76	256	9 Oct. *57
384	E. viii	143	28 Sep. 170	162	28 Sep. 151	181	28 Sep. 132	200	28 Sep. *113	219	29 Sep. 94	238	29 Sep. 75	257	29 Sep. 56
354	ix	144	16 Oct. 169	163	17 Oct. 150	182	17 Oct. 131	201	17 Oct. 112	220	17 Oct. *93	239	18 Oct. 74	258	18 Oct. 55
354	x	145	5 Oct. 168	164	5 Oct. *149	183	6 Oct. 130	202	6 Oct. 111	221	6 Oct. 92	240	6 Oct. *73	259	7 Oct. 54
385	E. xi	146	24 Sep. 167	165	24 Sep. 148	184	24 Sep. *129	203	25 Sep. 110	222	25 Sep. 91	241	25 Sep. 72	260	25 Sep. *53
354	xii	147	14 Oct. 166	166	14 Oct. 147	185	14 Oct. 128	204	14 Oct. *109	223	15 Oct. 90	242	15 Oct. 71	261	15 Oct. 52
384	E. xiii	148	2 Oct. *165	167	3 Oct. 146	186	3 Oct. 127	205	3 Oct. 108	224	3 Oct. *89	243	4 Oct. 70	262	4 Oct. 51
354	xiv	149	21 Oct. 164	168	21 Oct. *145	187	22 Oct. 126	206	22 Oct. 107	225	22 Oct. 88	244	22 Oct. *69	263	23 Oct. 50
354	xv	150	10 Oct 163	169	10 Oct. 144	188	10 Oct. *125	207	11 Oct. 106	226	11 Oct. 87	245	11 Oct. 68	264	11 Oct. *49
384	E. xvi	151	29 Sep. 162	170	29 Sep. 143	189	29 Sep. 124	208	29 Sep. *105	227	30 Sep. 86	246	30 Sep. 67	265	30 Sep. 48
354	xvii	152	17 Oct. *161	171	18 Oct. 142	190	18 Oct. 123	209	18 Oct. 104	228	18 Oct. *85	247	19 Oct. 66	266	19 Oct. 47
355	xviii	153	6 Oct. 160	172	6 Oct. *141	191	7 Oct. 122	210	7 Oct. 103	229	7 Oct. 84	248	7 Oct. *65	267	8 Oct. 46
384	E. xix	154	26 Sep. 159	173	26 Sep. 140	192	27 Sep. *121	211	27 Sep. 102	230	27 Sep. 83	249	27 Sep. 64	268	28 Sep. *45

6,940 days in 19 years.

* The stars denote leap years of Julian reckoning.

TABLE VII.—(Contd.)

SELEUKIDAN ERA.

Initial Days—CYCLE OF METON.

Days in Year.	Years of Cycle.	XV CYCLE. An Sel		B. C.	XVI CYCLE. An Sel		B. C.	XVII CYCLE. An Sel		B. C.	XVIII CYCLE. An Sel		A. D.	XIX CYCLE. An Sel		A. D.	XX CYCLE. An Sel		A. D.	XXI CYCLE. An Sel		A. D.
Days.																						
355	i	269	16 Oct.	44	288	16 Oct.	*25	307	17 Oct.	6	326	17 Oct.	14	345	17 Oct.	33	364	17 Oct.	*52	383	18 Oct.	71
354	ii	270	6 Oct.	43	289	6 Oct.	24	308	6 Oct.	*5	327	7 Oct.	15	346	7 Oct.	34	365	7 Oct.	53	384	7 Oct.	*72
384	E. iii	271	25 Sep.	42	290	25 Sep.	23	309	25 Sep.	4	328	25 Sep.	*16	347	26 Sep.	35	366	26 Sep.	54	385	26 Sep.	73
354	iv	272	13 Oct.	*41	291	14 Oct.	22	310	14 Oct.	3	329	14 Oct.	17	348	14 Oct.	*36	367	15 Oct.	55	386	15 Oct.	74
384	E. v	273	2 Oct.	40	292	2 Oct.	*21	311	3 Oct.	2	330	3 Oct.	18	349	3 Oct.	37	368	3 Oct.	*56	387	4 Oct.	75
354	vi	274	21 Oct.	39	293	21 Oct.	20	312	21 Oct.	*1	331	22 Oct.	19	350	22 Oct.	38	369	22 Oct.	57	388	22 Oct.	*76
355	vii	275	10 Oct.	38	294	10 Oct.	19	313	10 Oct.	A.D. 1	332	10 Oct	*20	351	11 Oct.	39	370	11 Oct.	58	389	11 Oct.	77
384	E. viii	276	29 Sep.	*37	295	30 Sep.	18	314	30 Sep.	2	333	30 Sep.	21	352	30 Sep.	*40	371	1 Oct.	59	390	1 Oct.	78
354	ix	277	18 Oct.	36	296	18 Oct.	*17	315	19 Oct	3	334	19 Oct.	22	353	19 Oct.	41	372	19 Oct.	*60	391	20 Oct.	79
354	x	278	7 Oct.	35	297	7 Oct.	16	316	7 Oct.	*4	335	8 Oct.	23	354	8 Oct.	42	373	8 Oct.	61	392	8 Oct.	*80
385	E. xi	279	26 Sep.	34	298	26 Sep.	15	317	26 Sep.	5	336	26 Sep.	*24	355	27 Sep.	43	374	27 Sep.	62	393	27 Sep.	81
354	xii	280	15 Oct.	*33	299	16 Oct.	14	318	16 Oct.	6	337	16 Oct.	25	356	16 Oct.	*44	375	17 Oct.	63	394	17 Oct.	82
384	E. xiii	281	4 Oct.	32	300	4 Oct.	*13	319	5 Oct.	7	338	5 Oct.	26	357	5 Oct.	45	376	5 Oct.	*64	395	6 Oct.	83
354	xiv	282	23 Oct.	31	301	23 Oct.	12	320	23 Oct.	*8	339	24 Oct.	27	358	24 Oct.	46	377	24 Oct.	65	396	24 Oct.	*84
354	xv	283	12 Oct.	30	302	12 Oct.	11	321	12 Oct.	9	340	12 Oct.	28	359	13 Oct.	47	378	13 Oct.	66	397	13 Oct.	85
384	E. xvi	284	30 Sep.	*29	303	1 Oct.	10	322	1 Oct.	10	341	1 Oct.	29	360	1 Oct.	*48	379	2 Oct.	67	398	2 Oct.	86
354	xvii	285	19 Oct.	28	304	19 Oct.	*9	323	20 Oct.	11	342	20 Oct.	30	361	20 Oct.	49	380	20 Oct.	*68	399	21 Oct.	87
355	xviii	286	8 Oct.	27	305	8 Oct.	8	324	8 Oct.	*12	343	9 Oct.	31	362	9 Oct.	50	381	9 Oct.	69	400	9 Oct.	*88
384	E. xix	287	28 Sep.	26	306	28 Sep.	7	325	28 Sep.	13	344	29 Sep.	*32	363	29 Sep.	51	382	29 Sep.	70	401	29 Sep.	89

6,940 days in 19 years.

* The stars denote leap years of Julian reckoning.

TABLE VII.—(Concld.)

SELEUKIDAN ERA.

Initial Days—CYCLE OF METON.

Days in Year.	Years of Cycle	XXII CYCLE. An Sel	XXII CYCLE. A. D.	XXIII CYCLE. An Sel	XXIII CYCLE. A. D.	XXIV CYCLE. An Sel	XXIV CYCLE. A. D.	XXV CYCLE. An Sel	XXV CYCLE. A. D.	XXVI CYCLE. An Sel	XXVI CYCLE. A. D.	XXVII CYCLE. An Sel	XXVII CYCLE. A. D.	XVIII CYCLE. An Sel	XVIII CYCLE. A. D.
355	i	402	18 Oct. 90	421	18 Oct. 109	440	18 Oct. *128	459	19 Oct. 147	478	19 Oct. 166	497	19 Oct. 185	516	19 Oct. *204
354	ii	403	8 Oct. 91	422	8 Oct. 110	441	8 Oct. 129	460	8 Oct. *148	479	9 Oct. 167	498	9 Oct. 186	517	9 Oct. 205
384	E. iii	404	26 Sep. *92	423	27 Sep. 111	442	27 Sep. 130	461	27 Sep. 149	480	27 Sep. *168	499	28 Sep. 187	518	28 Sep. 206
354	iv	405	15 Oct. 93	424	15 Oct. *112	443	16 Oct. 131	462	16 Oct. 150	481	16 Oct. 169	500	17 Oct. *188	519	17 Oct. 207
384	E. v	406	4 Oct. 94	425	4 Oct. 113	444	4 Oct. *132	463	5 Oct. 151	482	5 Oct. 170	501	5 Oct. 189	520	5 Oct. *208
354	vi	407	23 Oct. 95	426	23 Oct. 114	445	23 Oct. 133	464	23 Oct. *152	483	24 Oct. 171	502	24 Oct. 190	521	24 Oct. 209
355	vii	408	11 Oct. *96	427	12 Oct. 115	446	12 Oct. 134	465	12 Oct. 153	484	12 Oct. *172	503	13 Oct. 191	522	13 Oct. 210
384	E. viii	409	1 Oct. 97	428	1 Oct. *116	447	2 Oct. 135	466	2 Oct. 154	485	2 Oct. 173	504	3 Oct. *192	523	3 Oct. 211
354	ix	410	20 Oct. 98	429	20 Oct. 117	448	20 Oct. *136	467	21 Oct. 155	486	21 Oct. 174	505	21 Oct. 193	524	21 Oct. *212
354	x	411	9 Oct. 99	430	9 Oct. 118	449	9 Oct. 137	468	9 Oct. *156	487	10 Oct. 175	506	10 Oct. 194	525	10 Oct. 213
385	E. xi	412	27 Sep. *100	431	28 Sep. 119	450	28 Sep. 138	469	28 Sep. 157	488	28 Sep. *176	507	29 Sep. 195	526	29 Sep. 214
354	xii	413	17 Oct. 101	432	17 Oct. *120	451	18 Oct. 139	470	18 Oct. 158	489	18 Oct. 177	508	18 Oct. *196	527	19 Oct. 215
384	E. xiii	414	6 Oct. 102	433	6 Oct. 121	452	6 Oct. *140	471	7 Oct. 159	490	7 Oct. 178	509	7 Oct. 197	528	7 Oct. *216
354	xiv	415	25 Oct. 103	434	25 Oct. 122	453	25 Oct. 141	472	25 Oct. *160	491	26 Oct. 179	510	26 Oct. 198	529	26 Oct. 217
354	xv	416	13 Oct. *104	435	14 Oct. 123	454	14 Oct. 142	473	14 Oct. 151	492	14 Oct. *180	511	15 Oct. 199	530	15 Oct. 218
384	E. xvi	417	2 Oct. 105	436	2 Oct. *124	455	3 Oct. 143	474	3 Oct. 162	493	3 Oct. 181	512	3 Oct. *200	531	4 Oct. 219
354	xvii	418	21 Oct. 106	437	21 Oct. 125	456	21 Oct. *144	475	22 Oct. 163	494	22 Oct. 182	513	22 Oct. 201	532	22 Oct. *220
355	xviii	419	10 Oct. 107	438	10 Oct. 126	457	10 Oct. 145	476	10 Oct. *164	495	11 Oct. 183	514	11 Oct. 202	533	11 Oct. 221
384	E. xix	420	30 Sep. *108	439	30 Sep. 127	458	30 Sep. 146	477	30 Sep. 165	496	1 Oct. *184	515	1 Oct. 203	534	1 Oct. 222

6,940 days in 19 years.

* The stars denote leap years of Julian reckoning.

TABLE VIII.

Number of days in the Hindu SOLAR year.

Days.	Vaisakha.	Jyeshtha.	Ashâdha.	Srâvana.	Bhâdra.	Aswina.	Kârtika.	Agrahayana.	Pausha.	Mâgha.	Phâlguna.	Chaitra.
1	1	32	63	95	126	157	188	218	247	277	306	336
2	2	33	64	96	127	158	189	219	248	278	307	337
3	3	34	65	97	128	159	190	220	249	279	308	338
4	4	35	66	98	129	160	191	221	250	280	309	339
5	5	36	67	99	130	161	192	222	251	281	310	340
6	6	37	68	100	131	162	193	223	252	282	311	341
7	7	38	69	101	132	163	194	224	253	283	312	342
8	8	39	70	102	133	164	195	225	254	284	313	343
9	9	40	71	103	134	165	196	226	255	285	314	344
10	10	41	72	104	135	166	197	227	256	286	315	345
11	11	42	73	105	136	167	198	228	257	287	316	346
12	12	43	74	106	137	168	199	229	258	288	317	347
13	13	44	75	107	138	169	200	230	259	289	318	348
14	14	45	76	108	139	170	201	231	260	290	319	349
15	15	46	77	109	140	171	202	232	261	291	320	350
16	16	47	78	110	141	172	203	233	262	292	321	351
17	17	48	79	111	142	173	204	234	263	293	322	352
18	18	49	80	112	143	174	205	235	264	294	323	353
19	19	50	81	113	144	175	206	236	265	295	324	354
20	20	51	82	114	145	176	207	237	266	296	325	355
21	21	52	83	115	146	177	208	238	267	297	326	356
22	22	53	84	116	147	178	209	239	268	298	327	357
23	23	54	85	117	148	179	210	240	269	299	328	358
24	24	55	86	118	149	180	211	241	270	300	329	359
25	25	56	87	119	150	181	212	242	271	301	330	360
26	26	57	88	120	151	182	213	243	272	302	331	361
27	27	58	89	121	152	183	214	244	273	303	332	362
28	28	59	90	122	153	184	215	245	274	304	333	363
29	29	60	91	123	154	185	216	246	275	305	334	364
30	30	61	92	124	155	186	217	...	276	...	335	365
31	31	62	93	125	156	187	...	...	...	...	...	...
32	...	...	94	...	...	...	...	...	...	...	...	...

TABLE IX.

Approximate Initial dates of Hindu SOLAR years.

JULIAN.

	Year	Date
B. C.	3110	16 February.
	2765	19 —
	1615	1 March.
	1385	3 —
	925	7 —
	580	10 —
	350	12 —
B. C.	10	15 —
A. D.	105	16 —
	220	17 —
	335	18 —
	450	19 —
	565	20 —
	680	21 —
	795	22 —
	910	23 —
	1025	24 —
	1140	25 —
	1255	26 —
	1370	27 —
	1485	28 —
	1600	29 —
	1715	30 —
	1830	31 —
	1945.	1 April.
	2060	2 —

GREGORIAN.

	Year	Date	
B. C.	3100	20 January.	B. C.
	3000	21 —	
	1500	16 February.	
	1200	21 —	
	900	26 —	
	720	1 March.	
	360	7 —	
	60	12 —	
	...	13 —	
A. D.	60	14 —	A. D.
	120	15 —	
	180	16 —	
	240	17 —	
	300	18 —	
	360	19 —	
	420	20 —	
	480	21 —	
	540	22 —	
	600	23 —	
	660	24 —	
	720	25 —	
	780	26 —	
	840	27 —	
	900	28 —	
	960	29 —	
	1020	30 —	
	1080	31 —	
	1140	1 April.	
	1200	2 —	
	1260	3 —	
	1320	4 —	
	1380	5 —	
	1440	6 —	
	1500	7 —	
	1560	8 —	
	1620	9 —	
	1680	10 —	
	1740	11 —	
	1800	12 —	
	1860	13 —	
	1920	14 —	

TABLE X.

Number of days in the Hindu LUNI-SOLAR year.

BADI.	Chaitra.	Vaisákha.	Jyeshtha.	Asháḍha.	Srávana.	Bhádra.	Aswina.	Kártika.	Agrahay.	Paush.	Mágha.	Phálgun.	Chaitra.
1	...	16	45	75	104	134	163	193	222	252	281	311	340
2	...	17	46	76	105	135	164	194	223	253	282	312	341
3	...	18	47	77	106	136	165	195	224	254	283	313	342
4	...	19	48	78	107	137	166	196	225	255	284	314	343
5	...	20	49	79	108	138	167	197	226	256	285	315	344
6	...	21	50	80	109	139	168	198	227	257	286	316	345
7	...	22	51	81	110	140	169	199	228	258	287	317	346
8	...	23	52	82	111	141	170	200	229	259	288	318	347
9	...	24	53	83	112	142	171	201	230	260	289	319	348
10	...	25	54	84	113	143	172	202	231	261	290	320	349
11	...	26	55	85	114	144	173	203	232	262	291	321	350
12	...	27	56	86	115	145	174	204	233	263	292	322	351
13	...	28	57	87	116	146	175	205	234	264	293	323	352
14	...	29	58	88	117	147	176	206	235	265	294	324	353
15	...	30	59	89	118	148	177	207	236	266	295	325	354
SUDI													
1	1	31	60	90	119	149	178	208	237	267	296	326	...
2	2	32	61	91	120	150	179	209	238	268	297	327	...
3	3	33	62	92	121	151	180	210	239	269	298	328	...
4	4	34	63	93	122	152	181	211	240	270	299	329	...
5	5	35	64	94	123	153	182	212	241	271	300	330	...
6	6	36	65	95	124	154	183	213	242	272	301	331	...
7	7	37	66	96	125	155	184	214	243	273	302	332	...
8	8	38	67	97	126	156	185	215	244	274	303	333	...
9	9	39	68	98	127	157	186	216	245	275	304	334	...
10	10	40	69	99	128	158	187	217	246	276	305	335	...
11	11	41	70	100	129	159	188	218	247	277	306	336	...
12	12	42	71	101	130	160	189	219	248	278	307	337	...
13	13	43	72	102	131	161	190	220	249	279	308	338	...
14	14	44	73	103	132	162	191	221	250	280	309	339	...
15	15	...	74	...	133	...	192	...	251	...	310	...	...

TABLE XI.

Solar Ahargana of ARYA-BHATA

Years.	Days.	☉	Years	Days.
1	365 2587		34	12,418 7948
2	730·5174		35	12,784 0535
3	1,095 7760		36	13,149 3124
4	1,461·0347		37	13,514 5711
5	1,826 2934		38	13,879 8297
6	2,191 5521		39	14,245 0884
7	2,556 8108		40	14,610 3476
8	2,922·0694		41	14 975 6059
9	3,287 3281		42	15,340 8648
10	3,652 5868		43	15,706 1234
11	4,017 8455		44	16,071 3820
12	4,383 1042		45	16,436 6407
13	4,748 3629		46	16,801 8994
14	5,113 6216		47	17,167 1581
15	5,478 7802		48	17,532 4168
16	5,844 1388		49	17,897 6654
17	6,209 3974		50	18,262 9340
18	6,574 6562		51	18,628 1926
19	6,939 9149		52	18,993 4516
20	7,305 1736		53	19,358 7103
21	7,670·4324		54	19,723 9686
22	8,035 6910		55	20,089 2272
23	8,400 9497		56	20,454 4860
24	8,766 2084		57	20,819 7450
25	9,131 4670		58	21,185·0036
26	9,496 7256		59	21,550 2622
27	9,861 9848		60	21,915 5208
28	10,227 2432		61	22,280 7795
29	10,592 5018		62	22,646 0382
30	10,957 7604		63	23,011 2968
31	11,323 0191		64	23,376 5554
32	11,688 2777		65	23,741 8140
33	12,053·5363		66	24,107·0726

TABLE XI.—(Continued).

Solar Ahargana of ARYA-BHATA.

⊙

Years.	Days.	Years.	Days.
67	24,472·3316	100	36,525·8680
68	24,837·5903	200	73,051·7513
69	25,202·8489	300	109,577·6042
70	25,568·2076	400	146,103·4722
71	25,933·3662	500	182,629·3403
72	26,298·6248	600	219,155·2083
73	26,663·8834	700	255,681·0764
74	27,029·1422	800	292,206·9444
75	27,394·4010	900	328,732·8124
76	27,759·6594	1000	365,258·6805
77	28,124·9181	2000	730,517·3611
78	28,490·1768	3000	1.095,776·0417
79	28,855·4355	3100	1.132,301·9097
80	29,220·6944	3200	1.168,827·7777
81	29,585·9530	3300	1.205,353·6457
82	29,951·2118	3400	1241,879·5137
83	30,316·4705	3500	1,278,405·3817
84	30,681·7296	3600	1314,931·2498
85	31,046·9883	3700	1351,457·1178
86	31,412·2468	3800	1387,982·9858
87	31,777·5054	3900	1424,508·8538
88	32,142·7640	4000	1.461,034·7222
89	32,508·0226	4100	1.497,560·5902
90	32,873·2812	4200	1.534,086·4582
91	33,238·5398	4300	1.570,612·3264
92	33,603·7985	4400	1607,138·1944
93	33,969·0571	4500	1643,664·0627
94	34,334·3162	4600	1680,189·9304
95	34,699·5749	4700	1716,715·7984
96	35,064·8336	4800	1753,241·6664
97	35,430·0922	4900	1789,767·5344
98	35,795·3308	5000	1.826,293·4027
99	36,160·5894	5100	1.862,819·2707

TABLE XII.

Solar Ahargana of SURYA-SIDDHANTA.

Years.	Days.	☉ Years.	Days.
1	365·2587	34	12,418·7977
2	730·5175	35	12,784·0564
3	1,095·7763	36	13,149·3152
4	1,461·0350	37	13,514·5739
5	1,826·2938	38	13,879·8327
6	2,191·5525	39	14,245·0915
7	2,556·8113	40	14,610·3502
8	2,922·0700	41	14,975·6090
9	3,287·3288	42	15,340·8677
10	3,652·5876	43	15,706·1265
11	4,017·8463	44	16,071·3852
12	4,383·1051	45	16,436·6440
13	4,748·3638	46	16,801·9027
14	5,113·6226	47	17,167·1615
15	5,478·8813	48	17,532·4203
16	5,844·1401	49	17,897·6790
17	6,209·3988	50	18,262·9378
18	6,574·6576	51	18,628·1966
19	6,939·9163	52	18,993·4553
20	7,305·1751	53	19,358·7140
21	7,670·4339	54	19,723·9728
22	8,035·6926	55	20,089·2315
23	8,400·9514	56	20,454·4903
24	8,766·2101	57	20,819·7491
25	9,131·4689	58	21,185·0078
26	9,496·7276	59	21,550·2666
27	9,861·9864	60	21,915·5254
28	10,227·2451	61	22,280·7841
29	10,602·5039	62	22,646·0428
30	10,957·7627	63	23,011·3016
31	11,323·0214	64	23,376·5604
32	11,688·2802	65	23,741·8191
33	12,053·5389	66	24,107·0778

TABLE XII.—(Continued.)

Solar Ahargana of SURYA-SIDDHANTA.

Years.	Days.	⊙	Years.	Days.
67	24,472·3366		100	36,525·8756
68	24,837·5954		200	73,051·7513
69	25,202·8542		300	109,577·6269
70	25,568·1129		400	146,103·5026
71	25,933·3717		500	182,629·3782
72	26,298·6304		600	219,155·2539
73	26,663·8892		700	255,681·1295
74	27,029·1479		800	292,207·0052
75	27,394·4067		900	328,732·8808
76	27,759·6654		1000	365,258·7565
77	28,124 9241		2000	730,517·5130
78	28,490·1830		3000	1,095,776·2694
79	28,855·4417		3100	1,132,302·1451
80	29,220·7004		3200	1,168,828·0207
81	29,585 9592		3300	1,205,353·8964
82	29,951·2180		3400	1,241,879·7720
83	30,316·4767		3500	1,278,405·6477
84	30,681·7354		3600	1,314,931·5233
85	31,046·9942		3700	1,351,457·3990
86	31,412·2530		3800	1,387,983·2746
87	31.777·5117		3900	1,424,509·1503
88	32,142·7704		4000	1,461,035·0259
89	32,508·0292		4100	1,497,560·9016
90	32,873 2880		4200	1,534,086·7772
91	33,238·5467		4300	1,570,612·6528
92	33,603·8054		4400	1,607,138·5285
93	33,969·0642		4500	1,643,664·4042
94	34,334·3230		4600	1,680,190·2798
95	34,699·5818		4700	1,716,716·1555
96	35,064·8406		4800	1,753,242·0311
97	35,430·0993		4900	1,789,767·9067
98	35,795·3580		5000	1,826,293·7824
99	36,160·6168		5100	1,862,819·6580

TABLE XIII.

Luni-Solar Ahargana.—SURYA-SIDDHANTA.

⊙

Years.	Days.	Years.	Days.
1	354·3670	34	12,048·4796
2	708·7341	35	12,402·8466
3	1,063·1012	36	12,757·2136
4	1,417·4682	37	13,111·5806
5	1,771·8353	38	13,465·9476
6	2,126·2023	39	13,820·3146
7	2,480·5694	40	14,174·6822
8	2,834·9364	41	14,529·0492
9	3,189·3035	42	14,883·4164
10	3,543·6706	43	15,237·7834
11	3,898·0376	44	15,592·1504
12	4,252·4046	45	15,946·5175
13	4,606·7716	46	16,300·8844
14	4,961·1388	47	16,655·2514
15	5,315·5058	48	17,009·6184
16	5,669·8728	49	17,363·9854
17	6,024·2398	50	17,718·3528
18	6,378·6068	51	18,072·7198
19	6,732·9738	52	18,427·0864
20	7,087·3412	53	18,781·4534
21	7,441·7082	54	19,135·8210
22	7,796·0752	55	19,490·1880
23	8,150·4422	56	19,844·5552
24	8,504·8092	57	20,198 9222
25	8,859·1765	58	20,553·2892
26	9,213·5432	59	20,907·6562
27	9,567·9105	60	21,262·0232
28	9,922·2776	61	21,616·3902
29	10,276·6446	62	21,970·7572
30	10,631·0116	63	22,325·1242
31	10,985·3786	64	22,679·4912
32	11,339·7456	65	23,033·8582
33	11,694·1128	66	23,388·2256

TABLE XIII.—(Continued.)

Luni-Solar Ahargana.—*SURYA-SIDDHANTA.*

Years.	Days.	⊙	Years.	Days.
67	23,742·5922		100	35,436·7055
68	24,096·9592		200	70,873·4111
69	24,451·3262		300	106,310·1166
70	24,805·6939		400	141,746·8221
71	25,160·0609		500	177,183·5277
72	25,514·4276		600	212,620·2332
73	25,868·7946		700	248,056·9387
74	26,223·1612		800	283,493·6443
75	26,577·5295		900	318,930·3498
76	26,931·8952		1000	354,367·0553
77	27,286·2622		2000	708,734·1107
78	27,640·6292		3000	1,063,101·1660
79	27,994·9962		3100	1,098,537·8715
80	28,349·3644		3200	1,133,974·5770
81	28,703·7314		3300	1,169,411·2826
82	29,058·0984		3400	1,204,847·9886
83	29,412·4654		3500	1,240,284·6941
84	29,766·8328		3600	1,275,721·3997
85	30,121·1998		3700	1,311,158·1047
86	30,475·5668		3800	1,346,594·8102
87	30,829·9338		3900	1,382,031·5157
88	31,184·3008		4000	1,417,468·2213
89	31,538·6678		4100	1,452,904·9268
90	31,893·0349		4200	1,488,341·6323
91	32,247·4019		4300	1,523,778·3379
92	32,601·7688		4400	1,559,215 0434
93	32,956·1358		4500	1,594,651·7489
94	33,310·5028		4600	1,630,088·4545
95	33,664·8698		4700	1,665,525·1690
96	34,019·2368		4800	1,700,961·8655
97	34,373·6038		4900	1,736,398·5710
98	34,727·9708		5000	1,771,835·2766
99	35,082·3378		5100	1,807,271·9821

TABLE XIV.

LUNATIONS.

Number.	Days.
1	29·5306
2	59·0612
3	88·5918
4	118·1224
5	147·6529
6	177·1835
7	206·7141
8	236·2447
9	265·7753
10	295·3058
11	324·8364
12	354·3670
13	383·8976
14	413·4282
15	442·9587
16	472·4894
17	502·0201
18	531·5508
19	561·0813
20	590·6117
21	620·1423
22	649·6728
23	679·2034
24	708·7341
25	738·2647
26	767·7952
27	797·3262
28	826·8564
29	856·3870
30	885·9176
31	915·4482
32	944·9788
33	974·5094
34	1,004·0402
35	1,033·5705
36	1,063·1011
37	1,092·6317
38	1,122·1626
39	1,151·6932
40	1,181·2235
41	1,210·7541
42	1,240·2846
43	1,269·8152
44	1,299·3456
45	1,328·8762
46	1,358·4068
47	1,387·9374
48	1,417·4682
49	1,446·9988
50	1,476·5294
51	1,506·0600
52	1,535·5904
53	1,565·1210
54	1,594·6524
55	1,624·1830
56	1,653·7128
57	1,683·2434
58	1,712·7740
59	1,742·3046
60	1,771·8353
61	1,801·3659
62	1,830·8964
63	1,860·4270
64	1,889·9576
65	1,919·4882
66	1,949·0188

TABLE XIV.—(Continued.)

LUNATIONS.

Number.	Days.	Number.	Days.
67	2,978·5493	100	2,953·0588
68	2,008·0801	200	5,906·1176
69	2,037·6106	300	8,859·2764
70	2,067·1411	400	11,812·2352
71	2,096·6716	500	14,765·2940
72	2,126·2023	600	17,718·3527
73	2,155·7329	700	20,671·4115
74	2,185·2634	800	23,624·4703
75	2,214·7940	900	26,577·5291
76	2,244·3245	1000	29,530·5879
77	2,273·8551	1100	32,483·6467
78	2,303·3858	1200	35,436·7054
79	2,332·9164	1300	38,389·7642
80	2,362·4470	1400	41,342·8230
81	2,391·9776	1500	44,295·8820
82	2,421·5082	1600	47,248·9406
83	2,451·0388	1700	50,201·9994
84	2,480·5692	1800	53,155·0582
85	2,510·0998	1900	56,108·1170
86	2,539·6304	2000	59,061·1759
87	2,569·1610	2100	62,014·2347
88	2,598·6912	2200	64,967·2935
89	2,628·2218	2300	67,920·3523
90	2,657·7529	2400	70,873·4108
91	2,687·2835	2500	73,826 4700
92	2,716·8136	2600	76,779·5284
93	2,746·3442	2700	79,732·5873
94	2,775·9748	2800	82,685 6460
95	2,805·5054	2900	85,638·7049
96	2,834·9364	3000	88,591·7638
97	2,864·4670	4000	118,122·3517
98	2,893·9976	5000	147,652·9397
99	2,923·5282	6000	177,183·5276

TABLE XV.

HIJRA CALENDAR.

Months and Days of the Hijra Year.

	S	Mo	Tu	We	Th	Fr	Sa	S	Mo	Tu	We	Th	Fr	Sa	
	Mo	Tu	We	Th	Fr	Sa	S	Mo	Tu	We	Th	Fr	Sa	S	
	Tu	We	Th	Fr	Sa	S	Mo	Tu	We	Th	Fr	Sa	S	Mo	
	We	Th	Fr	Sa	S	Mo	Tu	We	Th	Fr	Sa	S	Mo	Tu	
	Th	Fr	Sa	S	Mo	Tu	We	Th	Fr	Sa	S	Mo	Tu	We	
	Fr	Sa	S	Mo	Tu	We	Th	Fr	Sa	S	Mo	Tu	We	Th	
MONTHS.	Sa	S	Mo	Tu	We	Th	Fr	Sa	S	Mo	Tu	We	Th	Fr	WEEKS.
Muharram ...	1	2	3	4	5	6	7	8	9	10	11	12	13	14	2
	15	16	17	18	19	20	21	22	23	24	25	26	27	28	4
Safar	29	30	1	2	3	4	5	6	7	8	9	10	11	12	6
	13	14	15	16	17	18	19	20	21	22	23	24	25	26	8
Rabia I	27	28	29	1	2	3	4	5	6	7	8	9	10	11	10
	12	13	14	15	16	17	18	19	20	21	22	23	24	25	12
Rabia II	26	27	28	29	30	1	2	3	4	5	6	7	8	9	14
	10	11	12	13	14	15	16	17	18	19	20	21	22	23	16
Jamâdi I ...	24	25	26	27	28	29	1	2	3	4	5	6	7	8	18
	9	10	11	12	13	14	15	16	17	18	19	20	21	22	20
Jamâdi II ...	23	24	25	26	27	28	29	30	1	2	3	4	5	6	22
	7	8	9	10	11	12	13	14	15	16	17	18	19	20	24
Rajab	21	22	23	24	25	26	27	28	29	1	2	3	4	5	26
	6	7	8	9	10	11	12	13	14	15	16	17	18	19	28
Shabân	20	21	22	23	24	25	26	27	28	29	30	1	2	3	30
	4	5	6	7	8	9	10	11	12	13	14	15	16	17	32
Ramzân	18	19	20	21	22	23	24	25	26	27	28	29	1	2	34
	3	4	5	6	7	8	9	10	11	12	13	14	15	16	36
	17	18	19	20	21	22	23	24	25	26	27	28	29	30	38
Shawâl	1	2	3	4	5	6	7	8	9	10	11	12	13	14	40
	15	16	17	18	19	20	21	22	23	24	25	26	27	28	42
Zilhada	29	1	2	3	4	5	6	7	8	9	10	11	12	13	44
	14	15	16	17	18	19	20	21	22	23	24	25	26	27	46
Zilhajja	28	29	30	1	2	3	4	5	6	7	8	9	10	11	48
	12	13	14	15	16	17	18	19	20	21	22	23	24	25	50
	26	27	28	29	30										

N.B.—Zilhajja has 30 days in Intercalary Years only.

TABLE XVI.

HIJRA CALENDAR.

Initial Days of Hijra Years.

I—CYCLE.

	Hijra	A.D.	Initial Days.		
	1	622	Fr	16	July
II	2	623	Tu	5	...
	3	624	S	24	June
	4	625	Th	13	...
V	5	626	Mo	2	...
	6	627	Sa	23	May
VII	7	628	We	11	...
*	8	629	Mo	1	...
	9	630	Fr	20	May
X	10	631	Tu	9	...
	11	632	S	29	Mar
	12	633	Th	18	...
XIII	13	634	Mo	7	...
	14	635	Sa	25	Feb
	15	636	We	14	...
XVI	16	637	S	2	...
	17	638	Fr	23	Jan
XVIII	18	639	Tu	12	...
*	19	640	S	2	...
	20	...	Th	21	Dec
XXI	21	641	Mo	10	...
	22	642	Sa	30	Nov
	23	643	We	19	...
XXIV	24	644	S	7	...
	25	645	Fr	28	Oct
XXVI	26	646	Tu	17	...
*	27	647	S	7	...
	28	648	Th	25	Sep
XXIX	29	649	Mo	14	...
	30	650	Sa	4	...

II—CYCLE.

	Hijra	A.D.	Initial Days.		
	31	651	We	24	Aug
II	32	652	S	12	...
	33	653	Fr	2	...
	34	654	Tu	22	July
V	35	655	Sa	11	...
	36	656	Th	30	June
VII	37	657	Mo	19	...
*	38	658	Sa	9	...
	39	659	We	29	May
X	40	660	S	17	...
	41	661	Fr	7	May
	42	662	Tu	26	April
XIII	43	663	Sa	15	...
	44	664	Th	4	...
	45	665	Mo	24	Mar
XVI	46	666	Fr	13	...
	47	667	We	3	...
XVIII	48	668	S	20	Feb
*	49	669	Fr	9	...
	50	670	Tu	29	Jan
XXI	51	671	Sa	18	...
	52	672	Tu	8	...
	53	...	Mo	27	Dec
XXIV	54	673	Fr	16	...
	55	674	We	6	...
XXVI	56	675	S	25	Nov
*	57	676	Fr	14	...
	58	677	Tu	3	...
XXIX	59	678	Sa	23	Oct
	60	679	Th	13	...

III—CYCLE.

	Hijra	A.D.	Initial Days.		
	61	680	Mo	1	...
II	62	681	Fr	20	Sep
	63	682	We	10	...
	64	683	S	30	Aug
V	65	684	Th	18	...
	66	685	Tu	8	...
VII	67	686	Sa	28	July
*	68	687	Th	18	...
	69	688	Mo	6	...
X	70	689	Fr	25	June
	71	690	We	15	...
	72	691	S	4	...
XIII	73	692	Th	23	May
	74	693	Tu	13	...
	75	694	Sa	2	...
XVI	76	695	We	21	April
	77	696	Mo	10	...
XVIII	78	697	Fr	30	Mar
*	79	698	We	20	...
	80	699	S	9	...
XXI	81	700	Th	26	Feb
	82	701	Tu	15	...
	83	702	Sa	4	...
XXIV	84	703	We	24	Jan
	85	704	Mo	14	...
XXVI	86	705	Fr	2	...
*	87	...	We	23	Dec
	88	706	S	12	...
XXIX	89	707	Th	1	...
	90	708	Tu	20	Nov

TABLE XVI.—(Continued.)

HIJRA CALENDAR.

Initial Days of Hijra Years.

IV—CYCLE.

	Hijra.	A.D.	Initial Days.		
	91	709	Sa	9	Nov
II	92	710	We	29	Oct
	93	711	Mo	19	...
	94	712	Fr	7	...
V	95	713	Tu	26	Sep
	96	714	S	16	...
VII	97	715	Th	5	...
*	98	716	Tu	25	Aug
	99	717	Sa	14	...
X	100	718	We	3	...
	101	719	Mo	24	July
	102	720	Fr	12	...
XIII	103	721	Tu	1	...
	104	722	S	21	June
	105	723	Th	10	...
XVI	106	724	Mo	29	May
	107	725	Sa	19	...
XVIII	108	726	We	8	...
*	109	727	Mo	28	April
	110	728	Fr	16	...
XXI	111	729	Tu	5	...
	112	730	S	26	Mar
	113	731	Tu	15	...
XXIV	114	732	Mo	3	...
	115	733	Sa	21	Feb
XXVI	116	734	We	10	...
*	117	735	Mo	31	Jan
	118	736	Fr	20	...
XXIX	119	737	Tu	8	...
	120	...	S	29	Dec

V—CYCLE.

	Hijra.	A.D.	Initial Days.		
	121	738	Th	18	Dec
II	122	739	Mo	7	...
	123	740	Sa	26	Nov
	124	741	We	15	...
V	125	742	S	4	...
	126	743	Fr	25	Oct
VII	127	744	Tu	13	...
*	128	745	S	3	...
	129	746	Th	22	Sep
X	130	747	Mo	11	...
	131	748	Sa	31	Aug
	132	749	We	20	...
XIII	133	750	S	9	...
	134	751	Fr	30	July
	135	752	Tu	18	...
XVI	136	753	Sa	7	...
	137	754	Th	27	June
XVIII	138	755	Mo	16	...
*	139	756	Sa	5	...
	140	757	We	25	May
XXI	141	758	S	14	...
	142	759	Fr	4	...
	143	760	Tu	22	April
XXIV	144	761	Sa	11	...
	145	762	Th	1	...
XXVI	146	763	Mo	21	Mar
*	147	764	Sa	10	...
	148	765	We	27	Feb
XXIX	149	766	S	16	...
	150	767	Fr	6	...

VI—CYCLE.

	Hijra.	A.D.	Initial Days.		
	151	768	Tu	26	Jan
II	152	769	Sa	14	...
	153	770	Th	4	...
	154	...	Mo	24	Dec
V	155	771	Fr	13	...
	156	772	We	2	...
VII	157	773	S	21	Nov
*	158	774	Fr	11	...
	159	775	Tu	31	Oct
X	160	776	Sa	19	...
	161	777	Th	9	Oct
	162	778	Mo	28	Sep
XIII	163	779	Fr	17	...
	164	780	We	6	...
	165	781	S	26	Aug
XVI	166	782	Th	15	...
	167	783	Tu	5	...
XVIII	168	784	Sa	24	July
*	169	785	Th	14	...
	170	786	Mo	3	...
XXI	171	787	Fr	22	June
	172	788	We	11	...
	173	789	S	31	May
XXIV	174	790	Th	20	...
	175	791	Tu	10	...
XXVI	176	792	Sa	28	April
*	177	793	Th	18	...
	178	794	Mo	7	...
XXIX	179	795	Fr	27	Mar
	180	796	We	16	...

TABLE XVI.—(Continued.)

HIJRA CALENDAR.

Initial Days of Hijra Years.

VII—CYCLE.

	Hijra.	A.D.	Initial Days.		
	181	797	S	5	...
II	182	798	Th	22	Feb
	183	799	Tu	12	...
	184	800	Sa	1	...
V	185	801	We	20	Jan
	186	802	Mo	10	...
VII	187	...	Fr	30	Dec
*	188	803	We	20	...
	189	804	S	8	...
X	190	805	Th	27	Nov
	191	806	Tu	17	...
	192	807	Sa	6	...
XIII	193	808	We	25	Oct
	194	809	Mo	15	...
	195	810	Fr	4	...
XVI	196	811	Tu	23	Sep
	197	812	S	12	...
XVIII	198	813	Th	1	...
*	199	814	Tu	22	Aug
	200	815	Sa	11	...
XXI	201	816	We	30	July
	202	817	Mo	20	...
	203	818	Fr	9	...
XXIV	204	819	Tu	28	June
	205	820	S	17	...
XXVI	206	821	Th	6	...
*	207	822	Tu	27	May
	208	823	Sa	16	...
XXIX	209	824	We	4	...
	210	825	Mo	24	April

VIII—CYCLE.

	Hijra.	A.D.	Initial Days.		
	211	826	Fr	13	...
II	212	827	Tu	2	...
	213	828	S	22	Mar
	214	829	Th	11	...
V	215	830	Mo	28	Feb
	216	831	Sa	18	...
VII	217	832	We	7	...
*	218	833	Mo	27	Jan
	219	834	Fr	16	...
X	220	835	Tu	5	...
	221	...	S	26	Dec
	222	836	Th	14	...
XIII	223	837	Mo	3	...
	224	838	Sa	23	Nov
	225	839	We	12	...
XVI	226	840	S	31	Oct
	227	841	Fr	21	...
XVIII	228	842	Tu	10	...
*	229	843	S	30	Sep
	230	844	Th	18	...
XXI	231	845	Mo	7	...
	232	846	Sa	28	Aug
	233	847	We	17	...
XXIV	234	848	S	5	...
	235	849	Fr	26	July
XXVI	236	850	Tu	15	...
*	237	851	S	5	...
	238	852	Th	23	June
XXIX	239	853	Mo	12	...
	240	854	Sa	2	...

IX—CYCLE.

	Hijra.	A.D.	Initial Days.		
	241	855	We	22	May
II	242	856	S	10	...
	243	857	Fr	30	April
	244	858	Tu	19	...
V	245	859	Sa	8	...
	246	860	Th	28	Mar
VII	247	861	Mo	17	...
*	248	862	Sa	7	...
	249	863	We	24	Feb
X	250	864	S	13	...
	251	865	Fr	2	...
	252	866	Tu	22	Jan
XIII	253	867	Sa	11	...
	254	868	Th	1	...
	255	...	Mo	20	Dec
XVI	256	869	Fr	9	...
	257	870	We	29	Nov
XVIII	258	871	S	18	...
*	259	872	Fr	7	...
	260	873	Tu	27	Oct
XXI	261	874	Sa	16	...
	262	875	Th	6	...
	263	876	Mo	24	Sep
XXIV	264	877	Fr	13	...
	265	878	We	3	...
XXVI	266	879	S	23	Aug
*	267	880	Fr	12	...
	268	881	Tu	1	...
XXIX	269	882	Sa	21	July
	270	883	Th	11	...

TABLE XVI.—(Continued.)

HIJRA CALENDAR.

Initial Days of Hijra Years.

X—CYCLE.

	Hijra.	A.D.	Initial	Days.	
	271	884	Mo	29	June
II	272	885	Fr	18	...
	273	886	We	8	...
	274	887	S	28	May
V	275	888	Th	16	...
	276	889	Tu	6	...
VII	277	890	Sa	25	April
*	278	891	Th	15	...
	279	892	Mo	3	...
X	280	893	Fr	23	March
	281	894	We	13	March
	282	895	S	2	...
XIII	283	896	Th	19	Feb
	284	897	Tu	8	...
	285	898	Sa	28	Jan
XVI	286	899	We	17	...
	287	900	Mo	7	...
XVIII	288	...	Fr	26	Dec
*	289	901	We	16	...
	290	902	S	5	...
XXI	291	903	Th	24	Nov
	292	904	Tu	13	...
	293	905	Sa	2	...
XXIV	294	906	We	22	Oct
	295	907	Mo	12	...
XXVI	296	908	Fr	30	Sep
*	297	909	We	20	...
	298	910	S	9	...
XXIX	299	911	Th	29	Aug
	300	912	Tu	18	...

XI—CYCLE.

	Hijra.	A.D.	Initial	Days.	
	301	913	Sa	7	...
II	302	914	We	27	July
	303	915	Mo	17	...
	304	916	Fr	5	...
V	305	917	Tu	24	June
	306	918	S	14	...
VII	307	919	Th	3	...
*	308	920	Tu	23	May
	309	921	Sa	12	...
X	310	922	We	1	...
	311	923	Mo	21	April
	312	924	Fr	9	...
XIII	313	925	Tu	29	Mar
	314	926	S	19	...
	315	927	Th	8	...
XVI	316	928	Mo	25	Feb
	317	929	Sa	14	...
XVIII	318	930	We	3	...
*	319	931	Mo	24	Jan
	320	932	Fr	13	...
XXI	321	933	Tu	1	Jan
	322	...	S	22	Dec
	323	934	Th	11	...
XXIV	324	935	Mo	30	Nov
	325	936	Sa	19	...
XXVI	326	937	We	8	...
*	327	938	Mo	29	Oct
	328	939	Fr	18	...
XXIX	329	940	Tu	6	...
	330	941	S	26	Sep

XII—CYCLE.

	Hijra.	A.D.	Initial	Days.	
	331	942	Th	15	...
II	332	943	Mo	4	...
	333	944	Sa	24	Aug
	334	945	We	13	...
V	335	946	S	2	...
	336	947	Fr	23	July
VII	337	948	Tu	11	...
*	338	949	S	1	...
	339	950	Th	20	June
X	340	951	Mo	9	...
	341	952	Sa	29	May
	342	953	We	18	...
XIII	343	954	S	7	...
	344	955	Fr	27	April
	345	956	Tu	15	...
XVI	346	957	Sa	4	...
	347	958	Th	25	Mar
XVIII	348	959	Mo	14	...
*	349	960	Sa	2	...
	350	961	We	20	Feb
XXI	351	962	S	9	...
	352	963	Fr	30	Jan
	353	964	Tu	19	...
XXIV	354	965	Sa	7	...
	355	...	Th	28	Dec
XXVI	356	966	Mo	17	...
*	357	967	Sa	7	...
	358	968	We	25	Nov
XXIX	359	969	S	14	...
	360	970	Fr	4	...

TABLE XVI.—(Continued.)

HIJRA CALENDAR.

Initial Days of Hijra Years.

XIII—CYCLE.

	Hijra.	A.D.	Initial	Days.	
	361	971	Tu	24	Oct
II	362	972	Sa	12	...
	363	973	Th	2	...
	364	974	Mo	21	Sep
V	365	975	Fr	10	...
	366	976	We	30	Aug
VII	367	977	S	19	...
*	368	978	Fr	9	...
	369	979	Tu	29	July
X	370	980	Sa	17	...
	371	981	Th	7	...
	372	982	Mo	26	June
XIII	373	983	Fr	15	...
	374	984	We	4	...
	375	985	S	24	May
XVI	376	986	Th	13	...
	377	987	Tu	3	...
XVIII	378	988	Sa	21	April
*	379	989	Th	11	...
	380	990	Mo	31	Mar
XXI	381	991	Fr	20	...
	382	992	We	8	...
	383	993	S	26	Feb
XXIV	384	994	Th	15	...
	385	995	Tu	5	...
XXVI	386	996	Sa	25	Jan
*	387	997	Th	14	...
	388	998	Mo	3	...
XXIX	389	...	Fr	23	Dec
	390	999	We	13	...

XIV—CYCLE.

	Hijra.	A.D.	Initial	Days.	
	391	1000	S	1	...
II	392	1001	Th	20	Nov
	393	1002	Tu	10	...
	394	1003	Sa	30	Oct
V	395	1004	We	18	...
	396	1005	Mo	8	...
VII	397	1006	Fr	27	Sep
*	398	1007	We	17	...
	399	1008	S	5	...
X	400	1009	Th	25	Aug
	401	1010	Tu	15	Aug
	402	1011	Sa	4	...
XIII	403	1012	We	23	July
	404	1013	Mo	13	...
	405	1014	Fr	2	...
XVI	406	1015	Tu	21	June
	407	1016	S	10	...
XVIII	408	1017	Th	30	May
*	409	1018	Tu	20	...
	410	1019	Sa	9	...
XXI	411	1020	We	27	April
	412	1021	Mo	17	...
	413	1022	Fr	6	...
XXIV	414	1023	Tu	26	May
	415	1024	S	15	...
XXVI	416	1025	Th	4	...
*	417	1026	Tu	22	Feb
	418	1027	Sa	11	...
XXIX	419	1028	We	31	Jan
	420	1029	Mo	20	...

XV—CYCLE.

	Hijra.	A.D.	Initial	Days.	
	421	1030	Fr	9	...
II	422	...	Tu	29	Dec
	423	1031	S	19	...
	424	1032	Th	7	...
V	425	1033	Mo	26	Nov
	426	1034	Sa	16	...
VII	427	1035	We	5	...
*	428	1036	Mo	25	Oct
	429	1037	Fr	14	...
X	430	1038	Tu	3	...
	431	1039	S	23	Sep
	432	1040	Th	11	...
XIII	433	1041	Mo	31	Aug
	434	1042	Sa	21	...
	435	1043	We	10	...
XVI	436	1044	S	29	July
	437	1045	Fr	19	...
XVIII	438	1046	Tu	8	...
*	439	1047	S	28	June
	440	1048	Th	16	...
XXI	441	1049	Mo	5	June
	442	1050	Sa	26	May
	443	1051	We	15	...
XXIV	444	1052	S	3	...
	445	1053	Fr	23	April
XXVI	446	1054	Tu	12	...
*	447	1055	S	2	...
	448	1056	Th	21	Mar
XXIX	449	1057	Mo	10	...
	450	1058	Sa	28	Feb

TABLE XVI.—(Continued.)

HIJRA CALENDAR.

Initial Days of Hijra Years.

XVI—CYCLE.

	Hijra.	A.D.	Initial Days.		
	451	1059	We	17	...
II	452	1060	S	6	...
	453	1061	Fr	26	Jan
	454	1062	Tu	15	...
V	455	1063	Sa	4	...
	456	...	Th	25	Dec
VII	457	1064	Mo	13	...
*	458	1065	Sa	3	...
	459	1066	We	22	Nov
X	460	1067	S	11	...
	461	1068	Fr	31	Oct
	462	1069	Tu	20	...
XIII	463	1070	Sa	9	...
	464	1071	Th	29	Sep
	465	1072	Mo	17	...
XVI	466	1073	Fr	6	..
	467	1074	We	27	Aug
XVIII	468	1075	S	16	...
*	469	1076	Th	4	...
	470	1077	Tu	25	July
XXI	471	1078	Sa	14	...
	472	1079	Th	4	...
	473	1080	Mo	22	June
XXIV	474	1081	Fr	11	...
	475	1082	We	1	...
XXVI	476	1083	S	21	May
*	477	1084	Fr	10	...
	478	1085	Tu	29	April
XXIX	479	1086	Sa	18	...
	480	1087	Th	8	...

XVII—CYCLE.

	Hijra.	A.D.	Initial Days.		
	481	1088	Mo	27	Mar
II	482	1089	Fr	16	...
	483	1090	We	6	...
	484	1091	S	23	Feb
V	485	1092	Th	12	...
	486	1093	Tu	1	...
VII	487	1094	Sa	21	Jan
*	488	1095	Th	11	...
	489	...	Mo	31	Dec
X	490	1096	Fr	19	...
	491	1097	We	9	...
	492	1098	S	28	Nov
XIII	493	1099	Th	17	...
	494	1100	Tu	6	...
	495	1101	Sa	26	Oct
XVI	496	1102	We	15	...
	497	1103	Mo	5	...
XVIII	498	1104	Fr	23	Sep
*	499	1105	We	13	...
	500	1106	S	2	..
XXI	501	1107	Th	22	Aug
	502	1108	Tu	11	...
	503	1109	Sa	31	July
XXIV	504	1110	We	20	...
	505	1111	Mo	10	...
XXVI	506	1112	Fr	28	June
*	507	1113	We	18	...
	508	1114	S	7	...
XXIX	509	1115	Th	27	May
	510	1116	Tu	16	...

XVIII—CYCLE.

	Hijra.	A.D.	Initial Days.		
	511	1117	Sa	5	...
II	512	1118	We	24	April
	513	1119	Mo	14	...
	514	1120	Fr	2	...
V	515	1121	Tu	22	Mar
	516	1122	S	12	...
VII	517	1123	Th	1	...
*	518	1124	Tu	19	Feb
	519	1125	Sa	7	...
X	520	1126	We	27	Jan
	521	1127	Mo	17	Jan
	522	1128	Fr	6	...
XIII	523	...	Tu	25	Dec
	524	1129	S	15	...
	525	1130	Th	4	...
XVI	526	1131	Mo	23	Nov
	527	1132	Sa	12	...
XVIII	528	1133	We	1	...
*	529	1134	Mo	29	Oct
	530	1135	Fr	11	...
XXI	531	1136	Tu	29	Sep
	532	1137	S	19	...
	533	1138	Th	8	...
XXIV	534	1139	Mo	28	Aug
	535	1140	Sa	17	...
XXVI	536	1141	We	6	...
*	537	1142	Mo	27	July
	538	1143	Fr	16	...
XXIX	539	1144	Tu	4	...
	540	1145	S	24	June

TABLE XVI.—(Continued.)

HIJRA CALENDAR.

Initial Days of Hijra Years.

XIX—CYCLE.

	Hijra.	A.D.	Initial	Days.
	541	1146	Th 13	...
II	542	1147	Mo 2	...
	543	1148	Sa 22	May
	544	1149	We 11	...
V	545	1150	S 30	April
	546	1151	Fr 20	...
VII	547	1152	Tu 8	...
*	548	1153	Sa 28	Mar
	549	1154	Th 18	...
X	550	1155	Mo 7	...
	551	1156	Sa 25	Feb
	552	1157	We 13	...
XIII	553	1158	S 2	...
	554	1159	Fr 23	Jan
	555	1160	Tu 12	...
XVI	556	...	Sa 31	Dec
	557	1161	Th 21	...
XVIII	558	1162	Mo 10	...
*	559	1163	Fr 29	Nov
	560	1164	We 18	...
XXI	561	1165	S 7	Nov
	562	1166	Fr 28	Oct
	563	1167	Tu 17	...
XXIV	564	1168	Sa 5	...
	565	1169	Th 25	Sep
XXVI	566	1170	Mo 14	...
*	567	1171	Fr 3	...
	568	1172	We 23	Aug
XXIX	569	1173	S 12	...
	570	1174	Fr 2	...

XX—CYCLE.

	Hijra.	A.D.	Initial	Days.
	571	1175	Tu 22	July
II	572	1176	Sa 10	...
	573	1177	Th 30	June
	574	1178	Mo 19	...
V	575	1179	Fr 8	...
	576	1180	We 28	May
VII	577	1181	S 17	...
*	578	1182	Th 6	...
	579	1183	Tu 26	April
X	580	1184	Sa 14	...
	581	1185	Th 4	...
	582	1186	Mo 24	Mar
XIII	583	1187	Fr 13	...
	584	1188	We 2	...
	585	1189	S 19	Feb
XVI	586	1190	Th 8	...
	587	1191	Tu 29	Jan
XVIII	588	1192	Sa 18	...
*	589	1193	We 6	...
	590	...	Mo 27	Dec
XXI	591	1194	Fr 16	...
	592	1195	We 6	...
	593	1196	S 24	Nov
XXIV	594	1197	Th 13	...
	595	1198	Tu 3	...
XXVI	596	1199	Sa 23	Oct
*	597	1200	We 11	...
	598	1201	Mo 1	...
XXIX	599	1202	Fr 20	Sep
	600	1203	We 10	...

XXI—CYCLE.

	Hijra.	A.D.	Initial	Days.
	601	1204	S 29	Aug
II	602	1205	Th 18	...
	603	1206	Tu 8	...
	604	1207	Sa 28	July
V	605	1208	We 16	...
	606	1209	Mo 6	...
VII	607	1210	Fr 25	June
*	608	1211	We 15	...
	609	1212	S 3	...
X	610	1213	Th 23	May
	611	1214	Tu 13	...
	612	1215	Sa 2	...
XIII	613	1216	We 20	April
	614	1217	Mo 10	...
	615	1218	Fr 30	Mar
XVI	616	1219	Tu 19	...
	617	1220	S 8	...
XVIII	618	1221	Th 25	Feb
*	619	1222	Tu 15	...
	620	1223	Sa 4	...
XXI	621	1224	We 24	Jan
	622	1225	Mo 13	...
	623	1226	Fr 2	...
XXIV	624	...	Tu 22	Dec
	625	1227	S 12	...
XXVI	626	1228	Th 30	Nov
*	627	1229	Tu 20	...
	628	1230	Sa 9	...
XXIX	629	1231	We 29	Oct
	630	1232	Mo 18	...

TABLE XVI.—(Continued.)

HIJRA CALENDAR.

Initial Days of Hijra Years.

XXII—CYCLE.

	Hijra.	A.D.	Initial		Days.
	631	1233	Fr	7	...
II	632	1234	Tu	26	Sep
	633	1235	S	16	...
	634	1236	Th	4	...
V	635	1237	Mo	24	Aug
	636	1238	Sa	14	...
VII	637	1239	We	3	...
*	638	1240	Mo	23	July
	639	1241	Fr	12	...
X	640	1242	Tu	1	...
	641	1243	S	21	June
	642	1244	Th	9	...
XIII	643	1245	Mo	29	May
	644	1246	Sa	19	...
	645	1247	We	8	...
XVI	646	1248	S	26	April
	647	1249	Fr	16	...
XVIII	648	1250	Tu	5	...
*	649	1251	S	26	Mar
	650	1252	Th	14	...
XXI	651	1253	Mo	3	...
	652	1254	Sa	21	Feb
	653	1255	We	10	...
XXIV	654	1256	S	30	Jan
	655	1257	Fr	19	...
XXVI	656	1258	Tu	8	...
*	657	...	S	29	Dec
	658	1259	Th	18	...
XXIX	659	1260	Mo	6	...
	660	1261	Sa	26	Nov

XXIII—CYCLE.

	Hijra.	A.D.	Initial		Days.
	661	1262	We	15	...
II	662	1263	S	4	...
	663	1264	Fr	24	Oct
	664	1265	Tu	13	...
V	665	1266	Sa	2	...
	666	1267	Th	22	Sep
VII	667	1268	Mo	10	...
*	668	1269	Sa	31	Aug
	669	1270	We	20	...
X	670	1271	S	9	...
	671	1272	Fr	29	July
	672	1273	Tu	18	...
XIII	673	1274	Sa	7	...
	674	1275	Th	27	June
	675	1276	Mo	15	...
XVI	676	1277	Fr	4	...
	677	1278	We	25	May
XVIII	678	1279	S	14	...
*	679	1280	Fr	3	...
	680	1281	Tu	22	April
XXI	681	1282	Sa	11	April
	682	1283	Th	1	...
	683	1284	Mo	20	Mar
XXIV	684	1285	Fr	9	...
	685	1286	We	27	Feb
XXVI	686	1287	S	16	...
*	687	1288	Fr	6	...
	688	1289	Tu	25	Jan
XXIX	689	1290	Sa	14	...
	690	1291	Th	4	...

XXIV—CYCLE.

	Hijra.	A.D.	Initial		Days.
	691	...	Mo	24	Dec
II	692	1292	Fr	12	...
	693	1293	We	2	...
	694	1294	S	21	Nov
V	695	1295	Th	10	...
	696	1296	Tu	30	Oct
VII	697	1297	Sa	19	...
*	698	1298	Th	9	...
	699	1299	Mo	28	Sep
X	700	1300	Fr	16	...
	701	1301	We	6	...
	702	1302	S	26	Aug
XIII	703	1303	Th	15	...
	704	1304	Tu	4	...
	705	1305	Sa	24	July
XVI	706	1306	We	13	...
	707	1307	Mo	3	...
XVIII	708	1308	Fr	21	June
*	709	1309	We	11	...
	710	1310	S	31	May
XXI	711	1311	Th	20	...
	712	1312	Tu	9	...
	713	1313	Sa	28	April
XXIV	714	1314	We	17	...
	715	1315	Mo	7	...
XXVI	716	1316	Fr	26	Mar.
*	717	1317	We	16	...
	718	1318	S	5	...
XXIX	719	1319	Th	22	Feb
	720	1320	Tu	12	...

TABLE XVI.—(Continued.)

HIJRA CALENDAR.

Initial Days of Hijra Years.

XXV—CYCLE.

	Hijra.	A.D.	Initial		Days.
	721	1321	Sa	31	Jan
II	722	1322	We	20	...
	723	1323	Mo	10	...
	724	...	Fr	30	Dec
V	725	1324	Tu	18	...
	726	1325	S	8	...
VII	727	1326	Th	27	Nov
*	728	1327	Tu	17	...
	729	1328	Sa	5	...
X	730	1329	We	25	Oct
	731	1330	Mo	15	...
	732	1331	Fr	4	...
XIII	733	1332	Tu	22	Sep
	734	1333	S	12	...
	735	1334	Th	1	...
XVI	736	1335	Mo	21	Aug
	737	1336	Sa	10	...
XVIII	738	1337	We	30	July
*	739	1338	Mo	20	...
	740	1339	Fr	9	...
XXI	741	1340	Tu	27	June
	742	1341	S	17	...
	743	1342	Th	6	...
XXIV	744	1343	Mo	24	May
	745	1344	Sa	15	...
XXVI	746	1345	We	4	...
*	747	1346	Mo	24	April
	748	1347	Fr	13	...
XXIX	749	1348	Tu	1	...
	750	1349	S	22	Mar

XXVI—CYCLE.

	Hijra.	A.D.	Initial		Days.
	751	1350	Th	11	...
II	752	1351	Mo	28	Feb
	753	1352	Sa	18	...
	754	1353	We	6	...
V	755	1354	S	26	Jan
	756	1355	Fr	16	...
VII	757	1356	Tu	5	...
*	758	...	S	25	Dec
	759	1357	Th	14	...
X	760	1358	Mo	3	...
	761	1359	Sa	23	Nov
	762	1360	We	11	...
XIII	763	1361	S	31	Oct
	764	1362	Fr	21	...
	765	1363	Tu	10	...
XVI	766	1364	Sa	28	Sep
	767	1365	Th	18	...
XVIII	768	1366	Mo	7	...
*	769	1367	Sa	28	Aug
	770	1368	We	16	...
XXI	771	1369	S	5	...
	772	1370	Fr	26	July
	773	1371	Tu	15	...
XXIV	774	1372	Sa	3	...
	775	1373	Th	23	June
XXVI	776	1374	Mo	12	...
*	777	1375	Sa	2	...
	778	1376	We	21	May
XXIX	779	1377	S	10	...
	780	1378	Fr	30	April

XXVII—CYCLE.

	Hijra.	A.D.	Initial		Days.
	781	1379	Tu	19	...
II	782	1380	Sa	7	...
	783	1381	Th	28	Mar
	784	1382	Mo	17	...
V	785	1383	Fr	6	...
	786	1384	We	24	Feb
VII	787	1385	S	12	...
*	788	1386	Fr	2	...
	789	1387	Tu	22	Jan
X	790	1388	Sa	11	...
	791	...	Th	31	Dec
	792	1389	Mo	20	...
XIII	793	1390	Fr	9	...
	794	1391	We	29	Nov
	795	1392	S	17	...
XVI	796	1393	Th	6	...
	797	1394	Tu	27	Oct
XVIII	798	1395	Sa	16	...
*	799	1396	Th	5	...
	800	1397	Mo	24	Sep
XXI	801	1398	Fr	13	Sep
	802	1399	We	3	...
	803	1400	S	22	Aug
XXIV	804	1401	Th	11	...
	805	1402	Tu	1	...
XXVI	806	1403	Sa	21	July
*	807	1404	Th	10	...
	808	1405	Mo	29	June
XXIX	809	1406	Fr	18	...
	810	1407	We	8	...

TABLE XVI.—(Continued.)

HIJRA CALENDAR.

Initial Days of Hijra Years.

XXVIII—CYCLE.

	Hijra.	A.D.	Initial Days.		
	811	1408	S	27	May
II	812	1409	Th	16	...
	813	1410	Tu	6	...
	814	1411	Sa	25	April
V	815	1412	We	13	...
	816	1413	Mo	3	...
VII	817	1414	Fr	23	Mar
*	818	1415	We	13	...
	819	1416	S	1	...
X	820	1417	Th	18	Feb
	821	1418	Tu	8	...
	822	1419	Sa	28	Jan
XIII	823	1420	We	17	...
	824	1421	Mo	6	...
	825	...	Fr	26	Dec
XVI	826	1422	Tu	15	...
	827	1423	S	5	...
XVIII	828	1424	Th	23	Nov
*	829	1425	Tu	13	...
	830	1426	Sa	2	...
XXI	831	1427	We	22	Oct
	832	1428	Mo	11	...
	833	1429	Fr	30	Sep
XXIV	834	1430	Tu	19	...
	835	1431	S	9	...
XXVI	836	1432	Th	28	Aug
*	837	1433	Tu	18	...
	838	1434	Sa	7	...
XXIX	839	1435	We	27	July
	840	1436	Mo	16	...

XXIX—CYCLE.

	Hijra.	A.D.	Initial Days.		
	841	1437	Fr	5	July
II	842	1438	Tu	24	June
	843	1439	S	14	...
	844	1440	Th	2	...
V	845	1441	Mo	22	May
	846	1442	Sa	12	...
VII	847	1443	We	1	...
*	848	1444	Mo	20	April
	849	1445	Fr	9	...
X	850	1446	Tu	29	Mar
	851	1447	S	19	...
	852	1448	Th	7	...
XIII	853	1449	Mo	24	Feb
	854	1450	Sa	14	...
	855	1451	We	3	...
XVI	856	1452	S	23	Jan
	857	1453	Fr	12	...
XVIII	858	1454	Tu	1	...
*	859	...	S	22	Dec
	860	1455	Th	11	...
XXI	861	1456	Mo	29	Nov
	862	1457	Sa	19	...
	863	1458	We	8	...
XXIV	864	1459	S	28	Oct
	865	1460	Fr	17	...
XXVI	866	1461	Tu	6	...
*	867	1462	S	26	Sep
	868	1463	Th	15	...
XXIX	869	1464	Mo	3	...
	870	1465	Sa	24	Aug

XXX—CYCLE.

	Hijra.	A.D.	Initial Days.		
	871	1466	We	13	...
II	872	1467	S	2	...
	873	1468	Fr	22	July
	874	1469	Tu	11	...
V	875	1470	Sa	30	June
	876	1471	Th	20	...
VII	877	1472	Mo	8	...
*	878	1473	Sa	29	May
	879	1474	We	18	...
X	880	1475	S	7	...
	881	1476	Fr	26	April
	882	1477	Tu	15	...
XIII	883	1478	Sa	4	...
	884	1479	Th	25	Mar
	885	1480	Mo	13	...
XVI	886	1481	Fr	2	...
	887	1482	We	20	Feb
XVIII	888	1483	S	9	...
*	889	1484	Fr	30	Jan
	890	1485	Tu	18	...
XXI	891	1486	Sa	7	...
	892	...	Th	28	Dec
	893	1487	Mo	17	...
XXIV	894	1488	Fr	5	...
	895	1489	We	25	Nov
XXVI	896	1490	S	14	...
*	897	1491	Fr	4	...
	898	1492	Tu	23	Oct
XXIX	899	1493	Sa	12	...
	900	1494	Th	2	...

TABLE XVI.—(Continued.)

HIJRA CALENDAR.

Initial Days of Hijra Years.

XXXI—CYCLE.

	Hijra.	A.D.	Initial Days.		
	901	1495	Mo	21	Sep
II	902	1496	Fr	9	...
	903	1497	We	30	Aug
	904	1498	S	19	...
V	905	1499	Th	8	...
	906	1500	Tu	28	July
VII	907	1501	S	17	...
*	908	1502	Th	7	...
	909	1503	Mo	26	June
X	910	1504	Fr	14	...
	911	1505	We	4	...
	912	1506	S	24	May
XIII	913	1507	Th	13	...
	914	1508	Tu	2	...
	915	1509	Sa	21	April
XVI	916	1510	We	10	...
	917	1511	Mo	31	Mar
XVIII	918	1512	Fr	19	...
*	919	1513	We	9	...
	920	1514	S	26	Feb
XXI	921	1515	Th	15	Feb
	922	1516	Tu	5	...
	923	1517	Sa	24	Jan
XXIV	924	1518	We	13	...
	925	1519	Mo	3	...
XXVI	926	...	Fr	23	Dec
*	927	1520	We	12	...
	928	1521	S	1	...
XXIX	929	1522	Th	20	Nov
	930	1523	Tu	10	...

XXXII—CYCLE.

	Hijra.	A.D.	Initial Days.		
	931	1524	Sa	29	Oct
II	932	1525	We	18	...
	933	1526	Mo	8	...
	934	1527	Fr	27	Sep
V	935	1528	Tu	15	...
	936	1529	S	5	...
VII	937	1530	Th	25	Aug
*	938	1531	Tu	15	...
	939	1532	Sa	8	...
X	940	1533	We	23	July
	941	1534	Mo	13	...
	942	1535	Fr	2	...
XIII	943	1536	Tu	20	June
	944	1537	S	10	...
	945	1538	Th	30	May
XVI	946	1539	Mo	19	...
	947	1540	Sa	8	...
XVIII	948	1541	We	27	April
*	949	1542	Mo	17	...
	950	1543	Fr	6	...
XXI	951	1544	Tu	25	Mar
	952	1545	S	15	...
	953	1546	Th	4	...
XXIV	954	1547	Mo	21	Feb
	955	1548	Sa	11	...
XXVI	956	1549	We	30	Jan
*	957	1550	Mo	20	...
	958	1551	Fr	9	...
XXIX	959	...	Tu	29	Dec
	960	1552	S	18	...

XXXIII—CYCLE.

	Hijra.	A.D.	Initial Days.		
	961	1553	Th	7	Dec
II	962	1554	Mo	26	Nov
	963	1555	Sa	16	...
	964	1556	We	4	...
V	965	1557	S	24	Oct
	966	1558	Fr	14	...
VII	967	1559	Tu	3	...
*	968	1560	S	22	Sep
	969	1561	Th	11	...
X	970	1562	Mo	31	Aug
	971	1563	Sa	21	...
	972	1564	We	9	...
XIII	973	1565	S	29	July
	974	1566	Fr	19	...
	975	1567	Tu	8	...
XVI	976	1568	Sa	26	June
	977	1569	Th	16	...
XVIII	978	1570	Mo	5	...
*	979	1571	Sa	26	May
	980	1572	We	14	...
XXI	981	1573	Sa	3	...
	982	1574	Fr	23	April
	983	1575	Tu	12	...
XXIV	984	1576	Sa	31	Mar
	985	1577	Th	21	...
XXVI	986	1578	Mo	10	...
*	987	1579	Sa	28	Feb
	988	1580	We	17	...
XXIX	989	1581	S	5	...
	990	1582	Fr	26	Jan

TABLE XVI.—(Continued.)
HIJRA CALENDAR.
Initial Days of Hijra Years.

	XXXIV—CYCLE.			
	Hijra.	A.D.	Initial Days.	
	991	1583	Tu 15	...
II	992	1584	Sa 4	...
	993	...	Th 24	Dec
	994	1585	Mo 13	...
V	995	1586	Fr 2	...
	996	1587	We 22	Nov
VII	997	1588	S 10	...
*	998	1589	Fr 31	Oct
	999	1590	Tu 20	...
X	1000	1591	Sa 9	...
	1001	1592	Th 28	Sep
	1002	1593	Mo 17	...
XIII	1003	1594	Fr 6	...
	1004	1595	We 27	Aug
	1005	1596	S 15	...
XVI	1006	1597	Th 5	...
	1007	1598	Tu 25	July
XVIII	1008	1599	Sa 14	...
*	1009	1600	Th 3	...
	1010	1601	Mo 22	June
XXI	1011	1602	Fr 11	...
	1012	1603	We 1	...
	1013	1604	S 20	May
XXIV	1014	1605	Th 9	...
	1015	1606	Tu 29	April
XXVI	1016	1607	Sa 18	...
	1017	1608	Th 7	...
	1018	1609	Mo 27	Mar
XXIX	1019	1610	Fr 16	...
	1020	1611	We 6	...

	XXXV—CYCLE.			
	Hijra.	A.D.	Initial Days.	
	1021	1612	S 23	Feb
II	1022	1613	Th 11	...
	1023	1614	Tu 1	...
	1024	1615	Sa 21	Jan
V	1025	1616	We 10	...
	1026	...	Mo 30	Dec
VII	1027	1617	Fr 19	...
*	1028	1618	We 9	...
	1029	1619	S 28	Nov
X	1030	1620	Th 16	...
	1031	1621	Tu 6	...
	1032	1622	Sa 26	Oct
XIII	1033	1623	We 15	...
	1034	1624	Mo 4	...
	1035	1625	Fr 23	Sep
XVI	1036	1626	Tu 12	...
	1037	1627	S 2	...
XVIII	1038	1628	Th 21	Aug
*	1039	1629	Tu 11	...
	1040	1630	Sa 31	July
XXI	1041	1631	We 20	July
	1042	1632	Mo 9	...
	1043	1633	Fr 28	June
XXIV	1044	1634	Tu 17	...
	1045	1635	S 7	...
XXVI	1046	1636	Th 26	May
*	1047	1637	Tu 16	...
	1048	1638	Sa 5	...
XXIX	1049	1639	We 24	April
	1050	1640	Mo 13	...

	XXXVI—CYCLE.			
	Hijra.	A.D.	Initial Days.	
	1051	1641	Fr 2	...
II	1052	1642	Tu 22	Mar
	1053	1643	S 12	...
	1054	1644	Th 29	Feb
V	1055	1645	Mo 17	...
	1056	1546	Sa 7	...
VII	1057	1647	We 27	Jan
*	1058	1648	Mo 17	...
	1059	1649	Fr 5	...
X	1060	...	Tu 25	Dec
	1061	1650	S 15	...
	1062	1651	Th 4	...
XIII	1063	1652	Mo 22	Nov
	1064	1653	Sa 12	...
	1065	1654	We 1	...
XVI	1066	1655	S 21	Oct
	1067	1656	Fr 10	...
XVIII	1068	1657	Tu 29	Sep
*	1069	1658	S 19	...
	1070	1659	Th 8	...
XXI	1071	1660	Mo 27	Aug
	1072	1661	Sa 17	...
	1073	1662	We 6	...
XXIV	1074	1663	S 26	July
	1075	1664	Fr 15	...
XXVI	1076	1665	Tu 4	...
*	1077	1666	S 24	June
	1078	1667	Th 13	...
XXIX	1079	1668	Mo 1	...
	1080	1669	S 22	May

TABLE XVI.—(Continued.)

HIJRA CALENDAR.

Initial Days of Hijra Years.

	XXXVII—CYCLE.				
	Hijra.	A.D.	Initial Days.		
	1081	1670	We	11	May
II	1082	1671	S	30	April
	1083	1672	Fr	19	...
	1084	1673	Tu	8	...
V	1085	1674	Sa	28	Mar
	1086	1675	Th	18	...
VII	1087	1676	Mo	6	...
*	1088	1677	Sa	24	Feb
	1089	1678	We	13	...
X	1090	1679	S	2	...
	1091	1680	Fr	23	Jan
	1092	1681	Tu	11	...
XIII	1093	...	Sa	31	Dec
	1094	1682	Th	21	...
	1095	1683	Mo	10	...
XVI	1096	1684	Fr	28	Nov
	1097	1685	We	18	...
XVIII	1098	1686	S	7	...
*	1099	1687	Fr	28	Oct
	1100	1688	Tu	16	...
XXI	1101	1689	Sa	5	...
	1102	1690	Th	25	Sep
	1103	1691	Mo	14	...
XXIV	1104	1692	Fr	2	...
	1105	1693	W	23	Aug
XXVI	1106	1694	S	12	...
*	1107	1695	Fr	2	...
	1108	1696	Tu	21	July
XXIX	1109	1697	Sa	10	...
	1110	1698	Th	30	June

	XXXVIII—CYCLE.				
	Hijra.	A.D.	Initial Days.		
	1111	1699	Mo	19	...
II	1112	1700	Fr	7	...
	1113	1701	We	28	May
	1114	1702	S	17	...
V	1115	1703	Th	6	...
	1116	1704	Tu	25	April
VII	1117	1705	Sa	14	...
*	1118	1706	Th	4	...
	1119	1707	Mo	24	Mar
X	1120	1708	Fr	12	...
	1121	1709	We	2	Mar
	1122	1710	S	19	Feb
XIII	1123	1711	Th	8	...
	1124	1712	Tu	29	Jan
	1125	1713	Sa	17	...
XVI	1126	1714	We	6	...
	1127	...	Mo	27	Dec
XVIII	1128	1715	Fr	16	...
*	1129	1716	We	5	...
	1130	1717	S	24	Nov
XXI	1131	1718	Th	13	...
	1132	1719	Tu	3	...
	1133	1720	Sa	22	Oct
XXIV	1134	1721	We	11	...
	1135	1722	Mo	1	...
XXVI	1136	1723	Fr	20	Sep
*	1137	1724	We	9	...
	1138	1725	S	29	Aug
XXIX	1139	1726	Th	18	...
	1140	1727	Tu	8	...

	XXXIX—CYCLE.					
	Hijra.	A.D.	Initial Days.			
	1141	1728	Sa	27	July	
II	1142	1729	We	16	...	
	1143	1730	Mo	6	...	
	1144	1731	Fr	25	June	
V	1145	1732	Tu	13	...	
	1146	1733	S	3	...	
VII	1147	1734	Th	23	May	
*	1148	1735	Tu	13	...	
	1149	1736	Sa	1	...	
X	1150	1737	We	20	April	
	1151	1738	Mo	10	...	
	1152	1739	Fr	30	Mar	
XIII	1153	1740	Tu	18	...	
	1154	1741	S	8	...	
	1155	1742	Th	25	Feb	
XVI	1156	1743	Mo	14	...	
	1157	1744	Sa	4	...	
XVIII	1158	1745	We	23	Jan	
*	1159	1746	Mo	13	...	
	1160	1747	Fr	2	...	
XXI	1161	...	Tu	22	Dec	
	1162	1748	S	11	...	
	1163	1749	Th	30	Nov	
XXIV	1164	1750	Mo	19	...	
	1165	1751	Sa	9	Nov	O S
XXVI	1166	1752	We	8	Nov	N S
*	1167	1753	Mo	29	Oct	
	1168	1754	Fr	18	...	
XXIX	1169	1755	Tu	7	...	
	1170	1756	S	26	Sep	

TABLE XVI.—(Continued.)

HIJRA CALENDAR.

Initial Days of Hijra Years.

XL—CYCLE.

	Hijra.	A.D	Initial Days.		
	1171	1757	Th	15	..
II	1172	1758	Mo	4	...
	1173	1759	Sa	25	Aug
	1174	1760	We	13	
V	1175	1761	S	2	
	1176	1762	Fr	23	July
VII	1177	1763	Tu	12	
*	1178	1764	S	1	
	1179	1765	Th	20	June
X	1180	1766	Mo	9	.
	1181	1767	Sa	30	May
	1182	1768	We	18	
XIII	1183	1769	S	7	
	1184	1770	Fr	27	April
	1185	1771	Tu	16	.
XVI	1186	1772	Sa	4	.
	1187	1773	Th	25	Mar
XVIII	1188	1774	Mo	14	.
*	1189	1775	Sa	4	.
	1190	1776	We	21	Feb
XXI	1191	1777	S	9	
	1192	1778	Fr	30	Jan
	1193	1779	Tu	19	
XXIV	1194	1780	Sa	8	
	1195		Th	28	Dec
XXVI	1196	1781	Mo	17	..
*	1197	1782	Sa	7	
	1198	1783	We	26	Nov
XXIX	1199	1784	S	14	..
	1200	1785	Fr	4	..

XLI—CYCLE.

	Hijra.	A D	Initial Days.		
	1201	1786	Tu	24	Oct
II	1202	1787	Sa	13	
	1203	1788	Th	2	
	1204	1789	Mo	21	Sep
V	1205	1790	Fr	10	
	1206	1791	We	31	Aug
VII	1207	1792	S	19	
*	1208	1793	Fr	9	
	1209	1794	Tu	29	July
X	1210	1795	Sa	18	.
	1211	1796	Th	7	
	1212	1797	Mo	26	June
XIII	1213	1798	Fr	15	
	1214	1799	We	5	
	1215	1800	S	25	May
XVI	1216	1801	Th	14	
	1217	1802	Tu	4	
XVIII	1218	1803	Sa	23	April
*	1219	1804	Th	12	..
	1220	1805	Mo	1	
XXI	1221	1806	Fr	21	Mar
	1222	1807	We	11	
	1223	1808	S	28	Feb
XXIV	1224	1809	Th	16	
	1225	1810	Tu	6	
XXVI	1226	1811	Sa	26	Jan
*	1227	1812	Th	16	
	1228	1813	Mo	4	
XXIX	1229		Fr	24	Dec
	1230	1814	We	14	.

XLII—CYCLE.

	Hijra.	A.D.	Initial Days		
	1231	1815	S	3	..
II	1232	1816	Th	21	Nov
	1233	1817	Tu	11	.
	1234	1818	Sa	31	Oct
V	1235	1819	We	20	
	1236	1820	Mo	9	
VII	1237	1821	Fr	28	Sep
*	1238	1822	We	18	
	1239	1823	S	7	.
X	1240	1824	Th	26	Aug
	1241	1825	Tu	16	
	1242	1826	Sa	5	.
XIII	1243	1827	We	25	July
	1244	1828	Mo	14	
	1245	1829	Fr	3	
XVI	1246	1830	Tu	22	June
	1247	1831	S	12	
XVIII	1248	1832	Th	31	May
*	1249	1833	Tu	21	.
	1250	1834	Sa	10	
XXI	1251	1835	We	29	April
	1252	1836	Mo	18	.
	1253	1837	Fr	7	
XXIV	1254	1838	Tu	27	Mar
	1255	1839	S	17	
XXVI	1256	1840	Th	5	
*	1257	1841	Tu	23	Feb
	1258	1842	Sa	12	.
XXIX	1259	1843	We	1	..
	1260	1844	Mo	22	Jan

TABLE XVI.—(Continued.)

HIJRA CALENDAR.

Initial Days of Hijra Years.

XLIII—CYCLE.

	Hijra.	A.D.	Initial Days.		
	1261	1845	Fr	10	...
II	1262	...	Tu	30	Dec
	1263	1846	S	20	...
	1264	1847	Th	9	...
V	1265	1848	Mo	27	Nov
	1266	1849	Sa	17	...
VII	1267	1850	We	6	...
*	1268	1851	Mo	27	Oct
	1269	1852	Fr	15	...
X	1270	1853	Tu	4	...
	1271	1854	S	24	Sep
	1272	1855	Th	13	...
XIII	1273	1856	Mo	1	...
	1274	1857	Sa	22	Aug
	1275	1858	We	11	...
XVI	1276	1859	S	31	July
	1277	1860	Fr	30	...
XVIII	1278	1861	Tu	9	...
*	1279	1862	S	29	June
	1280	1863	Th	18	...
XXI	1281	1864	Mo	6	June
	1282	1865	Sa	27	May
	1283	1866	We	16	...
XXIV	1284	1867	S	5	...
	1285	1868	Fr	24	April
XXVI	1286	1869	Tu	13	...
*	1287	1870	S	3	...
	1288	1871	Th	23	Mar
XXIX	1289	1872	Mo	11	...
	1290	1873	Sa	1	...

XLIV—CYCLE.

	Hijra.	A.D.	Initial Days.		
	1291	1874	We	18	Feb
II	1292	1875	S	7	...
	1293	1876	Fr	28	Jan
	1294	1877	Tu	16	..
V	1295	1878	S	5	...
	1296	...	Th	26	Dec
VII	1297	1879	Mo	15	...
*	1298	1880	Sa	4	...
	1299	1881	We	23	Nov
X	1300	1882	S	12	...
	1301	1883	Fr	2	...
	1302	1884	Tu	21	Oct
XIII	1303	1885	Sa	10	...
	1304	1886	Th	30	Sep
	1305	1887	Mo	19	...
XVI	1306	1888	Fr	7	...
	1307	1889	We	28	Aug
XVIII	1308	1890	S	17	...
*	1309	1891	Fr	7	...
	1310	1892	Tu	26	July
XXI	1311	1893	Sa	15	...
	1312	1894	Th	5	...
	1313	1895	Mo	24	June
XXIV	1314	1896	Fr	12	...
	1315	1897	We	2	...
XXVI	1316	1898	S	22	May
*	1317	1899	Fr	12	...
	1318	1900	Tu	1	...
XXIX	1319	1901	Sa	20	April
	1320	1902	Th	10	...

XLV—CYCLE.

	Hijra.	A.D.	Initial Days.		
	1321	1903	Mo	30	Mar
II	1322	1904	Fr	18	...
	1323	1905	We	8	...
	1324	1906	S	25	Feb
V	1325	1907	Th	14	...
	1326	1908	Tu	4	...
VII	1327	1909	Sa	23	Jan
*	1328	1910	Th	13	...
	1329	1911	Mo	2	...
X	1330	...	Fr	22	Dec
	1331	1912	We	11	...
	1332	1913	S	30	Nov
XIII	1333	1914	Th	19	...
	1334	1915	Tu	9	...
	1335	1916	Sa	28	Oct
XVI	1336	1917	We	17	...
	1337	1918	Mo	7	...
XVIII	1338	1919	Fr	26	Sep
*	1339	1920	We	15	...
	1340	1921	S	4	...
XXI	1341	1922	Th	24	Aug
	1342	1923	Tu	14	...
	1343	1924	Sa	2	...
XXIV	1344	1925	We	22	July
	1345	1926	Mo	12	...
XXVI	1346	1927	Fr	1	...
*	1347	1928	We	20	June
	1348	1929	S	9	...
XXIX	1349	1930	Th	29	May
	1350	1931	Tu	19	...

TABLE XVI.—(Concluded.)

HIJRA CALENDAR.

Initial Days of Hijra Years.

XLVI—CYCLE.

	Hijra.	A.D.	Initial Days.		
	1351	1932	Sa	7	...
II	1352	1933	We	26	April
	1353	1934	Mo	16	...
	1354	1935	Fr	5	...
V	1355	1936	Tu	24	Mar
	1356	1937	S	14	...
VII	1357	1938	Th	3	...
*	1358	1939	Tu	21	Feb
	1359	1940	Sa	10	...
X	1360	1941	We	29	Jan
	1361	1942	Mo	19	Jan
	1362	1943	Fr	8	...
XIII	1363	...	Tu	28	Dec
	1364	1944	S	17	...
	1365	1945	Th	6	...
XVI	1366	1946	Mo	25	Nov
	1367	1947	Sa	15	...
XVIII	1368	1948	We	3	...
*	1369	1949	Mo	24	Oct
	1370	1950	Fr	13	...
XXI	1371	1951	Tu	2	...
	1372	1952	S	21	Sep
	1373	1953	Th	10	...
XXIV	1374	1954	Mo	30	Aug
	1375	1955	Sa	20	...
XXVI	1376	1956	We	8	...
*	1377	1957	Mo	29	July
	1378	1958	Fr	18	...
XXIX	1379	1959	Tu	7	...
	1380	1960	S	26	June

XLVII—CYCLE.

	Hijra.	A.D.	Initial Days.		
	1381	1961	Th	15	...
II	1382	1962	Mo	4	...
	1383	1963	Sa	25	May
	1384	1964	We	13	...
V	1385	1965	S	2	...
	1386	1966	Fr	22	April
VII	1387	1967	Tu	11	...
*	1388	1968	S	31	Mar
	1389	1969	Th	20	...
X	1390	1970	Mo	9	...
	1391	1971	Sa	27	Feb
	1392	1972	We	16	...
XIII	1393	1973	S	4	...
	1394	1974	Fr	25	Jan
	139	1975	Tu	14	...
XVI	1396	1976	Sa	3	...
	1397	...	Th	23	Dec
XVIII	1398	1977	Mo	12	...
*	1399	1978	Sa	2	...
	1400	1979	We	21	Nov
XXI	1401	1980	S	9	Nov
	1402	1981	Fr	30	Oct
	1403	1982	Tu	19	...
XXIV	1404	1983	Sa	8	...
	1405	1984	Th	27	Sep
XXVI	1406	1985	Mo	16	...
*	1407	1986	Sa	6	...
	1408	1987	We	26	Aug
XXIX	1409	1988	S	14	...
	1410	1989	Fr	4	...

XLVIII—CYCLE.

	Hijra.	A.D.	Initial Days.		
	1411	1990	Tu	24	July
II	1412	1991	Sa	13	...
	1413	1992	Th	2	...
	1414	1993	Mo	21	June
V	1415	1994	Fr	10	...
	1416	1995	We	31	May
VII	1417	1996	S	19	
*	1418	1997	Fr	9	...
	1419	1998	Tu	28	April
X	1420	1999	Sa	17	...
	1421	2000	Th	6	...
	1422	2001	Mo	26	Mar
XIII	1423	2002	Fr	15	...
	1424	2003	We	5	...
	1425	2004	S	22	Feb
XVI	1426	2005	Th	10	...
	1427	2006	Tu	31	Jan
XVIII	1428	2007	Sa	20	...
*	1429	2008	Th	10	...
	1430	...	Mo	29	Dec
XXI	1431	2009	Fr	18	...
	1432	2010	We	8	...
	1433	2011	S	27	Nov
XXIV	1434	2012	Th	15	...
	1435	2013	Tu	5	...
XXVI	1436	2014	Sa	25	Oct
*	1437	2015	Th	15	...
	1438	2016	Mo	3	...
XXIX	1439	2017	Fr	22	Sep
	1440	2018	We	12	...

TABLE XVII.

General Table of Corresponding Dates.

B. C.	Solar-Year.		Luni-Solar-Year.				Jupiter-Cycles.			Sapt. Rishi.	Sel. Era.
	Kali Yuga.	Initial Day.	Vik Sam	Intercal. Month.	Sak Sal.	Initial Day.	60 Years. S. Sid.	60 Years. Tel.	12 Years.		
60	3042	13 Mar.	...				52.44	51.55	Phâl	17	253
59	43	14 —	...				45	56	Chait	18	254
58	44	14 —	0				46	57	Vais	19	255
* 57	45	13 —	1				47	58	Jyesh	20	256
56	46	13 —	2				48	59	Ashad	21	257
55	47	14 —	3				49	60	Srâv	22	258
54	48	14 —	4				50	52. 1	Bhâd	23	259
* 53	49	13 —	5				51	2	Aswa	24	260
52	50	13 —	6				52	3	Kârt	25	261
51	3051	14 —	7				53	4	Agra	26	262
50	3052	14 Mar.	8				54	5	Paush	27	263
* 49	53	13 —	9				55	6	Mâgh	28	264
48	54	14 —	10				56	7	Phâl	29	265
47	55	14 —	11				57	8	Chait	30	266
46	56	14 —	12				58	9	Vais	31	267
* 45	57	13 —	13				59	10	Jyesh	32	268
44	58	14 —	14				60	11	Ashad	33	269
43	59	14 —	15				53. 1	12	Srâv	34	270
42	60	14 —	16				2	13	Bhâd	35	271
* 41	3061	13 —	17				3	14	Aswa	36	272
40	3062	14 Mar.	18				4	15	Kârt	37	273
39	63	14 —	19				5	16	Agra	38	274
38	64	14 —	20				6	17	Paush	39	275
* 37	65	13 —	21				7	18	Mâgh	40	276
36	66	14 —	22				8	19	Phâl	41	277
35	67	14 —	23				9	20	Chait	42	278
34	68	14 —	24				10	21	Vais	43	279
* 33	69	13 —	25				11	22	Jyesh	44	280
32	70	14 —	26				12	23	Ashad	45	281
31	3071	14 —	27				14	52.24	Bhâd	46	282

TABLE XVII.—(Continued.)

General Table of Corresponding Dates.

B. C.	Solar-Year. Kali Yuga.	Solar-Year. Initial Day.	Luni-Solar-Year. Vik Sam	Luni-Solar-Year. Intercal. Month.	Luni-Solar-Year. Sak Sal.	Luni-Solar-Year. Initial Day.	Jupiter-Cycles. 60 Years. S. Sid.	Jupiter-Cycles. 60 Years. Tel.	Jupiter-Cycles. 12 Years.	Sapt. Rishi.	Sel. Era.	Gupta Kål.
30	3072	14 Mar	28				53.15	52.25	Aswa	47	283	
*29	73	13 —	29				16	26	Kårt	48	284	
28	74	14 —	30				17	27	Agra	49	285	
27	75	14 —	31				18	28	Paush	50	286	
26	76	14 —	32				19	29	Mågh	51	287	
*25	77	13 —	33				20	30	Phål	52	288	
24	78	14 —	34				21	31	Chait	53	289	
23	79	14 —	35				22	32	Vais	54	290	
22	80	14 —	36				23	33	Jyesh	55	291	
*21	3081	13 —	37				24	34	Ashad	56	292	
20	3082	14 Mar	38				25	35	Srâv	57	293	
19	83	14 —	39				26	36	Bhåd	58	294	
18	84	14 —	40				27	37	Aswa	59	295	
*17	85	13 —	41				28	38	Kårt	60	296	
16	86	14 —	42				29	39	Agra	61	297	
15	87	14 —	43				30	40	Paush	62	298	
14	88	14 —	44				31	41	Mågh	63	299	
*13	89	13 —	45				32	42	Phål	64	300	
12	90	14 —	46				33	43	Chait	65	301	
11	3091	14 —	47				34	44	Vais	66	302	
10	3092	14 Mar	48				35	45	Jyesh	67	303	
*9	93	13 —	49				36	46	Ashad	68	304	
8	94	14 —	50				37	47	Srâv	69	305	
7	95	14 —	51				38	48	Bhåd	70	306	
6	96	14 —	52				39	49	Aswa	71	307	
*5	97	13 —	53				40	50	Kårt	72	308	
4	98	14 —	54				41	51	Agra	73	309	
3	3099	14 —	55				42	52	Paush	74	310	
2	3100	14 —	56				43	53	Mågh	75	311	
*1	3101	13 —	57				44	54	Phål	76	312	

TABLE XVII.—(Continued.)

General Table of Corresponding Dates.

A. D.	Solar-Year. Kali Yuga.	Solar-Year. Initial Day.	Luni-Solar-Year. Vik Sam	Luni-Solar-Year. Intercal. Month.	Luni-Solar-Year. Sak Sal.	Luni-Solar-Year. Initial Day.	Jupiter-Cycles. 60 Years. S. Sid.	Jupiter-Cycles. 60 Years. Tel.	Jupiter-Cycles. 12 Years.	Sapt. Rishi.	Sel. Era.	Gupt. Kâl.
1	3102	14 Mar	58	...			53. 45	52. 55	Chait	77	313	
2	03	14 —	59	Srâv			46	56	Vais	78	314	
3	04	14 —	60	...			47	57	Jyesh	79	315	
*4	05	13 —	61	...			48	58	Ashad	80	316	
5	06	14 —	62	Ashad			49	59	Srâv	81	317	
6	07	14 —	63	...			50	60	Bhâd	82	318	
7	08	14 —	64	...			51	53. 1	Aswa	83	319	
*8	09	14 —	65	Vais			52	2	Kârt	84	320	
9	10	14 —	66	...			53	3	Agra	85	321	
10	3111	14 —	67	Srâv			54	4	Paush	86	322	
11	3112	14 Mar	68	...			55	5	Mâgh	87	323	
*12	13	14 —	69	...			56	6	Phâl	88	324	
13	14	14 —	70	Ashad			57	7	Chait	89	325	
14	15	14 —	71	...			58	8	Vais	90	326	
15	16	14 —	72	Jyesh			59	9	Jyesh	91	327	
*16	17	14 —	73	...			60	10	Ashad	92	328	
17	18	14 —	74	...			54. 1	11	Srâv	93	329	
18	†19	14 —	75	Kar Phal			2	12	Bhâd	94	330	
19	20	14 —	76	...			3	13	Aswa	95	331	
*20	3121	14 —	77	...			4	14	Kârt	96	332	
21	3122	14 Mar	78	Srâv			5	15	Agra	97	333	
22	23	14 —	79	...			6	16	Paush	98	334	
23	24	14 —	80	...			7	17	Mâgh	99	335	
*24	25	14 —	81	Ashad			8	18	Phâl	100	336	
25	26	14 —	82	...			9	19	Chait	1	337	
26	27	14 —	83	...			10	20	Vais	2	338	
27	28	14 —	84	Vais			11	21	Jyesh	3	339	
*28	29	14 —	85	...			12	22	Ashad	4	340	
29	30	14 —	86	Srâv			13	23	Srâv	5	341	
30	3131	14 —	87	...			14	24	Bhâd	6	342	

† Agrahayana omitted.

TABLE XVII.—(Continued)

General Table of Corresponding Dates

A D	Solar-Year: Kali Yuga	Solar-Year: Initial Day	Luni Solar Year: Vik Sam	Luni Solar Year: Intercal Month	Luni Solar Year: Sak Sal.	Luni Solar Year: Initial Day	Jupiter-Cycles: 60 Years: S Sid	Jupiter-Cycles: 60 Years: Tel	Jupiter-Cycles: 12 Years	Sapt. Rishi.	Sel Era	Gupt. Kāl
31	3132	15 Mar	88				54 15	53 25	Aswa	7	343	
*32	33	14 —	89	Ashad			16	26	Kārt	8	344	
33	34	15 —	90				17	27	Agra	9	345	
34	35	15 —	91				18	28	Paush	10	346	
35	36	15 —	92	Jyesh			19	29	Māgh	11	347	
*36	37	14 —	93				20	30	Phāl	12	348	
37	†38	15 —	94	{ Aswa Phal }			21	31	Chait	13	349	
38	39	15 —	95				22	32	Vais	14	350	
39	40	15 —	96				23	33	Jyesh	15	351	
*40	3141	14 —	97	Srāv			24	34	Ashad	16	352	
41	3142	14 Mar	98				25	35	Srāv	17	353	
42	43	14 —	99				26	36	Bhād	18	354	
43	44	15 —	100	Ashad			27	37	Aswa	19	355	
*44	45	14 —	101				28	38	Kārt	20	356	
45	46	15 —	102				29	39	Agra	21	357	
46	47	15 —	103	Vais			30	40	Paush	22	358	
47	48	15 —	104				31	41	Māgh	23	359	
*48	49	14 —	105	Srāv			32	42	Phāl	24	360	
49	50	15 —	106				33	43	Chait	25	361	
50	3151	15 —	107				34	44	Vais	26	362	
51	3152	15 Mar	108	Ashad			35	45	Jyesh	27	363	
*52	53	14 —	109				36	46	Ashad	28	364	
53	54	15 —	110				37	47	Srāv	29	365	
54	55	15 —	111				38	48	Bhād	30	366	
55	56	15 —	112				40	49	Kārt	31	367	
*56	‡57	14 —	113	{ Bhād Phāl }			41	50	Agra	32	368	
57	58	15 —	114				42	51	Paush	33	369	
58	59	15 —	115				43	52	Māgh	34	370	
59	60	15 —	116	Srāv			44	53	Phāl	35	371	
*60	3161	14 —	117	..			45	54	Chait	36	372	

† Agrahyana omitted ‡ Pausha omitted.

TABLE XVII.—(Continued.)

General Table of Corresponding Dates.

A. D.	Solar-Year. Kali Yuga.	Solar-Year. Initial Day.	Luni-Solar Year. Vik Sam	Luni-Solar Year. Intercal Month.	Luni-Solar Year. Sak Sal.	Luni-Solar Year. Initial Day.	Jupiter Cycles. 60 Years. S. Sid.	Jupiter Cycles. 60 Years. Tel.	Jupiter Cycles. 12 Years.	Sapt. Rishi.	Sel Era.	Gupt. Kál.
61	3162	15 Mar	118	...			46	53. 55	Vais	37	373	
62	63	15 —	119	Ashad			46	56	Jyesh	38	374	
63	64	15 —	120	...			47	57	Ashad	39	375	
*64	65	14 —	121	...			48	58	Srâv	40	376	
65	66	15 —	122	Chait			49	59	Bhâd	41	377	
66	67	15 —	123	...			50	60	Aswa	42	378	
67	68	15 —	124	Srâv			51	54. 1	Kârt	43	379	
*68	69	14 —	125	...			52	2	Agra	44	380	
69	70	15 —	126	...			53	3	Paush	45	381	
70	3171	15 —	127	Ashad			54	4	Mâgh	46	382	
71	3172	15 Mar	128	...			55	6	Phâl	47	383	
*72	73	14 —	129	...			56	6	Chait	48	384	
73	74	15 —	130	Vais			57	7	Vais	49	385	
74	75	15 —	131	...			58	8	Jyesh	50	386	
75	76	15 —	132	Bhâd			59	9	Ashad	51	387	
*76	77	14 —	133	...			1. 1	10	Srâv	52	388	
77	78	15 —	134	...			2	11	Bhâd	53	389	
78	79	15 —	135	...	0	Sa 14 Mar	3	12	Aswa	54	390	
79	80	15 —	136	Srâv	1	Th 18 Feb	3	13	Kârt	55	391	
*80	3181	14 —	137	...	2	Th 9 Mar	4	14	Agra	56	392	
81	3182	15 Mar	138	...	3	Mo 26 Feb	5	15	Paush	57	393	
82	83	15 —	139	Jyesh	4	Fr 15 Feb	6	16	Mâgh	58	394	
83	84	15 —	140	...	5	Th 6 Mar	7	17	Phâl	59	395	
*84	85	14 —	141	...	6	Mo 23 Feb	8	18	Chait	60	396	
85	86	14 —	142	Chait	7	We 12 Feb	9	19	Vais	61	397	
86	87	15 —	143	...	8	Fr 3 Mar	10	20	Jyesh	62	398	
87	88	15 —	144	Srâv	9	Tu 20 Feb	11	21	Ashad	63	399	
*88	89	14 —	145	...	10	Th 11 Mar	12	22	Srâv	64	400	
89	90	15 —	146	...	11	Sa 28 Feb	13	23	Bhâd	65	401	
90	3191	15 —	147	Ashad	12	We 17 Feb	1. 15	54. 24	Aswa	66	402	

TABLE XVII.—(Continued.)

General Table of Corresponding Dates.

A. D.	Solar-Year.		Luni-Solar-Year.				Jupiter-Cycles.			Sapt. Rishi.	Sel. Era.	Gupt. Kâl.
							60 Years.					
	Kali Yuga.	Initial Day.	Vik. Sam	Intercal Month.	Sak Sal.	Initial Days.	S. Sid.	Tel.	12 Years.			
91	3192	15 Mar	148	...	13	Tu 8 Mar	1. 16	54. 25	Kârt	67	403	
*92	93	15 —	149	...	14	Sa 25 Feb	17	26	Agra	68	404	
93	94	15 —	150	Vais	15	Th 14 Feb	18	27	Paush	69	405	
94	95	15 —	151	...	16	We 5 Mar	19	28	Mâgh	70	406	
95	96	15 —	152	Bhâd	17	Sa 21 Feb	20	29	Phâl	71	407	
*96	97	15 —	153	...	18	Sa 12 Mar	21	30	Chait	72	408	
97	98	15 —	154	...	19	We 1 Mar	22	31	Vais	73	409	
98	3199	15 —	155	Srâv	20	S 18 Feb	23	32	Jyesh	74	410	
99	3200	15 —	156	...	21	Sa 9 Mar	24	33	Ashad	75	411	
*100	3201	15 —	157	...	22	We 26 Feb	25	34	Srâv	76	412	
101	3202	15 Mar	158	Jyesh	23	Mo 15 Feb	26	35	Bhad	77	413	
102	03	15 —	159	...	24	S 6 Mar	27	36	Aswa	78	414	
103	04	15 —	160	...	25	Th 23 Feb	28	37	Kârt	79	415	
*104	05	15 —	161	Chait	26	Mo 12 Feb	29	38	Agra	80	416	
105	06	15 —	162	...	27	Mo 3 Mar	30	39	Paush	81	417	
106	07	15 —	163	Srâv	28	Fr 20 Feb	31	40	Mâgh	82	418	
107	08	15 —	164	...	29	Th 11 Mar	32	41	Phâl	83	419	
*108	09	15 —	165	...	30	Mo 28 Feb	33	42	Chait	84	420	
109	10	15 —	166	Ashad	31	Sa 17 Feb	34	43	Vais	85	421	
110	3211	15 —	167	...	32	Fr 8 Mar	35	44	Jyesh	86	422	
111	3212	15 Mar	168	...	33	Tu 25 Feb	36	45	Ashad	87	423	
*112	13	15 —	169	Vais	34	Sa 14 Feb	37	46	Srâv	88	424	
113	14	15 —	170	...	35	Sa 5 Mar	38	47	Bhâd	89	425	
114	15	15 —	171	Bhâd	36	Tu 21 Feb	39	48	Aswa	90	426	
115	16	15 —	172	...	37	Mo 12 Mar	40	49	Kârt	91	427	
*116	17	15 —	173	...	38	Sa 1 Mar	41	50	Agra	92	428	
117	18	15 —	174	Srâv	39	We 18 Feb	42	51	Paush	93	429	
118	19	15 —	175	...	40	Tu 9 Mar	43	52	Mâgh	94	430	
119	20	15 —	176	...	41	Sa 26 Feb	44	53	Phâl	95	431	
*120	3221	15 —	177	Jyesh	42	We 15 Feb	1. 45	54. 54	Chait	96	432	

TABLE XVII.—(Continued.)

General Table of Corresponding Dates.

A.D.	Solar-Year.		Luni-Solar-Year.				Jupiter-Cycles.			Sapt. Rishi.	Sel. Era.	Gupt. Kál.
	Kali Yuga.	Initial Day.	Vik. Sam	Intercal Month.	Sak Sal.	Initial Day.	60 Years. S. Sid.	60 Years. Tel.	12 Years.			
121	3222	15 Mar	178	...	43	We 6 Mar	1. 46	54. 55	Vais	97	433	
122	23	15 —	179	† ...	44	S 23 Feb	47	56	Jyesh	98	434	
123	24	15 —	180	Chait	45	Th 12 Feb	48	57	Ashad	99	435	
*124	25	15 —	181	...	46	Th 3 Mar	49	58	Srâv	100	436	
125	26	15 —	182	Srâv	47	Mo 20 Feb	50	59	Bhâd	1	437	
126	27	15 —	183	...	48	S 11 Mar	51	60	Aswa	2	438	
127	28	15 —	184	...	49	Mo 28 Feb	52	55. 1	Kârt	3	439	
*128	29	15 —	185	Ashad	50	Fr 17 Feb	53	2	Agra	4	440	
129	30	15 —	186	...	51	Mo 8 Mar	54	3	Paush	5	441	
130	3231	15 —	187	...	52	Fr 25 Feb	55	4	Mâgh	6	442	
131	3232	15 Mar	188	Vais	53	Tu 14 Feb	56	5	Phâl	7	443	
*132	33	15 —	189	...	54	S 5 Mar	57	6	Chait	8	444	
133	34	15 —	190	Bhâd	55	Fr 21 Feb	58	7	Vais	9	445	
134	35	15 —	191	...	56	Th 12 Mar	59	8	Jyesh	10	446	
135	36	15 —	192	..	57	Mo 1 Mar	60	9	Ashad	11	447	
*136	37	15 —	193	Srâv	58	Fr 18 Feb	2. 1	10	Srâv	12	448	
137	38	15 —	194	...	59	Fr 9 Mar	2	11	Bhâd	13	449	
138	39	15 —	195	...	60	Tu 26 Feb	3	12	Aswa	14	450	
139	40	15 —	196	Jyesh	61	Tu 15 Feb	4	13	Kârt	15	451	
*140	3241	15 —	197	...	62	Sa 6 Mar	6	14	Paush	16	452	
‡141	3242	15 Mar	198	Aswa	63	We 23 Feb	7	15	Mâgh	17	453	
142	43	15 —	199	...	64	We 12 Feb	8	16	Phâl	18	454	
143	44	15 —	200	...	65	Sa 3 Mar	9	17	Chait	19	455	
*144	45	15 —	201	Srâv	66	Sa 20 Feb	10	18	Vais	20	456	
145	46	15 —	202	...	67	We 11 Mar	11	19	Jyesh	21	457	
146	47	15 —	203	...	68	We 28 Feb	12	20	Ashad	22	458	
147	48	15 —	204	Jyesh	69	S 17 Feb	13	21	Srâv	23	459	
*148	49	15 —	205	...	70	Th 8 Mar	14	22	Bhâd	24	460	
149	50	15 —	206	...	71	Mo 25 Feb	15	23	Aswa	25	461	
150	3251	15 —	207	Vais	72	Mo 14 Feb	2. 16	55. 24	Kârt	26	462	

† Kartik omitted, and Aswa intercalary. ‡ Margasiras, or Agrahayana, omitted.

TABLE XVII.—(Continued.)

General Table of Corresponding Dates.

A. D.	Solar-Year.		Luni-Solar-Year.				Jupiter-Cycles.			Sapt. Rishi.	Sel. Era.	Gupt. Kâl.
	Kali Yuga.	Initial Day.	Vik Sam	Intercal Month.	Sak Sal.	Initial Day.	60 Years. S. Sid.	60 Years. Tel.	12 Years.			
151	3252	15 Mar	208	...	73	Th 5 Mar	2. 17	55. 25	Agra	27	463	
*152	53	15 —	209	Bhâd	74	We 21 Feb	18	26	Paush	28	464	
153	54	15 —	210	...	75	We 12 Mar	19	27	Mâgh	29	465	
154	55	15 —	211	...	76	Th 1 Mar	20	28	Phâl	30	466	
155	56	15 —	212	Ashad	77	Mo 18 Feb	21	29	Chait	31	467	
*156	57	15 —	213	...	78	Mo 9 Mar	22	30	Vais	32	468	
157	58	15 —	214	...	79	Fr 26 Feb	23	31	Jyesh	33	469	
158	59	15 —	215	Jyesh	80	Tu 15 Feb	24	32	Ashad	34	470	
159	60	15 —	216	...	81	Mo 6 Mar	25	33	Srâv	35	471	
*160	3261	15 —	217	Aswa	82	Fr 23 Feb	26	34	Bhâd	36	472	
161	3262	15 Mar	218	...	83	Fr 14 Mar	27	35	Aswa	37	473	
162	63	15 —	219	...	84	Tu 3 Mar	28	36	Kârt	38	474	
163	64	15 —	220	Srâv	85	Sa 20 Feb	29	37	Agra	39	475	
*164	65	15 —	221	...	86	Sa 11 Mar	30	38	Paush	40	476	
165	66	15 —	222	...	87	We 28 Feb	31	39	Mâgh	41	477	
166	67	15 —	223	Jyesh	88	S 17 Feb	32	40	Phâl	42	478	0
167	68	15 —	224	...	89	Sa 8 Mar	33	41	Chait	43	479	1
*168	69	15 —	225	...	90	We 25 Feb	34	42	Vais	44	480	2
169	70	15 —	226	Vais	91	Mo 14 Feb	35	43	Jyesh	45	481	3
170	3271	15 —	227	...	92	S 5 Mar	36	44	Ashad	46	482	4
171	3272	15 Mar	228	Bhâd	93	We 21 Feb	37	45	Srâv	47	483	5
*172	73	15 —	229	...	94	We 12 Mar	83	46	Bhâd	48	484	6
173	74	16 —	230	...	95	S 1 Mar	39	47	Aswa	49	485	7
174	75	16 —	231	Ashad	96	Th 18 Feb	40	48	Kârt	50	486	8
175	76	16 —	232	...	97	We 9 Mar	41	49	Agra	51	487	9
*176	77	15 —	233	...	98	S 26 Feb	42	50	Paush	52	488	10
177	78	16 —	234	Jyesh	99	Fr 15 Feb	43	51	Mâgh	53	489	11
178	79	16 —	235	...	100	Th 6 Mar	44	52	Phâl	54	490	12
179	80	16 —	236	Aswa	101	Mo 23 Feb	45	53	Chait	55	491	13
*180	3281	15 —	237	...	102	Mo 14 Mar	2. 46	55. 54	Vais	56	492	14

TABLE XVII.—(Continued.)

General Table of Corresponding Dates.

A. D.	Solar-Year. Kali Yuga.	Solar-Year. Initial Day.	Luni-Solar-Year. Vik Sam	Luni-Solar-Year. Intercal Month.	Luni-Solar-Year. Sak Sal.	Luni-Solar-Year. Initial Day.	Jupiter-Cycles. 60 Years. S. Sid.	Jupiter-Cycles. 60 Years. Tel.	Jupiter-Cycles. 12 Years.	Sapt. Rishi.	Sel. Era.	Gupt. Kâl.
181	3282	16 Mar	238	...	103	Fr 3 Mar	2. 47	55. 55	Jyesh	67	493	15
182	83	16 —	239	Srâv	104	Tu 20 Feb	48	56	Ashad	68	494	16
183	84	16 —	240	...	105	Mo 11 Mar	49	57	Srâv	69	495	17
*184	85	15 —	241	...	106	Fr 28 Feb	50	58	Bhâd	60	496	18
185	86	16 —	242	Jyesh	107	We 17 Feb	51	59	Aswa	61	497	19
186	87	16 —	243	...	108	Tu 8 Mar	52	60	Kârt	62	498	20
187	88	16 —	244	...	109	Sa 25 Feb	53	56. 1	Agran	63	499	21
*188	89	15 —	245	Vais	110	We 14 Feb	54	2	Paush	64	500	22
189	90	16 —	246	...	111	We 5 Mar	55	3	Mâgh	65	501	23
190	3291	16 —	247	Bhâd	112	Sa 21 Feb	56	4	Phâl	66	502	24
191	3292	16 Mar	248	...	113	Fr 12 Mar	57	5	Chait	67	503	25
*192	93	15 —	249	...	114	We 1 Mar	58	6	Vais	68	504	26
193	94	16 —	250	Ashad	115	S 18 Feb	59	7	Jyesh	69	505	27
194	95	16 —	251	...	116	Sa 9 Mar	60	8	Ashad	70	506	28
195	96	16 —	252	...	117	We 26 Feb	3. 1	9	Srâv	71	507	29
*196	97	15 —	253	Jyesh	118	S 15 Feb	2	10	Bhâd	72	508	30
197	98	16 —	254	...	119	S 6 Mar	3	11	Aswa	73	509	31
198	3299	16 —	255	Aswa	120	Th 23 Feb	4	12	Kârt	74	510	32
199	3300	16 —	256	...	121	We 14 Mar	5	13	Agra	75	511	33
*200	3301	15 —	257	...	122	Mo 3 Mar	6	14	Paush	76	512	34
201	3302	16 Mar	258	Srâv	123	Fr 20 Feb	7	15	Mâgh	77	513	35
202	03	16 —	259	...	124	Th 11 Mar	8	16	Phâl	78	514	36
203	04	16 —	260	...	125	Mo 28 Feb	9	17	Chait	79	515	37
*204	05	15 —	261	Jyesh	126	Fr 17 Feb	10	18	Vais	80	516	38
205	06	16 —	262	...	127	Fr 8 Mar	11	19	Jyesh	81	517	39
206	07	16 —	263	...	128	Tu 25 Feb	12	20	Ashad	82	518	40
207	08	16 —	264	Chait	129	Sa 14 Feb	13	21	Srâv	83	519	41
*208	09	15 —	265	...	130	Sa 5 Mar	14	22	Bhâd	84	520	42
209	10	16 —	266	Srâv	131	Tu 21 Feb	15	23	Aswa	85	521	43
210	3311	16 —	267	...	132	Mo 12 Mar	3. 16	56. 24	Kârt	86	522	44

TABLE XVII.—(Continued.)

General Table of Corresponding Dates.

A. D.	Solar-Year.		Luni-Solar-Year.				Jupiter-Cycles.			Sapt. Rishi.	Sel. Era.	Gupt. Kâl.
	Kali Yuga.	Initial Day.	Vik Sam	Intercal Month.	Sak Sal.	Initial Day.	60 Years. S. Sid.	60 Years. Tel.	12 Years.			
211	3312	16 Mar	268	...	133	Fr 1 Mar	S. 17	56. 25	Agra	87	523	45
* 212	13	16 —	269	Ashad	134	Tu 18 Feb	18	26	Paush	88	524	46
213	14	16 —	270	...	135	Tu 9 Mar	19	27	Mâgh	89	525	47
214	15	16 —	271	...	136	Sa 26 Feb	20	28	Phâl	90	526	48
215	16	16 —	272	Jyesh	137	We 15 Feb	21	29	Chait	91	527	49
* 216	17	16 —	273	...	138	We 6 Mar	22	30	Vais	92	528	50
217	18	16 —	274	Aswa	139	S 23 Feb	23	31	Jyesh	93	529	51
218	19	16 —	275	...	140	Sa 14 Mar	24	32	Ashad	94	530	52
219	20	16 —	276	...	141	We 3 Mar	25	33	Srâv	95	531	53
* 220	3321	16 —	277	Srâv	142	S 20 Feb	26	34	Bhâd	96	532	54
221	3322	16 Mar	278	...	143	S 11 Mar	27	35	Aswa	97	533	55
222	23	16 —	279	...	144	Th 28 Feb	28	36	Kârt	98	534	56
223	24	16 —	280	Jyesh	145	Mo 17 Feb	29	37	Agra	99	535	57
* 224	25	16 —	281	...	146	Mo 8 Mar	30	38	Paush	100	536	58
225	26	16 —	282	...	147	Fr 25 Feb	32	39	Phâl	1	537	59
226	27	16 —	283	Chait	148	Tu 14 Feb	33	40	Chait	2	538	60
227	28	16 —	284	...	149	Mo 5 Mar	34	41	Vais	3	539	61
* 228	29	16 —	285	Srâv	150	Th 21 Feb	35	42	Jyesh	4	540	62
229	30	16 —	286	...	151	Th 12 Mar	36	43	Ashad	5	541	63
230	3331	16 —	287	...	152	Mo 1 Mar	37	44	Srâv	6	542	64
231	3332	16 Mar	288	Ashad	153	Fr 18 Feb	38	45	Bhâd	7	543	65
* 232	33	16 —	289	...	154	Fr 9 Mar	39	46	Aswa	8	544	69
233	34	16 —	290	...	155	Tu 26 Feb	40	47	Kârt	9	545	67
234	35	16 —	291	Vais	156	Tu 15 Feb	41	48	Agra	10	546	68
235	36	16 —	292	...	157	Mo 6 Mar	42	49	Paush	11	547	69
* 236	37	16 —	293	Bhâd	158	Fr 23 Feb	43	50	Mâgh	12	548	70
237	38	16 —	294	...	159	Fr 14 Mar	44	51	Phâl	13	549	71
238	39	16 —	295	...	160	Tu 3 Mar	45	52	Chait	14	550	72
239	40	16 —	296	Srâv	161	We 20 Feb	46	53	Vais	15	...	73
*240	3341	16 —	297	...	162	We 11 Mar	S. 47	56. 54	Jyesh	16	...	74

TABLE XVII.—(Continued.)

General Table of Corresponding Dates.

A. D.	Solar-Year. Kali Yuga.	Solar-Year. Initial Day.	Luni-Solar-Year. Vik Sam	Luni-Solar-Year. Intercal Month.	Luni-Solar-Year. Sak Sal.	Luni-Solar-Year. Initial Day.	Jupiter-Cycles. 60 Years. S. Sid.	Jupiter-Cycles. 60 Years. Tel.	Jupiter-Cycles. 12 Years.	Sapt. Rishi.	Chedi Sam.	Gupt. Kâl.
241	3342	16 Mar	298	...	163	S 28 Feb	3.48	56.55	Ashad	17	...	75
242	43	16 —	299	Jyesh	164	We 17 Feb	49	56	Srâv	18	...	76
243	44	16 —	300	...	165	We 8 Mar	50	57	Bhâd	19	...	77
*244	45	16 —	301	...	166	S 25 Feb	51	58	Aswa	20	...	78
245	46	16 —	302	Chait	167	Fr 14 Feb	52	59	Kârt	21	...	79
246	47	16 —	303	...	168	Th 5 Mar	53	60	Agra	22	...	80
247	48	16 —	304	Srâv	169	S 21 Feb	54	57. 1	Paush	23	...	81
*248	49	16 —	305	...	170	S 12 Mar	55	2	Mâgh	24	...	82
249	50	16 —	306	...	171	Th 1 Mar	56	3	Phâl	25	0	83
250	3351	16 —	307	Ashad	172	Mo 18 Feb	57	4	Chait	26	1	84
251	3352	16 Mar	308	...	173	S 9 Mar	58	5	Vais	27	2	85
*252	53	16 —	309	...	174	Th 26 Feb	59	6	Jyesh	28	3	86
253	54	16 —	310	Vais	175	Tu 15 Feb	60	7	Ashad	29	4	87
254	55	16 —	311	...	176	Mo 6 Mar	4. 1	8	Srâv	30	5	88
255	56	16 —	312	Bhâd	177	Fr 23 Feb	2	9	Bhâd	31	6	89
*256	57	16 —	313	...	178	Fr 14 Mar	3	10	Aswa	32	7	90
257	58	16 —	314	...	179	Tu 3 Mar	4	11	Kârt	33	8	91
258	59	16 —	315	Srâv	180	Sa 20 Feb	5	12	Agra	34	9	92
259	60	16 —	316	...	181	Fr 11 Mar	6	13	Paush	35	10	93
*260	3361	16 —	317	...	182	Tu 28 Feb	7	14	Mâgh	36	11	94
261	3362	16 Mar	318	Jyesh	183	S 17 Feb	8	15	Phâl	37	12	95
262	63	16 —	319	...	184	Sa 8 Mar	9	16	Chait	38	13	96
263	64	16 —	320	†...	185	We 25 Feb	10	17	Vais	39	14	97
*264	65	16 —	321	Chait	186	S 14 Feb	11	18	Jyesh	40	15	98
265	66	16 —	322	...	187	S 5 Mar	12	19	Ashad	41	16	99
266	67	16 —	323	Srâv	188	We 21 Feb	13	20	Srâv	42	17	100
267	68	16 —	324	...	189	Tu 12 Mar	14	21	Bhâd	43	18	101
*268	69	16 —	325	...	190	S 1 Mar	15	22	Aswa	44	19	102
269	70	16 —	326	Ashad	191	Th 18 Feb	16	23	Kârt	45	20	103
270	3371	17 —	327	...	192	We 9 Mar	4.17	57.24	Agra	46	21	104

† Kartika omitted, and Kartika intercalary.

TABLE XVII.—(Continued.)

General Table of Corresponding Dates.

A. D.	Solar-Year. Kali Yuga.	Solar-Year. Initial Day.	Luni-Solar-Year. Vik Sam	Luni-Solar-Year. Intercal Month.	Luni-Solar-Year. Sak Sal	Luni-Solar-Year. Initial Day.	Jupiter-Cycles. 60 Years. S. Sid.	Jupiter-Cycles. 60 Years. Tel.	Jupiter-Cycles. 12 Years.	Sapt. Rishi.	Chedi Sam.	Gupt. Kál.
271	3372	17 Mar	328	...	193	S 26 Feb	4.18	57.25	Paush	47	22	105
* 272	73	16 —	329	Vais	194	Th 15 Feb	19	26	Mágh	48	23	106
273	74	17 —	330	...	195	Th 6 Mar	20	27	Phál	49	24	107
274	75	17 —	331	Bhád	196	Mo 23 Feb	21	28	Chait	50	25	108
275	76	17 —	332	...	197	Mo 14 Mar	22	29	Vais	51	26	109
* 276	77	16 —	333	...	198	Fr 3 Mar	23	30	Jyesh	52	27	110
277	78	17 —	334	Sráv	199	Tu 20 Feb	24	31	Ashad	53	28	111
278	79	17 —	335	...	200	Mo 11 Mar	25	32	Sráv	54	29	112
279	80	17 —	336	...	201	Fr 28 Feb	26	33	Bhád	55	30	113
* 280	3381	16 —	337	Jyesh	202	Tu 17 Feb	27	34	Aswa	56	31	114
281	3382	17 Mar	338	...	203	Tu 8 Mar	28	35	Kárt	57	32	115
282	83	17 —	339	†...	204	Sa 25 Feb	29	36	Agra	58	33	116
283	84	17 —	340	Chait	205	We 14 Feb	30	37	Paush	59	34	117
* 284	85	16 —	341	...	206	We 5 Mar	31	38	Mágh	60	35	118
285	86	17 —	342	Sráv	207	Sa 21 Feb	32	39	Phál	61	36	119
286	87	17 —	343	...	208	Fr 12 Mar	33	40	Chait	62	37	120
287	88	17 —	344	...	209	Tu 1 Mar	34	41	Vais	63	38	121
* 288	89	16 —	345	Jyesh	210	Sa 18 Feb	35	42	Jyesh	64	39	122
289	90	17 —	346	...	211	Sa 9 Mar	36	43	Ashad	66	40	123
290	3391	17 —	347	...	212	We 26 Feb	37	44	Sráv	67	41	124
291	3392	17 Mar	348	Vais	213	S 15 Feb	38	45	Bhád	67	42	125
* 292	93	16 —	349	...	214	S 6 Mar	39	46	Aswa	68	43	126
293	94	17 —	350	Bhád	215	Th 23 Feb	40	47	Kárt	69	44	127
294	95	17 —	351	...	216	We 14 Mar	41	48	Agra	70	45	128
295	96	17 —	352	...	217	S 3 Mar	42	49	Paush	71	46	129
* 296	97	16 —	353	Ashad	218	Th 20 Feb	43	50	Mágh	72	47	130
297	98	17 —	354	...	219	Th 11 Mar	44	51	Phál	73	48	131
298	99	17 —	355	...	220	Mo 28 Feb	45	52	Chait	74	49	132
299	3400	17 —	356	Jyesh	221	Fr 17 Feb	46	53	Vais	75	50	133
* 300	3401	16 —	357	...	222	Fr 8 Mar	4.47	57.54	Jyesh	76	51	134

† Agrahayna omitted and Aswina intercalary.

TABLE XVII.—(Continued.)

General Table of Corresponding Dates.

A. D.	Solar-Year. Kali Yuga.	Solar-Year. Initial Day.	Luni-Solar-Year. Vik. Sam	Luni-Solar-Year. Intercal Month.	Luni-Solar-Year. Sak Sal.	Luni-Solar-Year. Initial Day.	Jupiter-Cycles. 60 Years. S. Sid.	Jupiter-Cycles. 60 Years. Tel.	Jupiter-Cycles. 12 Years.	Sapt. Rishi.	Chedi Sam.	Gupt. Kâl.
801	3402	17 Mar	358	Aswa	223	Tu 26 Feb	4.48	57.55	Ashad	77	52	135
802	03	17 —	359	...	224	Mo 16 Mar	49	56	Srâv	78	53	136
803	04	17 —	360	...	225	Fr 5 Mar	50	57	Bhâd	79	54	137
*804	05	16 —	361	Srâv	226	Mo 21 Feb	51	58	Aswa	80	55	138
805	06	17 —	362	...	227	Mo 12 Mar	52	59	Kârt	81	56	139
806	07	17 —	363	...	228	Fr 1 Mar	53	60	Agra	82	57	140
807	08	17 —	364	Jyesh	229	Tu 18 Feb	54	58.1	Paush	83	58	141
*808	09	16 —	365	...	230	Tu 9 Mar	55	2	Mâgh	84	59	142
809	10	17 —	366	...	231	Sa 26 Feb	56	3	Phâl	85	60	143
810	3411	17 —	367	Vais	232	We 15 Feb	● 58	4	● Vais	86	61	144
811	3412	17 Mar	368	...	233	S 6 Mar	59	5	Jyesh	87	62	145
*812	13	16 —	369	Bhâd	234	Sa 23 Feb	60	6	Ashad	88	63	146
813	14	17 —	370	...	235	Sa 14 Mar	5. 1	7	Srâv	89	64	147
814	15	17 —	371	...	236	We 3 Mar	2	8	Bhâd	90	65	148
815	16	17 —	372	Vais	237	S 20 Feb	3	9	Aswa	91	66	149
*816	17	16 —	373	...	238	S 11 Mar	4	10	Kârt	92	67	150
817	18	17 —	374	...	239	Th 28 Feb	5	11	Agra	93	68	151
818	19	17 —	375	Jyesh	240	Mo 17 Feb	6	12	Paush	94	69	152
819	20	17 —	376	...	241	S 8 Mar	7	13	Mâgh	95	70	153
*820	3421	17 —	377	Aswa	242	Th 25 Feb	8	14	Phâl	96	71	154
821	3422	—	378	...	243	Th 16 Mar	9	15	Chait	97	72	155
822	23	—	379	...	244	Mo 5 Mar	10	16	Vais	98	73	156
823	24	—	380	Srâv	245	Th 21 Feb	11	17	Jyesh	99	74	157
*824	25	—	381	...	246	Th 12 Mar	12	18	Ashad	100	75	158
825	26	—	382	...	247	Mo 1 Mar	13	19	Srâv	1	76	159
826	27	—	383	Jyesh	248	Fr 18 Feb	14	20	Bhâd	2	77	160
827	28	—	384	...	249	Th 9 Mar	15	21	Aswa	3	78	161
*828	29	—	385	...	250	Mo 26 Feb	16	22	Kârt	4	79	162
829	30	—	386	Vais	251	Sa 15 Feb	17	23	Agra	5	80	163
830	3431	—	387	...	252	Fr 6 Mar	5.18	58.24	Paush	6	81	164

TABLE XVII.—(Continued.)

General Table of Corresponding Dates.

A.D.	Solar-Year. Kali Yuga.	Solar-Year. Initial Day.	Luni-Solar-Year. Vik. Sam	Luni-Solar-Year. Intercal Month.	Luni-Solar-Year. Sak Sal.	Luni-Solar-Year. Initial Day.	Jupiter-Cycles. 60 Years. S. Sid.	Jupiter-Cycles. 60 Years. Tel.	Jupiter-Cycles. 12 Years.	Sapt. Rishi.	Chedi Sam.	Gupt. Kál.
331	3432	17 Mar	388	Bhâd	253	Tu 23 Feb	5.19	58.25	Mâgh	7	82	165
*332	33	—	389	...	254	Tu 14 Mar	20	26	Phâl	8	83	166
333	34	—	390	...	255	Sa 3 Mar	21	27	Chait	9	84	167
334	35	—	391	Ashad	256	We 20 Feb	22	28	Vais	10	85	168
335	36	—	392	...	257	Tu 11 Mar	23	29	Jyesh	11	86	169
*336	37	—	393	...	258	Sa 28 Feb	24	30	Ashad	12	87	170
337	38	—	394	Jyesh	259	S 17 Feb	25	31	Srâv	13	88	171
338	39	—	395	...	260	We 8 Mar	26	32	Bhâd	14	89	172
339	40	—	396	Aswa	261	S 25 Feb	27	33	Aswa	15	90	173
*340	3441	—	397	...	262	S 16 Mar	28	34	Kârt	16	91	174
341	3442	—	398	...	263	Th 5 Mar	29	35	Agra	17	92	175
342	43	—	399	Srâv	264	Th 21 Feb	30	36	Paush	18	93	176
343	44	—	400	...	265	Sa 12 Mar	31	37	Mâgh	19	94	177
*344	45	—	401	...	266	Th 1 Mar	32	38	Phâl	20	95	178
345	46	—	402	Jyesh	267	Mo 18 Feb	33	39	Chait	21	96	179
346	47	—	403	...	268	S 9 Mar	34	40	Vais	22	97	180
347	48	—	404	...	269	Th 26 Feb	35	41	Jyesh	23	98	181
*348	49	—	405	Chait	270	Mo 15 Feb	36	42	Ashad	24	99	182
349	50	—	406	...	271	Mo 6 Mar	37	43	Srâv	25	100	183
350	3451	—	407	Srâv	272	Fr 23 Feb	38	44	Bhâd	26	101	184
351	3452	—	408	...	273	Th 14 Mar	39	45	Aswa	27	102	185
*352	53	—	409	...	274	Tu 3 Mar	40	46	Kârt	28	103	186
353	54	—	410	Ashad	275	Sa 20 Feb	41	47	Agra	29	104	187
354	55	—	411	...	276	Fr 11 Mar	42	48	Paush	30	105	188
355	56	—	412	...	277	Tu 28 Feb	43	49	Mâgh	31	106	189
*356	57	—	413	Jyesh	278	Sa 17 Feb	44	50	Phâl	32	107	190
357	58	—	414	...	279	Sa 8 Mar	45	51	Chait	33	108	191
358	59	—	415	Aswa	280	We 25 Feb	46	52	Vais	34	109	192
359	60	—	416	...	281	Tu 16 Mar	47	53	Jyesh	35	110	193
*360	3461	—	417	...	282	S 5 Mar	5.48	58.54	Ashad	36	111	194

TABLE XVII.—(Continued.)

General Table of Correspondng Dates.

A.D.	Solar-Year.		Luni-Solar-Year.				Jupiter-Cycles.			Sapt. Rishi.	Chedi Sam.	Gupt. Kál.
	Kali Yuga.	Initial Day.	Vik. Sam	Intercal Month.	Sak Sal.	Initial Day.	60 Years. S. Sid.	60 Years. Tel.	12 Years.			
361	3462	17 Mar	418	Ashad	283	We 21 Feb	5.49	58.55	Srâv	37	112	195
362	63	—	419	...	284	Tu 12 Mar	50	56	Bhâd	38	113	196
363	64	—	420	...	285	Sa 1 Mar	51	57	Aswa	39	114	197
*364	65	—	421	Jyesh	286	We 18 Mar	52	58	Kârt	40	115	198
365	66	—	422	...	287	We 9 Mar	53	59	Agra	41	116	199
366	67	—	423	Phâl	288	S 26 Feb	54	60	Paush	42	117	200
367	68	—	424	...	289	Sa 17 Mar	55	59. 1	Mâgh	43	118	201
*368	69	—	425	Srâv	290	We 6 Mar	56	2	Phâl	44	119	202
369	70	—	426	...	291	Mo 23 Feb	57	3	Chait	45	120	203
370	3471	—	427	...	292	S 14 Mar	58	4	Vais	46	121	204
371	3472	—	428	...	293	Th 3 Mar	59	5	Jyesh	47	122	205
*372	73	—	429	Ashad	294	Mo 20 Feb	60	6	Ashad	48	123	206
373	74	—	430	...	295	Mo 11 Mar	6. 1	7	Srâv	49	124	207
374	75	—	431	...	296	Fr 28 Feb	2	8	Bhâd	50	125	208
375	76	—	432	Vais	297	Tu 17 Feb	3	9	Aswa	51	126	209
*376	77	—	433	...	298	Tu 8 Mar	4	10	Kârt	52	127	210
377	78	—	434	Bhâd	299	Sa 25 Feb	5	11	Agra	53	128	211
378	79	—	435	...	300	Fr 16 Mar	6	12	Paush	54	129	212
379	80	—	436	...	301	Tu 5 Mar	7	13	Mâgh	55	130	213
*380	3481	—	437	Ashad	302	Fr 21 Feb	8	14	Phâl	56	131	214
381	3482	—	438	...	303	Fr 12 Mar	9	15	Chait	57	132	215
382	83	—	439	...	304	Tu 1 Mar	10	16	Vais	58	133	216
383	84	—	440	Jyesh	305	Sa 18 Feb	11	17	Jyesh	59	134	217
*384	85	—	441	...	306	Sa 9 Mar	12	18	Ashad	60	135	218
385	86	—	442	Phâl	307	We 26 Feb	13	19	Srâv	61	136	219
386	87	—	443	...	308	Tu 17 Mar	14	20	Bhâd	62	137	220
387	88	—	444	...	309	Sa 6 Mar	15	21	Aswa	63	138	221
*388	89	—	445	Srâv	310	We 23 Feb	16	22	Kârt	64	139	222
389	90	—	446	...	311	We 14 Mar	17	23	Agra	65	140	223
390	3491	—	447	...	312	S 3 Mar	6.18	59.24	Paush	66	141	224

TABLE XVII.—(Continued.)

General Table of Corresponding Dates.

A. D.	Solar-Year.		Luni-Solar-Year.				Jupiter-Cycles.			Sapt. Rishi.	Chedi Sam.	Gupt. Kal.
	Kali Yuga.	Initial Day.	Vik. Sam	Intercal Month.	Sak Sal.	Initial Day.	60 Years. S. Sid.	60 Years. Tel.	12 Years.			
391	3492	17 Mar	448	Ashad	313	Th 20 Feb	6.19	59.25	Mâgh	67	142	225
*392	93	—	449	...	314	Th 11 Mar	20	26	Phâl	68	143	226
393	94	—	450	...	315	Mo 28 Feb	21	27	Chait	69	144	227
394	95	—	451	Vais	316	Fr 17 Feb	22	28	Vais	70	145	228
395	96	—	452	...	317	Th 8 Mar	●24	29	●Ashad	71	146	229
*396	97	—	453	Bhâd	318	Mo 25 Feb	25	30	Srâv	72	147	230
397	98	—	454	...	319	Mo 16 Mar	26	31	Bhâd	73	148	231
398	99	—	455	...	320	Fr 5 Mar	27	32	Aswa	74	149	232
399	3500	—	456	Ashad	321	Mo 21 Feb	28	33	Kârt	75	150	233
*400	3501	17 —	457	...	322	Mo 12 Mar	29	34	Agra	76	151	234
401	3502	18 —	458	...	323	Fr 1 Mar	30	35	Paush	77	152	235
402	03	18 —	459	Jyesh	324	Tu 18 Feb	31	36	Mâgh	78	153	236
403	04	18 —	460	...	325	Mo 9 Mar	32	37	Phâl	79	154	237
*404	05	17 —	461	†...	326	Fr 26 Feb	33	38	Chait	80	155	238
405	06	18 —	462	Chait	327	We 15 Feb	34	39	Vais	81	156	239
406	07	18 —	463	...	328	Tu 6 Mar	35	40	Jyesh	82	157	240
407	08	18 —	464	Srâv	329	Sa 23 Feb	36	41	Ashad	83	158	241
*408	09	17 —	465	...	330	Sa 14 Mar	37	42	Srâv	84	159	242
409	10	18 —	466	...	331	We 3 Mar	38	43	Bhâd	85	160	243
410	3511	18 —	467	Ashad	332	S 20 Feb	39	44	Aswa	86	161	244
411	3512	18 —	468	...	333	Sa 11 Mar	40	45	Kârt	87	162	245
*412	13	17 —	469	...	334	We 28 Feb	41	46	Agra	88	163	246
413	14	18 —	470	Vais	335	Mo 17 Feb	42	47	Paush	89	164	247
414	15	18 —	471	...	336	S 8 Mar	43	48	Mâgh	90	165	248
415	16	18 —	472	Bhâd	337	Th 25 Feb	44	49	Phâl	91	166	249
*416	17	18 —	473	...	338	Th 16 Mar	45	50	Chait	92	167	250
417	18	18 —	474	...	339	Mo 5 Mar	46	51	Vais	93	168	251
418	19	18 —	475	Ashad	340	S 21 Feb	47	52	Jyesh	94	169	252
419	20	18 —	476	...	341	We 12 Mar	48	53	Ashad	95	170	253
*420	3521	18 —	477	...	342	Mo 1 Mar	6.49	59.54	Srâv	96	171	254

† Kârtika retrenched and Kârtika intercalary.

TABLE XVII.—(Continued.)

General Table of Corresponding Dates.

A.D.	Solar-Year.		Luni-Solar-Year.				Jupiter-Cycles.			Sapt. Rishi.	Ghedi Sam.	Gupt. Kál.
	Kali Yuga.	Initial Day.	Vik Sam	Intercal Month.	Sak Sal.	Initial Day.	60 Years. S. Sid.	60 Years. Tel.	12 Years.			
421	3522		478	Jyesh	343	Fr 18 Feb	6.50	59.55	Bhâd	97	172	255
422	23		479	...	344	Th 9 Mar	51	56	Aswa	98	173	256
423	24		480	†...	345	Mo 26 Feb	52	57	Kârt	99	174	257
*424	25		481	Chait	346	Fr 15 Feb	53	58	Agra	100	175	258
425	26		482	...	347	Fr 6 Mar	54	59	Paush	1	176	259
426	27		483	Srâv	348	Tu 23 Feb	55	60	Mâgh	2	177	260
427	28		484	...	349	Mo 14 Mar	56	60.1	Phâl	3	178	261
*428	29		485	...	350	Sa 3 Mar	57	2	Chait	4	179	262
429	30		486	Jyesh	351	We 20 Feb	58	3	Vais	5	180	263
430	3531		487	...	352	Tu 11 Mar	59	4	Jyesh	6	181	264
431	3532		488	...	353	Sa 28 Feb	60	5	Ashad	7	182	265
*432	33		489	Vais	354	We 17 Feb	7. 1	6	Srâv	8	183	266
433	34		490	...	355	We 8 Mar	2	7	Bhâd	9	184	267
434	35		491	Bhâd	356	S 25 Feb	3	8	Aswa	10	185	268
435	36		492	...	357	Sa 16 Mar	4	9	Kârt	11	186	269
*436	37		493	...	358	Th 5 Mar	5	10	Agra	12	187	270
437	38		494	Ashad	359	S 21 Feb	6	11	Paush	13	188	271
438	39		495	...	360	Sa 12 Mar	7	12	Mâgh	14	190	272
439	40		496	...	361	We 1 Mar	8	13	Phâl	15	190	273
*440	3541		497	Jyesh	362	S 18 Feb	9	14	Chait	16	191	274
441	3542		498	...	363	S 9 Mar	10	15	Vais	17	192	275
442	43		499	Bhâd	364	Th 26 Feb	11	16	Jyesh	18	193	276
443	44		500	...	365	We 17 Mar	12	17	Ashad	19	194	277
*444	45		501	...	366	Mo 6 Mar	13	18	Srâv	20	195	278
445	46		502	Srâv	367	Fr 23 Feb	14	19	Bhâd	21	196	279
446	47		503	...	368	Th 14 Mar	15	20	Aswa	22	197	280
447	48		504	...	369	Mo 3 Mar	16	21	Kârt	23	198	281
*448	49		505	Jyesh	370	Fr 20 Feb	17	22	Agra	24	199	282
449	50		506	...	371	Fr 11 Mar	18	23	Paush	25	200	283
450	3551		507	...	372	Tu 28 Feb	7.19	60.24	Mâgh	26	201	284

† Agrahayana omitted, Aswina intercalary.

TABLE XVII.—(Continued.)

General Table of Corresponding Dates.

A. D.	Solar-Year.		Luni-Solar-Year.				Jupiter-Cycles.			Sapt. Rishi.	Chedi Sam.	Gupt. Kâl.
	Kali Yuga.	Initial Day.	Vik Sam	Intercal Month.	Sak Sal.	Initial Day.	60 Years. S. Sid.	60 Years. Tel.	12 Years.			
451	3552		508	Vais	373	Sa 17 Feb	7.20	60.25	Phâl	27	202	285
*452	53		509	...	374	Sa 8 Mar	21	26	Chait	28	203	286
453	54		510	Bhâd	375	We 25 Feb	22	27	Vais	29	204	287
453	55		511	...	376	Tu 16 Mar	23	28	Jyesh	30	205	288
455	56		512	...	377	Sa 5 Mar	24	29	Ashad	31	206	289
*456	57		513	Ashad	378	Tu 21 Feb	25	30	Srâv	32	207	290
457	58		514	...	379	Tu 12 Mar	26	31	Bhad	33	208	291
458	59		515	...	380	Sa 1 Mar	27	32	Aswa	34	209	292
459	60		516	Jyesh	381	We 18 Feb	28	33	Kârt	35	210	293
*460	3561		517	...	382	We 9 Mar	29	34	Agra	36	211	294
461	3562		518	Bhâd	383	S 26 Feb	30	35	Paush	37	212	295
462	63		519	...	384	Fr 16 Mar	31	36	Mâgh	38	213	296
463	64		520	...	385	We 6 Mar	32	37	Phâl	39	214	297
*464	65		521	Srâv	386	S 23 Feb	33	38	Chait	40	215	298
465	66		522	...	387	S 14 Mar	34	39	Vais	41	216	299
466	67		523	...	388	Th 3 Mar	35	40	Jyesh	42	217	300
467	68		524	Jyesh	389	Mo 20 Feb	36	41	Ashad	43	218	301
*468	69		525	...	390	Mo 11 Mar	37	42	Srâv	44	219	302
469	70		526	†...	391	Fr 28 Feb	38	43	Bhâd	45	220	303
470	3571		527	Vais	392	Tu 17 Feb	39	44	Aswa	46	221	304
471	3572		528	...	393	Th 8 Mar	40	45	Kârt	47	222	305
*472	73		529	Bhâd	394	Fr 25 Feb	41	46	Agra	48	223	306
473	74		530	...	395	Fr 16 Mar	42	47	Paush	49	224	307
474	75		531	...	396	Tu 5 Mar	43	48	Mâgh	50	225	308
475	76		532	Ashad	397	Fr 21 Feb	44	49	Phâl	51	226	309
*476	77		533	...	398	Fr 12 Mar	45	50	Chait	52	227	310
477	78		534	...	399	Tu 1 Mar	46	51	Vais	53	228	311
478	79		535	Jyesh	400	Sa 18 Feb	47	52	Jyesh	54	229	312
479	80		536	...	401	Fr 9 Mar	7.48	53	Ashad	55	230	313
*480	3581		537	Aswa	402	Tu 26 Feb	● 50	60.54	●Bhâd	56	231	314

† Kârtika omitted, and Kârtika intercalary.

TABLE XVII.—(Continued.)

General Table of Corresponding Dates.

A.D.	Solar-Year.		Luni-Solar-Year.				Jupiter-Cycles.			Sapt. Rishi.	Chedi Sam.	Gupt. Kâl.
	Kali Yuga.	Initial Day.	Vik Sam	Intercal Month.	Sak Sal.	Initial Day.	60 Years. S. Sid.	60 Years. Tel.	12 Years.			
481	3582		538	...	403	Tu 17 Mar	7.51	60.55	Aswa	57	232	315
482	83		539	...	404	Sa 6 Mar	52	56	Kârt	58	233	316
483	84		540	Srâv	405	We 23 Feb	53	57	Agra	59	234	317
*484	85		541	...	406	We 14 Mar	54	58	Paush	60	235	318
485	86		542	...	407	S 3 Mar	55	59	Mâgh	61	236	319
486	87		543	Jyesh	408	Th 20 Feb	56	60	Phâl	62	237	320
487	88		544	...	409	We 11 Mar	57	61.1	Chait	63	238	321
*488	89		545	†...	410	Mo 28 Feb	58	2	Vais	64	239	322
489	90		546	Chait	411	Fr 17 Feb	59	3	Jyesh	65	240	323
490	3591		547	...	412	Th 8 Mar	60	4	Ashad	66	241	324
491	3592		548	Bhâd	413	Mo 25 Feb	8. 1	5	Srâv	67	242	325
*492	93		549	...	414	Mo 16 Mar	2	6	Bhâd	68	243	326
493	94		550	...	415	Fr 5 Mar	3	7	Aswa	69	244	327
494	95		551	Ashad	416	Mo 21 Feb	4	8	Kârt	70	245	328
495	96		552	...	417	S 12 Mar	5	9	Agra	71	246	329
*496	97		553	...	418	Fr 1 Mar	6	10	Paush	72	247	330
497	98		554	Jyesh	419	Tu 18 Feb	7	11	Mâgh	73	248	331
498	99		555	...	420	Mo 9 Mar	8	12	Phâl	74	249	332
499	3600		556	Aswa	421	Fr 26 Feb	9	13	Chait	75	250	333
*500	3601		557	...	422	Fr 17 Mar	10	14	Vais	76	251	334
501	3602		558	...	423	Tu 6 Mar	11	15	Jyesh	77	252	335
502	03		559	Ashad	424	Sa 23 Feb	12	16	Ashad	78	253	336
503	04		560	...	425	Fr 14 Mar	13	17	Srâv	79	254	337
*504	05		561	...	426	We 3 Mar	14	18	Bhâd	80	255	338
505	06		562	Jyesh	427	S 20 Feb	15	19	Aswa	81	256	339
506	07		563	...	428	Sa 11 Mar	16	20	Kârt	82	257	340
507	‡08		564	Phâl	429	We 28 Feb	17	21	Agra	83	258	341
*508	09		565	...	430	We 19 Mar	18	22	Paush	84	259	342
509	10		566	...	431	S 8 Mar	19	23	Mâgh	85	260	343
510	3611		567	Srâv	432	Th 25 Feb	8.20	61.24	Phâl	86	261	344

† Agrahayana omitted, and Kârtika intercalary. ‡ Pausha omitted, and Kârtika intercalary.

TABLE XVII.—(Continued.)

General Table of Corresponding Dates.

A. D.	Solar-Year: Kali Yuga.	Solar-Year: Initial Day.	Luni-Solar-Year: Vik Sam	Luni-Solar-Year: Intercal Month.	Luni-Solar-Year: Sak Sal.	Luni-Solar-Year: Initial Day.	Jupiter-Cycles: 60 Years. S. Sid.	Jupiter-Cycles: 60 Years. Tel.	Jupiter-Cycles: 12 Years.	Sapt. Rishi.	Chedi Sam.	Gupt. Kâl.
511	3612		568	...	433	We 16 Mar	8.21	61.25	Chait	87	262	345
*512	13		569	...	434	Mo 5 Mar	22	26	Vais	88	263	346
513	14		570	Ashad	435	Th 21 Feb	23	27	Jyesh	89	264	347
514	15		571	...	436	We 12 Mar	24	28	Ashad	90	265	348
515	16		572	...	437	S 1 Mar	25	29	Srâv	91	266	349
*516	17		573	Vais	438	Th 18 Feb	26	30	Bhâd	92	267	350
517	18		574	...	439	Th 9 Mar	27	31	Aswa	93	268	351
518	19		575	Bhâd	440	Mo 26 Feb	28	32	Kârt	94	269	352
519	20		576	...	441	S 17 Mar	29	33	Agra	95	270	353
*520	3621		577	...	442	Fr 6 Mar	30	34	Paush	96	271	354
521	3622		578	Ashad	443	Tu 23 Feb	31	35	Mâgh	97	272	355
522	23		579	...	444	Th 14 Mar	32	36	Phâl	98	273	356
523	24		580	...	445	Fr 3 Mar	33	37	Chait	99	274	357
*524	25		581	Jyesh	446	Tu 20 Feb	34	38	Vais	100	275	358
525	26		582	...	447	Tu 11 Mar	35	39	Jyesh	1	276	359
526	†27		583	Phâl	448	Sa 28 Feb	36	40	Ashad	2	277	360
527	28		584	...	449	Fr 19 Mar	37	41	Srâv	3	278	361
*528	29		585	...	450	We 8 Mar	38	42	Bhâd	4	279	362
529	30		586	Srâv	451	S 25 Feb	39	43	Aswa	5	280	363
530	3631		587	...	452	Sa 16 Mar	40	44	Kârt	6	281	364
531	3632		588	...	453	We 5 Mar	41	45	Agra	7	282	365
*532	33		589	Ashad	454	Sa 21 Feb	42	46	Paush	8	283	366
533	34		590	...	455	Sa 12 Mar	43	47	Mâgh	9	284	367
534	35		591	...	456	We 1 Mar	44	48	Phâl	10	285	368
535	36		592	Vais	457	S 18 Feb	45	49	Chait	11	286	369
*536	37		593	...	458	S 9 Mar	46	50	Vais	12	287	370
537	38		594	Bhâd	459	Th 26 Feb	47	51	Jyesh	13	288	371
538	39		595	...	460	We 17 Mar	48	52	Ashad	14	289	372
539	40		596	...	461	S 6 Mar	49	53	Srâv	15	290	373
*540	3641		597	Ashad	462	Th 23 Feb	8.50	61.54	Bhâd	16	291	374

† Agrahayana omitted, and Kârtika intercalary.

TABLE XVII.—(Continued.)

General Table of Corresponding Dates.

A. D.	Solar-Year.		Luni-Solar-Year.				Jupiter-Cycles.			Sapt. Rishi.	Chedi Sam.	Gupt. Kál.
	Kali Yuga.	Initial Day.	Vik Sam	Intercal Month.	Sak Sal.	Initial Day.	60 Years. S. Sid.	60 Years. Tel-	12 Years.			
541	3642	19 Mar	598	...	463	Th 14 Mar	8.51	61.55	Aswa	17	292	375
542	43	19 —	599	...	464	Mo 3 Mar	52	56	Kârt	18	293	376
543	44	19 —	600	Jyesh	465	Fr 20 Feb	53	57	Agra	19	294	377
*544	45	19 —	601	...	466	Fr 11 Mar	54	58	Paush	20	295	378
545	†46	19 —	602	Phâl	467	We 1 Mar	55	59	Mâgh	21	296	379
546	47	19 —	603	...	468	Mo 19 Mar	56	60	Phâl	22	297	380
547	48	19 —	604	...	469	Fr 8 Mar	57	62.1	Chait	23	298	381
*548	49	19 —	605	Srâv	470	We 26 Feb	58	2	Vais	24	299	382
549	50	19 —	606	...	471	Tu 16 Mar	59	3	Jyesh	25	300	383
550	3651	19 —	607	...	472	Sa 5 Mar	60	4	Ashad	26	301	384
551	3652	19 Mar	608	Ashad	473	We 22 Feb	9. 1	5	Srâv	27	302	385
*552	53	19 —	609	...	474	We 13 Mar	2	6	Bhâd	28	303	386
553	54	19 —	610	...	475	S 2 Mar	3	7	Aswa	29	304	387
554	55	19 —	611	Vais	476	Th 19 Feb	4	8	Kârt	30	305	388
555	56	19 —	612	...	477	Tu 9 Mar	5	9	Agra	31	306	389
*556	57	19 —	613	Bhâd	478	S 27 Feb	6	10	Paush	32	307	390
557	58	19 —	614	...	479	Sa 17 Mar	7	11	Mâgh	33	308	391
558	59	19 —	615	...	480	Th 7 Mar	8	12	Phâl	34	309	392
559	60	19 —	616	Ashad	481	Mo 24 Feb	9	13	Chait	35	310	393
*560	3661	19 —	617	...	482	S 14 Mar	10	14	Vais	36	311	394
561	3662	19 Mar	618	...	483	Th 3 Mar	11	15	Jyesh	37	312	395
562	63	19 —	619	Jyesh	484	Fr 21 Feb	12	16	Ashad	38	313	396
563	64	19 —	620	...	485	S 11 Mar	13	17	Srâv	39	314	397
*564	‡65	19 —	621	Aswa	486	Fr 29 Feb	14	18	Bhâd	40	315	398
565	66	19 —	622	...	487	Th 19 Mar	16	19	Kârt	41	316	399
566	67	19 —	623	..	488	Mo 8 Mar	17	20	Agra	42	317	400
567	68	19 —	624	Srâv	489	Fr 25 Feb	18	21	Paush	43	318	401
*568	69	19 —	625	...	490	Fr 16 Mar	19	22	Mâgh	44	319	402
569	70	19 —	626	...	491	Tu 5 Mar	20	23	Phâl	45	320	403
570	3671	19 —	627	Jyesh	492	Fr 21 Feb	9.21	62.24	Chait	46	321	404

† Agrahayana omitted, and Kârtika intercalary.

‡ Pausha omitted, and Phâlguna intercalary.

TABLE XVII.—(Continued.)

General Table of Corresponding Dates.

A. D.	Solar-Year.		Luni-Solar-Year.				Jupiter-Cycles.			Sapt. Rishi.	Chedi Sam.	Gupta. Kál.
	Kali Yuga.	Initial Day.	Vik Sam	Intercal Month.	Sak Sal.	Initial Day.	60 Years. S. Sid.	60 Years. Tel.	12 Years.			
571	3672	20 Mar	628	...	493	Fr 13 Mar	9.22	62.25	Vais	47	322	405
*572	73	19 —	629	...	494	We 2 Mar	23	26	Jyesh	48	323	406
573	74	19 —	630	Vais	495	Sa 18 Feb	24	27	Ashad	49	324	407
574	75	19 —	631	...	496	Fr 9 Mar	25	28	Srâv	50	325	408
575	76	20 —	632	Bhâd	497	We 27 Feb	26	29	Bhâd	51	326	409
*576	77	20 —	633	...	498	Tu 18 Mar	27	30	Aswa	52	327	410
577	78	19 —	634	...	499	Sa 6 Mar	28	31	Kârt	53	328	411
578	79	20 —	635	Ashad	500	Th 24 Feb	29	32	Agra	54	329	412
579	80	20 —	636	...	501	We 15 Mar	30	33	Paush	55	330	413
*580	3681	19 —	637	...	502	S 3 Mar	31	34	Mâgh	56	331	414
581	3682	19 Mar	638	Vais	503	Th 20 Feb	32	35	Phâl	57	332	415
582	83	20 —	639	...	504	Th 12 Mar	33	36	Chait	58	333	416
583	84	20 —	640	Bhâd	505	Sa 27 Feb	34	37	Vais	59	334	417
*584	85	19 —	641	...	506	S 19 Mar	35	38	Jyesh	60	335	418
585	86	20 —	642	...	507	F 9 Mar	36	39	Ashad	61	336	419
586	87	20 —	643	Srâv	508	Tu 26 Feb	37	40	Srâv	62	337	420
587	88	20 —	644	...	509	S 16 Mar	38	41	Bhâd	63	338	421
*588	89	19 —	645	...	510	Fr 5 Mar	39	42	Aswa	64	339	422
589	90	20 —	646	Jyesh	511	Mo 21 Feb	40	43	Kârt	65	340	423
590	3691	20 —	647	...	512	Mo 13 Mar	41	44	Agra	66	341	424
591	3692	20 Mar	648	...	513	Fr 2 Mar	42	45	Paush	67	342	425
*592	93	19 —	649	Vais	514	Tu 19 Feb	43	46	Mâgh	68	343	426
593	94	19 —	650	...	515	Mo 9 Mar	44	47	Phâl	69	344	427
594	95	20 —	651	Bhâd	516	Sa 27 Feb	45	48	Chait	70	345	428
595	96	20 —	652	...	517	Fr 18 Mar	46	49	Vais	71	346	429
*596	97	19 —	653	...	518	Tu 6 Mar	47	50	Jyesh	72	347	430
597	98	19 —	654	Ashad	519	Sa 23 Feb	48	51	Ashad	73	348	431
598	99	20 —	655	...	520	Sa 15 Mar	49	52	Srâv	74	349	432
599	3700	20 —	656	...	521	We 4 Mar	50	53	Bhâd	75	350	433
*600	3701	19 —	657	Vais	522	Sa 20 Feb	9.51	62.54	Aswa	76	351	434

TABLE XVII.—(Continued.)

General Table of Corresponding Dates.

A. D.	Solar-Year. Kali Yuga.	Solar-Year. Initial Day.	Luni-Solar-Year. Vik Sam	Luni-Solar-Year. Intercal Month.	Luni-Solar-Year. Sak Sal.	Luni-Solar-Year. Initial Day.	Jupiter-Cycles. 60 Years. S. Sid.	Jupiter-Cycles. 60 Years. Tel.	Jupiter-Cycles. 12 Years.	Sapt. Rishi.	Chedi Sam.	Harsha Kâl.
601	3702	20 Mar	658	...	523	Sa 11 Mar	9.52	62.55	Kârt	77	352	...
602	03	20 —	659	Bhâd	524	We 28 Feb	53	56	Agra	78	353	...
603	04	20 —	660	...	525	Tu 19 Mar	54	57	Paush	79	354	...
*604	05	19 —	661	...	526	S 8 Mar	55	58	Mâgh	80	355	...
605	06	20 —	662	Srâv	527	Fr 26 Feb	56	59	Phâl	81	356	...
606	07	20 —	663	...	528	We 16 Mar	57	60	Chait	82	357	0
607	08	20 —	664	...	529	S 5 Mar	58	63.1	Vais	83	358	1
*608	09	19 —	665	Jyesh	530	We 21 Feb	59	2	Jyesh	84	359	2
609	10	19 —	666	...	531	We 12 Mar	60	3	Ashad	85	360	3
610	3711	20 —	667	†...	532	Mo 2 Mar	10. 1	4	Srâv	86	361	4
611	3712	20 Mar	668	Vais	533	Th 18 Feb	2	5	Bhâd	87	362	5
*612	13	19 —	669	...	534	Th 9 Mar	3	6	Aswa	88	363	6
613	14	20 —	670	Bhâd	535	Mo 26 Feb	4	7	Kârt	89	364	7
614	15	20 —	671	...	536	Mo 18 Mar	5	8	Agra	90	365	8
615	16	20 —	672	...	537	S 5 Mar	6	9	Paush	91	366	9
*616	17	19 —	673	Ashad	538	Tu 24 Feb	7	10	Mâgh	92	367	10
617	18	20 —	674	...	539	Tu 15 Mar	8	11	Phâl	93	368	11
618	19	20 —	675	...	540	Sa 4 Mar	9	12	Chait	94	369	12
619	20	20 —	676	Vais	541	We 21 Feb	10	13	Vais	95	370	13
*620	3721	20 —	677	...	542	Tu 11 Mar	11	14	Jyesh	96	371	14
621	3722	20 Mar	678	Bhâd	543	Mo 1 Mar	12	15	Ashad	97	372	15
622	23	20 —	679	...	544	Fr 19 Mar	13	16	Srâv	98	373	16
623	24	20 —	680	...	545	Tu 8 Mar	14	17	Bhâd	99	374	17
*624	25	19 —	681	Srâv	546	Sa 25 Feb	15	18	Aswa	100	375	18
625	26	20 —	682	...	547	Sa 16 Mar	16	19	Kârt	1	376	19
626	27	20 —	683	...	548	We 5 Mar	17	20	Agra	2	377	20
627	28	20 —	684	Jyesh	549	S 22 Feb	18	21	Paush	3	378	21
*628	29	19 —	685	...	550	Sa 12 Mar	19	22	Mâgh	4	379	22
629	30	20 —	686	‡...	551	Th 2 Mar	20	23	Phâl	5	380	23
630	3731	20 —	687	Chait	552	Tu 20 Feb	10.21	63.24	Chait	6	381	24

† Kârtika omitted, and Kârtika intercalary ‡ Pausha omitted, and Kârtika intercalary.

TABLE XVII.—(Continued.)

General Table of Corresponding Dates.

A.D.	Solar-Year. Kali Yuga.	Solar-Year. Initial Day.	Luni-Solar-Year. Vik Sam	Luni-Solar-Year. Intercal Month.	Luni-Solar-Year. Sak Sal.	Luni-Solar-Year. Initial Day.	Jupiter-Cycles. 60 Years. S. Sid.	Jupiter-Cycles. 60 Years. Tel.	Jupiter-Cycles. 12 Years.	Sapt. Rishi.	Chedi Sam.	Harsha Kâl.
631	3732	20 Mar	688	...	553	We 10 Mar	10.22	63.25	Vais	7	382	25
*632	33	20 —	689	Bhâd	554	Fr 28 Feb	23	26	Jyesh	8	383	26
633	34	20 —	690	...	555	We 17 Mar	24	27	Ashad	9	384	27
634	35	20 —	691	...	556	Mo 7 Mar	25	28	Srâv	10	385	28
635	36	20 —	692	Ashad	557	Fr 24 Feb	26	29	Bhâd	11	386	29
*636	37	20 —	693	...	558	Th 14 Mar	27	30	Aswa	12	387	30
637	38	20 —	694	...	559	Tu 4 Mar	28	31	Kârt	13	388	31
638	39	20 —	695	Vais	560	Sa 21 Feb	29	32	Agra	14	389	32
639	40	20 —	696	...	561	Th 11 Mar	30	33	Paush	15	390	33
*640	3741	20 —	697	Bhâd	562	Tu 29 Feb	31	34	Mâgh	16	391	34
641	3742	20 Mar	698	...	563	Mo 19 Mar	32	35	Phâl	17	392	35
642	43	20 —	699	...	564	Fr. 8 Mar	33	36	Chait	18	393	36
643	44	20 —	700	Ashad	565	Tu 25 Feb	34	37	Vais	19	394	37
*644	45	20 —	701	...	566	Tu 16 Mar	35	38	Jyesh	20	395	38
645	46	20 —	702	...	567	Sa 5 Mar	36	39	Ashad	21	396	39
646	47	20 —	703	Jyesht	568	We 22 Feb	37	40	Srâv	22	397	40
647	48	20 —	704	...	569	Tu 13 Mar	38	41	Bhâd	23	398	41
*648	49	20 —	705	Kârt	570	S 2 Mar	39	42	Aswa	24	399	42
649	50	20 —	706	...	571	Fr 20 Mar	40	43	Kârt	25	400	43
650	3751	20 —	707	...	572	Tu 9 Mar	● 42	44	● Paush	26	401	44
651	3752	20 Mar	708	Srâv	573	S 27 Feb	43	45	Mâgh	27	402	45
*652	53	20 —	709	...	574	Sat 17 Mar	44	46	Phâl	28	403	46
653	54	20 —	710	...	575	We 6 Mar	45	47	Chait	29	404	47
654	55	20 —	711	Ashad	576	Mo 24 Feb	46	48	Vais	30	405	48
655	56	20 —	712	...	577	Sat 14 Mar	47	49	Jyesh	31	406	49
*656	57	20 —	713	...	578	Th 3 Mar	48	50	Ashad	32	407	50
657	58	20 —	714	Vais	579	Mo 20 Feb	49	51	Srâv	33	408	51
658	59	20 —	715	...	580	S 11 Mar	50	52	Bhâd	34	409	52
659	60	20 —	716	Bhâd	581	Fr 1 Mar	51	53	Aswa	35	410	53
*660	3761	20 —	717	...	582	Th 19 Mar	10.52	63.54	Kârt	36	411	54

TABLE XVII.—(Continued.)

General Table of Corresponding Dates.

A. D.	Solar-Year.		Luni-Solar-Year.				Jupiter-Cycles.			Sapt. Rishi.	Chedi Sam.	Harsha Kâl.
	Kali Yuga.	Initial Day.	Vik Sam	Intercal Month.	Sak Sal.	Initial Day.	60 Years. S. Sid.	60 Years. Tel.	12 Years.			
661	3762	20 Mar	718	...	583	Mo 8 Mar	10.53	63.55	Agra	37	412	55
662	63	20 —	719	Ashad	584	Fr 25 Feb	54	56	Paush	38	413	56
663	64	21 —	720	...	585	Fr 17 Mar	55	57	Mâgh	39	414	57
*664	65	20 —	721	...	586	Tu 5 Mar	56	58	Phâl	40	415	58
665	66	20 —	722	Jyesh	587	Sa 22 Feb	57	59	Chait	41	416	59
666	67	20 —	723	...	588	Th 12 Mar	58	60	Vais	42	417	60
667	68	21 —	724	Kârt	589	Tu 2 Mar	59	64.1	Jyesh	43	418	61
*668	69	20 —	725	...	590	Mo 20 Mar	60	2	Ashad	44	419	62
669	70	20 —	726	...	591	Fr 9 Mar	11. 1	3	Srâv	45	420	63
670	3771	21 —	727	Srâv	592	We 27 Feb	2	4	Bhâd	46	421	64
671	3772	20 Mar	728	...	593	Mo 17 Mar	3	5	Aswa	47	422	65
*672	73	20 —	729	...	594	Sa 6 Mar	4	6	Kârt	48	423	66
673	74	20 —	730	Ashad	595	We 23 Feb	5	7	Agra	49	424	67
674	75	20 —	731	...	596	Tu 14 Mar	6	8	Paush	50	425	68
675	76	21 —	732	...	597	S 4 Mar	7	9	Mâgh	51	426	69
*676	77	20 —	733	Chait	598	Th 21 Feb	8	10	Phâl	52	427	70
677	78	20 —	734	...	599	We 11 Mar	9	11	Chait	53	428	71
678	79	20 —	735	Bhâd	600	S 28 Feb	10	12	Vais	54	429	72
679	80	21 —	736	...	601	Tu 19 Mar	11	13	Jyesh	55	430	73
*680	3781	20 —	737	...	602	Th 8 Mar	12	14	Ashad	56	431	74
681	3782	20 Mar	738	Ashad	603	Mo 25 Feb	13	15	Srâv	57	432	75
682	83	20 —	739	...	604	Sa 15 Mar	14	16	Bhâd	58	433	76
683	84	20 —	740	...	605	We 4 Mar	15	17	Aswa	59	434	77
*684	85	20 —	741	Jyesh	606	Tu 23 Feb	16	18	Kârt	60	435	78
685	86	20 —	742	...	607	S 12 Mar	17	19	Agra	61	436	79
686	87	21 —	743	Aswa	608	Fr 2 Mar	18	20	Paush	62	437	80
687	88	21 —	744	...	609	Th 21 Mar	19	21	Mâgh	63	438	81
*688	89	20 —	745	...	610	Mo 9 Mar	20	22	Phâl	64	439	82
689	90	20 —	746	Srâv	611	Fr 26 Feb	21	23	Chait	65	440	83
690	3791	21 —	747	...	612	Fr 18 Mar	11.22	64.24	Vais	66	441	84

TABLE XVII.—(Continued.)

General Table of Corresponding Dates.

A. D.	Solar-Year.		Luni-Solar-Year.				Jupiter-Cycles.			Sapt. Rishi.	Chedi Sam.	Harsha Kâl.
	Kali Yuga.	Initial Day.	Vik Sam	Intercal Month.	Sak Sal	Initial Day.	60 Years. S. Sid.	60 Years. Tel.	12 Years.			
691	3792	21 Mar	748	...	613	Tu 7 Mar	11.23	64.25	Jyesh	67	442	85
*692	93	21	749	Ashad	614	Sa 24 Feb	24	26	Ashad	68	443	86
693	94	20	750	...	615	Fr 14 Mar	25	27	Srâv	69	444	87
694	95	20	751	...	616	Tu 3 Mar	26	28	Bhâd	70	445	88
695	96	21	752	Chait	617	S 21 Feb	27	29	Aswa	71	446	89
*696	97	20	753	...	618	Sa 11 Mar	28	30	Kârt	72	447	90
697	98	20	754	Bhâd	619	Wed 28 Feb	29	31	Agra	73	448	91
698	99	21	755	...	620	Fr 19 Mar	30	32	Paush	74	449	92
699	3800	21	756	...	621	Sa 8 Mar	31	33	Mâgh	75	450	93
*700	3801	21	757	Ashad	622	We 25 Feb	32	34	Phâl	76	451	94
701	3802	21 Mar	758	...	623	Wed 16 Mar	33	35	Chait	77	452	95
702	03	21 —	759	...	624	S 5 Mar	34	36	Vais	78	453	96
703	04	21 —	760	Jyesh	625	Th 22 Feb	35	37	Jyesh	79	454	97
*704	05	20 —	761	...	626	We 12 Mar	36	38	Ashad	80	455	98
705	06	20 —	762	Aswa	627	S 1 Mar	37	39	Srâv	81	456	99
706	07	21 —	763	...	628	Mo 21 Mar	38	40	Bhâd	82	457	100
707	08	22 —	764	...	629	Fr 10 Mar	39	41	Aswa	83	458	101
*708	09	21	765	Srâv	630	Tu 28 Feb	40	42	Kârt	84	459	102
709	10	21	766	...	631	Tu 18 Mar	41	43	Agra	85	460	103
710	3811	21	767	...	632	Sa 7 Mar	42	44	Paush	86	461	104
711	3812	21 Mar	768	Jyesh	633	Mo 23 Feb	43	45	Mâgh	87	462	105
*712	13	21	769	...	634	Tu 14 Mar	44	46	Phâl	88	463	106
713	14	21	770	...	635	Mo 3 Mar	45	47	Chait	89	464	107
714	15	21	771	Chait	636	Tu 20 Feb	46	48	Vais	90	465	108
715	16	21	772	...	637	Mo 11 Mar	47	49	Jyesh	91	466	109
*716	17	21	773	Srâv	638	Fr 28 Feb	48	50	Ashad	92	467	110
717	18	21	774	...	639	Fr 19 Mar	49	51	Srâv	93	468	111
718	19	21	775	...	640	Tu 8 Mar	50	52	Bhâd	94	469	112
719	20	21	776	...	641	Sa 25 Feb	51	53	Aswa	95	470	113
*720	3821	21	777	Ashad	642	Sa 16 Mar	11.52	64.54	Kârt	96	471	114

TABLE XVII.—(Continued.)

General Table of Corresponding Dates.

A. D.	Solar-Year.		Luni-Solar-Year.				Jupiter-Cycles.			Sapt. Rishi.	Chedi Sam.	Harsha Kâl.
	Kali Yuga.	Initial Day.	Vik Sam	Intercal Month.	Sak Sal.	Initial Day.	60 Years. S. Sid.	60 Years. Tel.	12 Years.			
721	3822	21 Mar	778	...	643	We 5 Mar	11.53	64.55	Agra	97	472	115
722	23	21 —	779	Vais	644	Sa 21 Feb	54	56	Paush	98	473	116
723	24	21 —	780	...	645	Sa 13 Mar	55	57	Mâgh	99	474	117
*724	25	21 —	781	Bhâd	646	Th 2 Mar	56	58	Phâl	100	475	118
725	26	21 —	782	...	647	Tu 20 Mar	57	59	Chait	1	476	119
726	27	21 —	783	...	648	Sa 9 Mar	58	60	Vais	2	477	120
727	28	21 —	784	Srâv	649	We 26 Feb	59	65. 1	Jyesh	3	478	121
*728	29	21 —	785	...	650	We 17 Mar	60	2	Ashad	4	479	122
729	30	21 —	786	...	651	S 6 Mar	12. 1	3	Srâv	5	480	123
730	3831	21 —	787	Jyesh	652	Th 23 Feb	2	4	Bhâd	6	481	124
731	3832	21 Mar	788	...	653	Fr 14 Mar	3	5	Aswa	7	482	125
*732	33	21 —	789	...	654	Mo 3 Mar	4	6	Kârt	8	483	126
733	34	21 —	790	Chait	655	Sa 21 Feb	5	7	Agra	9	484	127
734	35	21 —	791	...	656	Th 11 Mar	6	8	Paush	10	485	128
735	36	21 —	792	Srâv	657	Mo 28 Feb	● 8	9	● Phâl	11	486	129
*736	37	21 —	793	...	658	S 18 Mar	9	10	Chait	12	487	130
737	38	21 —	794	...	659	Fr 8 Mar	10	11	Vais	13	488	131
738	39	21 —	795	Ashad	660	Tu 25 Feb	11	12	Jyesh	14	489	132
739	40	21 —	796	...	661	Mo 16 Mar	12	13	Ashad	15	490	133
*740	3841	21 —	797	...	662	Fr 4 Mar	13	14	Srâv	16	491	134
741	3842	21 Mar	798	Vais	663	We 22 Feb	14	15	Bhâd	17	492	135
742	43	21 —	799	...	664	Mo 12 Mar	15	16	Aswa	18	493	136
743	44	21 —	800	Bhâd	665	Fr 1 Mar	16	17	Kârt	19	494	137
*744	45	21 —	801	...	666	Fr 20 Mar	17	18	Agra	20	495	138
745	46	21 —	802	...	667	Tu 9 Mar	18	19	Paush	21	496	139
746	47	21 —	803	Srâv	668	Sa 26 Feb	19	20	Mâgh	22	497	140
747	48	21 —	804	...	669	Fr 17 Mar	20	21	Phâl	23	498	141
*748	49	21 —	805	...	670	We 6 Mar	21	22	Chait	24	499	142
749	50	21 —	806	Jyesh	671	S 23 Feb	22	23	Vais	25	500	143
750	3851	21 —	807	...	672	S 14 Mar	12.23	65.24	Jyesh	26	501	144

TABLE XVII.—(Continued.)

General Table of Corresponding Dates.

A. D.	Solar-Year.		Luni-Solar-Year.				Jupiter-Cycles.			Sapt. Rishi.	Chedi Sam.	Harsha Kâl.
							60 Years.					
	Kali Yuga.	Initial Day.	Vik Sam	Intercal Month.	Sak Sal.	Initial Day.	S. Sid.	Tel.	12 Years.			
751	3852	21 Mar.	808	† ...	673	We 3 Mar	12.24	65.25	Ashad	27	502	145
*752	53	21 —	809	Chait	674	Mo 21 Feb	25	26	Srâv	28	503	146
753	54	21 —	810	...	675	S 11 Mar	26	27	Bhâd	29	504	147
754	55	21 —	811	Srâv	676	Th 28 Feb	27	28	Aswa	30	505	148
755	56	21 —	812	...	677	We 19 Mar	28	29	Kârt	31	506	149
*756	57	21 —	813	...	678	Mo 8 Mar	29	30	Agra	32	507	150
757	58	21 —	814	Ashad	679	Fr 25 Feb	30	31	Paush	33	508	151
758	59	21 —	815	...	680	We 15 Mar	31	32	Mâgh	34	509	152
759	60	21 —	816	...	681	S 4 Mar	32	33	Phâl	35	510	153
*760	3861	21 —	817	Vais	682	Sa 22 Feb	33	34	Chait	36	511	154
761	3862	21 Mar.	818	...	683	Th 12 Mar	34	35	Vais	37	512	155
762	63	21 —	819	Bhâd	684	Mo 1 Mar	35	36	Jyesh	38	513	156
763	64	21 —	820	...	685	S 20 Mar	36	37	Ashad	39	514	157
*764	65	21 —	821	...	686	Fr 9 Mar	37	38	Srâv	40	515	158
765	66	21 —	822	Srâv	687	Tu 26 Feb	38	39	Bhâd	41	516	159
766	67	21 —	823	...	688	Mo 17 Mar	39	40	Aswa	42	517	160
767	68	21 —	824	...	689	Fr 6 Mar	40	41	Kârt	43	518	161
*768	69	21 —	825	Jyesh	690	We 24 Feb	41	42	Agra	44	519	162
769	70	21 —	826	...	691	Tu 14 Mar	42	43	Paush	45	520	163
770	3871	21 —	827	‡ ...	692	Sa 3 Mar	43	44	Mâgh	46	521	164
771	3872	21 Mar.	828	Chait	693	We 20 Feb	44	45	Phâl	47	522	165
*772	73	21 —	829	...	694	We 11 Mar	45	46	Chait	48	523	166
773	74	21 —	830	Srâv	695	S 28 Feb	46	47	Vais	49	524	167
774	75	21 —	831	...	696	Fr 18 Mar	47	48	Jyesh	50	525	168
775	76	21 —	832	...	697	Tu 7 Mar	48	49	Ashad	51	526	169
*776	77	21 —	833	Ashad	698	S 25 Feb	49	50	Srâv	52	527	170
777	78	21 —	834	...	699	Sa 15 Mar	50	51	Bhâd	53	528	171
778	79	21 —	835	...	700	We 4 Mar	51	52	Aswa	54	529	172
779	80	22 —	836	Vais	701	Mo 22 Feb	52	53	Kârt	55	530	173
*780	3881	21 —	837	...	702	S 12 Mar	12.53	65.54	Agra	56	531	174

† Kârtika omitted, and Kârtika intercalary. ‡ Agrahayana omitted, and Aswina intercalary.

TABLE XVII.—(Continued.)

General Table of Corresponding Dates.

A. D.	Solar-Year: Kali Yuga.	Solar-Year: Initial Day.	Luni-Solar-Year: Vik Sam	Luni-Solar-Year: Intercal Month.	Luni-Solar-Year: Sak Sal.	Luni-Solar-Year: Initial Day.	Jupiter-Cycles: 60 Years: S. Sid.	Jupiter-Cycles: 60 Years: Tel.	Jupiter-Cycles: 12 Years.	Sapt. Rishi.	Chedi Sam.	Harsha Kâl.
781	3882	21 Mar	838	Bhâd	703	Th 1 Mar	12.54	65.55	Paush	57	532	175
782	83	21 —	839	...	704	We 20 Mar	55	56	Mâgh	58	533	176
783	84	22 —	840	...	705	S 9 Mar	56	57	Phâl	59	534	177
*784	85	21 —	841	Ashad	706	Th 26 Feb	57	58	Chait	60	535	178
785	86	21 —	842	...	707	Th 17 Mar	58	59	Vais	61	536	179
786	87	21 —	843	...	708	Mo 6 Mar	59	60	Jyesh	62	537	180
787	88	22 —	844	Jyesh	709	Sa 24 Feb	60	66. 1	Ashad	63	538	181
*788	89	21 —	845	...	710	Th 13 Mar	13. 1	2	Srâv	64	539	182
789	90	21 —	846	Aswa	711	Th 3 Mar	2	3	Bhâd	65	540	183
790	3891	21 —	847	...	712	S 21 Mar	3	4	Aswa	66	541	184
791	3892	21 Mar	848	...	713	Th 10 Mar	4	5	Kârt	67	542	185
*792	93	22 —	849	Srâv	714	We 29 Feb	5	6	Agra	68	543	186
793	94	21 —	850	...	715	Mo 18 Mar	6	7	Paush	69	544	187
794	95	22 —	851	...	716	Sa 8 Mar	7	8	Mâgh	70	545	188
795	96	22 —	852	Ashad	717	We 25 Feb	8	9	Phâl	71	546	189
*796	97	21 —	853	...	718	Tu 15 Mar	9	10	Chait	72	547	190
797	98	21 —	854	...	719	Sa 4 Mar	10	11	Vais	73	548	191
798	99	21 —	855	Vais	720	We 21 Feb	11	12	Jyesh	74	549	192
799	3900	22 —	856	...	721	Tu 12 Mar	12	13	Ashad	75	550	193
*800	3901	21 —	857	Bhâd	722	S 2 Mar	13	14	Srâv	76	551	194
801	3902	21 Mar	858	...	723	Sa 20 Mar	14	15	Bhâd	77	552	195
802	03	21 —	859	...	724	We 9 Mar	15	16	Aswa	78	553	196
803	04	22 —	860	Ashad	725	Mo 27 Feb	16	17	Kârt	79	554	197
*804	05	21 —	861	...	726	Sa 16 Mar	17	18	Agra	80	555	198
805	06	21 —	862	...	727	We 5 Mar	18	19	Paush	81	556	199
806	07	22 —	868	Jyesh	728	Mo 23 Feb	19	20	Mâgh	82	557	200
807	08	22 —	864	...	729	S 14 Mar	20	21	Phâl	83	558	201
*808	09	21 —	865	Aswa	730	Th 2 Mar	21	22	Chait	84	559	202
809	10	21 —	866	...	731	We 21 Mar	22	23	Vais	85	560	203
810	3911	22 —	867	...	732	Mo 12 Mar	13.23	66.24	Jyesh	86	561	204

TABLE XVII.—(Continued.)

General Table of Corresponding Dates.

A. D.	Solar-Year.		Luni-Solar-Year.					Jupiter-Cycles.			Sapt. Rishi.	Chedi Sam.	Harsha Kâl.
	Kali Yuga.	Initial Day.	Vik Sam	Intercal Month.	Sak Sal	Initial Day.		60 Years.		12 Years.			
								S. Sid.	Tel.				
811	3912	22 Mar	868	Srâv	733	Fr	28 Feb	13.24	66.25	Ashad	87	562	205
*812	13	21 —	869	...	734	Th	18 Mar	25	26	Srâv	88	563	206
813	14	21 —	870	...	735	Mo	7 Mar	26	27	Bhâd	89	564	207
814	15	21 —	871	Ashad	736	Fr	24 Feb	27	28	Aswa	90	565	208
815	16	22 —	872	...	737	Fr	16 Mar	28	29	Kârt	91	566	209
*816	17	22 —	873	...	738	We	5 Mar	29	30	Agra	92	567	210
817	18	21 —	874	Vais	739	Sa	21 Feb	30	31	Paush	93	568	211
818	19	22 —	875	...	740	Sa	13 Mar	31	32	Mâgh	94	569	212
819	20	22 —	876	Bhâd	741	We	2 Mar	32	33	Phâl	95	570	213
*820	3921	21 —	877	...	742	Mo	19 Mar	34	34	Vais	96	571	214
821	3922	21 Mar	878	...	743	Sa	9 Mar	35	35	Jyesh	97	572	215
822	23	22 —	879	Ashad	744	Th	27 Feb	36	36	Ashad	98	573	216
823	24	22 —	880	...	745	Tu	17 Mar	37	37	Srâv	99	574	217
*824	25	21 —	881	...	746	Sa	5 Mar	38	38	Bhâd	100	575	218
825	26	21 —	882	Jyesh	747	Th	23 Feb	39	39	Aswa	1	576	219
826	27	22 —	883	...	748	We	14 Mar	40	40	Kârt	2	577	220
827	28	22 —	884	Ashad	749	S	3 Mar	41	41	Agra	3	578	221
*828	29	22 —	885	...	750	S	22 Mar	42	42	Paush	4	579	222
829	30	21 —	886	...	751	We	10 Mar	43	43	Mâgh	5	580	223
830	3931	22 —	887	Srâv	752	Mo	28 Feb	44	44	Phâl	6	581	224
831	3932	22 Mar	888	...	753	S	19 Mar	45	45	Chait	7	582	225
*832	33	22 —	889	...	754	Fr	8 Mar	46	46	Vais	8	583	226
833	34	22 —	890	Ashad	755	Tu	25 Feb	47	47	Jyesh	9	584	227
834	35	22 —	891	...	756	Mo	16 Mar	48	48	Ashad	10	585	228
835	36	22 —	892	...	757	Fr	5 Mar	49	49	Srâv	11	586	229
*836	37	22 —	893	Chait	758	We	23 Feb	50	50	Bhâd	12	587	230
837	38	22 —	894	...	759	Mo	12 Mar	51	51	Aswa	13	588	231
838	39	22 —	895	Srâv	760	Fr	1 Mar	52	52	Kârt	14	589	232
839	40	22 —	896	...	761	Th	20 Mar	53	53	Agra	15	590	233
*840	3941	21 —	897	...	762	Mo	8 Mar	13.54	66.54	Paush	16	591	234

TABLE XVII.—(Continued.)

General Table of Corresponding Dates.

A. D.	Solar-Year.		Luni-Solar-Year.				Jupiter-Cycles.			Sapt. Rishi.	Chedi Sam.	Harsha Kâl.
	Kali Yuga.	Initial Day.	Vik Sam	Intercal Mouth.	Sak Sal.	Initial Day.	60 Years. S. Sid.	60 Years. Tel.	12 Years			
841	3942	22 Mar	898	Ashad	763	Sa 26 Feb	13.55	66.55	Mâgh	17	592	235
842	43	22 —	899	...	764	Fr 17 Mar	56	56	Phâl	18	593	236
843	44	22 —	900	...	765	Tu 6 Mar	57	57	Chait	19	594	237
*844	45	21 —	901	Jyesh	766	Sa 23 Feb	58	58	Vais	20	595	238
845	46	22 —	902	...	767	Sa 14 Mar	59	59	Jyesh	21	596	239
846	47	22 —	903	Ashad	768	We 3 Mar	60	60	Ashad	22	597	240
847	48	22 —	904	...	769	Mo 22 Mar	14. 1	67. 1	Srâv	23	598	241
*848	49	21 —	905	...	770	Sa 10 Mar	2	2	Bhâd	24	599	242
849	50	22 —	906	Srâv	771	Th 28 Feb	3	3	Aswa	25	600	243
850	3951	22 —	907	...	772	Tu 18 Mar	4	4	Kârt	26	601	244
851	3952	22 Mar	908	...	773	Sa 7 Mar	5	5	Agra	27	602	245
*852	53	21 —	909	Ashad	774	Th 25 Feb	6	6	Paush	28	603	246
853	54	22 —	910	...	775	We 15 Mar	7	7	Mâgh	29	604	247
854	55	22 —	911	...	776	S 4 Mar	8	8	Phâl	30	605	248
855	56	22 —	912	Chait	777	Fr 22 Feb	9	9	Chait	31	606	249
*856	57	21 —	913	...	778	We 11 Mar	10	10	Vais	32	607	250
857	58	22 —	914	Srâv	779	Mo 1 Mar	11	11	Jyesh	33	608	251
858	59	22 —	915	...	780	S 20 Mar	12	12	Ashad	34	609	252
859	60	22 —	916	...	781	Th 9 Mar	13	13	Srâv	35	610	253
*860	3961	22 —	917	Ashad	782	Tu 27 Feb	14	14	Bhâd	36	611	254
861	3962	22 Mar	918	...	783	Th 17 Mar	15	15	Aswa	37	612	255
862	63	22 —	919	...	784	Fr 6 Mar	16	16	Kârt	38	613	256
863	64	22 —	920	Vais	785	Tu 23 Feb	17	17	Agra	39	614	257
*864	65	22 —	921	...	786	Tu 14 Mar	18	18	Paush	40	615	258
865	66	22 —	922	Bhâd	787	Sa 3 Mar	19	19	Mâgh	41	616	259
866	67	22 —	923	...	788	Th 21 Mar	20	20	Phâl	42	617	260
867	68	22 —	924	...	789	Mo 10 Mar	21	21	Chait	43	618	261
*868	69	22 —	925	Srâv	790	Sa 28 Feb	22	22	Vais	44	619	262
869	70	22 —	926	...	791	Fr 18 Mar	23	23	Jyesh	45	620	263
870	3971	22 —	927	...	792	Tu 7 Mar	14.24	67.24	Ashad	46	621	264

TABLE XVII.—(Continued.)

General Table of Corresponding Dates.

A. D.	Solar-Year.		Luni-Solar-Year.				Jupiter-Cycles.			Sapt. Rishi.	Chedi Sam.	Harsha Kal.
	Kali Yuga.	Initial Day.	Vik Sam	Intercal Month.	Sak Sal.	Initial Day.	60 Years. S. Sid.	60 Years. Tel.	12 Years.			
871	3972	22 Mar	928	Jyesh	793	Sa 24 Feb	14.25	67.25	Srâv	47	622	265
*872	73	22 —	929	...	794	Sa 15 Mar	26	26	Bhâd	48	623	266
873	74	22 —	930	...	795	We 4 Mar	27	27	Aswa	49	624	267
874	75	22 —	931	Chait	796	Mo 22 Feb	28	28	Kârt	50	625	268
875	76	22 —	932	...	797	Tu 12 Mar	29	29	Agra	51	626	269
*876	77	22 —	933	Srâv	798	Th 1 Mar	30	30	Paush	52	627	270
877	78	22 —	934	...	799	We 20 Mar	31	31	Mâgh	53	628	271
878	79	22 —	935	...	800	S 9 Mar	32	32	Phâl	54	629	272
879	80	22 —	936	Ashad	801	Th 26 Feb	33	33	Chait	55	630	273
*880	3981	22 —	937	...	802	We 16 Mar	34	34	Vais	56	631	274
881	3982	22 Mar	938	...	803	Mo 6 Mar	35	35	Jyesh	57	632	275
882	83	22 —	939	Vais	804	Fr 23 Feb	36	36	Ashad	58	633	276
883	84	22 —	940	...	805	We 13 Mar	37	37	Srâv	59	634	277
*884	85	22 —	941	Bhâd	806	Tu 3 Mar	38	38	Bhâd	60	635	278
885	86	22 —	942	...	807	S 21 Mar	39	39	Aswa	61	636	279
886	87	22 —	943	...	808	Th 10 Mar	40	40	Kârt	62	637	280
887	88	22 —	944	Srâv	809	Mo 27 Feb	41	41	Agra	63	638	281
*888	89	22 —	945	...	810	Mo 18 Mar	42	42	Paush	64	639	282
889	90	22 —	946	...	811	Fr 7 Mar	43	43	Mâgh	65	640	283
890	3991	22 —	947	Jyesh	812	Tu 24 Feb	44	44	Phâl	66	641	284
891	3992	22 Mar	948	...	813	Mo 15 Mar	45	45	Chait	67	642	285
*892	93	22 —	949	†	814	Sa 4 Mar	46	46	Vais	68	643	286
893	94	22 —	950	Chait	815	We 21 Feb	47	47	Jyesh	69	644	287
894	95	22 —	951	...	816	Fr 12 Mar	48	48	Ashad	70	645	288
895	96	22 —	952	Srâv	817	Sa 1 Mar	49	49	Srâv	71	646	289
*896	97	22 —	953	...	818	Sa 20 Mar	50	50	Bhâd	72	647	290
897	98	22 —	954	...	819	We 9 Mar	51	51	Aswa	73	648	291
898	99	22 —	955	Ashad	820	S 26 Feb	52	52	Kârt	74	649	292
899	4000	23 —	956	...	821	Sa 17 Mar	53	53	Agra	75	650	293
*900	4001	23 —	957	...	822	We 6 Mar	14.54	67.54	Paush	76	651	294

† Kârtika omitted, and Kârtika intercalary.

TABLE XVII.—(Continued.)

General Table of Corresponding Dates.

A. D.	Solar-Year. Kali Yuga.	Solar-Year. Initial Day.	Luni-Solar-Year. Vik Sam	Luni-Solar-Year. Intercal Month.	Luni-Solar-Year. Sak Sal.	Luni-Solar-Year. Initial Day.	Jupiter-Cycles. 60 Years. S. Sid.	Jupiter-Cycles. 60 Years. Tel.	Jupiter-Cycles. 12 Years.	Sapt. Rishi.	Chedi Sam.	Harsha Kâl.
901	4002	22 Mar	958	Vais	823	S 22 Feb	14.55	67.55	Mâgh	77	652	295
902	03	23 —	959	...	824	S 14 Mar	56	56	Phâl	78	653	296
903	04	23 —	960	Bhâd	825	Th 3 Mar	57	57	Chait	79	654	297
*904	05	22 —	961	...	826	We 21 Mar	58	58	Vais	80	655	298
905	06	22 —	962	...	827	S 10 Mar	60	59	Ashad	81	656	299
906	07	23 —	963	Srâv	828	Fr 28 Feb	15. 1	60	Srâv	82	657	300
907	08	23 —	964	...	829	Th 19 Mar	2	68. 1	Bhâd	83	658	301
*908	09	22 —	965	...	830	Mo 7 Mar	3	2	Aswa	84	659	302
909	10	22 —	966	Jyesh	831	Fr 24 Feb	4	3	Kârt	85	660	303
910	4011	23 —	967	...	832	Th 15 Mar	5	4	Agra	86	661	304
911	4012	23 Mar	968	†...	833	Tu 5 Mar	6	5	Paush	87	662	305
*912	13	22 —	969	Chait	834	S 23 Feb	7	6	Mâgh	88	663	306
913	14	23 —	970	...	835	Sa 13 Mar	8	7	Phâl	89	664	307
914	15	22 —	971	Srâv	836	Tu 1 Mar	9	8	Chait	90	665	308
915	16	23 —	972	...	837	Mo 20 Mar	10	9	Vais	91	666	309
*916	17	22 —	973	...	838	Fr 8 Mar	11	10	Jyesh	92	667	310
917	18	22 —	974	Ashad	839	Tu 25 Feb	12	11	Ashad	93	668	311
918	19	22 —	975	...	840	Mo 16 Mar	13	12	Srâv	94	669	312
919	20	23 —	976	...	841	Sa 6 Mar	14	13	Bhâd	95	670	313
*920	4021	22 —	977	Vais	842	We 23 Feb	15	14	Aswa	96	671	314
921	4022	22 Mar	978	...	843	Tu 13 Mar	16	15	Kârt	97	672	315
922	23	22 —	979	Bhâd	844	Sa 2 Mar	17	16	Agra	98	673	316
923	24	23 —	980	...	845	Sa 22 Mar	18	17	Paush	99	674	317
*924	25	22 —	981	...	846	We 10 Mar	19	18	Mâgh	100	675	318
925	26	22 —	982	Ashad	847	S 27 Feb	20	19	Phâl	1	676	319
926	27	22 —	983	...	848	Sa 18 Mar	21	20	Chait	2	677	320
927	28	23 —	984	...	849	Th 8 Mar	22	21	Vais	3	678	321
*928	29	22 —	985	Jyesh	850	Mo 25 Feb	23	22	Jyesh	4	679	322
929	30	22 —	986	...	851	Sa 14 Mar	24	23	Ashad	5	680	323
930	4031	22 —	987	Aswa	852	Th 4 Mar	15.25	68.24	Srâv	6	681	324

† Agrahayana omitted, and Aswina intercalary.

TABLE XVII.—(Continued.)

General Table of Corresponding Dates.

A. D.	Solar-Year. Kali Yuga.	Solar-Year. Initial Day.	Luni-Solar-Year. Vik Sam	Luni-Solar-Year. Intercal Month.	Luni-Solar-Year. Sak Sal.	Luni-Solar-Year. Initial Day.	Jupiter-Cycles. 60 Years. S. Sid.	Jupiter-Cycles. 60 Years. Tel.	Jupiter-Cycles. 12 Years.	Sapt. Rishi.	Chedi Sam.	Harsha Kâl.
931	4032	23 Mar.	988	...	853	We 23 Mar	15.26	68.25	Bhâd	7	682	325
*932	33	23 —	989	...	854	Mo 12 Mar	27	26	Aswa	8	683	326
933	34	22 —	990	Srâv	855	Fr 1 Mar	28	27	Kârt	9	684	327
934	35	23 —	991	...	856	Th 20 Mar	29	28	Agra	10	685	328
935	36	23 —	992	...	857	Mo 9 Mar	30	29	Paush	11	686	329
*936	37	23 —	993	Ashad	858	Sa 27 Feb	31	30	Mâgh	12	687	330
937	38	22 —	994	...	859	Th 16 Mar	32	31	Phâl	13	688	331
938	39	23 —	995	...	860	Tu 6 Mar	33	32	Chait	14	689	332
939	40	23 —	996	Vais	861	Sa 23 Feb	34	33	Vais	15	690	333
*940	4041	22 —	997	...	862	Fr 13 Mar	35	34	Jyesh	16	691	334
941	4042	22 Mar.	998	Bhâd	863	Tu 2 Mar	36	35	Ashad	17	692	335
942	43	23 —	999	...	864	Mo 21 Mar	37	36	Srâv	18	693	336
943	44	23 —	1000	...	865	Fr 10 Mar	38	37	Bhâd	19	694	337
*944	45	22 —	1001	Ashad	866	We 28 Feb	39	38	Aswa	20	695	338
945	46	23 —	1002	...	867	Tu 18 Mar	40	39	Kârt	21	696	339
946	47	23 —	1003	...	868	S 7 Mar	41	40	Agra	22	697	340
947	48	23 —	1004	Jyesh	869	We 24 Feb	42	41	Paush	23	698	341
*948	49	22 —	1005	...	870	Mo 14 Mar	43	42	Mâgh	24	699	342
949	50	22 —	1006	Aswa	871	Sa 3 Mar	44	43	Phâl	25	700	343
950	4051	23 —	1007	...	872	Sa 23 Mar	45	44	Chait	26	701	344
951	4052	23 Mar.	1008	...	873	We 12 Mar	46	45	Vais	27	702	345
*952	53	22 —	1009	Srâv	874	S 29 Feb	47	46	Jyesh	28	703	346
953	54	22 —	1010	...	875	Sa 19 Mar	48	47	Ashad	29	704	347
954	55	23 —	1011	...	876	Th 9 Mar	49	48	Srâv	30	705	348
955	56	23 —	1012	Jyesh	877	Mo 26 Feb	50	49	Bhâd	31	706	349
*956	57	22 —	1013	...	878	S 16 Mar	51	50	Aswa	32	707	350
957	58	22 —	1014	...	879	Th 5 Mar	52	51	Kârt	33	708	351
958	59	23 —	1015	Vais	880	Tu 23 Feb	53	52	Agra	34	709	352
959	60	23 —	1016	...	881	Mo 14 Mar	54	53	Paush	35	710	353
*960	4061	22 —	1017	Bhâd	882	Fr 2 Mar	15.55	68.54	Mâgh	36	711	354

TABLE XVII.—(Continued.)

General Table of Corresponding Dates.

A. D.	Solar-Year.		Luni-Solar-Year.				Jupiter-Cycles.			Sapt. Rishi.	Chedi Sam.	Harsha Kâl.
	Kali Yuga.	Initial Day.	Vik Sam	Intercal Month.	Sak Sal.	Initial Day.	60 Years. S. Sid.	60 Years. Tel.	12 Years.			
961	4062	23 Mar	1018	...	883	Th 21 Mar	15.56	68.55	Phâl	37	712	355
962	63	23 —	1019	...	884	Mo 10 Mar	57	56	Chait	38	713	356
963	64	23 —	1020	Ashad	885	Fr 27 Feb	58	57	Vais	39	714	357
*964	65	22 —	1021	...	886	Th 17 Mar	59	58	Jyesh	40	715	358
965	66	23 —	1022	...	887	Tu 7 Mar	60	59	Ashad	41	716	359
966	67	23 —	1023	Jyesh	888	Sa 24 Feb	16. 1	60	Srâv	42	717	360
967	68	23 —	1024	...	889	Fr 15 Mar	2	69. 1	Bhâd	43	718	361
*968	69	22 —	1025	Aswa	890	Tu 3 Mar	3	2	Aswa	44	719	362
969	70	23 —	1026	...	891	Tu 23 Mar	4	3	Kârt	45	720	363
970	4071	23 —	1027	...	892	Sa 12 Mar	5	4	Agra	46	721	364
971	4072	23 Mar	1028	Srâv	893	We 1 Mar	6	5	Paush	47	722	365
*972	73	22 —	1029	...	894	Tu 19 Mar	7	6	Mâgh	48	723	366
973	74	23 —	1030	...	895	S 9 Mar	8	7	Phâl	49	724	367
974	75	23 —	1031	Jyesh	896	Mo 26 Feb	9	8	Chait	50	725	368
975	76	23 —	1032	...	897	Tu 16 Mar	10	9	Vais	51	726	369
*976	77	22 —	1033	...	898	S 5 Mar	11	10	Jyesh	52	727	370
977	78	23 —	1034	Chait	899	Fr 23 Feb	12	11	Ashad	53	728	371
978	79	23 —	1035	...	900	We 13 Mar	13	12	Srâv	54	729	372
979	80	23 —	1036	Bhâd	901	S 2 Mar	14	13	Bhâd	55	730	373
*980	4081	22 —	1037	...	902	Sa 20 Mar	15	14	Aswa	56	731	374
981	4082	23 Mar	1038	...	903	Th 10 Mar	16	15	Kârt	57	732	375
982	83	23 —	1039	Ashad	904	Mo 27 Feb	17	16	Agra	58	733	376
983	84	23 —	1040	...	905	S 18 Mar	18	17	Paush	59	734	377
*984	85	23 —	1041	...	906	Th 6 Mar	19	18	Mâgh	60	735	378
985	86	23 —	1042	Jyesh	907	Tu 24 Feb	20	19	Phâl	61	736	379
986	87	23 —	1043	...	908	Mo 15 Mar	21	20	Chait	62	737	380
987	88	23 —	1044	Aswa	909	Fr 4 Mar	22	21	Vais	63	738	381
*988	89	23 —	1045	...	910	Th 22 Mar	23	22	Jyesh	64	739	382
989	90	23 —	1046	...	911	Tu 12 Mar	16.24	23	Ashad	65	740	383
990	4091	23 —	1047	Srâv	912	Sa 1 Mar	26	69.24	Bhâd	66	741	384

TABLE XVII.—(Continued.)

General Table of Corresponding Dates.

A. D.	Solar-Year.		Luni-Solar-Year.				Jupiter-Cycles.			Sapt. Rishi.	Chedi Sam.	Harsha Kâl.
							60 Years.					
	Kali Yuga.	Initial Day.	Vik Sam	Intercal Month	Sak Sal.	Initial Day.	S. Sid.	Tel.	12 Years.			
991	4092	23 Mar	1048	...	913	Th 19 Mar	16.27	69.25	Aswa	67	742	385
*992	93	23 —	1049	...	914	Tu 8 Mar	28	26	Kârt	68	743	386
993	94	23 —	1050	Jyesh	915	Sa 25 Feb	29	27	Agra	69	744	387
994	95	23 —	1051	...	916	Fr 16 Mar	30	28	Paush	70	745	388
995	96	23 —	1052	...	917	We 6 Mar	31	29	Mâgh	71	746	389
*996	97	23 —	1053	Chait	918	Mo 24 Feb	32	30	Phâl	72	747	390
997	98	23 —	1054	...	919	Sa 13 Mar	33	31	Chait	73	748	391
998	99	23 —	1055	Srâv	920	We 2 Mar	34	32	Vais	74	749	392
999	4100	23 —	1056	...	921	Tu 21 Mar	35	33	Jyesh	75	750	393
*1000	4101	23 —	1057	...	922	S 10 Mar	36	34	Ashad	76	751	394
1001	4102	23 Mar	1058	Ashad	923	We 26 Feb	37	35	Srâv	77	752	395
1002	03	23 —	1059	...	924	We 18 Mar	38	36	Bhâd	78	753	396
1003	04	23 —	1060	...	925	S 7 Mar	39	37	Aswa	79	754	397
*1004	05	23 —	1061	Vais	926	Fr 25 Feb	40	38	Kârt	80	755	398
1005	06	23 —	1062	...	927	Th 15 Mar	41	39	Agra	81	756	399
1006	07	23 —	1063	Bhâd	928	Mo 4 Mar	42	40	Paush	82	757	400
1007	08	23 —	1064	...	929	Sa 22 Mar	43	41	Mâgh	83	758	401
*1008	09	28 —	1065	...	930	Th 11 Mar	44	42	Phâl	84	759	402
1009	10	23 —	1066	Srâv	931	Mo 28 Feb	45	43	Chait	85	760	403
1010	4111	23 —	1067	...	932	S 19 Mar	46	44	Vais	86	761	404
1011	4112	23 Mar	1068	...	933	Th 8 Mar	47	45	Jyesh	87	762	405
*1012	13	23 —	1069	Jyesh	934	Tu 26 Feb	48	46	Ashad	88	763	406
1013	14	23 —	1070	...	935	Mo 16 Mar	49	47	Srâv	89	764	407
1014	15	23 —	1071	...	936	Fr 5 Mar	50	48	Bhâd	90	765	408
1015	16	23 —	1072	Chait	937	Th 24 Feb	51	49	Aswa	91	766	409
*1016	17	23 —	1073	...	938	Tu 13 Mar	52	50	Kârt	92	767	410
1017	18	23 —	1074	Srâv	939	Sa 2 Mar	53	51	Agra	93	768	411
1018	19	23 —	1075	...	940	Fr 21 Mar	54	52	Paush	94	769	412
1019	20	24 —	1076	...	941	Tu 10 Mar	55	53	Mâgh	95	770	413
*1020	4121	23 —	1077	Ashad	942	S 28 Feb	16.56	69.54	Phâl	96	771	414

TABLE XVII.—(Continued.)

General Table of Corresponding Dates.

A. D.	Solar-Year.		Luni-Solar-Year.				Jupiter-Cycles.			Sapt. Rishi.	Chedi Sam.	Harsha Kal.
	Kali Yuga.	Initial Day.	Vik Sam	Intercal Month.	Sak Sal.	Initial Day.	60 Years. S. Sid	60 Years. Tel.	12 Years.			
1021	4122	23 Mar.	1078	...	943	Fr 17 Mar	16·57	69·55	Chait	97	772	415
1022	23	23 —	1079	...	944	We 7 Mar	58	56	Vais	98	773	416
1023	24	24 —	1080	Vais	945	S 24 Feb	59	57	Jyesh	99	774	417
*1024	25	23 —	1081	...	946	Sa 14 Mar	60	58	Ashad	100	775	418
1025	26	23 —	1082	Bhâd	947	We 3 Mar	17·1	59	Srâv	1	776	419
1026	27	23 —	1083	...	948	Tu 22 Mar	2	60	Bhâd	2	777	420
1027	28	24 —	1084	...	949	S 12 Mar	3	70·1	Aswa	3	778	421
*1028	29	23 —	1085	Srâv	950	Th 29 Feb	4	2	Kârt	4	779	422
1029	30	23 —	1086	...	951	We 19 Mar	5	3	Agra	5	780	423
1030	4131	23 —	1087	...	952	S 8 Mar	6	4	Paush	6	781	424
1031	4132	24 Mar	1088	Jyesh	953	Fr 26 Feb	7	5	Mâgh	7	782	425
*1032	33	23 —	1089	...	954	Th 16 Mar	8	6	Phâl	8	783	426
1033	34	23 —	1090	...	955	Mo 5 Mar	9	7	Chait	9	784	427
1034	35	23 —	1091	Chait	956	Fr 22 Feb	10	8	Vais	10	785	428
1035	36	24 —	1092	...	957	Th 13 Mar	11	9	Jyesh	11	786	429
*1036	37	23 —	1093	Srâv	958	Tu 2 Mar	12	10	Ashad	12	787	430
1037	38	24 —	1094	...	959	Mo 21 Mar	13	11	Srâv	13	788	431
1038	39	24 —	1095	...	960	Fr 10 Mar	14	12	Bhâd	14	789	432
1039	40	24 —	1096	Ashad	961	Tu 27 Feb	15	13	Aswa	15	790	433
*1040	4141	23 —	1097	...	962	S 17 Mar	16	14	Kârt	16	791	434
1041	4142	24 Mar	1098	...	963	Sa 7 Mar	17	15	Agra	17	792	435
1042	43	24 —	1099	Vais	964	We 24 Feb	18	16	Paush	18	793	436
1043	44	24 —	1100	...	965	Tu 15 Mar	19	17	Mâgh	19	794	437
*1044	45	23 —	1101	Bhâd	966	Sa 3 Mar	20	18	Phâl	20	795	438
1045	46	23 —	1102	...	967	Fr 22 Mar	21	19	Chait	21	796	439
1046	47	24 —	1103	...	968	We 12 Mar	22	20	Vais	22	797	440
1047	48	24 —	1104	Srâv	969	S 1 Mar	23	21	Jyesh	23	798	441
*1048	49	23 —	1105	...	970	Sa 19 Mar	24	22	Ashad	24	799	442
1049	50	24 —	1106	...	971	Th 9 Mar	25	23	Srâv	25	800	443
1050	4151	24 —	1107	Jyesh	972	Mo 26 Feb	17·26	70·24	Bhâd	26	801	444

TABLE XVII.—(Continued.)

General Table of Corresponding Dates.

A. D.	Solar-Year.		Luni-Solar-Year.				Jupiter-Cycles.			Sapt. Rishi.	Chedi Sam.	Harsha Kál.
	Kali Yuga.	Initial Day.	Vik Sam	Intercal Month.	Sak Sal.	Initial Day.	60 Years. S. Sid.	60 Years. Tel.	12 Years.			
1051	4152	24 Mar	1108	...	973	S 17 Mar	17.27	70.25	Aswa	27	802	445
*1052	†53	23 —	1109	...	974	Th 5 Mar	28	26	Kârt	28	803	446
1053	54	23 —	1110	Chait	975	Mo 22 Feb	29	27	Agra	29	804	447
1054	55	24 —	1111	...	976	S 13 Mar	30	28	Paush	30	805	448
1055	56	24 —	1112	Srâv	977	Th 2 Mar	31	29	Mâgh	31	806	449
*1056	57	23 —	1113	...	978	We 20 Mar	32	30	Phâl	32	807	450
1057	58	23 —	1114	...	979	S 9 Mar	33	31	Chait	33	808	451
1058	59	24 —	1115	Jyesh	980	Fr 27 Feb	34	32	Vais	34	809	452
1059	60	24 —	1116	...	981	Th 18 Mar	35	33	Jyesh	35	810	453
*1060	4161	23 —	1117	...	982	Mo 6 Mar	36	34	Ashad	36	811	454
1061	4162	24 Mar	1118	Vais	983	Sa 24 Feb	37	35	Srâv	37	812	455
1062	63	24 —	1119	...	984	Fr 15 Mar	38	36	Bhâd	38	813	456
1063	64	24 —	1120	Bhâd	985	Tu 4 Mar	39	37	Aswa	39	814	457
*1064	65	23 —	1121	...	986	Mo 22 Mar	40	38	Kârt	40	815	458
1065	66	23 —	1122	...	987	Fr 11 Mar	41	39	Agra	41	816	459
1066	67	24 —	1123	Ashad	988	We 1 Mar	42	40	Paush	42	817	460
1067	68	24 —	1124	...	989	Mo 19 Mar	43	41	Mâgh	43	818	461
*1068	69	23 —	1125	...	990	Fr 8 Mar	44	42	Phâl	44	819	462
1069	70	24 —	1126	Jyesh	991	Th 26 Feb	45	43	Chait	45	820	463
1070	4171	24 —	1127	...	992	Tu 16 Mar	46	44	...	46	821	464
1071	4172	24 Mar	1128	Aswa	993	Sa 5 Mar	47	45	Jyesh	47	822	465
*1072	73	23 —	1129	...	994	Fr 23 Mar	48	46	Ashad	48	823	466
1073	74	24 —	1130	...	995	We 13 Mar	49	47	Srâv	49	824	467
1074	75	24 —	1131	Srâv	996	S 2 Mar	50	48	Bhâd	50	825	468
1075	76	24 —	1132	...	997	Sa 21 Mar	52	49	Kârt	51	826	469
*1076	77	23 —	1133	...	998	We 9 Mar	53	50	Agra	52	827	470
1077	78	24 —	1134	Jyesh	999	Mo 27 Feb	54	51	Paush	53	828	471
1078	79	24 —	1135	...	1000	S 18 Mar	55	52	Mâgh	54	829	472
1079	80	24 —	1136	...	1001	Th 7 Mar	56	53	Phâl	55	830	473
*1080	4181	23 —	1137	Vais	1002	Mo 24 Feb	17.57	70.54	Chait	56	831	474

† Agrahayana omitted, and Aswina intercalary.

TABLE XVII.—(Continued.)

General Table of Corresponding Dates.

A. D.	Solar-Year. Kali Yuga.	Solar-Year. Initial Day.	Luni-Solar-Year. Vik Sam	Luni-Solar-Year. Intercal Month.	Luni-Solar-Year. Sak Sal.	Luni-Solar-Year. Initial Day.	Jupiter-Cycles. 60 Years. S. Sid.	Jupiter-Cycles. 60 Years. Tel.	Jupiter-Cycles. 12 Years.	Sapt. Rishi.	Chedi Sam.	Harsha Kâl.
1081	4182	24 Mar	1138	...	1003	Mo 15 Mar	17.58	70.55	Vais	57	832	475
1082	83	24 —	1139	Bhâd	1004	Fr 4 Mar	59	56	Jyesh	58	833	476
1083	84	24 —	1140	...	1005	We 22 Mar	60	57	Ashad	59	834	477
*1084	85	24 —	1141	...	1006	Mo 11 Mar	18· 1	58	Srâv	60	835	478
1085	86	24 —	1142	Ashad	1007	Fr 28 Feb	2	59	Bhâd	61	836	479
1086	87	24 —	1143	...	1008	Th 19 Mar	3	60	Aswa	62	837	480
1087	88	24 —	1144	...	1009	Mo 8 Mar	4	71. 1	Kârt	63	838	481
*1088	89	24 —	1145	Jyesh	1010	Sa 26 Feb	5	2	Agra	64	839	482
1089	90	24 —	1146	...	1011	Fr 16 Mar	6	3	Paush	65	840	483
1090	4191	24 —	1147	Aswa	1012	Tu 5 Mar	7	4	Mâgh	66	841	484
1091	4192	24 Mar	1148	...	1013	Mo 24 Mar	8	5	Phâl	67	842	485
*1092	93	24 —	1149	...	1014	Sa 13 Mar	9	6	Chait	68	843	486
1093	94	24 —	1150	Srâv	1015	We 2 Mar	10	7	Vais	69	844	487
1094	95	24 —	1151	...	1016	Tu 21 Mar	11	8	Jyesh	70	845	488
1095	96	24 —	1152	...	1017	Sa 10 Mar	12	9	Ashad	71	846	489
*1096	97	24 —	1153	Jyesh	1018	Th 28 Feb	13	10	Srâv	72	847	490
1097	98	24 —	1154	...	1019	We 18 Mar	14	11	Bhâd	73	848	491
1098	99	24 —	1155	...	1020	S 7 Mar	15	12	Aswa	74	849	492
1099	4200	24 —	1156	Vais	1021	Th 24 Feb	16	13	Kârt	75	850	493
*1100	4201	24 —	1157	...	1022	We 14 Mar	17	14	Agra	76	851	494
1101	4202	24 Mar	1158	Bhâd	1023	S 3 Mar	18	15	Paush	77	852	495
1102	03	24 —	1159	...	1024	Sa 22 Mar	19	16	Mâgh	78	853	496
1103	04	24 —	1160	...	1025	We 11 Mar	20	17	Phâl	79	854	497
*1104	05	24 —	1161	Ashad	1026	Mo 29 Feb	21	18	Chait	80	855	498
1105	06	24 —	1162	...	1027	S 19 Mar	22	19	Vais	81	856	499
1106	07	24 —	1163	...	1028	Th 8 Mar	23	20	Jyesh	82	857	500
1107	08	24 —	1164	Jyesh	1029	Mo 25 Feb	24	21	Ashad	83	858	501
*1108	09	84 —	1165	...	1030	Mo 16 Mar	25	22	Srâv	84	859	502
1109	10	24 —	1166	Aswa	1031	Fr 5 Mar	26	23	Bhâd	85	860	503
1110	4211	24 —	1167	...	1032	Th 24 Mar	18.27	71.24	Aswa	86	861	504

TABLE XVII.—(Continued.)

General Table of Corresponding Dates.

A.D.	Solar-Year.		Luni-Solar-Year.				Jupiter-Cycles.			Sapt. Rishi.	Chedi Sam.	Harsha Kâl.
							60 Years.					
	Kali Yuga.	Initial Day.	Vik Sam	Intercal Month.	Sak Sal.	Initial Day.	S. Sid.	Tel.	12 Years.			
1111	4212	24 Mar	1168	...	1033	Mo 13 Mar	18.28	71.25	Kârt	87	862	505
*1112	13	24 —	1169	Srâv	1034	We 2 Mar	29	26	Agra	88	863	506
1113	14	24 —	1170	...	1035	Th 20 Mar	30	27	Paush	89	864	507
1114	15	24 —	1171	...	1036	Tu 10 Mar	31	28	Mâgh	90	865	508
1115	16	24 —	1172	Jyesh	1037	Sa 27 Feb	32	29	Phâl	91	866	509
*1116	17	24 —	1173	...	1038	Fr 17 Mar	33	30	Chait	92	867	510
1117	18	24 —	1174	...	1039	Tu 6 Mar	34	1	Vais	93	868	511
1118	19	24 —	1175	Chait	1040	Sa 23 Feb	35	2	Jyesh	94	869	512
1119	20	24 —	1176	...	1041	Fr 14 Mar	36	3	Ashad	95	870	513
*1120	4221	24 —	1177	Bhâd	1042	We 3 Mar	37	4	Srâv	96	871	514
1121	4222	24 Mar	1178	...	1043	Tu 22 Mar	38	5	Bhâd	97	872	515
1122	23	24 —	1179	...	1044	Sa 11 Mar	39	6	Aswa	98	873	516
1123	24	24 —	1180	Ashad	1045	We 28 Feb	40	7	Kârt	99	874	517
*1124	25	24 —	1181	...	1046	We 19 Mar	41	8	Agra	100	875	518
1125	26	24 —	1182	...	1047	S 8 Mar	42	9	Paush	1	876	519
1126	27	24 —	1183	Jyesh	1048	Th 25 Feb	43	0	Mâgh	2	877	520
1127	28	24 —	1184	...	1049	We 16 Mar	44	1	Phâl	3	878	521
*1128	29	24 —	1185	Aswa	1050	Mo 5 Mar	45	2	Chait	4	879	522
1129	30	24 —	1186	..	1051	S 23 Mar	46	3	Vais	5	880	523
1130	4231	24 —	1187	...	1052	Th 13 Mar	47	4	Jyesh	6	881	524
1131	4232	24 Mar	1188	Ashad	1053	Mo 2 Mar	48	5	Ashad	7	882	525
*1132	33	24 —	1189	...	1054	S 2 Mar	49	6	Srâv	8	883	526
1133	34	24 —	1190	...	1055	Th 9 Mar	50	7	Bhâd	9	884	527
1134	35	24 —	1191	Jyesh	1056	Mo 26 Feb	51	8	Aswa	10	885	528
1135	36	25 —	1192	...	1057	Mo 18 Mar	52	9	Kârt	11	886	529
*1136	37	24 —	1193	...	1058	Fr 6 Mar	53	50	Agra	12	887	530
1137	38	24 —	1194	Chait	1059	Tu 23 Feb	54	1	Paush	13	888	531
1138	39	24 —	1195	...	1060	Th 14 Mar	55	2	Mâgh	14	889	532
1139	40	24 —	1196	Srâv	1061	Fr 3 Mar	56	3	Phâl	15	890	533
*1140	4241	24 —	1197	...	1062	Fr 22 Mar	18·57	71·4	Chait	16	891	534

TABLE XVII.—(Continued.)

General Table of Corresponding Dates.

A. D.	Solar-Year. Kali Yuga.	Solar-Year. Initial Day.	Luni-Solar-Year. Vik. Sam	Luni-Solar-Year. Intercal Month.	Luni-Solar-Year. Sak Sal.	Luni-Solar-Year. Initial Day.	Jupiter-Cycles. 60 Years. S. Sid.	Jupiter-Cycles. 60 Years. Tel.	Jupiter-Cycles. 12 Years.	Sapt. Rishi.	Chedi Sam.	Harsha Kâl.
1141	4242	24 Mar	1198	...	1063	Tu 13 Mar	18.58	71.55	Vais	17	892	535
1142	43	24 —	1199	Ashad	1064	Sa 28 Feb	59	56	Jyesh	18	893	536
1143	44	25 —	1200	...	1065	Fr 19 Mar	60	57	Ashad	19	894	537
*1144	45	24 —	1201	...	1066	We 8 Mar	19. 1	58	Srâv	20	895	538
1145	46	24 —	1202	Vais	1067	S 25 Feb	2	59	Bhâd	21	896	539
1146	47	25 —	1203	...	1068	Sa 16 Mar	3	60	Aswa	22	897	540
1147	48	25 —	1204	Bhâd	1069	We 5 Mar	4	72. 1	Kârt	23	898	541
*1148	49	24 —	1205	...	1070	Tu 23 Mar	5	2	Agra	24	899	542
1149	50	24 —	1206	...	1071	Sa 12 Mar	6	3	Paush	25	900	543
1150	4251	24 —	1207	Ashad	1072	We 1 Mar	7	4	Mâgh	26	901	544
1151	4252	25 Mar	1208	...	1073	We 21 Mar	8	5	Phâl	27	902	545
*1152	53	24 —	1209	...	1074	S 9 Mar	9	6	Chait	28	903	546
1153	54	24 —	1210	Jyesh	1075	Th 26 Feb	10	7	Vais	29	904	547
1154	55	24 —	1211	...	1076	We 17 Mar	11	8	Jyesh	30	905	548
1155	56	25 —	1212	...	1077	Mo 7 Mar	12	9	Ashad	31	906	549
*1156	57	24 —	1213	Chait	1078	Fr 24 Feb	13	10	Srâv	32	907	550
1157	58	24 —	1214	...	1079	Th 14 Mar	14	11	Bhâd	33	908	551
1158	59	24 —	1215	Srâv	1080	Mo 3 Mar	15	12	Aswa	34	909	552
1159	60	25 —	1216	...	1081	S 22 Mar	16	13	Kârt	35	910	553
*1160	4261	24 —	1217	...	1082	Fr 11 Mar	● 18	14	● Paush	36	911	554
1161	4262	24 Mar	1218	Ashad	1083	Tu 28 Feb	19	15	Mâgh	37	912	555
1162	63	25 —	1219	...	1084	Mo 19 Mar	20	16	Phâl	38	913	556
1163	64	25 —	1220	...	1085	Fr 8 Mar	21	17	Chait	39	914	557
*1164	65	24 —	1221	Vais	1086	We 26 Feb	22	18	Vais	40	915	558
1165	66	24 —	1222	...	1087	Mo 15 Mar	23	19	Jyesh	41	916	559
1166	67	25 —	1223	Bhâd	1088	Sa 5 Mar	24	20	Ashad	42	917	560
1167	68	25 —	1224	...	1089	Fr 24 Mar	25	21	Srâv	43	918	561
*1168	69	24 —	1225	...	1090	Tu 12 Mar	26	22	Bhâd	44	919	562
1169	70	24 —	1226	Srâv	1091	Sa 1 Mar	27	23	Aswa	45	920	563
1170	4271	25 —	1227	...	1092	Sa 21 Mar	19.28	72.24	Kârt	46	921	564

TABLE XVII.—(Continued.)

General Table of Corresponding Dates.

A. D.	Solar-Year.		Luni-Solar-Year.				Jupiter-Cycles.			Sapt. Rishi.	Chedi Sam.	Harsha Kál.
	Kali Yuga.	Initial Day.	Vik Sam	Intercal Month.	Sak Sal.	Initial Day.	60 Years. S. Sid.	60 Years. Tel.	12 Years.			
1171	4272	25 Mar	1228	...	1093	We 10 Mar	19.29	72.25	Agra	47	922	565
*1172	73	24 —	1229	Jyesh	1094	S 27 Feb	30	26	Paush	48	923	566
1173	74	24 —	1230	...	1095	Sa 17 Mar	31	27	Mâgh	49	924	567
1174	75	25 —	1231	...	1096	Th 7 Mar	32	28	Phâl	50	925	568
1175	76	25 —	1232	Chait	1097	Mo 24 Feb	33	29	Chait	51	926	569
*1176	77	24 —	1233	...	1098	Sa 13 Mar	34	30	Vais	52	927	570
1177	78	24 —	1234	Srâv	1099	We 2 Mar	35	31	Jyesh	53	928	571
1178	79	25 —	1235	...	1100	We 22 Mar	36	32	Ashad	54	929	572
1179	80	25 —	1236	...	1101	S 11 Mar	37	33	Srâv	55	930	573
*1180	4281	24 —	1237	Ashad	1102	Th 28 Feb	38	34	Bhâd	56	931	574
1181	4282	24 Mar	1238	...	1103	We 18 Mar	39	35	Aswa	57	932	575
1182	83	25 —	1239	...	1104	Mo 8 Mar	40	36	Kârt	58	933	576
1183	84	25 —	1240	Vais	1105	Fr 25 Feb	41	37	Agra	59	934	577
*1184	85	24 —	1241	...	1106	Th 15 Mar	42	38	Paush	60	935	578
1185	86	24 —	1242	Bhâd	1107	Mo 4 Mar	43	39	Mâgh	61	936	579
1186	87	25 —	1243	...	1108	Mo 24 Mar	44	40	Phâl	62	937	580
1187	88	25 —	1244	...	1109	Fr 13 Mar	45	41	Chait	63	938	581
*1188	89	24 —	1245	Srâv	1110	Tu 1 Mar	46	42	Vais	64	939	582
1189	90	24 —	1246	...	1111	Mo 20 Mar	47	43	Jyesh	65	940	583
1190	4291	25 —	1247	...	1112	Sa 10 Mar	48	44	Ashad	66	941	584
1191	4292	25 Mar	1248	Jyesh	1113	We 27 Feb	49	45	Srâv	67	942	585
*1192	93	24 —	1249	...	1114	Mo 16 Mar	50	46	Bhâd	68	943	586
1193	94	25 —	1250	†...	1115	Sa 6 Mar	51	47	Aswa	69	944	587
1194	95	25 —	1251	Chait	1116	We 23 Feb	52	48	Kârt	70	945	588
1195	96	25 —	1252	...	1117	Tu 14 Mar	53	49	Agra	71	946	589
*1196	97	24 —	1253	Srâv	1118	Sa 2 Mar	54	50	Paush	72	947	590
1197	98	25 —	1254	...	1119	Sa 22 Mar	55	51	Mâgh	73	948	591
1198	99	25 —	1255	...	1120	We 11 Mar	56	52	Phâl	74	949	592
1199	4300	25 —	1256	Jyesh	1121	S 28 Feb	57	53	Chait	75	950	593
*1200	4301	24 —	1257	...	1122	Sa 18 Mar	19.58	72.54	Vais	76	951	594

† Agrahayana omitted, and Aswina intercalary.

TABLE XVII.—(Continued.)

General Table of Corresponding Dates.

A. D.	Solar-Year.		Luni-Solar-Year.				Jupiter-Cycles.			Sapt. Rishi.	Cheli Sam.	Harsha Kâl.
	Kali Yuga.	Initial Day.	Vik Sam	Intercal Month.	Sak Sal.	Initial Day.	60 Years. S. Sid.	60 Years. Tel.	12 Years.			
1201	4302	25 Mar	1257	...	1123	Th 8 Mar	19.59	72.55	Jyesh	77	952	595
1202	03	25 —	1258	Vais	1124	Mo 25 Feb	60	56	Ashad	78	953	596
1203	04	25 —	1259	...	1125	S 16 Mar	20. 1	57	Srâv	79	954	597
*1204	05	24 —	1260	Bhâd	1126	Th 4 Mar	2	58	Bhâd	80	955	598
1205	06	25 —	1261	...	1127	Th 24 Mar	3	59	Aswa	81	956	599
1206	07	25 —	1262	...	1128	Mo 13 Mar	4	60	Kârt	82	957	600
1207	08	25 —	1263	Ashad	1129	Fr 2 Mar	5	73. 1	Agra	83	958	601
*1208	09	24 —	1264	...	1130	We 19 Mar	6	2	Paush	84	959	602
1209	10	25 —	1265	...	1131	Mo 9 Mar	7	3	Mâgh	85	960	603
1210	4311	25 —	1266	Jyesh	1132	Fr 26 Feb	8	4	Phâl	86	961	604
1211	4312	25 Mar	1267	...	1133	Th 17 Mar	9	5	Chait	87	962	605
*1212	13	25 —	1268	Aswa	1134	Tu 6 Mar	10	6	Vais	88	963	606
1213	14	25 —	1269	...	1135	Mo 25 Mar	11	7	Jyesh	89	964	607
1214	15	25 —	1270	...	1136	Fr 14 Mar	12	8	Ashad	90	965	608
1215	16	25 —	1271	Srâv	1137	Tu 3 Mar	13	9	Srâv	91	966	609
*1216	17	25 —	1272	...	1138	Tu 22 Mar	14	10	Bhâd	92	967	610
1217	18	25 —	1273	...	1139	Sa 11 Mar	15	11	Aswa	93	968	611
1218	19	25 —	1274	Jyesh	1140	We 28 Feb	16	12	Kârt	94	969	612
1219	20	25 —	1275	...	1141	Tu 19 Mar	17	13	Agra	95	970	613
*1220	4321	25 —	1276	...	1142	S 8 Mar	18	14	Paush	96	971	614
1221	4322	25 Mar	1277	Vais	1143	We 24 Feb	19	15	Mâgh	97	972	615
1222	23	25 —	1278	...	1144	We 16 Mar	20	16	Phâl	98	973	616
1223	24	25 —	1279	Bhâd	1145	S 5 Mar	21	17	Chait	99	974	617
*1224	25	25 —	1280	...	1146	Sa 23 Mar	22	18	Vais	100	975	618
1225	26	25 —	1281	...	1147	We 12 Mar	23	19	Jyesh	1	976	619
1226	27	25 —	1282	Ashad	1148	We 1 Mar	24	20	Ashad	2	977	620
1227	28	25 —	1283	...	1149	Sa 20 Mar	25	21	Srâv	3	978	621
*1228	29	25 —	1284	...	1150	Th 9 Mar	26	22	Bhâd	4	979	622
1229	30	25 —	1285	Jyesh	1151	Mo 26 Feb	27	23	Aswa	5	980	623
1230	4331	25 —	1286	...	1152	S 17 Mar	20.28	73.24	Kârt	6	981	624

TABLE XVII.—(Continued.)

General Table of Corresponding Dates.

A. D.	Solar-Year. Kali Yuga.	Solar-Year. Initial Day.	Luni-Solar-Year. Vik Sam	Luni-Solar-Year. Intercal Month.	Luni-Solar-Year. Sak Sal.	Luni-Solar-Year. Initial Day.	Jupiter-Cycles. 60 Years. S. Sid.	Jupiter-Cycles. 60 Years. Tel.	Jupiter-Cycles. 12 Years.	Sapt. Rishi.	Chedi Sam.	Harsha Kâl.
1231	4332	25 Mar	1288	Aswa	1153	Th 6 Mar	20.29	73. 25	Agra	7	982	625
*1232	33	25 —	1289	...	1154	Th 25 Mar	30	26	Paush	8	983	626
1233	34	25 —	1290	...	1155	Mo 14 Mar	31	27	Mâgh	9	984	627
1234	35	25 —	1291	Srâv	1156	Fr 3 Mar	32	28	Phâl	10	985	628
1235	36	25 —	1292	...	1157	Th 22 Mar	33	29	Chait	11	986	629
*1236	37	25 —	1293	...	1158	Tu 11 Mar	34	30	Vais	12	987	630
1237	38	25 —	1294	Jyesh	1159	Sa 28 Feb	35	31	Jyesh	13	988	631
1238	39	25 —	1295	...	1160	Mo 19 Mar	36	32	Ashad	14	989	632
1239	40	25 —	1296	...	1161	Tu 8 Mar	37	33	Srâv	15	990	633
*1240	4341	25 —	1297	Vais	1162	S 26 Feb	38	34	Bhâd	16	991	634
1241	4342	25 Mar	1298	...	1163	Fr 15 Mar	39	35	Aswa	17	992	635
1252	43	25 —	1299	Bhâd	1164	Tu 4 Mar	40	36	Kârt	18	993	636
1243	44	25 —	1300	...	1165	Mo 23 Mar	41	37	Agra	19	994	637
*1244	45	25 —	1301	...	1166	Sa 12 Mar	42	38	Paush	20	995	638
1245	46	25 —	1302	Ashad	1167	We 1 Mar	44	39	Phâl	21	996	639
1246	47	25 —	1303	...	1168	Tu 20 Mar	45	40	Chait	22	997	640
1247	48	25 —	1304	...	1169	Sa 9 Mar	46	41	Vais	23	998	641
*1248	49	25 —	1305	Jyesh	1170	We 26 Feb	47	42	Jyesh	24	999	642
1249	50	25 —	1306	...	1171	We 17 Feb	48	43	Ashad	25	1000	643
1250	4351	25 —	1307	Aswa	1172	S 6 Mar	49	44	Srâv	26	1001	644
1251	4352	26 Mar	1308	...	1173	Sa 25 Mar	50	45	Bhâd	27	1002	645
*1252	53	25 —	1309	...	1174	Th 14 Mar	51	46	Aswa	28	1003	646
1253	54	25 —	1310	Srâv	1175	Mo 3 Mar	52	47	Kârt	29	1004	647
1254	55	26 —	1311	...	1176	S 22 Feb	53	48	Agra	30	1005	648
1255	56	26 —	1312	...	1177	Th 11 Mar	54	49	Paush	31	1006	649
*1256	57	25 —	1313	Jyesh	1178	Mo 28 Feb	55	50	Mâgh	32	1007	650
1257	58	25 —	1314	...	1179	S 18 Mar	56	51	Phâl	33	1008	651
1258	59	25 —	1315	†...	1180	Th 7 Mar	57	52	Chait	34	1009	652
1259	60	26 —	1316	Chait	1181	Tu 25 Feb	58	53	Vais	35	1010	653
*1260	4361	25 —	1317	...	1182	Mo 15 Mar	20.59	73. 54	Jyesh	36	1011	654

† Agrahayana omitted, and Agrahayana intercalary.

TABLE XVII.—(Continued.)

General Table of Corresponding Dates.

A. D.	Solar-Year.		Luni-Solar-Year.				Jupiter-Cycles.			Sapt. Rishi.	Chedi Sam.
							60 Years.		12 Years.		
	Kali Yuga.	Initial Day.	Vik Sam	Intercal Mouth.	Sak Sal.	Initial Day.	S. Sid.	Tel.			
1261	4362	25 Mar	1318	Bhâd	1183	Fr 4 Mar	20.60	73.55	Ashad	37	1012
1262	63	25 —	1319	...	1184	Th 23 Mar	21. 1	56	Srâv	38	1013
1263	64	26 —	1320	...	1185	Mo 12 Mar	2	57	Bhâd	39	1014
*1264	65	25 —	1321	Ashad	1186	Sa 1 Mar	3	58	Aswa	40	1015
1265	66	25 —	1322	...	1187	Fr 20 Mar	4	59	Kârt	41	1016
1266	67	25 —	1323	...	1188	Tu 9 Mar	5	60	Agra	42	1017
1267	68	26 —	1324	Jyesh	1189	S 27 Feb	6	74. 1	Paush	43	1018
*1268	69	25 —	1325	...	1190	Sa 17 Mar	7	2	Mâgh	44	1019
1269	70	25 —	1326	Aswa	1191	We 6 Mar	8	3	Phâl	45	1020
1270	4371	26 —	1327	...	1192	Tu 25 Mar	9	4	Chait	46	1021
1271	4372	26 Mar	1328	...	1193	Sa 14 Mar	10	5	Vais	47	1022
*1272	73	25 —	1329	Ashad	1194	Fr 2 Mar	11	6	Jyesh	48	1023
1273	74	25 —	1330	...	1195	Tu 21 Mar	12	7	Ashad	49	1024
1274	75	25 —	1331	...	1196	Sa 10 Mar	13	8	Srâv	50	1025
1275	76	26 —	1332	Jyesh	1197	Th 28 Feb	14	9	Bhâd	51	1026
*1276	77	25 —	1333	...	1198	We 18 Mar	15	10	Aswa	52	1027
1277	† 78	25 —	1334	Phâl	1199	S 7 Mar	16	11	Kârt	53	1028
1278	79	26 —	1335	...	1200	Sa 26 Mar	17	12	Agra	54	1029
1279	80	26 —	1336	...	1201	Th 16 Mar	18	13	Paush	55	1030
*1280	4381	25 —	1337	Srâv	1202	Mo 4 Mar	19	14	Mâgh	56	1031
1281	4382	25 Mar	1338	...	1203	S 23 Mar	20	15	Phâl	57	1032
1282	83	26 —	1339	...	1204	Th 12 Mar	21	16	Chait	58	1033
1283	84	26 —	1340	Ashad	1205	Tu 2 Mar	22	17	Vais	59	1034
*1284	85	25 —	1341	...	1206	S 19 Mar	23	18	Jyesh	60	1035
1285	86	25 —	1342	...	1207	Fr 9 Mar	24	19	Ashad	61	1036
1286	87	26 —	1343	Vais	1208	Tu 26 Feb	25	20	Srâv	62	1037
1287	88	26 —	1344	...	1209	Mo 17 Mar	26	21	Bhâd	63	1038
*1288	89	25 —	1345	Bhâd	1210	Fr 5 Mar	27	22	Aswa	64	1039
1289	90	25 —	1346	...	1211	Th 24 Mar	28	23	Kârt	65	1040
1290	4391	26 —	1347	...	1212	Tu 14 Mar	21.29	74.24	Agra	66	1041

† Pausha omitted, and Agrahayana intercalary.

TABLE XVII.—(Continued.)

General Table of Corresponding Dates.

A. D.	Solar-Year. Kali Yuga.	Solar-Year. Initial Day.	Luni-Solar-Year. Vik Sam	Luni-Solar-Year. Intercal Month.	Luni-Solar-Year. Sak Sal.	Luni-Solar-Year. Initial Day.	Jupiter-Cycles. 60 Years. S. Sid.	Jupiter-Cycles. 60 Years. Tel.	Jupiter-Cycles. 12 Years.	Sapt. Rishi.	Chedi Sam.
1291	4392	26 Mar	1348	Ashad	1213	Sa 3 Mar	21.30	74.25	Paush	67	1042
*1292	93	25 —	1349	...	1214	Fr 21 Mar	31	26	Mâgh	68	1043
1293	94	25 —	1350	...	1215	Tu 10 Mar	32	27	Phâl	69	1044
1294	95	26 —	1351	Jyesh	1216	S 28 Feb	33	28	Chait	70	1045
1295	96	26 —	1352	...	1217	Sa 19 Mar	34	29	Vais	71	1046
*1296	†97	25 —	1353	Phâl	1218	Th 8 Mar	35	30	Jyesh	72	1047
1297	98	25 —	1354	...	1219	Tu 26 Mar	36	31	Ashad	73	1048
1298	99	26 —	1355	...	1220	S 16 Mar	37	32	Srâv	74	1049
1299	4400	26 —	1356	Srâv	1221	Fr 6 Mar	38	33	Bhâd	75	1050
*1300	4401	25 —	1357	...	1222	We 23 Mar	39	34	Aswa	76	1051
1301	4402	26 Mar	1358	...	1223	S 12 Mar	40	35	Kârt	77	1052
1302	03	26 —	1359	Ashad	1224	Th 1 Mar	41	36	Agra	78	1053
1303	04	26 —	1360	...	1225	We 20 Mar	42	37	Paush	79	1054
*1304	05	25 —	1361	...	1226	S 8 Mar	43	38	Mâgh	80	1055
1305	06	26 —	1362	Vais	1227	Fr 26 Mar	44	39	Phâl	81	1056
1306	07	26 —	1363	...	1228	Th 17 Mar	45	40	Chait	82	1057
1307	08	26 —	1364	Bhâd	1229	Mo 6 Mar	46	41	Vais	83	1058
*1308	09	25 —	1365	...	1230	S 24 Mar	47	42	Jyesh	84	1059
1309	10	26 —	1366	...	1231	Fr 14 Mar	48	43	Ashad	85	1060
1310	4411	26 —	1367	Ashad	1232	Tu 3 Mar	49	44	Srâv	86	1061
1311	4412	26 Mar	1368	...	1233	Mo 22 Mar	50	45	Bhâd	87	1062
*1312	13	25 —	1369	...	1234	Fr 10 Mar	51	46	Aswa	88	1063
1313	14	26 —	1370	Jyesh	1235	We 28 Feb	52	47	Kârt	89	1064
1314	15	26 —	1371	...	1236	Mo 18 Mar	53	48	Agra	90	1065
1315	‡16	26 —	1372	Phâl	1237	Fr 7 Mar	54	49	Paush	91	1066
*1316	17	25 —	1373	...	1238	Th 25 Mar	55	50	Mâgh	92	1067
1317	18	26 —	1374	...	1239	Tu 15 Mar	56	51	Phâl	93	1068
1318	19	26 —	1375	Srâv	1240	S 4 Mar	57	52	Chait	94	1069
1319	20	26 —	1376	...	1241	Fr 23 Mar	58	53	Vais	95	1070
*1320	4421	26 —	1377	...	1242	We 12 Mar	21.59	74.54	Jyesh	96	1071

†Agrahayana omitted, and Agrahayana intercalary. ‡ Agrahayana omitted, and Kârtika intercalary.

TABLE XVII.—(Continued.)

General Table of Corresponding Dates.

A. D.	Solar-Year.		Luni-Solar-Year.				Jupiter-Cycles.			Sapt. Rishi.	Chedi Sam.
	Kali Yuga.	Initial Day.	Vik Sam	Intercal Month.	Sak Sal.	Initial Day.	60 Years. S. Sid.	60 Years. Tel.	12 Years.		
1321	4422	26 Mar.	1378	Ashad	1243	S 1 Mar	21.60	74.55	Ashad	97	1072
1322	23	26 —	1379	...	1244	Sa 20 Mar	22. 1	56	Srâv	98	1073
1323	24	26 —	1380	...	1245	We 9 Mar	2	57	Bhâd	99	1074
*1324	25	26 —	1381	Vais	1246	Mo 27 Feb	3	58	Aswa	100	1075
1325	26	26 —	1382	...	1247	S 17 Mar	4	59	Kârt	1	1076
1326	27	26 —	1383	Bhâd	1248	Th 6 Mar	5	60	Agra	2	1077
1327	28	26 —	1384	...	1249	We 25 Mar	6	75. 1	Paush	3	1078
*1328	29	26 —	1385	...	1250	Mo 14 Mar	7	2	Mâgh	4	1079
1329	30	26 —	1386	Ashad	1251	Fr 3 Mar	8	3	Phâl	5	1080
1330	4431	26 —	1387	...	1252	We 21 Mar	10	4	Vais	6	1081
1331	4432	26 Mar.	1388	...	1253	S 10 Mar	11	5	Jyesh	7	1082
*1332	33	26 —	1389	Jyesh	1254	Fr 28 Feb	12	6	Ashad	8	1083
1333	34	26 —	1390	...	1255	Th 18 Mar	13	7	Srâv	9	1084
1334	35	26 —	1391	Aswa	1256	Mo 7 Mar	14	8	Bhâd	10	1085
1335	36	26 —	1392	...	1257	S 26 Mar	15	9	Aswa	11	1086
*1336	37	26 —	1393	...	1258	Fr 15 Mar	16	10	Kârt	12	1087
1337	38	26 —	1394	Srâv	1259	Tu 4 Mar	17	11	Agra	13	1088
1338	39	26 —	1395	...	1260	Mo 23 Mar	18	12	Paush	14	1089
1339	40	26 —	1396	...	1261	Fr 12 Mar	19	13	Mâgh	15	1090
*1340	4441	26 —	1397	Ashad	1262	We 1 Mar	20	14	Phâl	16	1091
1341	4442	26 Mar.	1398	...	1263	Tu 20 Mar	21	15	Chait	17	1092
1342	43	26 —	1399	...	1264	Sa 9 Mar	22	16	Vais	18	1093
1343	44	26 —	1400	Vais	1265	We 26 Feb	23	17	Jyesh	19	1094
*1344	45	26 —	1401	...	1266	Th 16 Mar	24	18	Ashad	20	1095
1345	46	26 —	1402	Bhâd	1267	S 6 Mar	25	19	Srâv	21	1096
1346	47	26 —	1403	...	1268	Fr 24 Mar	26	20	Bhâd	22	1097
1347	48	26 —	1404	...	1269	Tu 13 Mar	27	21	Aswa	23	1098
*1348	49	26 —	1405	Ashad	1270	S 3 Mar	28	22	Kârt	24	1099
1349	50	26 —	1406	...	1271	Sa 21 Mar	29	23	Agra	25	1100
1350	4451	26 —	1407	...	1272	We 10 Mar	22.30	75.24	Paush	26	1101

TABLE XVII.—(Continued.)

General Table of Corresponding Dates.

A. D.	Solar-Year. Kali Yuga.	Solar-Year. Initial Day.	Luni-Solar-Year. Vik Sam	Luni-Solar-Year. Intercal Month.	Luni-Solar-Year. Sak Sal.	Luni-Solar-Year. Initial Day.	Jupiter-Cycles. 60 Years. S. Sid.	Jupiter-Cycles. 60 Years. Tel.	Jupiter-Cycles. 12 Years.	Sapt. Rishi.	Chedi Sam.
1351	4452	26 Mar.	1408	Vais	1273	S 27 Feb	22.31	75.25	Mâgh	27	1102
*1352	53	26 —	1409	...	1274	S 18 Mar	32	26	Phâl	28	1103
1353	54	26 —	1410	Bhâd	1275	Th 7 Mar	33	27	Chait	29	1104
1354	55	26 —	1411	...	1276	We 26 Mar	34	28	Vais	30	1105
1355	56	26 —	1412	...	1277	S 15 Mar	35	29	Jyesh	31	1106
*1356	57	26 —	1413	Srâv	1278	Fr 4 Mar	36	30	Ashad	32	1107
1357	58	26 —	1414	...	1279	Th 23 Mar	37	31	Srâv	33	1108
1358	59	26 —	1415	...	1280	Mo 12 Mar	38	32	Bhâd	34	1109
1359	60	26 —	1416	Jyesh	1281	Fr 1 Mar	39	33	Aswa	35	1110
*1360	4461	26 —	1417	...	1282	Th 20 Mar	40	34	Kârt	36	1111
1361	4462	25 Mar.	1418	...	1283	Tu 9 Mar	41	35	Agra	37	1112
1362	63	26 —	1419	Vais	1284	Sa 26 Feb	42	36	Paush	38	1113
1363	64	27 —	1420	...	1285	Fr 17 Mar	43	37	Mâgh	39	1114
*1364	65	26 —	1421	Bhâd	1286	Tu 5 Mar	44	38	Phâl	40	1115
1365	66	26 —	1422	...	1287	Mo 24 Mar	45	39	Chait	41	1116
1366	67	26 —	1423	...	1288	Fr 13 Mar	46	40	Vais	42	1117
1367	68	26 —	1424	Ashad	1289	Tu 2 Mar	47	41	Jyesh	43	1118
*1368	69	26 —	1425	...	1290	Tu 21 Mar	48	42	Ashad	44	1119
1369	70	26 —	1426	...	1291	Sa 10 Mar	49	43	Srâv	45	1120
1370	4471	26 —	1427	Vais	1292	We 27 Feb	50	44	Bhâd	46	1121
1371	4472	27 Mar.	1428	...	1293	We 19 Mar	51	45	Aswa	47	1122
*1372	73	26 —	1429	Bhâd	1294	S 7 Mar	52	46	Kârt	48	1123
1373	74	26 —	1430	...	1295	Sa 26 Mar	53	47	Agra	49	1124
1374	75	26 —	1431	...	1296	We 15 Mar	54	48	Paush	50	1125
1375	76	27 —	1432	Srâv	1297	S 4 Mar	55	49	Mâgh	51	1126
*1376	77	26 —	1433	...	1298	Sa 22 Mar	56	50	Phâl	52	1127
1377	78	26 —	1434	...	1299	We 11 Mar	57	51	Chait	53	1128
1378	79	26 —	1435	Jyesh	1300	Mo 1 Mar	58	52	Vais	54	1129
1379	80	72 —	1436	...	1301	S 20 Mar	59	53	Jyesh	55	1130
*1380	4481	26 —	1437	† ...	1302	Th 8 Mar	22.60	75.54	Ashad	56	1131

† Kârtika omitted, and Kârtika intercalary.

TABLE XVII.—(Continued.)

General Table of Corresponding Dates.

A. D.	Solar-Year. Kali Yuga.	Solar-Year. Initial Day.	Luni-Solar-Year. Vik Sam	Luni-Solar-Year. Intercal Month.	Luni-Solar-Year. Sak Sal.	Luni-Solar-Year. Initial Day.	Jupiter-Cycles. 60 Years. S. Sid.	Jupiter-Cycles. 60 Years. Tel.	Jupiter-Cycles. 12 Years.	Sapt. Rishi.	Chedi Sam.
1381	4482	26 Mar	1438	Vais	1303	Mo 25 Feb	23. 1	75.55	Srâv	57	1132
1382	83	26 —	1439	...	1304	S 16 Mar	2	56	Bhâd	58	1133
1383	84	26 —	1440	Bhâd	1305	Th 5 Mar	3	57	Aswa	59	1134
*1384	85	26 —	1441	...	1306	Th 24 Mar	4	58	Kârt	60	1135
1385	86	26 —	1442	...	1307	Mo 13 Mar	5	59	Agra	61	1136
1386	87	26 —	1443	Ashad	1308	Fr 2 Mar	6	60	Paush	62	1137
1387	88	27 —	1444	...	1309	Fr 22 Mar	7	76. 1	Mâgh	63	1138
*1388	89	26 —	1445	...	1310	Tu 10 Mar	8	2	Phâl	64	1139
1389	90	26 —	1446	Jyesh	1311	Sa 27 Feb	9	3	Chait	65	1140
1390	4491	26 —	1447	...	1312	Mo 18 Mar	10	4	Vais	66	1141
1391	4492	27 Mar	1448	Bhâd	1313	Tu 7 Mar	11	5	Jyesh	67	1142
*1392	93	26 —	1449	...	1314	Mo 25 Mar	12	6	Ashad	68	1143
1393	94	26 —	1450	...	1315	Fr 14 Mar	13	7	Srâv	69	1144
1394	95	26 —	1451	Srâv	1316	Tu 3 Mar	14	8	Bhâd	70	1145
1395	96	26 —	1452	...	1317	Mo 22 Mar	15	9	Aswa	71	1146
*1396	97	26 —	1453	...	1318	Sa 11 Mar	16	10	Kârt	72	1147
1397	98	26 —	1454	Jyesh	1319	We 28 Feb	17	11	Agra	73	1148
1398	99	26 —	1455	...	1320	Tu 19 Mar	18	12	Paush	74	1149
1399	4500	27 —	1456	† ...	1321	Sa 8 Mar	19	13	Mâgh	75	1150
*1400	4501	26 —	1457	Chait	1322	Th 26 Feb	20	14	Phâl	76	1151
1401	4502	26 Mar	1458	...	1323	We 16 Mar	21	15	Chait	77	1152
1402	03	27 —	1459	Bhâd	1324	Mo 6 Mar	22	16	Vais	78	1153
1403	04	27 —	1460	...	1325	S 25 Mar	23	17	Jyesh	79	1154
*1404	05	26 —	1461	...	1326	Th 13 Mar	24	18	Ashad	80	1155
1405	06	26 —	1462	Ashad	1327	Mo 2 Mar	25	19	Srâv	81	1156
1406	07	27 —	1463	...	1328	Mo 22 Mar	26	20	Bhâd	82	1157
1407	08	27 —	1464	...	1329	Fr 11 Mar	27	21	Aswa	83	1158
*1408	09	26 —	1465	Vais	1330	Tu 28 Feb	28	22	Kârt	84	1159
1409	10	26 —	1466	...	1331	S 17 Mar	29	23	Agra	85	1160
1410	4511	27 —	1467	Bhâd	1332	Fr 7 Mar	23.30	76.24	Paush	86	1161

† Agrahayana omitted, and Kârtika intercalary.

TABLE XVII.—(Continued.)

General Table of Corresponding Dates.

A. D.	Solar-Year.		Luni-Solar-Year.				Jupiter-Cycles.			Sapt. Rishi.	Chedi Sam.
	Kali Yuga.	Initial Day.	Vik Sam	Intercal Month.	Sak Sal.	Initial Day.	60 Years. S. Sid.	60 Years. Tel.	12 Years		
1411	4512	27 Mar	1468	...	1333	Th 26 Mar	23.31	76.25	Mâgh	87	1162
*1412	13	26 —	1469	...	1334	Mo 14 Mar	32	26	Phâl	88	1163
1413	14	26 —	1470	Ashad	1335	Fr 3 Mar	33	27	Chait	89	1164
1414	15	27 —	1471	...	1336	Fr 23 Mar	34	28	Vais	90	1165
1415	16	27 —	1472	...	1337	Tu 12 Mar	36	29	Ashad	91	1166
*1416	17	26 —	1473	Jyesh	1338	Sa 29 Feb	37	30	Srâv	92	1167
1417	18	26 —	1474	...	1339	Fr 19 Mar	38	31	Bhâd	93	1168
1418	19	27 —	1475	Kârt	1340	We 9 Mar	39	32	Aswa	94	1169
1419	20	27 —	1476	...	1341	Mo 27 Mar	40	33	Kârt	95	1170
*1420	4521	26 —	1477	...	1342	Sa 16 Mar	41	34	Agra	96	1171
1421	4522	26 Mar	1478	Srâv	1343	We 5 Mar	42	35	Paush	97	1172
1422	23	27 —	1479	...	1344	Tu 24 Mar	43	36	Mâgh	98	1173
1423	24	27 —	1480	...	1345	Sa 13 Mar	44	37	Phâl	99	1174
*1424	25	26 —	1481	Ashad	1346	Th 2 Mar	45	38	Chait	100	1175
1425	26	27 —	1482	...	1347	We 21 Mar	46	39	Vais	1	1176
1426	27	27 —	1483	...	1348	S 10 Mar	47	40	Jyesh	2	1177
1427	28	27 —	1484	Vais	1349	Th 27 Feb	48	41	Ashad	3	1178
*1428	29	26 —	1485	...	1350	We 17 Mar	49	42	Srâv	4	1179
1429	30	27 —	1486	Bhâd	1351	Mo 7 Mar	50	43	Bhâd	5	1180
1430	4531	27 —	1487	...	1352	S 26 Mar	51	44	Aswa	6	1181
1431	4532	27 Mar	1488	...	1353	Th 15 Mar	52	45	Kârt	7	1182
*1432	33	26 —	1489	Ashad	1354	Mo 3 Mar	53	46	Agra	8	1183
1433	34	27 —	1490	...	1355	Mo 23 Mar	54	47	Paush	9	1184
1434	35	27 —	1491	...	1356	Fr 12 Mar	55	48	Mâgh	10	1185
1435	36	27 —	1492	Jyesh	1357	Tu 1 Mar	56	49	Phâl	11	1186
*1436	37	26 —	1493	...	1358	Mo 19 Mar	57	50	Chait	12	1187
1437	38	27 —	1494	Kârt	1359	Sa 9 Mar	58	51	Vais	13	1188
1438	39	27 —	1495	...	1360	Th 27 Mar	59	52	Jyesh	14	1189
1439	40	27 —	1396	...	1361	Mo 16 Mar	23.60	53	Ashad	15	1190
*1440	4541	26 —	1497	Srâv	1362	Sa 5 Mar	24. 1	76.54	Srâv	16	1191

TABLE XVII.—(Continued.)

General Table of Corresponding Dates

A. D	Solar-Year: Kali Yuga	Solar-Year: Initial Day	Luni-Solar Year: Vik Sam	Luni-Solar Year: Intercal Month	Luni-Solar Year: Sak Sal	Luni-Solar Year: Initial Day	Jupiter Cycles: 60 Years Sid	Jupiter Cycles: 60 Years Tel	Jupiter Cycles: 12 Years	Sapt Rishi	Chedi Sam
1441	4542	27 Mar	1498		1363	Fr 24 Mar	24 2	76 55	Bhad	17	1192
1442	43	27 —	1499		1364	Tu 13 Mar	3	56	Aswa	18	1193
1443	44	27 —	1500	Ashad	1365	Sa 2 Mar	4	57	Kart	19	1194
*1444	45	26 —	1501		1366	Fr 20 Mar	5	58	Agra	20	1195
1445	46	27 —	1502		1367	We 10 Mar	6	59	Paush	21	1196
1446	47	27 —	1503	Vais	1368	S 27 Feb	7	60	Magh	22	1197
1447	48	27 —	1504		1369	Sa 15 Mar	8	77 1	Phâl	23	1198
*1448	49	27 —	1505	Bhâd	1370	Th 7 Mar	9	2	Chait	24	1199
1449	50	27 —	1506		1371	Th 26 Mar	10	3	Vais	25	1200
1450	4551	27 —	1507		1372	S 15 Mar	11	4	Jyesh	26	1201
1451	4552	27 Mar	1508	Ashad	1373	Th 4 Mar	12	5	Ashad	27	1202
*1452	53	27 —	1509		1374	We 22 Mar	13	6	Srav	28	1203
1453	54	27 —	1510		1375	Mo 12 Mar	14	7	Bhad	29	1204
1454	55	27 —	1511	Jyesh	1376	Fr 1 Mar	15	8	Aswa	30	1205
1455	56	27 —	1512		1377	We 19 Mar	16	9	Kart	31	1206
*1456	57	27 —	1513	Kart	1378	Mo 6 Mar	17	10	Agra	32	1207
1457	58	27 —	1514		1379	S 27 Mar	18	11	Paush	33	1208
1458	59	27 —	1515		1380	Th 16 Mar	19	12	Magh	34	1209
1459	60	27 —	1516	Srâv	1381	Mo 5 Mar	20	13	Phal	35	1210
*1460	4561	27 —	1517	.	1382	Mo 24 Mar	21	14	Chait	36	1211
1461	4562	27 Mar	1518		1383	Fr 13 Mar	22	15	Vais	37	1212
1462	63	27 —	1519	Ashad	1384	Tu 2 Mar	23	16	Jyesh	38	1213
1463	64	27 —	1520		1385	Mo 21 Mar	24	17	Ashad	39	1214
*1464	65	27 —	1521		1386	Sa 10 Mar	25	18	Srav	40	1215
1465	66	27 —	1522	Chait	1387	We 27 Feb	26	19	Bhad	41	1216
1466	67	27 —	1523		1388	We 18 Mar	27	20	Aswa	42	1217
1467	68	27 —	1524	Bhâd	1389	Sa 7 Mar	28	21	Kârt	43	1218
*1468	69	27 —	1525		1390	Fr 25 Mar	29	22	Agra	44	1219
1469	70	27 —	1526	.	1391	We 15 Mar	30	23	Paush	45	1220
1470	4571	27 —	1527	Ashad	1392	S 4 Mar	24.31	77 24	Mâgh	46	1221

TABLE XVII.—(Continued.)

General Table of Corresponding Dates.

A. D.	Solar-Year. Kali Yuga.	Solar-Year. Initial Day.	Luni-Solar-Year. Vik Sam	Luni-Solar-Year. Intercal Month.	Luni-Solar-Year. Sak Sal.	Luni-Solar-Year. Initial Day.	Jupiter-Cycles. 60 Years. S. Sid.	Jupiter-Cycles. 60 Years. Tel.	Jupiter-Cycles. 12 Years.	Sapt. Rishi.	Chedi Sam.
1471	4572	27 Mar	1528	...	1393	Fr 22 Mar	24.32	77.25	Phâl	47	1222
*1472	73	27 —	1529	...	1394	We 11 Mar	33	26	Chait	48	1223
1473	74	27 —	1530	Jyesh	1395	S 28 Feb	34	27	Vais	49	1224
1474	75	27 —	1531	...	1396	Sa 19 Mar	35	28	Jyesh	50	1225
1475	76	27 —	1532	Aswa	1397	We 8 Mar	36	29	Ashad	51	1226
*1476	77	27 —	1533	...	1398	We 27 Mar	37	30	Srâv	52	1227
1477	78	27 —	1534	...	1399	S 16 Mar	38	31	Bhâd	53	1228
1478	79	27 —	1535	Srâv	1400	Th 5 Mar	39	32	Aswa	54	1229
1479	80	27 —	1536	...	1401	We 24 Mar	40	33	Kârt	55	1230
*1480	4581	27 —	1537	...	1402	Mo 13 Mar	41	34	Agra	56	1231
1481	4582	27 Mar	1538	Ashad	1403	Fr 2 Mar	42	35	Paush	57	1232
1482	83	27 —	1539	...	1404	Th 21 Mar	43	36	Mâgh	58	1233
1483	84	28 —	1540	...	1405	Tu 11 Mar	44	37	Phâl	59	1234
*1484	85	27 —	1541	Chait	1406	Sa 28 Feb	45	38	Chait	60	1235
1485	86	27 —	1542	...	1407	Th 17 Mar	46	39	Vais	61	1236
1486	87	27 —	1543	Srâv	1408	Tu 7 Mar	47	40	Jyesh	62	1237
1487	88	28 —	1544	...	1409	Mo 26 Mar	48	41	Ashad	63	1238
*1488	89	27 —	1545	..	1410	Fr 14 Mar	49	42	Srâv	64	1239
1489	90	27 —	1546	Ashad	1411	Tu 3 Mar	50	43	Bhâd	65	1240
1490	4591	27 —	1547	...	1412	Mo 22 Mar	51	44	Aswa	66	1241
1491	4592	28 Mar	1548	...	1413	Sa 12 Mar	52	45	Kàrt	67	1242
*1492	93	27 —	1549	Vais	1414	We 29 Feb	53	46	Agra	68	1243
1493	94	27 —	1550	...	1415	Tu 19 Mar	54	47	Paush	69	1244
1494	95	28 —	1551	Bhâd	1416	S 9 Mar	55	48	Mâgh	70	1245
1495	96	28 —	1452	...	1417	Fr 27 Mar	56	49	Phâl	71	1246
*1496	97	27 —	1553	...	1418	We 16 Mar	57	50	Chait	72	1247
1497	98	27 —	1554	Srâv	1419	S 5 Mar	58	51	Vais	73	1248
1498	99	27 —	1555	...	1420	Sa 24 Mar	59	52	Jyesh	74	1249
1499	4600	28 —	1556	...	1421	Th 14 Mar	24.60	53	Ashad	75	1250
*1500	4601	27 —	1557	Jyesh	1422	Mo 2 Mar	2	77.54	Bhâd	76	1251

TABLE XVII.—(Continued.)

General Table of Corresponding Dates.

A. D.	Solar-Year. Kali Yuga.	Solar-Year. Initial Day.	Luni-Solar-Year. Vik Sam	Luni-Solar-Year. Intercal Month.	Luni-Solar-Year. Sak Sal.	Luni-Solar-Year. Initial Day.	Jupiter-Cycles. 60 Years. S. Sid.	Jupiter-Cycles. 60 Years. Tel.	Jupiter-Cycles. 12 Years.	Sapt. Rishi.	Chedi Sam.
1501	4602	27 Mar	1558	...	1423	Sa 20 Mar	25. 3	77.55	Aswa	77	1252
1502	03	27 —	1559	...	1424	Th 10 Mar	4	56	Kârt	78	1253
1503	04	28 —	1560	Chait	1425	Mo 27 Feb	5	57	Agra	79	1254
*1504	05	27 —	1561	...	1426	S 17 Mar	6	58	Paush	80	1255
1505	06	27 —	1562	Srâv	1427	Th 6 Mar	7	59	Mâgh	81	1256
1506	07	27 —	1563	...	1428	We 25 Mar	8	60	Phâl	82	1257
1507	08	28 —	1564	...	1429	Mo 15 Mar	9	78. 1	Chait	83	1258
*1508	09	27 —	1565	Ashad	1430	Fr 3 Mar	10	2	Vais	84	1259
1509	10	27 —	1566	...	1431	Th 22 Mar	11	3	Jyesh	85	1260
1510	4611	27 —	1567	...	1432	Mo 11 Mar	12	4	Ashad	86	1261
1511	4612	28 Mar	1568	Vais	1433	Sa 1 Mar	13	5	Srâv	87	1262
*1512	13	27 —	1569	...	1434	Fr 19 Mar	14	6	Bhâd	88	1263
1513	14	27 —	1570	Bhâd	1435	Tu 8 Mar	15	7	Aswa	89	1264
1514	15	28 —	1571	...	1436	Mo 27 Mar	16	8	Kârt	90	1265
1515	16	28 —	1572	...	1437	Fr 16 Mar	17	9	Agra	91	1266
*1516	17	27 —	1573	Srâv	1438	We 5 Mar	18	10	Paush	92	1267
1517	18	27 —	1574	...	1439	Mo 23 Mar	19	11	Mâgh	93	1268
1518	19	27 —	1575	...	1440	Fr 12 Mar	20	12	Phâl	94	1269
1519	20	28 —	1576	Jyesh	1441	We 2 Mar	21	13	Chait	95	1270
*1520	4621	27 —	1577	...	1442	Tu 20 Mar	22	14	Vais	96	1271
1521	4622	27 Mar	1578	†...	1443	Sa 9 Mar	23	15	Jyesh	97	1272
1522	23	28 —	1579	Vais	1444	Th 27 Feb	24	16	Ashad	98	1273
1523	24	28 —	1580	...	1445	We 18 Mar	25	17	Srâv	99	1274
*1524	25	27 —	1581	Bhâd	1446	S 6 Mar	26	18	Bhâd	100	1275
1525	26	27 —	1582	...	1447	Sa 25 Mar	27	19	Aswa	1	1276
1526	27	28 —	1583	...	1448	Th 15 Mar	28	20	Kârt	2	1277
1527	28	28 —	1584	Ashad	1449	Mo 4 Mar	29	21	Agra	3	1278
*1528	29	27 —	1585	...	1450	S 22 Mar	30	22	Paush	4	1279
1529	30	27 —	1586	...	1451	Th 11 Mar	31	23	Mâgh	5	1280
1530	4631	28 —	1587	Vais	1452	Mo 28 Feb	25.32	78.24	Phâl	6	1281

† Kârtika omitted, and Kârtika intercalary.

TABLE XVII.—(Continued.)

General Table of Corresponding Dates.

A. D.	Solar-Year.		Luni-Solar-Year.				Jupiter-Cycles.			Sapt. Rishi.	Chedi Sam.	Fasli.
	Kali Yuga.	Initial Day.	Vik Sam	Intercal Month.	Sak Sal.	Initial Day.	60 Years. S. Sid.	60 Years. Tel.	12 Years.			
1531	4632	28 Mar	1588	...	1453	S 19 Mar	25. 33	78. 25	Chait	7	1282	
*1532	33	27 —	1589	Bhâd	1454	Fr 8 Mar	34	26	Vais	8	1283	
1533	34	27 —	1590	...	1455	We 26 Mar	35	27	Jyesh	9	1284	
1534	35	28 —	1591	...	1456	Mo 16 Mar	36	28	Ashad	10	1285	
1535	36	28 —	1592	Srâv	1457	Fr 5 Mar	37	29	Srâv	11	1286	
*1536	37	27 —	1593	...	1458	Th 23 Mar	38	30	Bhâd	12	1287	
1537	38	28 —	1594	...	1459	Tu 13 Mar	39	31	Aswa	13	1288	
1538	39	28 —	1595	Jyesh	1460	Sa 2 Mar	40	32	Kârt	14	1289	
1539	40	28 —	1596	...	1461	Fr 21 Mar	41	33	Agra	15	1290	
*1540	4641	27 —	1597	† ...	1462	Tu 9 Mar	42	34	Paush	16	1291	
1541	4642	28 Mar	1598	Chait	1463	S 27 Feb	43	35	Mâgh	17	1292	
1542	43	28 —	1599	...	1464	Sa 18 Mar	44	36	Phâl	18	1293	
1543	44	28 —	1600	Srâv	1465	We 7 Mar	45	37	Chait	19	1294	
*1544	45	27 —	1601	...	1466	Tu 25 Mar	46	38	Vais	20	1295	
1545	46	28 —	1602	...	1467	S 15 Mar	47	39	Jyesh	21	1296	
1546	47	28 —	1603	Ashâd	1468	Th 4 Mar	48	40	Ashad	22	1297	
1547	48	28 —	1604	...	1469	We 23 Mar	49	41	Srâv	23	1298	
*1548	49	27 —	1605	...	1470	S 11 Mar	50	42	Bhâd	24	1299	
1549	50	28 —	1606	Vais	1471	Fr 1 Mar	51	43	Aswa	25	1300	
1550	4651	28 —	1607	...	1472	We 19 Mar	52	44	Kârt	26	1301	
1551	4652	28 Mar	1608	Bhâd	1473	S 8 Mar	53	45	Agra	27	1302	
*1552	53	27 —	1609	...	1474	Sa 26 Mar	54	46	Paush	28	1303	
1553	54	28 —	1610	...	1475	Th 16 Mar	55	47	Mâgh	29	1304	
1554	55	28 —	1611	Ashad	1476	Mo 5 Mar	56	48	Phâl	30	1305	
1555	56	28 —	1612	...	1477	S 24 Mar	57	49	Chait	31	1306	963
*1556	57	27 —	1613	...	1478	Th 12 Mar	58	50	Vais	32	1307	964
1557	58	28 —	1614	Jyesh	1479	Tu 2 Mar	59	51	Jyesh	33	1308	965
1558	59	28 —	1615	...	1480	Mo 21 Mar	60	52	Ashad	34	1309	966
1559	60	28 —	1616	Aswa	1481	Fr 10 Mar	1	53	Srâv	35	1310	967
*1560	4661	27 —	1617	...	1482	We 27 Mar	26. 2	78. 54	Bhâd	36	1311	968

† Pausha omitted, and Aswina intercalary.

TABLE XVII.—(Continued.)

General Table of Corresponding Dates.

A. D.	Solar-Year. Kali Yuga.	Solar-Year. Initial Day.	Luni-Solar-Year. Vik. Sam	Luni-Solar-Year. Intercal Month.	Luni-Solar-Year. Sak Sal.	Luni-Solar-Year. Initial Day.	Jupiter-Cycles. 60 Years. S. Sid.	Jupiter-Cycles. 60 Years. Tel.	Jupiter-Cycles. 12 Years.	Sapt. Rishi.	Chedi Sam.	Fasli.
1561	4662	28 Mar	1618	...	1483	Tu 18 Mar	26. 3	78.55	Aswa	37	1312	969
1562	63	28 —	1619	Srâv	1484	Sa 7 Mar	4	56	Kârt	38	1313	970
1563	64	28 —	1620	...	1485	Th 25 Mar	5	57	Agra	39	1314	971
*1564	65	28 —	1621	...	1486	Tu 14 Mar	6	58	Paush	40	1315	972
1565	66	28 —	1622	Ashad	1487	Sa 3 Mar	7	59	Mâgh	41	1316	973
1566	67	28 —	1623	...	1488	Fr 22 Mar	8	60	Phâl	42	1317	974
1567	68	28 —	1624	...	1489	Tu 11 Mar	9	79. 1	Chait	43	1318	975
*1568	69	28 —	1625	Vais	1490	S 29 Feb	10	2	Vais	44	1319	976
1569	70	28 —	1626	...	1491	Sa 19 Mar	11	3	Jyesh	45	1320	977
1570	4671	28 —	1627	Bhâd	1492	We 8 Mar	12	4	Ashad	46	1321	978
1571	4672	28 Mar	1628	...	1493	Tu 27 Mar	13	5	Srâv	47	1322	979
*1572	73	28 —	1629	...	1494	S 16 Mar	14	6	Bhâd	48	1323	980
1573	74	28 —	1630	Ashad	1495	Th 5 Mar	15	7	Aswa	49	1324	981
1574	75	28 —	1631	...	1496	We 24 Mar	16	8	Kârt	50	1325	982
1575	76	28 —	1632	...	1497	S 13 Mar	17	9	Agra	51	1326	983
*1576	77	28 —	1633	Jyesh	1498	Fr 2 Mar	18	10	Paush	52	1327	984
1577	78	28 —	1634	...	1499	We 20 Mar	19	11	Mâgh	53	1328	985
1578	79	28 —	1635	Aswa	1500	Mo 10 Mar	20	12	Phâl	54	1329	986
1579	80	28 —	1636	...	1501	Sa 28 Mar	21	13	Chait	55	1330	987
*1580	4681	28 —	1637	...	1502	Th 17 Mar	22	14	Vais	56	1331	988
1581	4682	28 Mar	1638	Srâv	1503	Mo 6 Mar	23	15	Jyesh	57	1332	989
1582	83	28 —	1639	...	1504	S 25 Mar	24	16	Ashad	58	1333	990
1583	84	28 —	1640	...	1505	Th 14 Mar	25	17	Srâv	59	1334	991
*1584	85	28 —	1641	Ashad	1506	Tu 3 Mar	26	18	Bhâd	60	1335	992
1585	86	28 —	1642	...	1507	Mo 22 Mar	28	19	Kârt	61	1336	993
1586	87	28 —	1643	...	1508	Fr 11 Mar	29	20	Agra	62	1337	994
1587	88	28 —	1644	Vais	1509	Tu 28 Feb	30	21	Paush	63	1338	995
*1588	89	28 —	1645	...	1510	Tu 19 Mar	31	22	Mâgh	64	1339	996
1589	90	28 —	1646	Bhâd	1511	Sa 8 Mar	32	23	Phâl	65	1340	997
1590	4691	28 —	1647	...	1512	Fr 27 Mar	26.33	79.24	Chait	66	1341	998

TABLE XVII.—(Continued.)

General Table of Corresponding Dates.

A. D.	Solar-Year. Kali Yuga.	Solar-Year. Initial Day.	Luni-Solar-Year. Vik Sam	Luni-Solar-Year. Intercal Month	Luni-Solar-Year. Sak Sal.	Luni-Solar-Year. Initial Day.	Jupiter-Cycles. 60 Years. S. Sid.	Jupiter-Cycles. 60 Years. Tel.	Jupiter-Cycles. 12 Years.	Sapt. Rishi.	Chedi Sam.	Fasli.
1591	4692	28 Mar	1648	...	1513	Tu 16 Mar	26.34	79.25	Vais	67	1342	999
*1592	93	28 —	1649	Ashad	1514	S 5 Mar	35	26	Jyesh	68	1343	1000
1593	94	28 —	1650	...	1515	Fr 23 Mar	36	27	Ashad	69	1344	1001
1594	95	28 —	1651	...	1516	Tu 12 Mar	37	28	Srâv	70	1345	1002
1595	96	28 —	1652	Jyesh	1517	S 2 Mar	38	29	Bhâd	71	1346	1003
*1596	97	28 —	1653	...	1518	Sa 20 Mar	39	30	Aswa	72	1347	1004
1597	98	28 —	1654	Aswa	1519	We 9 Mar	40	31	Kârt	73	1348	1005
1598	99	28 —	1655	...	1520	Tu 28 Mar	41	32	Agra	74	1349	1006
1599	4700	29 —	1656	...	1521	S 18 Mar	42	33	Paush	75	1350	1007
*1600	4701	28 —	1657	Srâv	1522	Th 6 Mar	43	34	Mâgh	76	1351	1008
1601	4702	28 Mar	1658	...	1523	We 25 Mar	44	35	Phâl	77	1352	1009
1602	03	28 —	1659	...	1524	S 14 Mar	45	36	Chait	78	1353	1010
1603	04	29 —	1660	Ashad	1525	Fr 4 Mar	46	37	Vais	79	1354	1011
*1604	05	28 —	1661	...	1526	Th 22 Mar	47	38	Jyesh	80	1355	1012
1605	06	28 —	1662	...	1527	Mo 11 Mar	48	39	Ashad	81	1356	1013
1606	07	28 —	1663	Chait	1528	Fr 28 Feb	49	40	Srâv	82	1357	1014
1607	08	29 —	1664	...	1529	Fr 20 Mar	50	41	Bhâd	83	1358	1015
*1608	09	28 —	1665	Bhâd	1530	Tu 8 Mar	51	42	Aswa	84	1359	1016
1609	10	28 —	1666	...	1531	S 26 Mar	52	43	Kârt	85	1360	1017
1610	4711	28 —	1667	...	1532	Th 15 Mar	53	44	Agra	86	1361	1018
1611	4712	29 Mar	1668	Ashad	1533	We 6 Mar	54	45	Paush	87	1362	1019
*1612	13	28 —	1669	...	1534	Mo 23 Mar	55	46	Mâgh	88	1363	1020
1613	14	28 —	1670	...	1535	Fr 12 Mar	56	47	Phâl	89	1364	1021
1614	15	28 —	1671	Jyesh	1536	Tu 1 Mar	57	48	Chait	90	1365	1022
1615	16	29 —	1672	...	1537	Tu 21 Mar	58	49	Vais	91	1366	1023
*1616	17	28 —	1673	Aswa	1538	Sa 9 Mar	59	50	Jyesh	92	1367	1024
1617	18	28 —	1674	...	1539	Fr 28 Mar	60	51	Ashad	93	1368	1025
1618	19	28 —	1675	...	1540	Tu 17 Mar	27. 1	52	Srâv	94	1369	1026
1619	20	29 —	1676	Srâv	1541	S 7 Mar	2	53	Bhâd	95	1370	1027
*1620	4721	28 —	1677	...	1542	Sa 25 Mar	3	79.54	Aswa	96	1371	1028

TABLE XVII.—(Continued.)

General Table of Corresponding Dates.

A. D.	Solar-Year. Kali Yuga.	Solar-Year. Initial Day.	Luni-Solar-Year. Vik Sam	Luni-Solar-Year. Intercal Month.	Luni-Solar-Year. Sak Sal.	Luni-Solar-Year. Initial Day.	Jupiter-Cycles. 60 Years. S. Sid	Jupiter-Cycles. 60 Years. Tel.	Jupiter-Cycles. 12 Years.	Sapt. Rishi.	Chedi Sam.	Fasli.
1621	4722	28 Mar	1678	...	1543	We 14 Mar	27·4	79·55	Kârt	97	1372	1029
1622	23	29 —	1679	Ashad	1544	Mo 4 Mar	5	56	Agra	98	1373	1030
1623	24	29 —	1680	...	1545	Sa 22 Mar	6	57	Paush	99	1374	1031
*1624	25	28 —	1681	...	1546	S 11 Mar	7	58	Mâgh	100	1375	1032
1625	26	28 —	1682	Chait	1547	Mo 28 Feb	8	59	Phâl	1	1376	1033
1626	27	29 —	1683	...	1548	S 19 Mar	9	60	Chait	2	1377	1034
1627	28	29 —	1684	Srâv	1549	Th 8 Mar	10	80·1	Vais	3	1378	1035
*1628	29	28 —	1685	...	1550	We 26 Mar	11	2	Jyesh	4	1379	1036
1629	30	28 —	1686	...	1551	S 15 Mar	12	3	Ashad	5	1380	1037
1630	4731	29 —	1687	Ashad	1552	Fr 5 Mar	13	4	Srâv	6	1381	1038
1631	4732	29 Mar	1688	...	1553	Th 24 Mar	14	5	Bhâd	7	1382	1039
*1632	33	28 —	1689	...	1554	Mo 12 Mar	15	6	Aswa	8	1383	1040
1633	34	28 —	1690	Vais	1555	Fr 1 Mar	16	7	Kârt	9	1384	1041
1634	35	29 —	1691	...	1556	Fr 21 Mar	17	8	Agra	10	1385	1042
1635	36	29 —	1692	Bhâd	1557	Tu 10 Mar	18	9	Paush	11	1386	1043
*1636	37	28 —	1693	...	1558	Mo 28 Mar	19	10	Mâgh	12	1387	1044
1637	38	28 —	1694	...	1559	Fr 17 Mar	20	11	Phâl	13	1388	1045
1638	39	29 —	1695	Srâv	1560	We 7 Mar	21	12	Chait	14	1389	1046
1639	40	29 —	1696	...	1561	Mo 25 Mar	22	13	Vais	15	1390	1047
*1640	4741	28 —	1697	...	1562	Fr 13 Mar	23	14	Jyesh	16	1391	1048
1641	4742	28 Mar	1698	Jyesh	1563	We 3 Mar	24	15	Ashad	17	1392	1049
1642	43	29 —	1699	...	1564	Tu 22 Mar	25	16	Srâv	18	1393	1050
1643	44	29 —	1700	...	1565	Sa 11 Mar	26	17	Bhâd	19	1394	1051
*1644	45	28 —	1701	Chait	1566	We 28 Feb	27	18	Aswa	20	1395	1052
1645	46	28 —	1702	...	1567	Tu 18 Mar	28	19	Kârt	21	1396	1053
1646	47	29 —	1703	Srâv	1568	S 8 Mar	29	20	Agra	22	1397	1054
1647	48	29 —	1704	...	1569	Sa 27 Mar	30	21	Paush	23	1398	1055
*1648	49	28 —	1705	...	1570	We 15 Mar	31	22	Mâgh	24	1399	1056
1649	50	28 —	1706	Ashad	1571	S 4 Mar	32	23	Phâl	25	1400	1057
1650	4751	29 —	1707	...	1572	S 24 Mar	27·33	80·24	Chait	26	1401	1058

TABLE XVII.—(Continued.)

General Table of Corresponding Dates.

A. D.	Solar-Year.		Luni-Solar-Year.				Jupiter-Cycles.			Sapt. Rishi.	Chedi Sam.	Fasli.
							60 Years.					
	Kali Yuga.	Initial Day.	Vik Sam	Intercal Month.	Sak Sal.	Initial Day.	S. Sid.	Tel.	12 Years.			
1651	4752	29 Mar	1708	...	1573	Th 13 Mar	27.34	80.25	Vais	27	1402	1059
*1652	53	28 —	1709	Vais	1574	Mo 1 Mar	35	26	Jyesh	28	1403	1060
1653	54	29 —	1710	...	1575	Mo 21 Mar	36	27	Ashad	29	1404	1061
1654	55	29 —	1711	Bhâd	1576	Fr 10 Mar	37	28	Srâv	30	1405	1062
1655	56	29 —	1712	...	1577	We 28 Mar	38	29	Bhâd	31	1406	1063
*1656	57	28 —	1713	...	1578	Sa 16 Mar	39	30	Aswa	32	1407	1064
1657	58	29 —	1714	Srâv	1579	Sa 7 Mar	40	31	Kârt	33	1408	1065
1658	59	29 —	1715	...	1580	Th 25 Mar	41	32	Agra	34	1409	1066
1659	60	29 —	1716	...	1581	Mo 14 Mar	42	33	Paush	35	1410	1067
*1660	4761	28 —	1717	Jyesh	1582	Fr 2 Mar	43	34	Mâgh	36	1411	1068
1661	4762	29 Mar	1718	...	1583	Fr 22 Mar	44	35	Phâl	37	1412	1069
1662	63	29 —	1719	...	1584	Tu 11 Mar	45	36	Chait	38	1413	1070
1663	64	29 —	1720	Chait	1585	Sa 28 Feb	46	37	Vais	39	1414	1071
*1664	65	28 —	1721	...	1586	Sa 19 Mar	47	38	Jyesh	40	1415	1072
1665	66	29 —	1722	Srâv	1587	Th 9 Mar	48	39	Ashad	41	1416	1073
1666	67	29 —	1723	...	1588	Tu 28 Mar	49	40	Srâv	42	1417	1074
1667	68	29 —	1724	...	1589	Sa 16 Mar	50	41	Bhâd	43	1418	1075
*1668	69	28 —	1725	Ashad	1590	We 4 Mar	51	42	Aswa	44	1419	1076
1669	70	29 —	1726	...	1591	Tu 23 Mar	52	43	Kârt	45	1420	1077
1670	4771	29 —	1727	...	1592	Sa 12 Mar	54	44	Paush	46	1421	1078
1671	4772	29 Mar	1728	Vais	1593	We 1 Mar	55	45	Mâgh	47	1422	1079
*1672	73	28 —	1729	...	1594	Tu 19 Mar	56	46	Phâl	48	1423	1080
1673	74	29 —	1730	Bhâd	1595	S 9 Mar	57	47	Chait	49	1424	1081
1674	75	29 —	1731	...	1596	Sa 28 Mar	58	48	Vais	50	1425	1082
1675	76	29 —	1732	...	1597	We 17 Mar	59	49	Jyesh	51	1426	1083
*1676	77	28 —	1733	Srâv	1598	S 5 Mar	60	50	Ashad	52	1427	1084
1677	78	29 —	1734	...	1599	S 25 Mar	28· 1	51	Srâv	53	1428	1085
1678	79	29 —	1735	...	1600	Th 14 Mar	2	52	Bhâd	54	1429	1086
1679	80	29 —	1736	Jyesh	1601	Mo 3 Mar	3	53	Aswa	55	1430	1087
*1680	4781	28 —	1737	...	1602	S 21 Mar	4	80.54	Kârt	56	1431	1088

TABLE XVII.—(Continued.)

General Table of Corresponding Dates.

A. D.	Solar-Year.		Luni-Solar-Year.				Jupiter-Cycles.			Sapt. Rishi.	Chedi Sam.	Fasli.
	Kali Yuga.	Initial Day.	Vik Sam	Intercal Month.	Sak Sal.	Initial Day.	60 Years. S. Sid.	60 Years. Tel.	12 Years.			
†1681	4782	29 Mar	1738	Bhâd	1603	Fr 11 Mar	28. 5	80.55	Agra	57	1432	1089
1682	83	29 —	1739	...	1604	We 29 Mar	6	56	Paush	58	1433	1090
1683	84	29 —	1740	...	1605	Mo 19 Mar	7	57	Mâgh	59	1434	1091
*1684	85	29 —	1741	Srâv	1606	Sa 8 Mar	8	58	Phâl	60	1435	1092
1685	86	29 —	1742	...	1607	Th 26 Mar	9	59	Chait	61	1436	1093
1686	87	29 —	1743	...	1608	Mo 15 Mar	10	60	Vais	62	1437	1094
1687	88	29 —	1744	Ashad	1609	Sa 5 Mar	11	81. 1	Jyesh	63	1438	1095
*1688	89	29 —	1745	...	1610	Fr 23 Mar	12	2	Ashad	64	1439	1096
1689	90	29 —	1746	...	1611	Tu 12 Mar	13	3	Srâv	65	1440	1097
1690	4791	29 —	1747	Vais	1612	Sa 1 Mar	14	4	Bhâd	66	1441	1098
1691	4792	29 Mar	1748	...	1613	Fr 20 Mar	15	5	Aswa	67	1442	1099
*1692	93	29 —	1749	Bhâd	1614	We 9 Mar	16	6	Kârt	68	1443	1100
1693	94	29 —	1750	...	1615	Tu 28 Mar	17	7	Agra	69	1444	1101
1694	95	29 —	1751	...	1616	Sa 17 Mar	18	8	Paush	70	1445	1102
1695	96	29 —	1752	Ashad	1617	We 6 Mar	19	9	Mâgh	71	1446	1103
*1696	97	29 —	1753	...	1618	We 25 Mar	20	10	Phâl	72	1447	1104
1697	98	29 —	1754	...	1619	S 14 Mar	21	11	Chait	73	1448	1105
1698	99	29 —	1755	Jyesh	1620	Th 3 Mar	22	12	Vais	74	1449	1106
1699	4800	29 —	1756	...	1621	We 22 Mar	23	13	Jyesh	75	1450	1107
*1700	4801	29 —	1757	Aswa	1622	Mo 11 Mar	24	14	Ashad	76	1451	1108
1701	4802	29 Mar	1758	...	1623	Sa 29 Mar	25	15	Srâv	77	1452	1109
1702	03	29 —	1759	...	1624	We 18 Mar	26	16	Bhâd	78	1453	1110
1703	04	29 —	1760	Srâv	1625	S 7 Mar	27	17	Aswa	79	1454	1111
*1704	05	29 —	1761	..	1626	S 26 Mar	28	18	Kârt	80	1455	1112
1705	06	29 —	1762	...	1627	Th 15 Mar	29	19	Agra	81	1456	1113
1706	07	29 —	1763	Jyesh	1628	Mo 4 Mar	30	20	Paush	82	1457	1114
1707	08	29 —	1764	...	1629	S 23 Mar	31	21	Mâgh	83	1458	1115
*1708	09	29 —	1765	...	1630	Fr 12 Mar	32	22	Phâl	84	1459	1116
1709	4810	29 —	1766	Vais	1631	Tu 1 Mar	33	23	Chait	85	1460	1117
1710	4811	29 —	1767	...	1632	Mo 20 Mar	28.34	81.24	Vais	86	1461	1118

† Agrahayana omitted, and Bhâdrapada intercalary.

TABLE XVII.—(Continued.)

General Table of Corresponding Dates.

A. D.	Solar-Year. Kali Yuga.	Solar-Year. Initial Day.	Luni-Solar-Year. Vik Sam	Luni-Solar-Year. Intercal Month.	Luni-Solar-Year. Sak Sal.	Luni-Solar-Year. Initial Day.	Jupiter-Cycles. 60 Years. S. Sid.	Jupiter-Cycles. 60 Years. Tel.	Jupiter-Cycles. 12 Years.	Sapt. Rishi.	Chedi Sam.	Fasli.
1711	4812	30 Mar	1768	Bhâd	1633	Sa 10 Mar	28.35	81.25	Jyesh	87	1462	1119
*1712	13	29 —	1769	...	1634	Fr 28 Mar	36	26	Ashad	88	1463	1120
1713	14	29 —	1770	...	1635	Tu 17 Mar	37	27	Srâv	89	1464	1121
1714	15	29 —	1771	Ashad	1636	Sa 6 Mar	38	28	Bhâd	90	1465	1122
1715	16	30 —	1772	...	1637	Fr 25 Mar	39	29	Aswa	91	1466	1123
*1716	17	29 —	1773	...	1638	We 14 Mar	40	30	Kârt	92	1467	1124
1717	18	29 —	1774	Jyesh	1639	S 3 Mar	41	31	Agra	93	1468	1125
1718	19	29 —	1775	...	1640	Fr 21 Mar	42	32	Paush	94	1469	1126
1719	20	30 —	1776	Aswa	1641	We 11 Mar	43	33	Mâgh	95	1470	1127
*1720	4821	29 —	1777	...	1642	Tu 29 Mar	44	34	Phâl	96	1471	1128
1721	4822	29 Mar	1778	...	1643	Sa 18 Mar	45	35	Chait	97	1472	1129
1722	23	29 —	1779	Srâv	1644	We 7 Mar	46	36	Vais	98	1473	1130
1723	24	30 —	1780	...	1645	We 27 Mar	47	37	Jyesh	99	1474	1131
*1724	25	29 —	1781	...	1646	S 15 Mar	48	38	Ashad	100	1475	1132
1725	26	29 —	1782	Ashad	1647	Th 4 Mar	49	39	Srâv	1	1476	1133
1726	27	29 —	1783	...	1648	We 23 Mar	50	40	Bhâd	2	1477	1134
1727	28	30 —	1784	...	1649	Mo 13 Mar	51	41	Aswa	3	1478	1135
*1728	29	29 —	1785	Vais	1650	Fr 1 Mar	52	42	Kârt	4	7479	1136
1729	30	29 —	1786	...	1651	Th 20 Mar	53	43	Agra	5	1480	1137
1730	4831	29 —	1787	Bhâd	1652	Mo 9 Mar	54	44	Paush	6	1481	1138
1731	4832	30 Mar	1788	...	1653	S 28 Mar	55	45	Mâgh	7	1482	1139
*1732	33	29 —	1789	...	1654	Fr 17 Mar	56	46	Phâl	8	1483	1140
1733	34	29 —	1790	Ashad	1655	Tu 6 Mar	57	47	Chait	9	1484	1141
1734	35	29 —	1791	...	1656	S 24 Mar	58	48	Vais	10	1485	1142
1735	36	29 —	1792	...	1657	Th 13 Mar	59	49	Jyesh	11	1486	1143
*1736	37	29 —	1793	Jyesh	1658	Tu 2 Mar	60	50	Ashad	12	1487	1144
1737	38	29 —	1794	...	1659	Mo 21 Mar	29. 1	51	Srâv	13	1488	1145
1738	39	30 —	1795	Aswa	1660	Sa 11 Mar	2	52	Bhâd	14	1489	1146
1739	40	30 —	1796	...	1661	Fr 30 Mar	3	53	Aswa	15	1490	1147
*1740	4841	29 —	1797	...	1662	Tu 18 Mar	4	81.54	Kârt	16	1491	1148

TABLE XVII.—(Continued.)

General Table of Corresponding Dates.

A. D.	Solar-Year. Kali Yuga.	Solar-Year. Initial Day.	Luni-Solar-Year. Vik Sam	Luni-Solar-Year. Intercal Month.	Luni-Solar-Year. Sak Sal.	Luni-Solar-Year. Initial Day.	Jupiter-Cycles. 60 Years. S. Sid	Jupiter-Cycles. 60 Years. Tel.	Jupiter-Cycles. 12 Years.	Sapt. Rishi.	Chedi Sam.	Fasli.
1741	4842	29 Mar	1798	Srâv	1663	Sa 7 Mar	29. 5	81.55	Agra	17	1492	1149
1742	43	30 —	1799	...	1664	Sa 27 Mar	6	56	Paush	18	1493	1150
1743	44	30 —	1800	...	1665	We 16 Mar	7	57	Mâgh	19	1494	1151
*1744	45	29 —	1801	Ashad	1666	S 4 Mar	8	58	Phâl	20	1495	1152
1745	46	29 —	1802	...	1667	Sa 23 Mar	9	59	Chait	21	1496	1153
1746	47	30 —	1803	...	1668	Th 13 Mar	10	60	Vais	22	1497	1154
1747	48	30 —	1804	Chait	1669	Mo 2 Mar	11	82. 1	Jyesh	23	1498	1155
*1748	49	29 —	1805	...	1670	Sa 19 Mar	12	2	Ashad	24	1499	1156
1749	50	29 —	1806	Bhâd	1671	Th 9 Mar	13	3	Srâv	25	1500	1157
1750	4851	30 —	1807	...	1672	We 28 Mar	14	4	Bhâd	26	1501	1158
1751	4852	30 Mar	1808	...	1673	S 17 Mar	15	5	Aswa	27	1502	1159
O·S·1752*	53	29 —	1809	Ashad	1674	Th 5 Mar	16	6	Kârt	28	1503	1160
N·S·1753	54	9 Apr	1810	...	1675	We 4 Apr	17	7	Agra	29	1504	1161
1754	55	10 —	1811	...	1676	Mo 25 Mar	18	8	Paush	30	1505	1162
1755	56	10 —	1812	Jyesh	1677	Fr 14 Mar	20	9	Phâl	31	1506	1163
*1756	57	9 —	1813	...	1678	Th 1 Apr	21	10	Chait	32	1507	1164
1757	58	9 —	1814	Aswa	1679	Mo 21 Mar	22	11	Vais	33	1508	1165
1758	59	10 —	1815	...	1680	S 9 Apr	23	12	Jyesh	34	1509	1166
1759	60	10 —	1816	...	1681	Fr 30 Mar	24	13	Ashad	35	1510	1167
*1760	4861	9 —	1817	Srâv	1682	Tu 18 Mar	25	14	Srâv	36	1511	1168
1761	4862	10 Apr	1818	...	1683	Fr 6 Apr	26	15	Bhâd	37	1512	1169
1762	63	10 —	1819	...	1684	Sa 27 Mar	27	16	Aswa	38	1513	1170
1763	64	10 —	1820	Jyesh	1685	We 16 Mar	28	17	Kârt	39	1514	1171
*1764	65	9 —	1821	...	1686	Mo 2 Apr	29	18	Agra	40	1515	1172
1765	66	10 —	1822	...	1687	Sa 23 Mar	30	19	Paush	41	1516	1173
1766	67	10 —	1823	Chait	1688	We 12 Mar	31	20	Mâgh	42	1517	1174
1767	68	10 —	1824	...	1689	Tu 31 Mar	32	21	Phâl	43	1518	1175
*1768	69	9 —	1825	Srâv	1690	Fr 19 Mar	33	22	Chait	44	1519	1176
1769	70	10 —	1826	...	1691	Sa 8 Apr	34	23	Vais	45	1520	1177
1770	4871	10 —	1827	...	1692	We 23 Mar	29.35	82.24	Jyesh	46	1521	1178

***N.B.*—New style is used from 1753 onwards.**

TABLE XVII.—(Continued.)

General Table of Corresponding Dates.

A. D.	Solar-Year. Kali Yuga.	Solar-Year. Initial Day.	Luni-Solar-Year. Vik Sam	Luni-Solar-Year. Intercal Month.	Luni-Solar-Year. Sak Sal.	Luni-Solar-Year. Initial Day.	Jupiter-Cycles. 60 Years. S. Sid.	Jupiter-Cycles. 60 Years. Tel.	Jupiter-Cycles. 12 Years.	Sapt. Rishi.	Chedi Sam.	Fasli.
1771	4872	10 Apr	1828	Ashad	1693	S 17 Mar	29.36	82.25	Ashad	47	1522	1179
*1772	73	9 —	1829	...	1694	Th 4 Mar	37	26	Srâv	48	1523	1180
1773	74	10 —	1830	...	1695	Th 25 Mar	38	27	Bhâd	49	1524	1181
1774	75	10 —	1831	Vais	1696	Mo 14 Mar	39	28	Aswa	50	1525	1182
1775	76	10 —	1832	...	1697	S 2 Apr	40	29	Kârt	51	1526	1183
*1776	77	9 —	1833	Bhâd	1698	Th 21 Mar	41	30	Agra	52	1527	1184
1777	78	10 —	1834	...	1699	We 9 Apr	42	31	Paush	53	1528	1185
1778	79	10 —	1835	...	1700	Mo 30 Mar	43	32	Mâgh	54	1529	1186
1779	80	10 —	1836	Srâv	1701	Fr 19 Mar	44	33	Phâl	55	1530	1187
*1780	4881	9 —	1837	...	1702	We 5 Apr	45	34	Chait	56	1531	1188
1781	4882	10 Apr	1838	...	1703	Mo 26 Mar	46	35	Vais	57	1532	1189
1782	83	10 —	1839	Jyesh	1704	Fr 15 Mar	47	36	Jyesh	58	1533	1190
1783	84	10 —	1840	...	1705	Th 3 Apr	48	37	Ashad	59	1534	1191
*1784	85	9 —	1841	...	1706	Mo 22 Mar	49	38	Srâv	60	1535	1192
1785	86	10 —	1842	Chait	1707	Sa 12 Mar	50	39	Bhâd	61	1536	1193
1786	87	10 —	1843	...	1708	Fr 31 Mar	51	40	Aswa	62	1537	1194
1787	88	10 —	1844	Srâv	1709	Tu 20 Mar	52	41	Kârt	63	1538	1195
*1788	89	10 —	1845	...	1710	Tu 8 Apr	58	42	Agra	64	1539	1196
1789	90	10 —	1846	...	1711	Sa 28 Mar	54	43	Paush	65	1540	1197
1790	4891	10 —	1847	Ashad	1712	We 17 Mar	55	44	Mâgh	66	1541	1198
1791	4892	10 Apr	1848	...	1713	Tu 5 Apr	56	45	Phâl	67	1542	1199
*1792	93	9 —	1849	...	1714	Sa 24 Mar	57	46	Chait	68	1543	1200
1793	94	10 —	1850	Vais	1715	Th 14 Mar	58	47	Vais	69	1544	1201
1794	95	10 —	1851	...	1716	Tu 1 Apr	59	48	Jyesh	70	1545	1202
1795	96	10 —	1852	Bhâd	1717	S 22 Mar	60	49	Ashad	71	1546	1203
*1796	97	10 —	1853	...	1718	Sa 9 Apr	30. 1	50	Srâv	72	1547	1204
1797	98	10 —	1854	...	1719	We 29 Mar	2	51	Bhâd	73	1548	1205
1798	99	10 —	1855	Srâv	1720	S 18 Mar	3	52	Aswa	74	1549	1206
1799	4900	10 —	1856	...	1721	Sa 6 Apr	4	53	Kârt	75	1550	1207
*1800	4901	11 —	1857	...	1722	Th 27 Mar	30. 5	82.54	Agra	76	1551	1208

TABLE XVII.—(Continued.)

General Table of Corresponding Dates.

A. D.	Solar-Year. Kali Yuga.	Solar-Year. Initial Day.	Luni-Solar-Year. Vik Sam	Luni-Solar-Year. Intercal Month.	Luni-Solar-Year. Sak Sal.	Luni-Solar-Year. Initial Day.	Jupiter-Cycles. 60 Years. S. Sid.	Jupiter-Cycles. 60 Years. Tel.	Jupiter-Cycles. 12 Years.	Sapt. Rishi.		Fasli.
1801	4902	11 Apr	1858	Jyesh	1723	Mo 16 Mar	30. 6	82. 55	Paush	77		1209
1802	03	11 —	1859	...	1724	S 4 Apr	7	56	Mâgh	78		1210
1803	04	11 —	1860	...	1725	Th 24 Mar	8	57	Phâl	79		1211
*1804	05	11 —	1861	Chait	1726	Tu 13 Mar	9	58	Chait	80		1212
1805	06	11 —	1862	...	1727	Mo 1 Apr	10	59	Vais	81		1213
1806	07	11 —	1863	Srâv	1728	Fr 21 Mar	11	60	Jyesh	82		1214
1807	08	11 —	1864	...	1729	Th 9 Apr	12	83. 1	Ashad	13		1215
*1808	09	11 —	1865	...	1730	Mo 29 Mar	13	2	Srâv	84		1216
1809	10	11 —	1866	Ashad	1731	Sa 18 Mar	14	3	Bhâd	85		1217
1810	4911	11 —	1867	...	1732	Th 5 Apr	15	4	Aswa	86		1218
1811	4912	11 Apr	1868		1733	Mo 25 Mar	16	5	Kârt	87		1219
*1812	13	11 —	1869	Vais	1734	Sa 14 Mar	17	6	Agra	88		1220
1813	14	11 —	1870	...	1735	Fr 2 Apr	18	7	Paush	89		1221
1814	15	11 —	1871	Bhâd	1736	Tu 22 Mar	19	8	Mâgh	90		1222
1815	16	11 —	1872	...	1737	Mo 10 Apr	20	9	Phâl	91		1223
*1816	17	11 —	1873	...	1738	Sa 30 Mar	21	10	Chait	92		1224
1817	18	11 —	1874	Srâv	1739	We 19 Mar	22	11	Vais	93		1225
1818	19	11 —	1875	...	1740	Tu 7 Apr	23	12	Jyesh	94		1226
1819	20	11 —	1876	...	1741	Sa 27 Mar		13	Ashad	95		1227
*1820	4921	11 —	1877	Jyesh	1742	Th 16 Mar	25	14	Srâv	96		1228
1821	4922	11 Apr	1878	...	1743	We 4 Apr	26	15	Bhâd	97		1229
1822	23	11 —	1879	...	1744	S 24 Mar	27	16	Aswa	98		1230
1823	†24	11 —	1880	Chait	1745	Th 13 Mar	28	17	Kârt	99		1231
*1824	25	11 —	1881	...	1746	We 31 Mar	29	18	Agra	100		1232
1825	26	11 —	1882	Srâv	1747	Mo 21 Mar	30	19	Paush	1		1233
1826	27	11 —	1883	...	1748	Sa 8 Apr	31	20	Mâgh	2		1234
1827	28	11 —	1884	...	1749	Th 29 Mar	32	21	Phâl	3		1235
*1828	29	11 —	1885	Ashad	1750	Mo 17 Mar	33	22	Chait	4		1236
1829	30	11 —	1886	...	1751	S 5 Apr	34	23	Vais	5		1237
1830	4931	11 —	1887	...	1752	Th 25 Mar	30. 35	83. 24	Jyesh	6		1238

† Agrahayana omitted, and Chaitra intercalary.

TABLE XVII.—(Continued.)

General Table of Corresponding Dates.

A. D.	Solar-Year.		Luni-Solar-Year.				Jupiter-Cycles.			Sapt Rishi.		Fasli.
	Kali Yuga.	Initial Day.	Vik Sam	Intercal Month.	Sak Sal.	Initial Day.	60 Years. S. Sid.	60 Years. Tel.	12 Years.			
1831	4932	12 Apr	1888	Vais	1753	Tu 15 Mar	30.36	83.25	Ashad	7		1239
*1832	33	11 —	1889	...	1754	Mo 2 Apr	37	26	Srâv	8		1240
1833	34	11 —	1890	Bhâd	1755	Fr 22 Mar	38	27	Bhâd	9		1241
1834	35	11 —	1891	...	1756	Th 10 Apr	39	28	Aswa	10		1242
1835	36	12 —	1892	...	1757	Tu 31 Mar	40	29	Kârt	11		1243
*1836	37	11 —	1893	Ashad	1758	Sa 19 Mar	41	30	Agra	12		1244
1837	38	11 —	1894	...	1759	Fr 7 Apr	42	31	Paush	13		1245
1838	39	11 —	1895	...	1760	Tu 27 Mar	43	32	Mâgh	14		1246
1839	40	12 —	1896	Jyesh	1761	S 17 Mar	44	33	Phâl	15		1247
*1840	4941	11 —	1897	...	1762	Fr 3 Apr	46	34	Vais	16		1248
†1841	4942	11 Apr	1898	Chait	1763	We 24 Mar	47	35	Jyesh	17		1249
1842	43	11 —	1899	...	1764	Mo 11 Apr	48	36	Ashad	18		1250
1843	44	12 —	1900	...	1765	Sa 1 Apr	49	37	Srâv	19		1251
*1844	45	11 —	1901	Srâv	1766	We 20 Mar	50	38	Bhâd	20		1252
1845	46	11 —	1902	...	1767	Th 8 Apr	51	39	Aswa	21		1253
1846	47	12 —	1903	...	1768	S 29 Mar	52	40	Kârt	22		1254
1847	48	12 —	1904	Jyesh	1769	Th 18 Mar	53	41	Agra	23		1255
*1848	49	11 —	1905	...	1770	We 5 Apr	54	42	Paush	24		1256
1849	50	11 —	1906	...	1771	S 25 Mar	55	43	Mâgh	25		1257
1850	4951	12 —	1907	Vais	1772	Fr 15 Mar	56	44	Phâl	26		1258
1851	4952	12 Apr	1908	...	1773	Th 3 Apr	57	45	Chait	27		1259
*1852	53	11 —	1909	Bhâd	1774	Mo 22 Mar	58	46	Vais	28		1260
1853	54	11 —	1910	...	1775	S 10 Apr	59	47	Jyesh	29		1261
1854	55	12 —	1911	...	1776	Fr 31 Mar	60	48	Ashad	30		1262
1855	56	12 —	1912	Srâv	1777	Tu 20 Mar	31. 1	49	Srâv	31		1263
*1856	57	11 —	1913	...	1778	S 6 Apr	2	50	Bhâd	32		1264
1857	58	11 —	1914	...	1779	Th 26 Mar	3	51	Aswa	33		1265
1858	59	12 —	1915	Jyesh	1780	Tu 16 Mar	4	52	Kârt	34		1266
1859	60	12 —	1916	...	1781	Mo 4 Apr	5	53	Agra	35		1267
*1860	4961	11 —	1917	...	1782	Fr 23 Mar	31. 6	83.54	Paush	36		1268

† Pausha omitted, and Chaitra intercalary.

TABLE XVII.—(Continued.)

General Table of Corresponding Dates.

A. D.	Solar-Year.		Luni-Solar-Year.				Jupiter-Cycles.			Sapt. Rishi.		Fasli.
	Kali Yuga.	Initial Day.	Vik Sam	Intercal Month	Sak Sal.	Initial Day.	60 Years. S. Sid.	60 Years. Tel.	12 Years.			
1861	4962	11 Apr	1918	...	1783	Th 11 Apr	31. 7	83.55	Mâgh	37		1269
1862	63	12 —	1919	...	1784	Tu 1 Apr	8	56	Phâl	38		1270
1863	64	12 —	1920	Srâv	1785	Sa 21 Mar	9	57	Chait	39		1271
*1864	65	11 —	1921	...	1786	Fr 8 Apr	10	58	Vais	40		1272
1865	66	11 —	1922	...	1787	Tu 28 Mar	11	59	Jyesh	41		1273
1866	67	12 —	1923	Jyesh	1788	S 18 Mar	12	60	Ashad	42		1274
1867	68	12 —	1924	...	1789	Fr 5 Apr	13	84. 1	Srâv	43		1275
*1868	69	11 —	1925	...	1790	We 25 Mar	14	2	Bhâd	44		1276
1869	70	11 —	1926	Vais	1791	S 14 Mar	15	3	Aswa	45		1277
1870	4971	12 —	1927	...	1792	Sa 2 Apr	16	4	Kârt	46		1278
1871	4972	12 Apr	1928	Bhâd	1793	Th 23 Mar	17	5	Agra	47		1279
*1872	73	11 —	1929	...	1794	Tu 9 Apr	18	6	Paush	48		1280
1873	74	12 —	1930	...	1795	S 30 Mar	19	7	Mâgh	49		1281
1874	75	12 —	1931	Ashad	1796	Th 19 Mar	20	8	Phâl	50		1282
1875	76	12 —	1932	...	1797	We 7 Apr	21	9	Chait	51		1283
*1876	77	11 —	1933	...	1798	S 26 Mar	22	10	Vais	52		1284
1877	78	12 —	1934	Jyesh	1799	Fr 16 Mar	23	11	Jyesh	53		1285
1878	79	12 —	1935	...	1800	Th 4 Apr	24	12	Ashad	54		1286
1879	80	12 —	1936	Aswa	1801	Mo 24 Mar	25	13	Srâv	55		1287
*1880	4981	11 —	1937	...	1802	S 11 Apr	26	14	Bhâd	56		1288
1881	4982	12 Apr	1938	...	1803	Fr 1 Apr	27	15	Aswa	57		1289
1882	83	12 —	1939	Srâv	1804	M 20 Mar	28	16	Kârt	58		1290
1883	84	12 —	1940	...	1805	S 8 Apr	29	17	Agra	59		1291
*1884	85	11 —	1941	...	1806	Fr 28 Mar	30	18	Paush	60		1292
1885	86	12 —	1942	Jyesh	1807	Sa 18 Mar	31	19	Mâgh	61		1293
1886	87	12 —	1943	...	1808	Mo 5 Apr	32	20	Phâl	62		1294
1887	88	12 —	1944	...	1809	Fr 25 Mar	33	21	Chait	63		1295
*1888	89	11 —	1945	Chait	1810	We 14 Mar	34	22	Vais	64		1296
1889	90	12 —	1946	...	1811	Tu 2 Apr	35	23	Jyesh	65		1297
1890	4991	12 —	1947	Bhâd	1812	Sa 22 Mar	31.36	84.24	Ashad	66		1298

TABLE XVII.—(Continued.)

General Table of Corresponding Dates.

A. D.	Solar-Year.		Luni-Solar-Year.				Jupiter-Cycles.			Sapt. Rishi.		Fasli.
	Kali Yuga.	Initial Day.	Vik Sam	Intercal Month.	Sak Sal.	Initial Day.	60 Years. S. Sid.	60 Years. Tel.	12 Years.			
1891	4992	12 Apr	1948	...	1813	Fr 10 Apr	31.37	84.25	Srâv	67		1270
*1892	93	12 —	1949	...	1814	We 30 Mar	38	26	Bhâd	68		1271
1893	94	12 —	1950	Ashad	1815	S 29 Mar	39	27	Aswa	69		1272
1894	95	12 —	1951	...	1816	Sa 7 Apr	40	28	Kârt	70		1273
1895	96	12 —	1952	...	1817	We 27 Mar	41	29	Agra	71		1274
*1896	97	12 —	1953	Jyesh	1818	S 16 Mar	42	30	Paush	72		1275
1897	98	12 —	1954	...	1819	S 4 Apr	43	31	Mâgh	73		1276
1898	4999	12 —	1955	Aswa	1820	Th 24 Mar	44	32	Phâl	74		1277
1899	5000	12 —	1956	...	1821	Tu 11 Apr	45	33	Chait	75		1278
*1900	5001	12 —	1957	...	1822	S 1 Apr	46	34	Vais	76		1279
1901	5002	13 Apr	1958	Srâv	1823	Fr 22 Mar	47	35	Jyesh	77		1280
1902	03	13 —	1959	...	1824	We 9 Apr	48	36	Ashad	78		1281
1903	04	13 —	1960	...	1825	S 29 Mar	49	37	Srâv	79		1282
*1904	05	12 —	1961	Jyesh	1826	Fr 18 Mar	50	38	Bhâd	80		1283
1905	06	13 —	1962	..	1827	Th 6 Apr	51	39	Aswa	81		1284
1906	07	13 —	1963	...	1828	Mo 26 Mar	52	40	Kârt	82		1285
1907	08	13 —	1964	Chait	1829	Sa 16 Mar	53	41	Agra	83		1286
*1908	09	13 —	1965	...	1830	Fr 3 Apr	54	42	Paush	84		1287
1909	10	13 —	1966	Srâv	1831	Tu 23 Mar	55	43	Mâgh	85		1288
1910	5011	13 —	1967	...	1832	Mo 11 Apr	56	44	Phâl	86		1289
1911	5012	13 Apr	1968	...	1833	Fr 31 Mar	57	45	Chait	87		1290
*1912	13	13 —	1969	Ashad	1834	We 20 Mar	58	46	Vais	88		1291
1913	14	13 —	1970	...	1835	Tu 8 Apr	59	47	Jyesh	89		1292
1914	15	13 —	1971	...	1836	Sa 28 Mar	60	48	Ashad	90		1293
1915	16	13 —	1972	Vais	1837	We 17 Mar	32. 1	49	Srâv	91		1294
*1916	17	13 —	1973	...	1838	Tu 4 Apr	2	50	Bhâd	92		1295
1917	18	13 —	1974	Bhâd	1839	Sa 25 Mar	3	51	Aswa	93		1296
1918	19	13 —	1975	...	1840	Fr 12 Apr	4	52	Kârt	94		1297
1919	20	13 —	1976	...	1841	Tu 1 Apr	5	53	Agra	95		1298
*1920	5021	13 —	1977	Srâv	1842	S 21 Mar	32. 6	84.54	Paush	96		1299

TABLE XVII.—(Continued.)

General Table of Corresponding Dates.

A. D.	Solar-Year.		Luni-Solar-Year.				Jupiter-Cycles.			Sapt. Rishi.		Fasli.
	Kali Yuga.	Initial Day.	Vik. Sam.	Intercal Month.	Sak Sal.	Initial Day.	60 Years. S. Sid.	60 Years. Tel.	12 Years.			
1921	5022	13 Apr	1978	...	1843	Sa 9 Apr	32. 7	84.55	Mâgh	97		1300
1922	23	13 —	1979	...	1844	We 29 Mar	8	56	Phâl	98		1301
1923	24	13 —	1980	Jyesh	1845	S 18 Mar	9	57	Chait	99		1302
*1924	25	13 —	1981	...	1846	S 6 Apr	10	58	Vais	100		1303
1925	26	13 —	1982	...	1847	Th 26 Mar	12	59	Ashad	1		1304
1926	27	13 —	1983	Chait	1848	Mo 15 Mar	13	60	Srâv	2		1305
1927	28	13 —	1984	...	1849	S 3 Apr	14	85. 1	Bhâd	3		1306
*1928	29	13 —	1985	Srâv	1850	Fr 23 Mar	15	2	Aswa	4		1307
1929	30	13 —	1986	...	1851	Th 11 Apr	16	3	Kârt	5		1308
1930	5031	13 —	1987	...	1852	Mo 31 Mar	17	4	Agra	6		1309
1931	5032	13 Apr	1988	Ashad	1853	Fr 20 Mar	18	5	Paush	7		1310
*1932	33	13 —	1989	...	1854	Th 7 Apr	19	6	Mâgh	8		1311
1933	34	13 —	1990	...	1855	Mo 27 Mar	20	7	Phâl	9		1312
1934	35	13 —	1991	Vais	1856	Sa 17 Mar	21	8	Chait	10		1313
1935	36	14 —	1992	...	1857	Fr 5 Apr	22	9	Vais	11		1314
*1936	37	13 —	1993	Bhâd	1858	Tu 24 Mar	23	10	Jyesh	12		1315
1937	38	13 —	1994	...	1859	Mo 12 Apr	24	11	Ashad	13		1316
1938	39	13 —	1995	...	1860	Fr 1 Apr	25	12	Srâv	14		1317
1939	40	14 —	1996	Srâv	1861	We 22 Mar	26	13	Bhâd	15		1318
*1940	5041	13 —	1997	...	1862	Tu 9 Apr	27	14	Aswa	16		1319
1941	5042	13 Apr	1998	...	1863	Sa 29 Mar	28	15	Kârt	17		1320
1942	43	13 —	1999	Jyesh	1864	We 18 Mar	29	16	Agra	18		1321
1943	44	14 —	2000	...	1865	We 7 Apr	30	17	Paush	19		1322
*1944	45	13 —	2001	...	1866	S 26 Mar	31	18	Mâgh	20		1323
1945	46	13 —	2002	Chait	1867	Th 15 Mar	32	19	Phâl	21		1324
1946	47	13 —	2003	...	1868	Tu 2 Apr	33	20	Chait	22		1325
1947	48	14 —	2004	Srâv	1869	S 23 Mar	34	21	Vais	23		1326
*1948	49	13 —	2005	...	1870	Sa 10 Apr	35	22	Jyesh	24		1327
1949	50	13 —	2006	...	1871	We 30 Mar	36	23	Ashad	25		1328
1950	5051	13 —	2007	Ashad	1872	Mo 20 Mar	32.37	85.24	Srâv	26		1329

TABLE XVII.—(Continued.)

General Table of Corresponding Dates

A. D	Solar-Year		Luni Solar Year				Jupiter-Cycles			Sapt Rishi		Fasli
	Kali Yuga	Initial Day	Vik Sam	Intercal Month	Sak Sal	Initial Day	60 Years B Sid	60 Years Tel.	12 Years			
1951	5052	14 Mar	2008	.	1873	S 8 Apr	32 38	85 25	Bhâd	27		1330
*1952	53	13 —	2009		1874	Th 27 Mar	39	26	Aswa	28		1331
1953	54	13 —	2010	Vais	1875	Mo 16 Mar	40	27	Kart	29		1332
1954	55	13 —	2011		1876	S 4 Apr	41	28	Agra	30		1333
1955	56	14 —	2012	Bhâd	1877	Fr 25 Mar	42	29	Paush	31		1334
*1956	57	13 —	2013		1878	Th 12 Apr	43	30	Mâgh	32		1335
1957	58	13 —	2014	.	1879	Mo 1 Apr	44	31	Phâl	33		1336
1958	59	13 —	2015	Srâv	1880	Tu 21 Mar	45	32	Chait	34		1337
1959	60	14 —	2016	.	1881	We 10 Apr	46	33	Vais	35		1338
*1960	5061	13 —	2017	.	1882	Tu 29 Mar	47	34	Jyesh	36		1339
1961	5062	13 Mar	2018	Jyesh	1883	Sa 18 Mar	48	35	Ashad	37		1340
1962	63	14 —	2019		1884	Fr 6 Apr	49	36	Srâv	38		1341
1963	64	14 —	2020		1885	Tu 26 Mar	50	37	Bhad	39		1342
*1964	65	13 —	2021	Chait	1886	S 15 Mar	51	38	Aswa	40		1343
1965	66	13 —	2022	.	1887	Fr 2 Apr	52	39	Kart	41		1344
1966	67	14 —	2023	Srâv	1888	We 23 Mar	53	40	Agra	42		1345
1967	68	14 —	2024	.	1889	Tu 11 Apr	54	41	Paush	43		1346
*1968	69	13 —	2025		1890	Sa 30 Mar	55	22	Magh	44		1347
1969	70	13 —	2026	Ashad	1891	We 19 Mar	56	43	Phâl	45		1348
1970	5071	14 —	2027	..	1892	We 8 Apr	57	44	Chait	46		1349
1971	5072	14 Apr	2028		1893	S 28 Mar	58	45	Vais	47		1350
*1972	73	13 —	2029	Vais	1894	Th 16 Mar	59	46	Jyesh	48		1351
1973	74	13 —	2030		1895	We 4 Apr	60	47	Ashad	49		1352
1974	75	14 —	2031	Bhâd	1896	Mo 25 Mar	33. 1	48	Srâv	50		1353
1975	76	14 —	2032		1897	S 13 Apr	2	49	Bhâd	51		1354
*1976	77	13 —	2033		1898	Th 1 Apr	3	50	Aswa	52		1355
1977	78	13 —	2034	Ashad	1899	Mo 21 Mar	4	51	Kârt	53		1356
1978	79	14 —	2035	.	1900	S 9 Apr	5	52	Agra	54		1357
1979	80	14 —	2036	..	1901	Fr 30 Mar	6	53	Paush	55		1358
*1980	5081	13 —	2037	Jyesh	1902	Tu 18 Mar	33 7	85 54	Mâgh	56		1359

TABLE XVII.—(Continued.)

General Table of Corresponding Dates.

A. D.	Solar-Year.		Luni-Solar-Year.				Jupiter-Cycles.			Sapt. Rishi.		Fasli.
	Kali Yuga.	Initial Day.	Vik Sam	Intercal Month.	Sak Sal.	Initial Day.	60 Years. S. Sid.	60 Years. Tel.	12 Years.			
1981	5082	13 Apr	2038	...	1903	S 5 Apr	33. 8	85.55	Phâl	57		1360
1982	83	14 —	2039	Aswa	1904	Fr 26 Mar	9	56	Chait	58		1361
1983	84	14 —	2040	...	1905	Th 14 Apr	10	57	Vais	59		1362
1984	85	13 —	2041	...	1906	Mo 2 Apr	11	58	Jyesh	60		1363
1985	86	13 —	2042	Srâv	1907	Mo 22 Mar	12	59	Ashad	61		1364
1986	87	14 —	2043	...	1908	Fr 11 Apr	13	60	Srâv	62		1365
1987	88	14 —	2044	...	1909	Tu 31 Mar	14	86. 1	Bhâd	63		1366
1988	89	13 —	2045	Jyesh	1910	Sa 19 Mar	15	2	Aswa	64		1367
1989	90	13 —	2046	...	1911	Fr 7 Apr	16	3	Kârt	65		1368
1990	5091	14 —	2047	...	1912	We 28 Mar	17	4	Agra	66		1369
1991	5092	14 Apr	2048	Vais	1913	S 17 Mar	18	5	Paush	67		1370
1992	93	13 —	2049	...	1914	Sa 4 Apr	19	6	Mâgh	68		1371
1993	94	14 —	2050	Bhâd	1915	Th 25 Mar	20	7	Phâl	69		1372
1994	95	14 —	2051	...	1916	Tu 12 Apr	21	8	Chait	70		1373
1995	96	14 —	2052	...	1917	Sa 1 Apr	22	9	Vais	71		1374
1996	97	13 —	2053	Ashad	1918	Th 21 Mar	23	10	Jyesh	72		1375
1997	98	14 —	2054	...	1919	We 9 Apr	24	11	Ashad	73		1376
1998	99	14 —	2055	...	1920	S 29 Mar	25	12	Srâv	74		1377
1999	5100	14 —	2056	Jyesh	1921	Th 18 Mar	26	13	Bhâd	75		1378
2000	5101	13 —	2057	...	1922	We 5 Apr	33.27	86.14	Aswa	76		1379

TABLE XVIII.

List of Eclipses.

A.D.	Lunar.	Solar.	A.D.	Lunar.	Solar.
1	24 June	10 June	51	14 Apr — 8 Oct	23 Sep
2	15 May — 9 Nov	23 Nov	52	——	19 Mar
3	4 May — 28 Oct	——	53	21 Feb — 18 Aug	9 Mar
4	23 Apr — 17 Oct	8 Apr	54	11 Feb — 7 Aug	23 July — 26 Feb
5	——	28 Mar — 22 Sep	55	31 Jan — 27 July	13 July
6	3 Mar — 27 Aug	11 Sep	56	10 Dec	1 July — 25 Dec
7	20 Feb — 17 Aug	6 Feb — 31 Aug	57	5 June — 29 Nov	——
8	9 Feb — 5 Aug	26 Jan	58	26 May — 19 Nov	11 May
9	20 Dec	15 Jan — 10 July	59	——	30 Apr — 25 Oct
10	15 June — 10 Dec	30 June — 24 Nov	60	4 Apr — 28 Sep	13 Oct
11	4 June — 29 Nov	14 Nov	61	24 Mar — 18 Sep	10 Mar — 2 Oct
12	24 May	9 May	62	13 Mar — 7 Sep	28 Feb
13	14 Apr — 7 Oct	28 Apr	63	——	17 Feb
14	4 Apr — 27 Sep	18 Apr	64	22 Jan — 17 July	1 Aug
15	24 Mar — 16 Sep	2 Sep	65	{11 Jan — 6 July 31 Dec}	16 Dec
16	——	21 Aug	66	26 June	——
17	30 Jan — 27 July	15 Feb	67	17 May — 9 Nov	31 May
18	20 Jan — 16 July	1 July	68	6 May — 29 Oct	19 May
19	9 Jan — 5 July	21 June — 15 Dec	69	25 Apr — 18 Oct	4 Oct
20	25 May — 19 Nov	10 June — 3 Dec	70	——	23 Sep
21	15 May — 8 Nov	23 Nov	71	4 Mar — 29 Aug	20 Mar
22	4 May — 28 Oct	19 Apr	72	22 Feb — 17 Aug	2 Aug
23	——	——	73	11 Feb — 6 Aug	23 July
24	14 Mar — 6 Sep	21 Sep	74	22 Dec	12 July
25	3 Mar — 27 Aug	10 Sep	75	17 June — 11 Dec	5 Jan — 26 Dec
26	20 Feb — 16 Aug	6 Feb	76	5 June — 29 Nov	21 May
27	31 Dec	26 Jan — 22 July	77	——	——
28	25 June — 20 Dec	10 July	78	16 Apr — 9 Oct	30 Apr — 24 Oct
29	14 June — 9 Dec	24 Nov	79	5 Apr — 29 Sep	13 Oct
30	4 June	21 May — 14 Nov	80	24 Mar — 17 Sep	10 Mar
31	25 Apr — 19 Oct	10 May	81	——	27 Feb — 23 Aug
32	14 Apr — 7 Oct	28 Apr	82	2 Feb — 28 July	12 Aug
33	3 Apr — 27 Sep	12 Sep	83	22 Jan — 17 July	2 Aug — 27 Dec
34	——	9 Mar — 1 Sep	84	11 Jan — 6 July	16 Dec
35	11 Feb — 7 Aug	——	85	27 May — 20 Nov	10 June
36	31 Jan — 26 July	16 Feb — 12 July	86	17 May — 9 Nov	31 May
37	20 Jan — 15 July	1 July — 25 Dec	87	6 May — 30 Oct	15 Oct
38	30 Nov	21 June	88	——	10 Apr — 3 Oct
39	26 May — 19 Nov	4 Dec	89	15 Mar — 8 Sep	30 Mar
40	15 May — 7 Nov	29 Apr	90	4 Mar — 28 Aug	20 Mar
41	——	19 Apr — 13 Oct	91	22 Feb — 17 Aug	3 Aug
42	25 Mar — 18 Sep	2 Oct	92	——	27 Jan — 27 July
43	14 Mar — 7 Sep	28 Feb	93	1 Jan — 21 Dec	——
44	2 Mar — 27 Aug	17 Feb	94	17 June — 10 Dec	5 Jan — 1 June
45	——	1 Aug	95	6 June	22 May
46	{11 Jan — 6 July 31 Dec}	22 July — 16 Dec	96	26 Apr — 20 Oct	10 May — 3 Nov
47	26 June — 21 Dec	——	97	15 Apr — 9 Oct	1 Apr
48	14 June	31 May — 24 Nov	98	4 Apr — 29 Sep	21 Mar
49	6 May — 29 Oct	20 May	99	——	3 Sep
50	25 Apr — 18 Oct	9 May	100	13 Feb — 7 Aug	23 Aug

TABLE XVIII.—(Continued.)

List of Eclipses.

A.D.	Lunar.	Solar.
101	1 Feb — 28 July	17 Jan — 12 Aug
102	22 Jan — 17 July	27 Dec
103	1 Dec	22 June
104	27 May — 19 Nov	10 June
105	16 May — 9 Nov	25 Oct
106	——	21 Apr
107	26 Mar — 20 Sep	11 Apr
108	15 Mar — 8 Sep	30 Mar — 24 Aug
109	4 Mar — 28 Aug	14 Aug
110	——	3 Aug
111	13 Jan — 8 July	27 Jan
112	1 Jan — 27 June	12 June
113	16 June	1 June — 26 Nov
114	31 Oct	22 May — 15 Nov
115	26 Apr — 21 Oct	4 Nov
116	14 Apr — 9 Oct	31 Mar
117	——	21 Mar
118	23 Feb — 18 Aug	3 Sep
119	13 Feb — 8 Aug	——
120	2 Feb — 28 July	18 Jan
121	11 Dec	2 July
122	7 June — 1 Dec	21 June
123	28 May — 21 Nov	6 Nov
124	——	1 May — 25 Oct
125	5 Apr — 30 Sep	21 Apr
126	26 Mar — 19 Sep	10 Apr — 4 Sep
127	16 Mar — 8 Sep	25 Aug
128	——	——
129	23 Jan — 19 July	6 Feb
130	12 Jan — 8 July	27 Jan — 23 June
131	1 Jan — 28 June	12 June
132	10 Nov	1 June — 25 Nov
133	6 May — 31 Oct	14 Nov
134	26 Apr	12 Apr
135	15 Apr	1 Apr — 25 Sep
136	6 Mar — 29 Aug	13 Sep
137	23 Feb — 18 Aug	3 Sep
138	12 Feb — 8 Aug	28 Jan
139	23 Dec	18 Jan
140	18 June — 11 Dec	2 July
141	7 June — 1 Dec	21 June — 16 Nov
142	27 May	13 May — 5 Nov
143	17 Apr — 11 Oct	2 May
144	5 Apr — 29 Sep	20 Apr
145	26 Mar — 18 Sep	4 Sep
146	——	28 Feb
147	3 Feb — 30 July	17 Feb
148	23 Jan — 19 July	3 July — 7 Feb
149	11 Jan — 8 July	23 June
150	22 Nov	12 June — 6 Dec
151	18 May — 11 Nov	25 Nov
152	6 May — 31 Oct	22 Apr
153	26 Apr	11 Apr
154	17 Mar — 9 Sep	31 Mar — 25 Sep
155	6 Mar — 30 Aug	14 Sep
156	24 Feb — 18 Aug	8 Feb
157	——	28 Jan — 24 June
158	2 Jan—29 June, 23 Dec	13 July
159	18 June — 12 Dec	——
160	6 June	23 May
161	22 Oct	12 May
162	17 Apr — 11 Oct	2 May
163	6 Apr — 30 Sep	16 Sep
164	——	4 Sep
165	13 Feb — 9 Aug	28 Feb
166	2 Feb — 30 July	18 Feb
167	23 Jan — 19 July	4 July
168	2 Dec	23 June — 17 Dec
169	28 May — 22 Nov	6 Dec
170	17 May — 11 Nov	3 May
171	7 May	22 Apr
172	27 Mar — 19 Sep	5 Oct
173	17 Mar — 9 Sep	——
174	6 Mar — 30 Aug	19 Feb
175	——	8 Feb — 4 Aug
176	13 Jan — 9 July	23 July
177	2 Jan—28 June, 23 Dec	13 July — 8 Dec
178	17 June	27 Nov
179	2 Nov	24 May
180	27 Apr — 21 Oct	12 May
181	17 Apr — 10 Oct	26 Sep
182	——	——
183	25 Feb — 21 Aug	11 Mar
184	14 Feb — 9 Aug	29 Feb
185	2 Feb — 30 July	14 July
186	14 Dec	8 Jan — 4 July, 28 Dec
187	8 June — 3 Dec	17 Dec
188	28 May — 21 Nov	14 May
189	17 May	3 May — 27 Oct
190	8 Apr	22 Apr
191	28 Mar — 20 Sep	6 Oct
192	16 Mar — 9 Sep	1 Mar
193	——	19 Feb
194	24 Jan — 20 July	4 Aug
195	13 Jan — 10 July	24 July — 19 Dec
196	3 Jan — 28 June	7 Dec
197	12 Nov	3 June
198	8 May — 1 Nov	23 May
199	28 Apr — 21 Oct	7 Oct
200	——	1 Apr

TABLE XVIII.—(Continued.)

List of Eclipses.

A.D.	LUNAR.	SOLAR.	A.D.	LUNAR.	SOLAR.
201	7 Mar — 31 Aug	22 Mar	251	——	9 Jan — 6 July
202	24 Feb — 20 Aug	11 Mar	252	9 June — 3 Dec	24 June
203	13 Feb — 10 Aug	25 July	253	30 May — 22 Nov	13 June
204	24 Dec	14 July	254	19 May — 12 Nov	4 May — 29 Oct
205	18 June — 13 Dec	28 Dec	255	8 Oct	23 Apr
206	8 June — 3 Dec	25 May	256	28 Mar	12 Apr
207	28 May	14 May	257	17 Mar — 11 Sep	26 Aug
208	18 Apr	2 May	258	7 Mar — 16 Aug	15 Aug
209	7 Apr — 1 Oct	16 Oct	259	26 Jan — 21 July	6 Aug
210	28 Mar — 20 Sep	13 Mar	260	16 Jan — 11 July	30 Jan
211	——	2 Mar — 25 Aug	261	4 Jan — 29 June	15 June
212	4 Feb — 31 July	14 Aug	262	——	4 June — 29 Nov
213	24 Jan — 20 July	3 Aug	263	10 May — 3 Nov	18 Nov
214	13 Jan — 9 July	——	264	28 Apr — 22 Oct	14 Apr
215	——	14 June	265	17 Apr — 12 Oct	3 Apr
216	19 May — 12 Nov	2 June	266	8 Mar	24 Mar — 16 Sep
217	8 May — 1 Nov	18 Oct	267	26 Feb — 22 Aug	5 Sep
218	28 Apr — 21 Oct	12 Apr — 7 Oct	268	15 Feb — 10 Aug	31 Jan
219	18 Mar — 11 Sep	2 Apr	269	——	16 July
220	6 Mar — 31 Aug	22 Mar	270	20 June — 15 Dec	5 July
221	24 Feb — 20 Aug	5 Aug	271	10 June — 4 Dec	24 June — 20 Nov
222	——	30 Jan — 25 July	272	30 May — 22 Nov	8 Nov
223	{4 Jan—30 June 25 Dec}	19 Jan	273	4 May — 13 Oct	4 May
224	18 June — 13 Dec	8 Jan — 4 June	274	8 Apr — 3 Oct	24 Apr
225	8 June	24 May — 17 Nov	275	29 Mar — 22 Sept	7 Sep
226	——	7 Nov	276	17 Mar	3 Mar — 26 Aug
227	19 Apr — 12 Oct	——	277	5 Feb — 1 Aug	20 Feb
228	7 Apr — 1 Oct	23 Mar	278	26 Jan — 21 July	9 Feb
229	——	13 Mar	279	15 Jan — 11 July	26 June — 21 Dec
230	14 Feb	25 Aug	280	——	14 June — 9 Dec
231	4 Feb — 11 Aug	15 Aug	281	21 May — 13 Nov	——
232	25 Jan — 19 July	10 Jan — 29 Dec	282	10 May — 3 Nov	25 Apr
233	——	25 June	283	29 April — 23 Oct	15 Apr — 8 Oct
234	30 May — 23 Nov	14 June	284	——	3 Apr — 26 Sep
235	20 May — 12 Nov	3 June — 29 Oct	285	8 Mar — 1 Sep	16 Sep
236	8 May — 31 Oct	23 Apr — 17 Oct	286	26 Feb — 21 Aug	11 Feb
237	22 Sep	——	287	10 Aug	31 Jan — 27 July
238	18 Mar — 11 Sep	2 Apr	288	1 July — 25 Dec	16 July
239	7 Mar — 1 Sep	16 Aug	289	20 June — 14 Dec	5 July — 30 Nov
240	10 Feb	5 Aug	290	10 June — 3 Dec	19 Nov
241	15 Jan — 10 July	29 Jan	291	25 Oct	15 May
242	{4 Jan—29 June 24 Dec}	15 June	292	19 Apr — 13 Oct	4 May
243	19 June	5 June	293	8 Apr — 2 Oct	17 Sep
244	——	24 May	294	28 Mar	14 Mar — 7 Sep
245	29 Apr — 22 Oct	7 Nov	295	17 Feb	3 Mar
246	18 Apr — 12 Oct	3 Apr	296	6 Feb — 31 July	——
247	2 Oct	24 Mar	297	25 Jan — 21 July	6 July — 31 Dec
248	26 Feb — 21 Aug	4 Sep	298	——	25 June — 20 Dec
249	14 Feb — 10 Aug	25 Aug	299	1 June — 24 Nov	10 Dec
250	4 Feb — 30 July	20 Jan	300	20 May — 13 Nov	5 May

TABLE XVIII.—(Continued.)

List of Eclipses.

A.D.	LUNAR.	SOLAR.
301	9 May — 3 Nov	25 Apr
302	——	8 Oct
303	19 Mar — 12 Sep	27 Sep
304	8 Mar — 31 Aug	22 Feb
305	21 Aug	10 Feb — 7 Aug
306	12 July	27 July
307	{ 5 Jan — 2 July 25 Dec }	16 July
308	20 June — 14 Dec	30 Nov
309	4 Nov	25 May
310	30 Apr — 25 Oct	15 May
311	19 Apr — 14 Oct	——
312	8 Apr	17 Sep
313	27 Feb	7 Sep
314	17 Feb — 12 Aug	3 Mar
315	6 Feb — 1 Aug	18 July
316	——	6 July — 31 Dec
317	11 June — 5 Dec	20 Dec
318	31 May — 24 Nov	16 May
319	20 May — 14 Nov	6 May
320	——	25 Apr — 18 Oct
321	30 Mar — 23 Sep	8 Oct
322	19 Mar — 12 Sep	4 Mar
323	1 Sep	21 Feb
324	22 July	6 Aug
325	16 Jan — 12 July	26 July — 22 Dec
326	{ 5 Jan — 1 July 25 Dec }	11 Dec
327	——	6 June
328	10 May — 4 Nov	25 May
329	29 Apr — 24 Oct	9 Oct
330	19 Apr — 13 Oct	28 Sep
331	10 Mar	25 Mar
332	28 Feb — 22 Aug	13 Mar
333	16 Feb — 12 Aug	28 July
334	1 Aug	17 July
335	22 June — 16 Dec	11 Jan
336	10 June — 5 Dec	27 May
337	31 May — 24 Nov	16 May
338	——	6 May
339	10 Apr — 4 Oct	19 Oct
340	30 Mar — 22 Sep	14 Mar
341	19 Mar — 11 Sep	4 Mar
342	3 Aug	17 Aug
343	27 Jan — 23 July	6 Aug
344	16 Jan — 12 July	2 Jan — 21 Dec
345	4 Jan	16 June
346	21 May — 15 Nov	6 June
347	11 May — 4 Nov	20 Oct
348	29 Apr — 23 Oct	9 Oct
349	21 Mar	1 Apr
350	10 Mar — 2 Sep	24 Mar

A.D.	LUNAR.	SOLAR.
351	27 Feb — 23 Aug	8 Aug
352	12 Aug	2 Feb — 27 July
353	3 July — 26 Dec	22 Jan — 17 July
354	22 June — 16 Dec	11 Jan — 7 June
355	11 June — 6 Dec	28 May
356	——	16 May — 9 Nov
357	20 Apr — 14 Oct	29 Oct
358	10 Apr — 3 Oct	26 Mar
359	31 Mar — 23 Sep	13 Mar
360	13 Aug	28 Aug
361	6 Feb — 3 Aug	17 Aug
362	26 Jan — 23 July	——
363	16 Jan	2 Jan
364	1 June — 26 Nov	16 June
365	21 May — 15 Nov	6 June
366	11 May — 4 Nov	20 Oct
367	——	15 Apr — 10 Oct
368	21 Mar — 13 Sep	3 Apr
369	10 Mar — 2 Sep	——
370	——	8 Aug
371	14 July	2 Feb — 28 July
372	{ 7 Jan — 2 July 26 Dec }	22 Jan
373	21 June — 16 Dec	7 June
374	——	27 May — 20 Nov
375	2 May — 26 Oct	10 Nov
376	20 Apr — 14 Oct	——
377	10 Apr — 3 Oct	25 Mar
378	——	15 Mar — 8 Sep
379	17 Feb — 14 Aug	28 Aug
380	7 Feb — 2 Aug	24 Jan
381	26 Jan	12 Jan — 8 July
382	12 June — 7 Dec	27 June
383	1 June — 26 Nov	11 Nov
384	21 May — 14 Nov	31 Oct
385	——	——
386	1 Apr — 24 Sep	15 Apr
387	21 Mar — 14 Sep	30 Aug
388	9 Mar — 2 Sep	18 Aug
389	——	12 Feb
390	17 Jan — 13 July	——
391	{ 7 Jan — 2 July 27 Dec }	18 June
392	——	7 June
393	12 May — 5 Nov	20 Nov
394	2 May — 25 Oct	16 Apr
395	21 Apr — 14 Oct	6 Apr
396	——	——
397	28 Feb — 24 Aug	——
398	17 Feb — 14 Aug	3 Feb
399	7 Feb	23 Jan — 19 July
400	22 June — 17 Dec	8 July

TABLE XVIII.—(Continued.)

List of Eclipses.

A.D.	Lunar.	Solar.
401	12 June — 6 Dec	27 June
402	1 June — 25 Nov	11 Nov
403	——	7 May — 31 Oct
404	11 Apr — 4 Oct	25 Apr
405	31 Mar — 24 Sep	15 Apr — 9 Sep
406	20 Mar — 14 Sep	6 Mar — 29 Aug
407	——	24 Feb — 19 Aug
408	29 Jan — 24 July	13 Feb
409	17 Jan — 13 July	29 June
410	7 Jan	18 June — 12 Dec
411	23 May — 16 Nov	——
412	12 May — 4 Nov	27 Apr
413	2 May — 25 Oct	16 Apr
414	——	6 Apr — 30 Sep
415	11 Mar — 5 Sep	19 Sep
416	28 Feb — 24 Aug	——
417	17 Feb — 13 Aug	3 Feb
418	29 Dec	19 July
419	23 June — 18 Dec	8 July — 3 Dec
420	12 June — 6 Dec	——
421	——	17 May — 11 Nov
422	22 Apr — 16 Oct	6 May
423	12 Apr — 5 Oct	26 Apr
424	31 Mar — 24 Sep	9 Sep
425	——	6 Mar — 29 Aug
426	8 Feb — 4 Aug	23 Feb
427	29 Jan — 24 July	10 July
428	18 Jan — 12 July	22 Dec
429	8 June — 27 Nov	12 Dec
430	23 May — 16 Nov	——
431	13 May — 5 Nov	27 Apr
432	——	16 Apr — 10 Oct
433	21 Mar — 15 Sep	29 Sep
434	11 Mar — 4 Sep	25 Feb
435	28 Feb — 24 Aug	14 Feb
436	——	3 Feb — 29 July
437	{8 Jan — 3 July 28 Dec}	13 Dec — 19 July
438	23 June — 17 Dec	3 Dec
439	——	——
440	3 May — 26 Oct	17 May
441	22 Apr — 16 Oct	6 May — 1 Oct
442	11 Apr — 5 Oct	20 Sep
443	——	17 Mar
444	19 Feb — 14 Aug	——
445	8 Feb — 3 Aug	20 July
446	28 Jan — 24 July	10 July
447	14 June — 8 Dec	29 June — 23 Dec
448	3 June — 26 Nov	——
449	23 May — 16 Nov	8 May
450	——	——
451	2 Apr — 26 Sep	——
452	21 Mar — 15 Sep	7 Mar
453	11 Mar — 4 Sep	24 Feb
454	——	13 Feb — 10 Aug
455	19 Jan — 15 July	30 July
456	{9 Jan — 3 July 27 Dec}	13 Dec
457	——	8 June — 3 Dec
458	14 May — 6 Nov	28 May
459	3 May — 27 Oct	18 May — 12 Oct
460	21 Apr — 16 Oct	30 Sep
461	——	27 Mar — 20 Sep
462	2 Mar — 25 Aug	17 Mar
463	19 Feb — 15 Aug	1 Aug
464	9 Feb — 3 Aug	20 July
465	24 June — 18 Dec	13 Jan — 9 July
466	14 June — 7 Dec	2 Jan
467	3 June — 27 Nov	19 May
468	——	8 May — 1 Nov
469	12 Apr — 7 Oct	21 Oct
470	1 Apr — 26 Sep	10 Oct
471	22 Mar — 15 Sep	7 Mar
472	——	20 Aug
473	30 Jan — 25 July	9 Aug
474	19 Jan — 15 July	4 Jan
475	8 Jan — 4 July	19 June
476	24 May — 17 Nov	7 June
477	13 May — 6 Nov	28 May
478	2 May — 27 Oct	12 Oct
479	——	8 Apr — 1 Oct
480	12 Mar — 5 Sep	27 Mar
481	2 Mar — 25 Aug	11 Aug
482	19 Feb — 14 Aug	31 July
483	6 July — 30 Dec	24 Jan
484	24 June — 18 Dec	14 Jan
485	14 June — 7 Dec	29 May
486	——	19 May — 12 Nov
487	23 Apr — 18 Oct	1 Nov
488	12 Apr — 6 Oct	29 Mar
489	1 Apr — 25 Sep	18 Mar
490	——	7 Mar
491	10 Feb — 5 Aug	21 Aug
492	30 Jan — 25 July	15 Jan
493	18 Jan — 15 July	4 Jan
494	5 June — 28 Nov	19 June
495	25 May — 18 Nov	8 June — 3 Nov
496	13 May — 6 Nov	22 Oct
497	——	18 Apr
498	23 Mar — 16 Sep	7 Apr
499	13 Mar — 5 Sep	22 Aug
500	1 Mar — 25 Aug	10 Aug

TABLE XVIII.—(Continued.)

List of Eclipses.

A.D.	Lunar.	Solar.
501	—	31 July
502	9 Jan — 6 July 29 Dec	24 Jan
503	25 June — 19 Dec	10 June
504	—	29 May
505	4 May — 28 Oct	—
506	28 Apr — 18 Oct	9 Apr
507	13 Apr — 7 Oct	29 Mar
508	—	17 Mar — 11 Sep
509	20 Feb — 16 Aug	31 Aug
510	9 Feb — 5 Aug	—
511	29 Jan — 26 July	15 Jan
512	15 June — 9 Dec	29 June
513	4 June — 28 Nov	19 June
514	24 May — 18 Nov	2 Nov
515	—	23 Oct
516	3 Apr — 26 Sep	18 Apr
517	23 Mar — 15 Sep	7 Apr
518	13 Mar — 5 Sep	22 Aug
519	—	16 Feb — 11 Aug
520	20 Jan — 16 July	5 Feb
521	8 Jan — 5 July 29 Dec	20 June
522	—	10 June — 4 Dec
523	15 May — 9 Nov	23 Nov
524	3 May — 28 Oct	11 Nov
525	23 Apr — 17 Oct	—
526	—	22 Sep
527	4 Mar — 27 Aug	11 Sep
528	21 Feb — 16 Aug	6 Feb
529	9 Feb — 5 Aug	25 Jan
530	20 Dec	15 Jan — 10 July
531	15 June — 10 Dec	30 June
532	3 June — 28 Nov	13 Nov
533	—	10 May
534	14 Apr — 8 Oct	29 Apr
535	4 Apr — 27 Sep	18 Apr — 13 Sep
536	23 Mar — 15 Sep	1 Sep
537	—	25 Feb — 21 Aug
538	31 Jan — 27 July	15 Feb
539	20 Jan — 17 July	1 July
540	9 Jan — 5 July	20 June — 14 Dec
541	25 May — 19 Nov	3 Dec
542	15 May — 8 Nov	—
543	4 May — 28 Oct	20 Apr
544	—	8 Apr
545	14 Mar — 6 Sep	22 Sep
546	3 Mar — 27 Aug	16 Feb
547	20 Feb — 17 Aug	6 Feb
548	30 Dec	21 July
549	25 June — 20 Dec	10 July — 5 Dec
550	15 June — 9 Dec	24 Nov

A.D.	Lunar.	Solar.
551	4 June	21 May
552	24 Apr — 18 Oct	9 May
553	14 Apr — 7 Oct	23 Sep
554	3 Apr — 27 Sep	—
555	—	—
556	11 Feb — 6 Aug	26 Feb
557	30 Jan — 27 July	15 Feb — 12 July
558	20 Jan — 16 July	1 July
559	30 Nov — 21 June	21 June
560	25 May — 19 Nov	3 Dec
561	15 May — 8 Nov	30 Apr
562	—	19 Apr — 14 Oct
563	25 Mar — 18 Sep	3 Oct
564	13 Mar — 6 Sep	28 Feb — 21 Sep
565	2 Mar — 27 Aug	16 Feb
566	—	1 Aug
567	11 Jan — 7 July 31 Dec	22 July — 16 Dec
568	25 June — 20 Dec	—
569	14 June	31 May — 24 Nov
570	6 May — 29 Oct	20 May
571	25 Apr — 18 Oct	9 May
572	14 Apr — 7 Oct	23 Sep
573	—	19 Mar — 12 Sep
574	21 Feb — 18 Aug	9 Mar
575	11 Feb — 7 Aug	23 July
576	31 Jan — 26 July	12 July
577	11 Dec	5 Jan — 25 Dec
578	5 June — 30 Nov	—
579	26 May — 19 Nov	11 May
580	—	29 Apr — 24 Oct
581	5 Apr — 28 Sep	13 Oct
582	25 Mar — 18 Sep	10 Mar — 2 Oct
583	14 Mar — 7 Sep	28 Feb
584	—	17 Feb — 11 Aug
585	21 Jan — 17 July	1 Aug
586	11 Jan — 6 July 31 Dec	16 Dec
587	25 June	11 June — 5 Dec
588	16 May — 9 Nov	31 May
589	6 May — 29 Oct	20 May — 15 Oct
590	25 Apr — 8 Oct	4 Oct
591	—	30 Mar — 23 Sep
592	4 Mar — 28 Aug	19 Mar
593	21 Feb — 17 Aug	2 Aug
594	10 Feb — 6 Aug	23 July
595	22 Dec	16 Jan — 12 July
596	15 June — 10 Dec	5 Jan — 25 Dec
597	5 June — 29 Nov	21 May
598	—	11 May
599	16 Apr — 9 Oct	30 Apr — 25 Oct
600	4 Apr — 28 Sep	—

TABLE XVIII.—(Continued.)

List of Eclipses.

A.D.	Lunar.	Solar.
601	24 Mar — 17 Sep	10 Mar
602	—	22 Aug
603	1 Feb — 28 July	12 Aug
604	22 Jan — 16 July	7 Jan — 1 Aug, 26 Dec
605	11 Jan — 6 July	22 June — 16 Dec
606	27 May — 20 Nov	11 June
607	17 May — 9 Nov	31 May — 26 Oct
608	5 May — 29 Oct	—
609	—	10 Apr
610	15 Mar — 8 Sep	30 Mar
611	4 Mar — 29 Aug	20 Mar
612	22 Feb — 17 Aug	2 Aug
613	—	23 July
614	1 Jan—27 June, 22 Dec	—
615	16 June — 11 Dec	5 Jan — 2 June
616	5 June	21 May — 15 Nov
617	26 Apr — 20 Oct	10 May — 4 Nov
618	15 Apr — 9 Oct	1 Apr — 24 Oct
619	4 Apr — 29 Sep	21 Mar
620	—	10 Mar — 2 Sep
621	12 Feb — 8 Aug	22 Aug
622	1 Feb — 28 July	17 Jan — 12 Aug
623	22 Jan — 17 July	27 Dec
624	8 June—30 Nov	21 June
625	27 May — 20 Nov	10 June
626	17 May — 9 Nov	26 Oct
627	—	21 Apr — 15 Oct
628	25 Mar — 19 Sep	10 Apr
629	15 Mar — 8 Sep	30 Mar — 24 Aug
630	4 Mar — 28 Aug	13 Aug
631	—	3 Aug
632	13 Jan — 7 July	27 Jan
633	1 Jan—27 June, 21 Dec	12 June
634	16 June	1 June
635	7 May — 31 Oct	15 Nov
636	26 Apr — 20 Oct	11 Apr — 8 Nov
637	15 Apr — 9 Oct	1 Apr
638	—	21 Mar
639	23 Feb — 19 Aug	3 Sep
640	13 Feb — 7 Aug	—
641	1 Feb — 27 July	17 Jan
642	12 Dec	2 July
643	7 June — 1 Dec	21 June
644	27 May — 19 Nov	5 Nov
645	—	1 May — 25 Oct
646	5 Apr — 30 Sep	21 Apr
647	26 Mar — 19 Sep	4 Sep
648	14 Mar — 7 Sep	24 Aug
649	—	17 Feb — 13 Aug
650	23 Jan — 18 July	6 Feb
651	12 Jan — 8 July	27 Jan — 23 June
652	1 Jan — 27 June	11 June
653	18 May — 10 Nov	1 June — 26 Nov
654	7 May — 31 Oct	—
655	26 Apr — 21 Oct	12 Apr
656	—	31 Mar — 23 Sep
657	5 Mar — 29 Aug	13 Sep
658	23 Feb — 18 Aug	8 Feb — 3 Sep
659	13 Feb — 8 Aug	28 Jan
660	22 Dec	18 Jan — 13 July
661	18 June — 11 Dec	2 July
662	7 June — 1 Dec	—
663	—	—
664	16 Apr — 10 Oct	1 May
665	5 Apr — 30 Sep	21 Apr
666	26 Mar — 19 Sep	4 Sep
667	—	28 Feb — 25 Aug
668	3 Feb — 29 July	17 Feb
669	23 Jan — 18 July	6 Feb
670	12 Jan — 8 July	23 June — 18 Dec
671	22 Nov	12 June — 7 Dec
672	17 May — 10 Nov	25 Nov
673	6 May — 31 Oct	22 Apr
674	—	12 Apr — 5 Oct
675	17 Mar — 9 Sep	25 Sep
676	5 Mar — 29 Aug	13 Sep
677	23 Feb — 18 Aug	—
678	—	23 Jan — 24 July
679	2 Jan—29 June, 23 Dec	13 July
680	17 June — 11 Dec	27 Nov
681	7 June	23 May — 16 Nov
682	27 Apr — 22 Oct	12 May
683	16 Apr — 11 Oct	2 May
684	5 Apr — 29 Sep	14 Sep
685	—	4 Sep
686	14 Feb — 9 Aug	28 Feb
687	3 Feb — 30 July	15 July
688	23 Jan — 18 July	3 July — 28 Dec
689	2 Dec	22 June — 17 Dec
690	28 May — 22 Nov	6 Dec
691	17 May — 11 Nov	3 May
692	6 May	22 Apr
693	27 Mar — 20 Sep	5 Oct
694	17 Mar — 9 Sep	—
695	6 Mar — 29 Aug	19 Feb
696	—	—
697	13 Jan — 9 July	23 July — 19 Dec
698	2 Jan—29 June, 22 Dec	13 July — 8 Dec
699	18 June	3 June — 27 Nov
700	1 Nov	23 May

TABLE XVIII.—(Continued.)

List of Eclipses.

A.D.	Lunar.	Solar.	A.D.	Lunar.	Solar.
701	27 Apr — 21 Oct	12 May	751	15 Feb — 11 Aug	25 Aug
702	16 Apr — 10 Oct	26 Sep	752	4 Feb — 31 July	14 Aug
703	———	22 Mar	753	24 Jan — 20 July	9 Jan — 29 Dec
704	25 Feb — 19 Aug	10 Mar	754	4 Dec	25 June
705	13 Feb — 9 Aug	28 Feb — 25 July	755	30 May — 23 Nov	14 June
706	2 Feb — 30 July	14 July	756	18 May — 11 Nov	28 Oct
707	13 Dec	4 July — 29 Dec	757	8 May	23 Apr
708	8 June — 2 Dec	17 Dec	758	29 Mar — 21 Sep	12 Apr
709	28 May — 22 Nov	14 May	759	18 Mar — 11 Sep	2 Apr
710	17 May	3 May — 27 Oct	760	6 Mar — 31 Aug	15 Aug
711	7 Apr — 1 Oct	16 Oct	761	———	5 Aug
712	27 Mar — 19 Sep	5 Oct	762	15 Jan — 10 July	30 Jan
713	17 Mar — 9 Sep	1 Mar	763	4 Jan—30 June, 25 Dec	18 Jan — 16 June
714	———	19 Feb — 15 Aug	764	18 June	4 June — 28 Nov
715	24 Jan — 21 July	4 Aug	765	9 May	24 May
716	13 Jan — 9 July	23 July	766	29 Apr — 22 Oct	7 Nov
717	2 Jan — 28 June	———	767	18 Apr — 12 Oct	3 Apr
718	12 Nov	3 June	768	———	23 Mar
719	8 May — 2 Nov	24 May	769	25 Feb — 22 Aug	5 Sep
720	27 Apr — 21 Oct	6 Oct	770	14 Feb — 11 Aug	25 Aug
721	———	1 Apr — 26 Sep	771	4 Feb — 31 July	———
722	7 Mar — 31 Aug	21 Mar	772	15 Dec	5 July
723	24 Feb — 20 Aug	11 Mar	773	9 June — 4 Dec	24 June
724	13 Feb — 9 Aug	25 July	774	30 May — 23 Nov	———
725	24 Dec	19 Jan — 14 July	775	19 May	4 May — 29 Oct
726	19 June — 13 Dec	8 Jan — 28 Dec	776	8 Apr — 2 Oct	———
727	8 June — 3 Dec	25 May	777	28 Mar — 21 Sep	12 Apr
728	27 May	13 May — 6 Nov	778	17 Mar — 11 Sep	26 Aug
729	18 Apr — 11 Oct	27 Oct	779	———	21 Feb — 16 Aug
730	7 Apr — 1 Oct	16 Oct	780	26 Jan — 21 July	10 Feb
731	28 Mar — 20 Sep	12 Mar	781	15 Jan — 10 July	29 Jan — 26 June
732	———	1 Mar — 25 Aug	782	4 Jan — 29 June	15 June
733	8 Feb — 31 July	14 Aug	783	———	29 Nov
734	24 Jan — 20 July	10 Jan — 3 Aug, 30 Dec	784	9 May — 2 Nov	17 Nov
735	13 Jan — 9 July	19 Dec	785	29 Apr — 22 Oct	13 Apr
736	23 Nov	———	786	12 Oct	3 Apr — 27 Sep
737	18 May — 12 Nov	3 June	787	8 Mar — 2 Sep	16 Sep
738	8 May — 1 Nov	18 Oct	788	26 Feb — 21 Aug	———
739	———	7 Oct	789	14 Feb — 10 Aug	31 Jan
740	18 Mar — 10 Sep	1 Apr	790	26 Dec	20 Jan
741	7 Mar — 31 Aug	———	791	20 June — 15 Dec	6 July
742	24 Feb — 20 Aug	5 Aug	792	9 June — 3 Dec	24 June — 19 Nov
743	———	30 Jan	793	30 May	8 Nov
744	4 Jan — 29 June, 24 Dec	19 Jan	794	13 Oct	4 May
745	18 June — 13 Dec	4 June	795	9 Apr — 3 Oct	23 Apr
746	8 June	25 May	796	28 Mar — 21 Sep	6 Sep
747	29 Apr	14 May — 7 Nov	797	———	3 Mar
748	18 Apr — 11 Oct	27 Oct	798	5 Feb — 1 Aug	20 Feb
749	7 Apr — 30 Sep	23 Mar	799	26 Jan — 21 July	9 Feb — 7 July
750	———	———	800	15 Jan — 10 July	26 June

TABLE XVIII.—(Continued.)

List of Eclipses.

A.D.	LUNAR.	SOLAR.
801	—	15 June — 9 Dec
802	21 May — 13 Nov	29 Nov
803	10 May — 2 Nov	25 Apr
804	22 Oct	13 Apr
805	19 Mar — 12 Sep	3 April — 26 Sep
806	8 Mar — 1 Sep	16 Sep
807	26 Feb — 21 Aug	11 Feb
808	—	31 Jan — 27 July
809	5 Jan — 1 July 25 Dec	16 July
810	20 Jan — 14 Dec	5 July — 30 Nov
811	10 June	—
812	23 Oct	14 May
813	19 Apr — 13 Oct	4 May
814	8 Apr — 3 Oct	17 Sep
815	28 Mar	7 Sep
816	17 Feb — 11 Aug	2 Mar
817	5 Feb — 31 July	19 Feb
818	26 Jan — 21 July	7 July
819	—	26 June
820	31 May — 23 Nov	9 Dec
821	20 May — 13 Nov	5 May
822	9 May — 2 Nov	25 Apr
823	24 Sep	8 Oct
824	18 Mar — 12 Sep	26 Sep
825	8 Mar — 1 Sep	—
826	—	7 Aug
827	17 Jan — 12 July	27 July
828	6 Jan — 1 July 25 Dec	15 July
829	20 June	30 Nov
830	4 Nov	25 May
831	30 Apr — 24 Oct	15 May
832	18 Apr — 13 Oct	—
833	8 Apr	25 Mar — 17 Sep
834	27 Feb	14 Mar — 7 Sep
835	17 Feb — 12 Aug	3 Mar
836	6 Feb — 31 July	17 July
837	—	10 Jan — 6 July 31 Dec
838	11 June — 5 Dce	—
839	1 June — 24 Nov	16 May
840	20 May — 13 Nov	5 May — 29 Oct
841	—	25 Apr — 18 Oct
842	30 Mar — 23 Sep	—
843	19 Mar — 12 Sep	5 Mar
844	—	22 Feb
845	27 Jan — 22 July	7 Aug
846	16 Jan — 12 July	27 July — 22 Dec
847	5 Jan — 2 July	11 Dec
848	14 Nov	5 June
849	11 May — 4 Nov	25 May
850	30 Apr — 24 Oct	9 Oct

A.D.	LUNAR.	SOLAR.
851	19 Apr	5 Apr
852	9 Mar	24 Mar — 17 Sep
853	27 Feb — 22 Aug	13 Mar
854	16 Feb — 12 Aug	28 July
855	—	17 July
856	22 June — 15 Dec	11 Jan — 31 Dec
857	11 June — 5 Dec	27 May
858	31 May — 24 Nov	—
859	—	6 May — 29 Oct
860	9 Apr — 3 Oct	18 Oct
861	30 Mar — 22 Sep	15 Mar
862	19 Mar — 11 Sep	4 Mar — 29 Aug
863	7 Feb — 3 Aug	18 Aug
864	27 Jan — 22 July	6 Aug
865	15 Jan — 12 July	1 Jan — 21 Dec
866	26 Nov	16 June
867	22 May — 15 Nov	6 June
868	10 May — 4 Nov	19 Oct
869	29 Apr	9 Oct
870	21 Mar	—
871	10 Mar — 2 Sep	24 Mar
872	28 Feb — 22 Aug	8 Aug
873	12 Aug	1 Feb — 28 July
874	3 July — 26 Dec	21 Jan — 17 July
875	22 June — 16 Dec	11 Jan — 7 June
876	10 June — 5 Dec	27 May
877	—	9 Nov
878	20 Apr — 15 Oct	29 Oct
879	10 Apr — 4 Oct	26 Mar
880	30 Mar — 22 Sep	14 Mar — 8 Sep
881	10 Feb — 13 Aug	28 Aug
882	7 Feb — 3 Aug	17 Aug
883	27 Jan — 23 July	—
884	16 Jan — 6 Dec	2 Jan — 26 June
885	1 June — 26 Nov	16 June
886	21 May — 15 Nov	6 June
887	11 May	20 Oct
888	31 Mar	15 Apr — 9 Oct
889	21 Mar — 13 Sep	4 Apr
890	10 Mar — 2 Sep	19 Aug
891	23 Aug	12 Feb
892	13 July	2 Feb
893	6 Jan — 2 July 26 Dec	17 June
894	22 June — 16 Dec	7 June
895	—	28 May — 20 Nov
896	1 May — 25 Oct	—
897	20 Apr — 14 Oct	5 Apr
898	10 Apr — 3 Oct	26 Mar
899	24 Aug	15 Mar
900	18 Feb — 13 Aug	—

TABLE XVIII.—(Continued.)

List of Eclipses.

A. D.	LUNAR.	SOLAR.	A.D.	LUNAR.	SOLAR.
901	6 Feb — 3 Aug	23 Jan	951	23 May — 16 Nov	8 May
902	26 Jan — 17 Dec	12 Jan — 8 July	952	12 May — 4 Nov	26 Apr
903	12 June — 7 Dec	27 June	953	———	16 Apr
904	31 May — 25 Nov	16 June — 10 Nov	954	22 Mar — 15 Sep	———
905	21 May	———	955	11 Mar — 4 Sep	
906	———	26 Apr	956	28 Feb	14 Feb — 8 Aug
907	1 Apr — 24 Sep	15 Apr	957	18 Jan	29 July
908	20 Mar — 13 Sep	29 Aug	958	{8 Jan — 3 July / 28 Dec}	19 July — 13 Dec
909	2 Sep	18 Aug	959	23 June	2 Dec
910	24 July	12 Feb	960	———	28 May
911	17 Jan — 14 July	2 Feb	961	3 May — 26 Oct	17 May
912	{7 Jan — 2 July / 26 Dec}	17 June	962	22 Apr — 16 Oct	1 Oct
913	———	7 June	963	11 Apr — 5 Oct	20 Sep
914	12 May — 5 Nov	20 Nov	964	———	16 Mar
915	2 May — 25 Oct	17 Apr	965	18 Feb — 15 Aug	6 Mar
916	20 Apr — 13 Oct	5 Apr	966	8 Feb — 4 Aug	20 July
917	———	19 Sep	967	28 Jan	10 July
918	28 Feb — 24 Oct	8 Sep	968	13 June — 7 Dec	22 Dec
919	17 Feb — 14 Aug	3 Feb	969	3 June — 26 Nov	19 May
920	7 Feb — 28 Dec	24 Jan — 18 July	970	23 May — 15 Nov	8 May
921	23 June — 17 Dec	8 July	971	———	27 Apr — 22 Oct
922	12 June — 7 Dec	27 June — 21 Nov	972	1 Apr — 25 Sep	10 Oct
923	1 June	11 Nov	973	21 Mar — 15 Sep	7 Mar
924	———	6 May	974	11 Mar — 4 Sep	25 Feb — 20 Aug
925	11 Apr — 4 Oct	25 Apr	975	———	10 Aug
926	1 Apr — 24 Sep	10 Sep	976	19 Jan — 14 July	29 July
927	14 Sep	6 Mar — 30 Aug	977	{8 Jan — 3 July / 28 Dec}	13 Dec
928	4 Aug	24 Feb — 18 Aug	978	———	8 June
929	27 Jan — 24 July	12 Feb	979	14 May — 6 Nov	28 May
930	17 Jan — 13 July	29 June	980	3 May — 26 Oct	17 May
931	7 Jan	18 June — 12 Dec	981	22 Apr — 16 Oct	30 Sep
932	22 May — 16 Nov	30 Nov	982	———	28 Mar — 20 Sep
933	12 May — 5 Nov	27 Apr	983	1 Mar — 26 Aug	17 Mar
934	2 May — 25 Oct	16 Apr — 11 Oct	984	19 Feb — 14 Aug	30 July
935	———	6 Apr — 30 Sep	985	8 Feb — 3 Aug	20 July
936	11 Mar — 4 Sep	18 Sep	986	24 June — 19 Dec	13 Jan
937	28 Feb — 24 Aug	13 Feb	987	14 June — 8 Dec	———
938	17 Feb	3 Feb	988	2 June — 26 Nov	18 May
939	{8 Jan — 4 July / 29 Dec}	19 July	989	———	8 May — 1 Nov
940	22 June — 17 Dec	8 July	990	12 Apr — 7 Oct	21 Oct
941	12 June	21 Nov	991	1 Apr — 26 Sep	18 Mar — 10 Oct
942	———	17 May — 11 Nov	992	21 Mar — 14 Sep	7 Mar
943	23 Apr — 16 Oct	7 May	993	———	24 Feb — 20 Aug
944	11 Apr — 4 Oct	25 Apr — 20 Sep	994	30 Jan — 25 July	9 Aug
945	24 Sep	16 Mar — 9 Sep	995	19 Jan — 14 July	4 Jan
946	———	6 Mar — 29 Aug	996	8 Jan	———
947	8 Feb — 4 Aug	———	997	24 May — 17 Nov	7 June
948	28 Jan — 23 July	9 July	998	14 May — 6 Nov	28 May — 23 Oct
949	17 Jan	28 June — 22 Dec	999	3 May — 27 Oct	12 Oct
950	3 June — 27 Nov	12 Dec	1000	———	7 Apr — 30 Sep

TABLE XVIII.—(Continued.)

List of Eclipses.

A.D.	Lunar.	Solar.
1001	12 Mar — 5 Sep	——
1002	1 Mar — 25 Aug	11 Aug
1003	19 Feb — 14 Aug	31 July
1004	4 July — 29 Dec	24 Jan — 20 July
1005	24 June — 18 Dec	13 Jan
1006	7 Dec	29 May
1007	——	19 May
1008	23 Apr — 17 Oct	——
1009	12 Apr — 6 Oct	29 Mar
1010	1 Apr — 26 Sep	18 Mar
1011	——	7 Mar — 31 Aug
1012	10 Feb — 4 Aug	20 Aug
1013	29 Jan — 25 July	14 Jan
1014	19 Jan — 14 July	4 Jan — 30 June
1015	5 June — 28 Nov	19 June
1016	24 May — 17 Nov	7 June — 2 Nov
1017	13 May — 6 Nov	22 Oct
1018	——	18 Apr
1019	23 Mar — 16 Sep	21 Aug
1020	12 Mar — 4 Sep	——
1021	1 Mar — 25 Aug	11 Aug
1022	16 July	31 July
1023	9 Jan — 5 July 29 Dec	24 Jan
1024	24 June — 18 Dec	9 June
1025	——	29 May — 23 Nov
1026	4 May — 28 Oct	12 Nov
1027	23 Apr — 18 Oct	9 Apr — 1 Nov
1028	12 Apr — 6 Oct	28 Mar
1029	——	11 Sep
1030	20 Feb — 16 Aug	31 Aug
1031	10 Feb — 5 Aug	——
1032	30 Jan — 25 July	15 Jan — 10 July
1033	15 June — 8 Dec	4 Jan — 29 June
1034	4 June — 28 Nov	18 June
1035	24 May — 18 Nov	——
1036	——	29 Apr — 22 Oct
1037	2 Apr — 27 Sep	18 Apr
1038	23 Mar — 16 Sep	1 Sep
1039	13 Mar — 5 Sep	22 Aug
1040	——	15 Feb
1041	20 Jan — 16 July	——
1042	9 Jan — 5 July 29 Dec	20 June
1043	——	9 June — 4 Dec
1044	14 May — 8 Nov	22 Nov
1045	3 May — 28 Oct	19 Apr — 11 Nov
1046	23 Apr — 17 Oct	9 Apr
1047	——	29 Mar — 22 Sep
1048	3 Mar — 6 Aug	10 Sep
1049	20 Feb — 15 Aug	5 Feb
1050	9 Feb — 5 Aug	——
1051	26 June — 20 Dec	15 Jan — 10 July
1052	15 June — 8 Dec	29 June — 24 Nov
1053	4 June — 28 Nov	13 Nov
1054	——	10 May
1055	14 Apr — 8 Oct	29 Apr
1056	2 Apr — 26 Sep	12 Sep
1057	23 Mar — 15 Sep	——
1058	——	25 Feb — 22 Aug
1059	31 Jan — 27 July	15 Feb
1060	20 Jan — 16 July	30 June
1061	8 Jan	20 June
1062	25 May — 19 Nov	——
1063	15 May — 8 Nov	1 May
1064	3 May — 28 Oct	19 Apr
1065	——	8 Apr
1066	14 Mar — 6 Sep	22 Sep
1067	3 Mar — 27 Aug	16 Feb
1068	21 Feb — 15 Aug	6 Feb
1069	7 July — 30 Dec	21 July
1070	26 June — 20 Dec	10 July — 5 Dec
1071	15 June — 9 Dec	24 Nov
1072	——	20 May
1073	24 Apr — 18 Oct	9 May
1074	14 Apr — 7 Oct	29 Apr
1075	3 Apr — 27 Sep	13 Sep
1076	——	1 Sep
1077	10 Feb — 6 Aug	25 Feb
1078	30 Jan — 27 July	11 July
1079	20 Jan	1 July — 26 Dec
1080	5 June — 29 Nov	20 June — 14 Dec
1081	25 May — 19 Nov	3 Dec
1082	14 May — 8 Nov	30 Apr
1083	——	14 Oct
1084	24 Mar — 16 Sep	2 Oct
1085	14 Mar — 6 Sep	——
1086	3 Mar — 27 Aug	16 Feb
1087	——	1 Aug
1088	11 Jan — 6 July 30 Dec	20 July
1089	25 June — 20 Dec	——
1090	——	24 Nov
1091	5 May — 30 Oct	21 May
1092	24 Apr — 18 Oct	9 May
1093	14 Apr — 7 Oct	23 Sep
1094	——	19 Mar
1095	22 Feb — 18 Aug	——
1096	11 Feb — 6 Aug	22 July
1097	30 Jan — 27 July	——
1098	11 Dec	5 Jan — 1 July 25 Dec
1099	5 June — 30 Nov	——
1100	25 May — 18 Nov	11 May

TABLE XVIII.—(Continued.)

List of Eclipses.

A.D.	LUNAR.	SOLAR.
1101	—	30 Apr — 24 Oct
1102	5 Apr — 28 Sep	—
1103	25 Mar — 17 Sep	10 Mar
1104	13 Mar — 6 Sep	—
1105	—	16 Feb
1106	21 Jan — 17 July	1 Aug — 27 Dec
1107	11 Jan — 6 July 31 Dec	16 Dec
1108	25 June	11 June
1109	16 Mar — 9 Nov	31 May
1110	5 May — 29 Oct	20 May — 15 Oct
1111	15 Apr — 18 Oct	—
1112	—	29 Mar — 22 Sep
1113	4 Mar — 28 Aug	19 Mar
1114	21 Feb — 18 Aug	2 Aug
1115	10 Feb — 7 Aug	23 July
1116	21 Dec	—
1117	16 June — 11 Dec	—
1118	5 June — 30 Nov	22 May
1119	—	11 May
1120	15 Apr — 8 Oct	24 Oct
1121	4 Apr — 28 Sep	20 Mar — 13 Oct
1122	24 Mar — 17 Sep	10 Mar
1123	—	22 Aug
1124	1 Feb — 28 July	11 Aug
1125	21 Jan — 17 July	6 Jan — 26 Dec
1126	11 Jan — 6 July	22 June
1127	27 May — 20 Nov	11 June
1128	16 May — 8 Nov	30 May — 25 Oct
1129	5 May — 29 Oct	15 Oct
1130	—	4 Oct
1131	15 Mar — 8 Sep	30 Mar
1132	3 Mar — 28 Aug	19 Mar
1133	21 Feb — 17 Aug	2 Aug
1134	—	27 Jan — 23 July
1135	1 Jan — 27 June 22 Dec	16 Jan
1136	15 June — 10 Dec	5 Jan — 1 June
1137	5 June	21 May — 15 Nov
1138	26 Apr — 20 Oct	4 Nov
1139	16 Apr — 9 Oct	—
1140	4 Apr — 28 Sep	20 Mar
1141	—	10 Mar — 2 Sep
1142	12 Feb — 8 Aug	—
1143	1 Feb — 28 July	12 Aug
1144	22 Jan — 16 July	6 Jan — 26 Dec
1145	6 Jan — 1 Dec	22 June
1146	27 May — 20 Nov	11 June — 6 Nov
1147	17 May — 9 Nov	26 Oct
1148	—	20 Apr — 14 Oct
1149	26 Mar — 19 Sep	9 Apr
1150	15 Mar — 8 Sep	24 Aug

A.D.	LUNAR.	SOLAR.
1151	4 Mar — 28 Aug	13 Aug
1152	—	7 Feb — 2 Aug
1153	12 Jan — 7 July	26 Jan
1154	1 Jan — 27 June 21 Dec	12 June
1155	16 June	1 June — 26 Nov
1156	7 May — 30 Oct	21 May
1157	26 Apr — 19 Oct	11 Apr — 4 Nov
1158	15 Apr — 9 Oct	—
1159	—	21 Mar
1160	13 Feb — 18 Aug	2 Sep
1161	12 Feb — 7 Aug	28 Jan
1162	1 Feb — 27 July	17 Jan
1163	18 June — 12 Dec	6 Jan — 3 July
1164	6 June — 30 Nov	21 June — 16 Nov
1165	27 May — 19 Nov	—
1166	—	1 May
1167	6 Apr — 30 Sep	21 Apr
1168	25 Mar — 19 Sep	9 Apr — 3 Sep
1169	14 Mar — 8 Sep	24 Aug
1170	—	—
1171	23 Jan — 18 July	—
1172	13 Jan	27 Jan — 23 June
1173	1 Jan — 27 June	12 June
1174	18 May — 10 Nov	1 June — 26 Nov
1175	7 May — 31 Oct	15 Nov
1176	25 Apr — 19 Oct	11 Apr
1177	—	23 Sep
1178	5 Mar — 30 Aug	13 Sep
1179	23 Feb — 19 Aug	8 Feb — 3 Sep
1180	13 Feb — 7 Aug	28 Jan
1181	22 Dec	17 Jan — 13 July
1182	18 June — 11 Dec	2 July
1183	7 June — 1 Dec	17 Nov
1184	—	5 Nov
1185	16 Apr — 10 Oct	1 May
1186	5 Apr — 30 Sep	21 Apr
1187	26 Mar — 19 Sep	4 Sep
1188	—	29 Feb — 24 Aug
1189	3 Feb — 29 July	17 Feb
1190	23 Jan — 18 July	6 Feb — 4 July
1191	12 Jan — 8 July	23 June — 18 Dec
1192	28 May — 21 Nov	11 June — 6 Dec
1193	18 May — 10 Nov	—
1194	7 May — 31 Oct	22 Apr
1195	—	12 Apr — 5 Oct
1196	16 Mar — 9 Sep	—
1197	5 Mar — 29 Aug	13 Sep
1198	23 Feb — 18 Aug	7 Feb
1199	—	28 Jan — 24 July
1200	3 Jan — 28 June 22 Dec	12 July — 8 Dec

TABLE XVIII.—(Continued.)

List of Eclipses.

A.D.	Lunar.	Solar.	A.D.	Lunar.	Solar.
1201	18 June — 11 Dec	27 Nov	1251	7 Apr — 1 Oct	16 Oct
1202	——	23 May	1252	27 Mar — 19 Sept	11 Mar
1203	27 Apr — 22 Oct	12 May	1253	——	1 Mar — 25 Aug
1204	16 Apr — 10 Oct	1 May	1254	4 Feb — 31 July	14 Aug
1205	5 Apr — 29 Sep	——	1255	24 Jan — 20 July	10 Jan — 20 Dec
1206	——	11 Mar — 4 Sep	1256	13 Jan — 9 July	18 Dec
1207	14 Feb — 9 Aug	28 Feb	1257	23 Nov	13 June
1208	3 Feb — 29 July	14 July	1258	18 May — 12 Nov	3 June
1209	22 Jan — 18 July	3 July — 28 Dec	1259	8 May — 1 Nov	——
1210	9 June — 2 Dec	17 Dec	1260	——	12 Apr — 6 Oct
1211	29 May — 22 Nov	——	1261	18 Mar — 10 Sep	1 Apr
1212	17 May — 10 Nov	2 May	1262	7 Mar — 31 Aug	——
1213	——	22 Apr	1263	24 Feb — 20 Aug	5 Aug
1214	27 Mar — 20 Sep	5 Oct	1264	——	30 Jan
1215	17 Mar — 9 Sep	2 Mar	1265	3 Jan—30 June 24 Dec	19 Jan
1216	5 Mar — 28 Aug	19 Feb	1266	19 June — 13 Dec	8 Jan — 4 June
1217	——	7 Feb — 4 Aug	1267	8 June	25 May
1218	13 Jan — 9 July	24 July — 19 Dec	1268	28 Apr — 22 Oct	13 May — 6 Nov
1219	2 Jan—29 June 22 Dec	——	1269	18 Apr — 11 Oct	——
1220	——	2 June	1270	7 Apr — 30 Sep	23 Mar
1221	8 May — 1 Nov	23 May	1271	——	12 Mar — 6 Sep
1222	27 Apr — 22 Oct	12 May — 6 Oct	1272	15 Feb — 10 Aug	25 Aug
1223	16 Apr — 11 Oct	26 Sep	1273	3 Feb — 31 July	20 Jan — 14 Aug
1224	——	21 Mar	1274	23 Jan — 20 July	——
1225	24 Feb — 19 Aug	——	1275	4 Dec	25 June
1226	14 Feb — 9 Aug	28 Feb — 25 July	1276	29 May — 23 Nov	13 June
1227	3 Feb — 30 July	15 July	1277	18 May — 12 Nov	28 Oct
1228	12 Dec	3 July — 28 Dec	1278	8 May	23 Apr
1229	8 June — 2 Dec	——	1279	29 Mar — 21 Sep	12 Apr
1230	28 May — 22 Nov	14 May	1280	18 Mar — 10 Sep	1 Apr
1231	——	3 May — 26 Oct	1281	7 Mar — 31 Aug	15 Aug
1232	6 Apr — 1 Oct	15 Oct	1282	——	5 Aug
1233	27 Mar — 20 Sep	5 Oct	1283	14 Jan — 11 July	30 Jan
1234	17 Mar — 9 Sep	1 Mar	1284	4 Jan—29 June 24 Dec	19 Jan — 15 June
1235	——	19 Feb — 15 Aug	1285	18 June	4 June — 28 Nov
1236	24 Jan — 20 July	3 Aug	1286	9 May — 2 Nov	17 Nov
1237	12 Jan — 9 July	19 Dec	1287	29 Apr — 22 Oct	7 Nov
1238	2 Jan — 29 June	8 Dec	1288	18 Apr — 11 Oct	2 Apr
1239	12 Nov	3 June	1289	——	23 Mar — 16 Sep
1240	7 May — 1 Nov	23 May	1290	25 Feb — 22 Aug	5 Sep
1241	27 Apr — 21 Oct	6 Oct	1291	14 Feb — 11 Aug	25 Aug
1242	——	26 Sep	1292	4 Feb — 30 July	21 Jan
1243	8 Mar — 31 Aug	22 Mar	1293	15 Dec	9 Jan — 5 July
1244	25 Feb — 19 Aug	10 Mar — 5 Aug	1294	9 June — 4 Dec	25 June
1245	13 Feb — 9 Aug	25 July	1295	30 May — 23 Nov	8 Nov
1246	24 Dec	19 Jan — 14 July	1296	18 May	28 Oct
1247	19 June — 13 Dec	8 Jan	1297	9 Apr — 2 Oct	23 Apr
1248	7 June — 2 Dec	24 May	1298	29 Mar — 21 Sep	12 Apr
1249	28 May	14 May — 6 Nov	1299	18 Mar — 11 Sep	27 Aug
1250	18 Apr — 12 Oct	——	1300	——	21 Feb — 15 Aug

TABLE XVIII.—(Continued.)

List of Eclipses.

A.D.	Lunar.	Solar.
1301	25 Jan — 21 July	9 Feb
1302	14 Jan — 10 July	26 June
1303	4 Jan — 29 June	15 June — 9 Dec
1304	20 May — 13 Nov	4 June — 28 Nov
1305	9 May — 2 Nov	17 Nov
1306	29 Apr — 22 Oct	13 Apr
1307	———	3 Apr
1308	8 Mar — 1 Sep	15 Sep
1309	25 Feb — 21 Aug	11 Feb
1310	14 Feb — 11 Aug	31 Jan
1311	26 Dec	20 Jan — 16 July
1312	19 June — 14 Dec	5 July
1313	9 June — 3 Dec	———
1314	30 May	15 May — 8 Nov
1315	20 Apr — 13 Oct	4 May
1316	8 Apr — 2 Oct	22 Apr
1317	28 Mar — 21 Sep	6 Sep
1318	———	3 Mar
1319	5 Feb — 1 Aug	21 Feb
1320	26 Jan — 20 July	10 Feb — 6 July
1321	14 Jan — 10 July	26 June
1322	24 Nov	15 June — 9 Dec
1323	21 May — 13 Nov	29 Nov
1324	9 May — 1 Nov	24 Apr
1325	———	13 Apr — 7 Oct
1326	19 Mar — 12 Sep	26 Sep
1327	8 Mar — 2 Sep	16 Sep
1328	25 Feb — 21 Aug	———
1329	———	27 July
1330	{5 Jan — 1 July, 26 Dec}	16 July
1331	20 June — 15 Dec	30 Nov
1332	9 June	25 May
1333	30 Apr — 23 Oct	14 May
1334	19 Apr — 13 Oct	4 May
1335	8 Apr — 3 Oct	———
1336	———	6 Sep
1337	15 Feb — 12 Aug	3 Mar
1338	5 Feb — 1 Aug	20 Feb — 18 July
1339	26 Jan — 21 July	7 July — 31 Dec
1340	4 Dec	———
1341	31 May — 23 Nov	9 Dec
1342	21 May — 13 Nov	5 May
1343	———	25 Apr — 19 Oct
1344	29 Mar — 23 Sep	7 Oct
1345	18 Mar — 12 Sep	26 Sep
1346	8 Mar — 1 Sep	22 Feb
1347	———	11 Feb — 7 Aug
1348	17 Jan — 11 July	26 July
1349	{5 Jan — 1 July, 25 Dec}	10 Dec
1350	20 June	30 Nov

A.D.	Lunar.	Solar.
1351	4 Nov	———
1352	30 Apr — 23 Oct	14 May
1353	19 Apr — 13 Oct	28 Sep
1354	———	25 Mar — 17 Sep
1355	27 Feb — 23 Aug	14 Mar — 6 Sep
1356	16 Feb — 11 Aug	28 July
1357	5 Feb — 31 July	17 July
1358	16 Dec	{10 Jan — 7 July, 31 Dec}
1359	11 June — 5 Dec	———
1360	31 May — 23 Nov	15 May
1361	20 May	5 May
1362	4 Oct	18 Oct
1363	30 Mar — 23 Sep	———
1364	18 Mar — 12 Sep	4 Mar
1365	———	21 Feb
1366	27 Jan — 22 July	7 Aug
1367	16 Jan — 12 July	27 July — 22 Dec
1368	5 Jan — 1 July	10 Dec
1369	14 Nov	5 June
1370	11 May — 4 Nov	25 May
1371	30 Apr — 24 Oct	9 Oct
1372	———	4 Apr — 27 Sep
1373	9 Mar — 2 Sep	24 Mar — 17 Sep
1374	27 Feb — 22 Aug	14 Mar — 8 Aug
1375	16 Feb — 12 Aug	29 July
1376	26 Dec	17 July
1377	22 June — 15 Dec	10 Jan — 31 Dec
1378	11 June — 4 Dec	27 May
1379	31 May — 24 Nov	16 May
1380	14 Oct	5 May
1381	9 Apr — 4 Oct	18 Oct
1382	29 Mar — 23 Sep	———
1383	———	29 Aug
1384	7 Feb — 2 Aug	17 Aug
1385	27 Jan — 22 July	6 Aug
1386	16 Jan — 12 July	1 Jan — 22 Dec
1387	25 Nov	16 June
1388	21 May — 14 Nov	5 June
1389	10 May — 4 Nov	———
1390	29 Apr	9 Oct
1391	20 Mar	5 Apr
1392	6 Mar — 2 Sept	24 Mar
1393	27 Feb — 22 Aug	8 Aug
1394	———	28 July
1395	{6 Jan — 3 July, 26 Dec}	———
1396	21 June — 15 Dec	11 Jan — 6 June
1397	11 June — 4 Dec	26 May
1398	26 Oct	16 May — 9 Nov
1399	20 Apr — 15 Oct	29 Oct
1400	9 Apr — 3 Oct	26 Mar

TABLE XVIII.—(Continued.)

List of Eclipses.

A.D.	Lunar.	Solar.	A.D.	Lunar.	Solar.
1401	30 Mar	15 Mar — 8 Sep	1451	17 Jan — 13 July	28 June
1402	13 Aug	4 Mar	1452	7 Jan — 27 Nov	17 June — 11 Dec
1403	7 Feb — 2 Aug	18 Aug	1453	22 May — 16 Nov	30 Nov
1404	27 Jan — 22 July	———	1454	12 May — 5 Nov	27 Apr
1405	6 Dec	1 Jan — 26 June	1455	1 May — 25 Oct	17 Apr — 11 Oct
1406	2 June — 25 Nov	16 June	1456	22 Mar	5 Apr
1407	22 May — 15 Nov	31 Oct	1457	11 Mar — 3 Sep	18 Sep
1408	10 May	26 Apr — 19 Oct	1458	28 Feb — 24 Aug	———
1409	31 Mar	15 Apr — 9 Oct	1459	———	3 Feb — 29 July
1410	21 Mar — 13 Sep	4 Apr	1460	{8 Jan — 3 July 28 Dec}	18 July
1411	10 Mar — 2 Sep	19 Aug	1461	22 June — 17 Dec	7 July — 2 Dec
1412	22 Aug	12 Feb — 7 Aug	1462	12 June	21 Nov
1413	17 Jan — 13 July	1 Feb	1463	———	18 May — 11 Nov
1414	{6 Jan — 3 July 26 Dec}	17 June	1464	22 Apr — 15 Oct	6 May —
1415	22 June — 16 Dec	7 June	1465	11 Apr — 4 Oct	20 Sep
1416	5 Nov	27 May — 19 Nov	1466	24 Sep	16 Mar
1417	1 May — 25 Oct	———	1467	15 Aug	6 Mar
1418	20 Apr — 14 Oct	6 Apr	1468	8 Feb — 4 Aug	———
1419	10 Apr	26 Mar	1469	27 Jan — 24 July	9 July
1420	29 Feb — 23 Aug	14 Mar — 8 Sep	1470	17 Jan — 8 Dec	28 June — 22 Dec
1421	17 Feb — 13 Aug	28 Aug	1471	3 June — 27 Nov	———
1422	6 Feb — 2 Aug	23 Jan	1472	22 May — 15 Nov	8 May
1423	17 Dec	8 July	1473	12 May — 4 Nov	27 Apr
1424	12 June — 6 Dec	26 June	1474	———	16 Apr — 11 Oct
1425	1 June — 25 Nov	10 Nov	1475	22 Mar — 15 Sep	30 Sep
1426	21 May	7 May	1476	10 Mar — 3 Sep	25 Feb
1427	11 Apr	20 Oct	1477	———	8 Aug
1428	31 Mar — 23 Sep	14 Apr	1478	18 Jan — 15 July	29 July
1429	20 Mar — 13 Sep	30 Aug	1479	{8 Jan — 4 July 29 Dec}	19 July — 13 Dec
1430	2 Sep	19 Aug	1480	22 June	———
1431	24 July	12 Feb — 8 Aug	1481	———	28 May
1432	17 Jan — 13 July	2 Feb — 27 June	1482	3 May — 26 Oct	17 May
1433	{6 Jan — 2 July 26 Dec}	17 June	1483	22 Apr — 16 Oct	2 Oct
1434	16 Nov	7 June — 30 Nov	1484	4 Oct	20 Sep
1435	12 May — 6 Nov	20 Nov	1485	25 Aug	16 Mar — 9 Sep
1436	30 Apr — 25 Oct	16 Apr	1486	18 Feb — 15 Aug	6 Mar
1437	20 Apr — 14 Oct	5 Apr — 30 Sep	1487	8 Feb — 4 Aug	20 July
1438	11 Mar — 3 Sep	19 Sep	1488	28 Jan	9 July
1439	1 Mar — 24 Aug	8 Sep	1489	13 June — 8 Dec	1 Jan — 22 Dec
1440	18 Feb — 13 Aug	3 Feb	1490	2 June — 27 Nov	———
1441	27 Dec	23 Jan — 18 July	1491	23 May — 16 Nov	8 May
1442	23 June — 17 Dec	7 July	1492	———	26 Apr — 21 Oct
1443	12 June — 7 Dec	27 June	1493	2 Apr — 25 Sep	10 Oct
1444	31 May	10 Nov	1494	22 Mar — 15 Sep	7 Mar
1445	———	7 May	1495	11 Mar — 4 Sep	25 Feb — 20 Aug
1446	11 Apr — 5 Oct	26 Apr	1496	30 Jan — 25 July	14 Feb — 8 Aug
1447	1 Apr — 24 Sep	10 Sep	1497	18 Jan — 14 July	29 July
1448	12 Sep	5 Mar — 29 Aug	1498	8 Jan — 3 July	13 Dec
1449	4 Aug	18 Aug	1499	———	8 June
1450	28 Jan — 24 July	12 Feb	1500	13 May — 6 Nov	28 May

TABLE XVIII.—(Continued.)

List of Eclipses.

A.D.	LUNAR.	SOLAR.
1501	3 May — 26 Oct	12 Oct
1502	22 Apr — 15 Oct	7 Apr — 1 Oct
1503	6 Sep	27 Mar — 20 Sep
1504	1 Mar — 25 Aug	16 Mar
1505	18 Feb — 14 Aug	30 July
1506	8 Feb	20 July
1507	24 June — 19 Dec	13 Jan
1508	13 June — 7 Dec	2 Jan — 29 May
1509	2 June — 26 Nov	18 May
1510	—	8 May
1511	13 Apr — 6 Oct	—
1512	1 Apr — 25 Sep	17 Mar
1513	30 Jan — 25 July	7 Mar
1514	9 Feb	20 Aug
1515	30 Jan — 25 July	9 Aug
1516	19 Jan — 13 July	4 Jan — 23 Dec
1517	—	19 June
1518	24 May — 17 Nov	8 June
1519	14 May — 6 Nov	28 May — 23 Oct
1520	2 May — 26 Oct	11 Oct
1521	—	7 Apr
1522	12 Mar — 5 Sep	27 Mar
1523	1 Mar — 26 Aug	11 Aug
1524	19 Feb	30 July
1525	4 July — 29 Dec	23 Jan
1526	24 June — 18 Dec	13 Jan
1527	14 June — 7 Dec	30 May
1528	—	18 May — 12 Nov
1529	23 Apr — 17 Oct	1 Nov
1530	12 Apr — 6 Oct	29 Mar
1531	1 Apr — 26 Sep	—
1532	—	30 Aug
1533	9 Feb — 4 Aug	20 Aug
1534	30 Jan — 25 July	14 Jan
1535	—	3 Jan — 30 June
1536	4 June — 27 Nov	18 June
1537	24 May — 17 Nov	7 June
1538	14 May — 6 Nov	23 Oct
1539	—	18 Apr — 12 Oct
1540	22 Mar — 16 Sep	7 Apr
1541	12 Mar — 5 Sep	21 Aug
1542	1 Mar — 25 Aug	11 Aug
1543	16 July	3 Feb
1544	{10 Jan — 4 July, 29 Dec}	24 Jan
1545	24 June — 18 Dec	9 June
1546	—	29 May — 23 Nov
1547	4 May — 28 Oct	12 Nov
1548	22 Apr — 17 Oct	8 Apr
1549	12 Apr — 6 Oct	29 Mar
1550	—	18 Mar
1551	20 Feb — 16 Aug	31 Aug
1552	10 Feb — 4 Aug	—
1553	25 July	14 Jan
1554	15 June — 9 Dec	29 June
1555	5 June — 28 Nov	19 June — 14 Nov
1556	24 May — 17 Nov	2 Nov
1557	—	28 Apr — 22 Oct
1558	2 Apr — 27 Sep	18 Apr
1559	23 Mar — 16 Sep	—
1560	12 Mar — 4 Sep	21 Aug
1561	26 July	14 Feb — 11 Aug
1562	20 Jan — 16 July	—
1563	{9 Jan — 5 July, 29 Dec}	20 June
1564	—	8 June
1565	15 May — 8 Nov	—
1566	4 May — 28 Oct	19 Apr
1567	23 Apr — 18 Oct	9 Apr
1568	—	28 Mar — 21 Sep
1569	3 Mar — 26 Aug	—
1570	20 Feb — 15 Aug	5 Feb
1571	10 Feb — 5 Aug	25 Jan — 22 July
1572	25 June — 19 Dec	15 Jan — 10 July
1573	15 June — 8 Dec	29 June — 24 Nov
1574	4 June — 28 Nov	13 Nov
1575	—	10 May
1576	13 Apr — 7 Oct	28 Apr
1577	2 Apr — 27 Sep	12 Sep
1578	23 Mar — 16 Sep	—
1579	—	25 Feb — 22 Aug
1580	31 Jan — 26 July	15 Feb
1581	19 Jan — 16 July	30 June
1582	8 Jan	20 June* — 25 Dec
1583	5 June — 29 Nov	14 Dec
1584	24 May — 18 Nov	10 May
1585	13 May — 7 Nov	29 Apr
1586	—	19 Apr — 12 Oct
1587	24 Mar — 16 Sep	2 Oct
1588	13 Mar — 5 Sep	26 Feb
1589	2 Mar — 25 Aug	15 Feb — 11 Aug
1590	17 July	4 Feb — 31 July
1591	{9 Jan — 6 July, 30 Dec}	20 July — 15 Dec
1592	24 June — 18 Dec	3 Dec
1593	—	30 May — 23 Nov
1594	4 May — 29 Oct	20 May
1595	24 Apr — 18 Oct	3 Oct
1596	12 Apr — 6 Oct	22 Sep
1597	—	17 Mar
1598	21 Feb — 16 Aug	7 Mar
1599	10 Feb — 6 Aug	22 July
1600	30 Jan	10 July

* From this year all the dates are given in the Gregorian Calendar, or New Style.

TABLE XVIII.—(Continued.)

List of Eclipses.

A.D.	Lunar.	Solar.
1601	15 June — 9 Dec	{4 Jan—30 June, 24 Dec}
1602	4 June — 29 Nov	21 May
1603	24 May — 18 Nov	11 May
1604	—	29 Apr
1605	3 Apr — 27 Sep	12 Oct
1606	24 Mar — 16 Sep	—
1607	13 Mar — 6 Sep	26 Feb
1608	27 July	10 Aug
1609	20 Jan — 16 July	30 July — 26 Dec
1610	{9 Jan — 6 July, 30 Dec}	15 Dec
1611	—	4 Dec
1612	14 May — 8 Nov	30 May
1613	4 May — 28 Oct	—
1614	24 Apr — 17 Oct	3 Oct
1615	—	29 Mar — 22 Sep
1616	3 Mar — 27 Aug	—
1617	20 Feb — 16 Aug	1 Aug
1618	9 Feb — 6 Aug	—
1619	26 June — 21 Dec	11 July
1620	15 June — 9 Dec	31 May
1621	4 June — 29 Nov	21 May
1622	—	10 May ... 3 Nov
1623	15 Apr — 8 Oct	—
1624	3 Apr — 26 Sep	19 Mar
1625	24 Mar — 16 Sep	—
1626	7 Aug	26 Feb — 21 Aug
1627	31 Jan — 28 July	11 Aug
1628	20 Jan — 16 July	6 Jan — 25 Dec
1629	9 Jan	21 June — 14 Dec
1630	26 May — 19 Nov	10 June
1631	15 May — 8 Nov	31 May — 25 Oct
1632	4 May — 27 Oct	—
1633	—	8 Apr — 3 Oct
1634	14 Mar — 7 Sep	29 Mar
1635	3 Mar — 28 Aug	12 Aug
1636	20 Feb — 16 Aug	1 Aug
1637	7 July — 31 Dec	26 Jan
1638	26 June — 21 Dec	15 Jan
1639	15 June — 10 Dec	1 June
1640	—	—
1641	26 Apr — 18 Oct	3 Nov
1642	15 Apr — 8 Oct	30 Mar
1643	4 Apr — 27 Sep	20 Mar
1644	—	1 Sep
1645	10 Feb — 7 Aug	21 Aug
1646	31 Jan — 27 July	17 Jan
1647	20 Jan	{5 Jan — 2 July, 26 Dec}
1648	5 June — 30 Nov	21 June
1649	26 May — 19 Nov	10 June — 4 Nov
1650	15 May — 8 Nov	25 Oct
1651	—	—
1652	25 Mar — 17 Sep	8 Apr
1653	14 Mar — 7 Sep	29 Mar
1654	3 Mar — 27 Aug	12 Aug
1655	—	6 Feb — 2 Aug
1656	{11 Jan — 6 July, 31 Dec}	26 Jan
1657	25 June — 20 Dec	11 June
1658	—	1 June — 24 Nov
1659	6 May — 30 Oct	14 Nov
1660	25 Apr — 18 Oct	3 Nov
1661	4 Apr — 8 Oct	30 Mar
1662	—	20 Mar — 12 Sep
1663	22 Feb — 18 Aug	—
1664	11 Feb — 6 Aug	28 Jan — 21 Aug
1665	31 Jan — 26 July	16 Jan
1666	16 June — 11 Dec	5 Jan — 2 July
1667	6 June — 30 Nov	21 June
1668	26 May — 18 Nov	4 Nov
1669	—	30 Apr
1670	5 Apr — 29 Sep	19 Apr
1671	25 Mar — 18 Sep	3 Sep
1672	13 Mar — 7 Sep	22 Aug
1673	—	12 Aug
1674	22 Jan — 17 July	—
1675	11 Jan — 7 July	23 June
1676	1 Jan — 25 June	11 June — 5 Dec
1677	17 May — 9 Nov	24 Nov
1678	6 May — 29 Oct	21 Apr — 14 Nov
1679	25 Apr — 19 Oct	10 Apr
1680	—	30 Mar
1681	4 Mar — 29 Aug	12 Sep
1682	21 Feb — 18 Aug	1 Sep
1683	11 Feb — 7 Aug	27 Jan — 24 July
1684	27 June — 21 Dec	12 July
1685	16 June — 10 Dec	1 July
1686	6 June — 29 Nov	—
1687	—	11 May — 5 Nov
1688	15 Apr — 9 Oct	30 Apr
1689	4 Apr — 29 Sep	13 Sep
1690	24 Mar — 18 Sep	3 Sep
1691	—	28 Feb
1692	2 Feb — 28 July	17 Feb
1693	22 Jan — 17 July	3 July
1694	11 Jan — 7 July	29 June — 16 Dec
1695	28 May — 20 Nov	o Dec
1696	16 May — 9 Nov	—
1697	6 May — 29 Oct	21 Apr
1698	—	4 Oct
1699	15 Mar — 9 Sep	23 Sep
1700	5 Mar — 29 Aug	19 Feb

TABLE XVIII.—(Continued.)

List of Eclipses.

A.D.	LUNAR.	SOLAR.
1701	22 Feb — 18 Aug	7 Feb — 4 Aug
1702	——	24 July
1703	3 Jan—29 June 23 Dec	14 July — 8 Dec
1704	17 June — 11 Dec	27 Nov
1705	——	——
1706	28 Apr — 21 Oct	12 May
1707	17 Apr — 11 Oct	2 May
1708	5 Apr — 29 Sep	14 Sep
1709	——	11 Mar — 4 Sep
1710	13 Feb — 9 Aug	28 Feb
1711	3 Feb — 29 July	15 July
1712	23 Jan — 18 July	3 July — 28 Dec
1713	8 June — 2 Dec	17 Dec
1714	29 May — 21 Nov	7 Dec
1715	18 May — 11 Nov	3 May
1716	——	22 Apr — 15 Oct
1717	27 Mar — 20 Sep	——
1718	16 Mar — 9 Sep	2 Mar — 24 Sep
1719	6 Mar — 29 Aug	19 Feb
1720	——	8 Feb — 4 Aug
1721	13 Jan — 9 July	24 July — 19 Dec
1722	2 Jan—29 June 19 Dec	8 Dec
1723		3 June
1724	8 May — 1 Nov	22 May
1725	27 Apr — 21 Oct	12 May — 6 Oct
1726	16 Apr — 11 Oct	25 Sep
1727	——	15 Sep
1728	25 Feb — 19 Aug	——
1729	13 Feb — 9 Aug	26 July
1730	3 Feb — 29 July	15 July
1731	20 Jan — 13 Dec	8 Jan — 4 July 29 Dec
1732	8 June — 1 Dec	17 Dec
1733	28 May — 21 Nov	13 May
1734	——	3 May
1735	7 Apr — 2 Oct	16 Oct
1736	26 Mar — 20 Sep	4 Oct
1737	16 Mar — 9 Sep	1 Mar
1738	——	15 Aug
1739	24 Jan — 20 July	4 Aug ... 30 Dec
1740	13 Jan — 9 July	18 Dec
1741	1 Jan	13 June — 8 Dec
1742	19 May — 12 Nov	3 June
1743	8 May — 2 Nov	23 May — 17 Oct
1744	26 Apr — 21 Oct	6 Oct
1745	——	2 Apr
1746	7 Mar — 30 Aug	22 Mar
1747	25 Feb — 20 Aug	11 Mar — 6 Aug
1748	14 Feb — 8 Aug	25 July
1749	30 June — 23 Dec	14 July
1750	19 June — 13 Dec	8 Jan

A.D.	LUNAR.	SOLAR.
1751	9 June — 2 Dec	25 May
1752	——	13 May — 6 Nov
1753	17 Apr — 12 Oct	26 Oct
1754	7 Apr — 1 Oct	23 Mar — 16 Oct
1755	28 Mar — 20 Sep	12 Mar
1756	——	1 Mar
1757	4 Feb — 30 July	14 Aug
1758	24 Jan — 20 July	30 Dec
1759	13 Jan — 10 July	19 Dec
1760	29 May — 22 Nov	13 June
1761	18 May — 12 Nov	3 June
1762	8 May — 1 Nov	17 Oct
1763	——	13 Apr — 7 Oct
1764	18 Mar — 10 Sep	1 Apr
1765	7 Mar — 30 Aug	16 Aug
1766	24 Feb — 20 Aug	5 Aug
1767	——	30 Jan
1768	4 Jan — 23 Dec	——
1769	19 June — 13 Dec	8 Jan — 4 June
1770	——	25 May — 17 Nov
1771	29 Apr — 23 Oct	——
1772	17 Apr — 11 Oct	3 Apr — 26 Oct
1773	7 Apr — 30 Sep	23 Mar
1774	——	12 Mar — 6 Sep
1775	15 Feb — 11 Aug	26 Aug
1776	4 Feb — 31 July	21 Jan
1777	23 Jan — 20 July	9 Jan — 5 July
1778	10 June — 4 Dec	10 June — 4 Dec
1779	30 May — 23 Nov	14 June — 8 Nov
1780	18 May — 12 Nov	27 Oct
1781	——	23 Apr — 17 Oct
1782	29 Mar — 21 Sep	12 Apr
1783	18 Mar — 10 Sep	——
1784	7 Mar — 30 Aug	16 Aug
1785	——	9 Feb — 5 Aug
1786	14 Jan — 11 July	30 Jan
1787	3 Jan—30 June 24 Dec	19 Jan — 15 June
1788	——	4 June
1689	9 May — 3 Nov	17 Nov
1790	29 Apr — 23 Oct	——
1791	18 Apr — 12 Oct	3 Apr
1792	——	16 Sep
1793	25 Feb — 21 Aug	5 Sep
1794	14 Feb — 11 Aug	31 Jan
1795	4 Feb — 31 July	21 Jan — 16 July
1796	14 Dec	10 Jan — 4 July
1797	9 June — 4 Dec	24 June
1798	29 May — 23 Nov	8 Nov
1799	——	——
1800	9 Apr — 2 Oct	24 Apr

TABLE XVIII.—(Continued.)

List of Eclipses.

A.D.	Lunar.	Solar.
1801	30 Mar — 22 Sep	13 Apr — 8 Sep
1802	19 Mar — 11 Sep	28 Aug
1803	—	17 Aug
1804	26 Jan — 22 July	11 Feb
1805	15 Jan — 11 July	26 June
1806	5 Jan — 30 June	16 June — 10 Dec
1807	21 May — 15 Nov	6 June — 29 Nov
1808	10 May — 3 Nov	18 Nov
1809	30 April — 23 Oct	—
1810	—	4 Apr
1811	10 Mar — 2 Sep	—
1812	27 Feb — 22 Aug	—
1813	15 Feb — 12 Aug	1 Feb
1814	26 Dec	21 Jan — 17 July
1815	21 June — 16 Dec	7 July
1816	10 June — 4 Dec	19 Nov
1817	30 May	16 May — 9 Nov
1818	21 Apr — 14 Oct	5 May
1819	10 Apr — 3 Oct	26 Apr — 19 Sep
1820	29 Mar — 22 Sep	7 Sep
1821	—	4 Mar
1822	6 Feb — 3 Aug	—
1823	26 Jan — 23 July	11 Feb — 8 July
1824	16 Jan — 11 July	26 June — 20 Dec
1825	1 June — 25 Nov	16 June
1826	21 May — 14 Nov	29 Nov
1827	11 May — 3 Nov	26 Apr
1828	—	14 Apr — 9 Oct
1829	20 Mar — 13 Sep	28 Sep
1830	9 Mar — 2 Sep	23 Feb
1831	26 Feb — 23 Aug	—
1832	—	27 July
1833	6 Jan — 2 July, 26 Dec	17 July
1834	21 June — 16 Dec	—
1835	10 June	27 May — 20 Nov
1836	1 May — 24 Oct	15 May
1837	20 Apr — 13 Oct	4 May
1838	10 Apr — 3 Oct	—
1839	—	15 Mar — 7 Sep
1840	17 Feb — 13 Aug	4 Mar
1841	6 Feb — 2 Aug	21 Feb — 18 July
1842	26 Jan — 22 July	8 July
1843	12 June — 7 Dec	21 Dec
1844	31 May — 25 Nov	—
1845	21 May — 14 Nov	6 May
1846	—	25 Apr — 20 Oct
1847	31 Mar — 24 Sep	9 Oct
1848	19 Mar — 13 Sep	27 Sep
1849	9 Mar — 2 Sep	23 Feb
1850	—	12 Feb — 7 Aug

A.D.	Lunar.	Solar.
1851	17 Jan — 13 July	28 July
1852	7 Jan — 1 July, 26 Dec	11 Dec
1853	21 June	—
1854	12 May — 4 Nov	—
1855	2 May — 25 Oct	16 May
1856	20 Apr — 13 Oct	29 Sep
1857	—	18 Sep
1858	27 Feb — 24 Aug	15 Mar
1859	17 Feb — 13 Aug	29 July
1860	7 Feb — 1 Aug	18 July
1861	17 Dec	11 Jan — 8 July, 31 Dec
1862	12 June — 6 Dec	21 Dec
1863	2 June — 25 Nov	17 May
1864	—	19 Oct — 6 May
1865	11 Apr — 4 Oct	19 Oct
1866	31 Mar — 24 Sep	16 Mar — 8 Oct
1867	20 Mar — 14 Sep	6 Mar
1868	—	23 Feb — 18 Aug
1869	28 Jan — 23 July	7 Aug
1870	17 Jan — 12 July	22 Dec
1871	6 Jan — 2 July	18 June — 12 Dec
1872	22 May — 15 Nov	6 June
1873	12 May — 4 Nov	26 May
1874	1 May — 25 Oct	10 Oct
1875	—	6 Apr — 29 Sep
1876	10 Mar — 3 Sep	—
1877	27 Feb — 23 Aug	15 Mar — 9 Aug
1878	17 Feb — 13 Aug	29 July
1879	28 Dec	22 Jan — 19 July
1880	22 June — 16 Dec	11 Jan — 31 Dec
1881	12 June — 5 Dec	28 May
1882	—	17 May — 11 Nov
1883	22 Apr — 16 Oct	31 Oct
1884	10 Apr — 4 Oct	27 Mar — 19 Oct
1885	30 Mar — 24 Sep	—
1886	—	29 Aug
1887	8 Feb — 3 Aug	19 Aug
1888	26 Jan — 23 July	—
1889	17 Jan — 12 July	22 Dec
1890	3 June — 26 Nov	17 June
1891	23 May — 16 Nov	6 June
1892	11 May — 4 Nov	—
1893	—	16 Apr
1894	21 Mar — 15 Sep	6 Apr — 29 Sep
1895	11 Mar — 4 Sep	26 Mar — 20 Aug
1896	28 Feb — 23 Aug	9 Aug
1897	—	—
1898	8 Jan — 3 July, 27 Dec	22 Jan
1899	23 June — 17 Dec	11 Jan — 8 June
1900	13 June	28 May — 22 Nov

TABLE XVIII.–(Concluded.)

List of Eclipses.

A.D.	LUNAR.	SOLAR.	A.D.	LUNAR.	SOLAR.
1901	3 May — 27 Oct	18 May — 11 Nov	1951	——	1 Sep
1902	22 Apr — 17 Oct	31 Oct	1952	10 Feb — 5 Aug	25 Feb — 20 Aug
1903	11 Apr — 6 Oct	29 Mar — 21 Sep	1953	29 Jan — 26 July	14 Feb — 11 July
1904	——	17 Mar	1954	19 Jan — 16 July	30 June — 25 Dec
1905	19 Feb — 15 Aug	30 Aug	1955	29 Nov	20 June — 14 Dec
1906	9 Feb — 4 Aug	20 Aug	1956	24 May — 18 Nov	2 Dec
1907	29 Jan — 25 July	14 Jan	1957	13 May — 7 Nov	23 Oct
1908	7 Dec	27 June — 23 Dec	1958	3 May	19 Apr
1909	4 June — 27 Nov	17 June	1959	24 Mar — 17 Sep	2 Oct
1910	24 May — 17 Nov	2 Nov	1960	13 Mar — 5 Sep	20 Sep
1911	——	22 Oct	1961	2 Mar — 26 Aug	11 Aug
1912	1 Apr — 26 Sep	17 Apr — 10 Oct	1962	——	4 Feb — 31 July
1913	22 Mar — 15 Sep	——	1963	{9 Jan — 6 July 30 Dec}	25 Jan
1914	11 Mar — 4 Sep	21 Aug	1964	25 June — 19 Dec	9 July — 4 Dec
1915	——	14 Feb — 10 Aug	1965	14 June	23 Nov
1916	18 Jan — 15 July	3 Feb	1966	4 May — 29 Oct	20 May — 12 Nov
1917	{8 Jan — 4 July 28 Dec}	23 Jan — 19 June	1967	24 Apr — 18 Oct	9 May
1918	24 June	8 June — 3 Dec	1968	{13 Apr — 22 Sep — 6 Oct}	——
1919	8 Nov	29 May — 22 Nov	1969	——	18 Mar
1920	3 May — 27 Oct	10 Nov	1970	21 Feb — 17 Aug	7 Mar
1921	22 Apr — 16 Oct	8 Apr — 1 Oct	1971	10 Feb — 6 Aug	25 Feb — 22 July
1922	——	28 Mar	1972	30 Jan — 26 July	——
1923	3 Mar — 26 Aug	17 Mar — 10 Sep	1973	10 Dec	{4 Jan — 30 June 24 Dec
1924	20 Feb — 14 Aug	30 Aug	1974	4 June — 29 Nov	13 Dec
1925	8 Feb — 4 Aug	24 Jan	1975	25 May — 18 Nov	11 May
1926	19 Dec	14 Jan — 8 July	1976	13 May	29 Apr — 23 Oct
1927	15 June — 8 Dec	29 June	1977	4 Apr — 27 Sep	18 Apr
1928	3 June — 27 Nov	19 May — 12 Nov	1978	24 Mar — 16 Sep	2 Oct
1929	23 May	9 May — 1 Nov	1979	13 Mar — 6 Sep	26 Feb
1930	13 Apr — 7 Oct	——	1980	——	16 Feb
1931	2 Apr — 26 Sep	17 Apr	1981	17 July	31 July
1932	22 Mar — 14 Sep	——	1982	{9 Jan — 6 July 30 Sep}	20 July — 15 Dec
1933	——	24 Feb — 21 Aug	1983	25 June	11 June — 4 Dec
1934	30 Jan — 26 July	14 Feb — 10 Aug	1984	——	30 May
1935	19 Jan — 16 July	——	1985	4 May — 28 Oct	12 Nov
1936	8 Jan — 4 July	19 June	1986	24 Apr — 17 Oct	——
1937	18 Nov	2 Dec	1987	——	29 Mar — 23 Sep
1938	14 May — 7 Nov	22 Nov	1988	27 Aug	18 May — 11 Sep
1939	3 May — 28 Oct	19 Apr	1989	20 Feb — 17 Aug	——
1940	22 Apr	1 Oct	1990	9 Feb — 6 Aug	22 July
1941	13 Mar — 5 Sep	21 Sep	1991	30 Jan — 31 Dec	——
1942	2 Mar — 26 Aug	10 Sep	1992	15 June — 9 Dec	24 Dec
1943	20 Feb — 15 Aug	4 Feb	1993	4 June — 29 Nov	21 May
1944	29 Dec	25 Jan — 20 July	1994	25 May	10 May — 3 Nov
1945	25 June — 19 Dec	14 Jan — 9 July	1995	15 Apr	29 Apr — 24 Oct
1946	14 June — 8 Dec	29 June	1996	3 Apr — 27 Sep	12 Oct
1947	3 June	20 May	1997	16 Sep	9 Mar
1948	23 Apr — 18 Oct	9 May — 1 Nov	1998	——	26 Feb — 22 Aug
1949	13 Apr — 7 Oct	28 Apr	1999	28 July	16 Feb — 11 Aug
1950	2 Apr — 26 Sep	12 Sep	2000	21 Jan — 16 July	31 July

TABLE XIX.

THE DAKHINI CYCLE OF JUPITER.

The Jovian cycle of 60 years, as used in Southern India, is a simple period of 60 solar years, in which year has a separate name. There are no omitted years as in the Northern reckoning, and the cycle has no longer any connection with Jupiter's revolution. The cycles begin in the following years A.D., with the year named Prabhava :

A. D.	7	—	—	—	—	—	—
	67	367	667	967	1267	1567	1867
	127	427	727	1027	1327	1627	1927
	187	487	787	1087	1387	1687	1987
	247	547	847	1147	1447	1747	2047
	307	607	907	1207	1507	1807	2107

The names of the 60 years of the cycle of Jupiter are the same both in Northern and Southern India. They are as follows :—

1	Prabhava.	16	Chitrabhânu.	31	Hemalamba.	46	Paridhâvin.
2	Vibhava.	17	Subhânu.	32	Vilambin.	47	Pramâdin.
3	Sukla.	18	Târana.	33	Vikârin.	48	Ananda.
4	Pramoda.	19	Pârthiva.	34	Sarvari.	49	Râkshasa.
5	Prajâpati.	20	Vyaya.	35	Plava.	50	Anala.
6	Angiras.	21	Sarvajit.	36	Sabhakrit.	51	Pingala.
7	Srimukha.	22	Sarvadhârin.	37	Sabhakrit.	52	Kalayutka.
8	Bhâva.	23	Virodhin.	38	Krodhin.	53	Siddhartha.
9	Yuvan.	24	Vikrita.	39	Viswâvasu.	54	Randra.
10	Dhâtar.	25	Khara.	40	Parâbhava.	55	Durmati.
11	Iswara.	26	Nandana.	41	Plavanga.	56	Dundubhi.
12	Bahudhânya.	27	Vijaya.	42	Kilaka.	57	Udgârin.
13	Pramâthin.	28	Jaya.	43	Saumya.	58	Raktaksha.
14	Vikrama.	29	Manmatha.	44	Sâdharana.	59	Krodha.
15	Vrisha.	30	Durmukha.	45	Virodhakrit.	60	Kshaya.

As an example of the use of this Dakhini cycle, I may cite the date of the Kurda inscription (Royal Asiat. Soc. Jour., III., 104), which is recorded as Sake 894 (A.D. 972), with the Jupiter year named Angiras. As this is the 6th name, we obtain the date intended by adding 5 years to the 1st year of the cycle, which began previously to A.D. 972. This is A.D. 967, to which adding 5 we get 972 A.D., in exact accordance with the Sake date of 894.

TABLE XX.

INITIAL DAYS OF ILAHI YEARS.

The Ilahi is a true solar year beginning with the Nauroz (in March). The initial days in the Hijra reckoning are taken from Dowson's Table as given by Abul Fazl. The corresponding Christian dates have been calculated, and a few palpable errors have been corrected.

ILAHI.	Months.		A. H.	March.		A. D.	ILAHI.	Months.		A. H.	March.		A. D.
1	27	Rabi II ...	963	Tues	10	1556	26	5	Safar ...	989	Sat	11	1581
2	9	Jumadi I...	964	Wed	10	1557	27	15	———	990	S	11	1582
3	20	———	965	Thur	10	1558	28	26	———	991	Mon	11	1583
4	2	Jumadi II	966	Frid	10	1559	29	8	Rabi I ...	992	Tues	10	1584
5	12	———	967	S	11	1560	30	19	———	993	Thur	11	1585
6	23	———	968	Tues	11	1561	31	29	———	994	Thur	10	1586
7	5	Rajab ...	969	Wed	11	1562	32	11	Rabi II ...	995	Sat	11	1587
8	16	———	970	Thur	11	1563	33	22	———	996	Mon	11	1588
9	27	———	971	Sat	10	1564	34	4	Jumadi I...	997	Tues	11	1589
10	8	Shabân ...	972	S	11	1565	35	14	———	998	Wed	11	1590
11	18	———	973	S	10	1566	36	24	———	999	Wed	10	1591
12	29	———	974	Tues	11	1567	37	5	Jumadi II	1000	Thur	10	1592
13	11	Ramzân ...	975	Wed	10	1568	38	17	———	1001	S	11	1593
14	22	———	976	Thur	10	1569	39	28	———	1002	Mon	11	1594
15	2	Shawâl ...	977	Frid	10	1570	40	9	Rajab ...	1003	Mon	10	1595
16	14	———	978	S	11	1571	41	20	———	1004	Wed	10	1596
17	25	———	979	Tues	11	1572	42	2	Shabân ...	1005	Frid	11	1597
18	6	Zilkada ...	980	Tues	10	1573	43	13	———	1006	Sat	11	1598
19	17	———	981	Wed	10	1574	44	23	———	1007	S	11	1599
20	27	———	982	Thur	10	1575	45	4	Ramzân ...	1008	S	9	1600
21	9	Zîl-hijja ...	983	Sat	10	1576	46	15	———	1009	Tues	10	1601
22	20	———	984	S	10	1577	47	26	———	1010	Wed	10	1602
23	2	Muharram	986	Tues	11	1578	48	6	Shawâl ...	1011	Wed	9	1603
24	12	———	987	Wed	11	1579	49	17	———	1012	Frid	9	1604
25	24	———	988	Frid	11	1580	50	28	———	1013	Sat	9	1605

TABLE XXI.

THE ABJAD.

A favourite mode of recording Hijra dates is by the numerical values of the letters in some short phrase, or chronogram, descriptive of the event commemorated. This system is called *Abjad*, from the first four letters of the Hebrew alphabet, from which the scheme was borrowed, namely, *a, b, j, d.* The whole scheme is as follows:—

Letters.	Values.	Letters.	Values.	Letters.	Values.
a	1	*i*	10	*ḳ*	100
b	2	*k*	20	*r*	200
j	3	*l*	30	*sh*	300
d	4	*m*	40	*t*	400
h	5	*n*	50	*ṣ*	500
o. w.	6	*s*	60	*kh*	600
z	7	*ain*	70	*z̈*	700
ḥ	8	*f*	80	*zw*	800
ṭ	9	*sw*	90	*ṡ*	900
				gh	1000

Occasionally the chronograms were very tersely and happily expressed, and the fortunate inventors were usually rewarded very liberally. The following are rather favourable specimens of these *Abjad* chronograms:

1.—*Wafât Firoz* records the "Death of Firoz" in A. H. 790.

2.—*Masjid Jâmi ul Shark* records the building of the Great Mosque at Jaunpur in A. H. 852.

3.—*Az âtash murd*, "he died by fire," records the date of the death of Sher Shah, who was killed at the siege of Kâlinjar by the bursting of a shell.

4.—*Zawâl Khusroan*, or the "Ruin of the Kings," was invented by Ghulam Ali Hindu Shah, the father of the historian Ferishta, to commemorate the deaths, in A. H. 961, of the three kings,*

Mahmud Shâh of Gujarât.
Burhân Nizâm Shah of Ahmednagar.
Islâm Shâh, Sûr, of Delhi.

5.—*Pul Muhammad Munim Khan*, or "Bridge of Muhammad Munîm Khan," at Jaunpur, gives the date A.H. 975.

---

* Brigg's Ferishta, Vol. IV, 152. Islam Shah died within a few days of the end of A.H. 960.

6.—In the old town of Hilsa in Bihâr, near the tomb of the holy Saint Jaman Madâri, there is an upright stone with the date of A.H. 1013, recorded in four different ways, as follows: *

In Arabic	... alf wa suls ashr = 1000 + 3 + 10	= 1013 A.H.
" Persian	... hazâr wa sis-dah = 1000 + 13	... = 1013
" Numerals	... 1013	... = 1013 "
" Abjad	... d . w . b . a . zw . z	
Values below	... 4 + 6 + 2 + 1 + 800 + 200	... = 1013 "

The values of the Abjad letters are engraved on the stone in numerals immediately below the letters.

* See Archæological Survey of India, Vol. XI, 164.